CHRONICLES OF THE ROYAL FAMILY OF BONAI (ODISHA)

STUDIES IN ORISSAN SOCIETY, CULTURE AND HISTORY

Editors: **HERMANN KULKE and BURKHARD SCHNEPEL**

Vol. 1: *Jagannatha Revisited: Studying Society, Religion and the State in Orissa*, **edited by Hermann Kulke and Burkhard Schnepel**

Vol. 2: *The Jungle Kings: Ethnohistorical Aspects of Politics and Ritual in Orissa*, **by Burkhard Schnepel**

Vol. 3: *Text and Context in the History, Literature and Religion of Orissa*, **edited by Angelika Malinar, Johannes Beltz and Heiko Frese**

Vol. 4: *Altar of Power: The Temple and the State in the Land of Jagannatha*, **by Yaaminey Mubayi**

Vol. 5: *The Aghria: A Peasant Caste on a Tribal Frontier*, **by Uwe koda**

Vol. 6: *Time in India: Concepts and Practices*, **edited by Angelika Malinar**

Vol. 7: *Periphery and Centre: Studies in Orissan History, Religion and Anthropology*, **edited by Georg Pfeffer**

Vol. 8: *Popular Religion and Ascetic Practices: New Studies on Mahima Dharma*, **edited by Ishita Banerjee-Dube and Johannes Beltz**

Vol. 9: *Bhima Bhoi: Verses from the Void–Mystic Poetry of an Oriya Saint*, **edited by Bettina Bäumer and Johannes Beltz**

Vol. 10: *Descriptive Topographical Catalogue of Orissan Inscriptions*, **by Snigdha Tripathy**

Vol. 11: *Centres Out There? Facets of Subregional Identities*, **edited by Hermann Kulke and Georg Berkemer**

Vol. 12: *Jagannatha and the Gajapati Kings of Orissa; A Compendium of Late Medieval Texts*, **edited by Gaganendra Nath Dash**

Vol. 13: *Chronicles of the Royal Family of Bonai (Odisha)*, **edited by Rashmi Pramanik and Uwe Skoda**

Chronicles of the Royal Family of Bonai (Odisha)

Edited by

RASHMI PRAMANIK AND UWE SKODA

MANOHAR
2013

First published 2013

ISBN 978-81-7304-979-8

Published by
Ajay Kumar Jain *for*
Manohar Publishers & Distributors
4753/23 Ansari Road, Daryaganj
New Delhi 110 002

Typeset by
Umesh Chand Nailwal
Delhi 110 092

Printed at
Salasar Imaging Systems
Delhi 110 035

Dedicated to
the memory of
SRI KADAMBA KESARI CHANDRA DEO,
Late Rajasahib of Bonai

Contents

Acknowledgements

This edition of the chronicles of the Bonai Rajfamily, would not have been possible without the help and encouragement of a number of people in and outside Bonai. We can name only a few here, but first and foremost we would like to thank the late Rajasahib of Bonai, Sri Kadamba Kesari Chandra Deo, who brought us into contact with his family chronicles, generously offered his hospitality, aroused our interest in these scriptures and blessed this venture. Likewise, we are grateful to his son, the new Raja of Bonai, Sri Bir Kesari Indra Deo, who equally supported the project and together with his father, read and commented on the English translation of the *Bansabali of Bonai Rajfamily*.

In addition to the royal family, in Bonaigarh, we also had long discussions with Sri Narayan Sathua, who has devoted immense energy and time to preserve the chronicles—as record-keeper *par excellence*—and who also guided us with his expertise in understanding these sources. Sri Madan Mohan Mishra, the Rajpurohit of Keonjhar and a truly knowledgeable pundit, added a perspective from outside, that is, an account based on a Sanskrit text from Keonjhar. We are also indebted to two other local experts on the history of Bonai: Sri Gananath Dandia (retd. OAS) and Sri Purna Chandra Mishra. All of them have been extremely kind and patient to share their knowledge and to answer our questions in a long process of venturing into the past—a venture that has also been facilitated by Sri John Deep, former Sub-Collector of Bonai, allowing us to get access to the local archive.

Sri Jagdish Mishra, descendant of the Rajpurohit family, and historian Dr. Kailash Chandra Dash contributed in a very direct way to this volume. Without them we could not have included the final few chapters in this compilation. They were thus instrumental in shaping the volume, in fact, they added a whole new textual dimension to the edition and broadened the historical horizon further. In the case of 'Chapter XIV', Jagdish Mishra agreed to digitalize the text and just a few weeks later the original was, by mistake, sold to a waste paper trader. Thus, in the process we were fortunate to play a role in the preservation of this text and were pleased to give a printout of it to him later. We are also grateful to Sambalpur University, and notably the Department of History, for granting us access to its archives, where a copy of Surendra Nath Mishra's synopsis of *Kadamba* is preserved.

Quite a few colleagues and friends were involved in the process of translating the Oriya texts by translating portions, revising them or advising us on certain terms. Sri Biswaranjan Purohit, Sri Minaketan Bag, Sri Atish Satpathy and Sri Pradipta Mishra were all directly involved in conducting the research in Bonai itself at different times, while in Sambalpur Sri Niranjan Pradhan, Sri Madan Biswal and Sri Abinash Sahu contributed in a decisive way to improve the quality of the text. We are also grateful to Sri Manto Pradhan who always supported the project with his remarkable talent to organize the crucial logistics.

A very special thanks goes to Professor Hermann Kulke, well known for his pioneering work on Orissan history and the field of kingship, who encouraged us to proceed with this book right from its inception, that is, during the Orissa Research Project, and also afterwards. Last, but not least, we would like to acknowledge our deepest gratitude to the German Research Council (DFG)—not only for supporting and funding the research that led to this volume in a very generous way, but also for financing this publication with an equally generous grant—a publication that was handled in a very professional manner by Manohar Publishers & Distributors of Delhi.

EDITORS

CHAPTER I

The Kingdom of Bonai and the Chronicles of its Royal Family: An Introduction

UWE SKODA

Whoever visits the former kingdom of Bonai, now a subdivision of Sundargarh district in north-western Orissa, and its capital and headquarter Bonaigarh, can hardly fail to notice the roads and highways always chock-a-block with trucks and dumpers (over-)loaded with iron-ore. Though it is well known that the area close to the borders of Jharkhand and Chhattisgarh is rich in minerals and iron-ore from here has been supplied to the Rourkela Steel Plant for decades, it was only in the wake of the most recent industrialization that the valley is seen dotted with sponge iron factories. In contrast to these new chimneys, one may easily pass and overlook the former fort (*garh*) with the palace located slightly away from the busy main road with a court, a high school, a bus stand and a market alongside. The picture was rather different when Colonel Dalton visited it in 1863-4, experiencing it as an isolated valley with the Raja's fort at the centre surrounded by almost uninhabited hills. He wrote:

> Bonai is a small hilly district lying very snugly isolated from all civilization, between Sarundah the wildest part of Singhbhoom and the Tributary Mehals of Keonjhur, Bamra, and Gangpore. It is 58 miles [*c*. 93 km—authors] in its greatest length from east to west and 37 miles [*c*. 60 km—authors] in greatest breadth from north to south, with an area of 1,297 square miles [*c*. 3359 km^2—authors]. It is for the most part a mass of uninhabited hills, only 11/12th of the whole being under cultivation, but about its centre, on both banks of the Brahmini river, which bisects it, there is a beautiful valley containing the sites of upwards of twenty good, and for the most part coterminous villages, houses well sheltered by very ancient mango and tamarind trees, with a due proportion of graceful palms.... On all sides, at the distance of a few miles, are hills, some nearly three thousand feet [around 900 m—authors] above the level of the valley, and thus a very pleasing and varied landscape is disclosed at every turn of the broad and rapid rock-broken stream....
>
> Bonaigurh, where the Rajah resides, is in the valley.... It has the river on three sides, and is surrounded by a mud wall and moat, within which are about

150 houses including those of the chief, his court-house, and jail: the village altogether, inside and outside the gurh, contains about 300 houses, but nothing that can be called a bazar. The inhabitants are the Brahmins and other retainers of the Rajah; his own family, including most of the collateral branches, legitimate and illegitimate; people practising trades—workers in brass and pewter, potters, weavers, smiths; and people of low caste, Gonds, Pahans, Ghassees and Domes. Ooriah is the language spoken, and the costume and customs followed are those of the Orissa provinces. (Dalton 1865: 1-2)

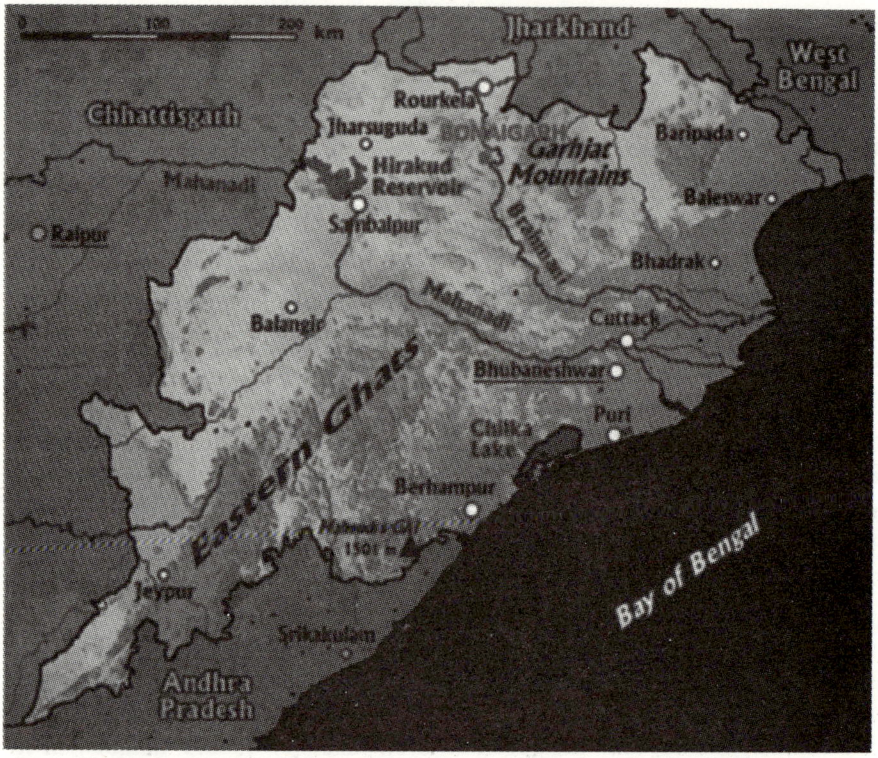

Topographical map of Orissa, © Eric Töpfer / www.suedasien.info

The history of the feudatory chiefs of Orissa appeared to Dalton as a Rajputization-process of rulers who were initially of tribal origin. Presumably inspired by the racial theories of his times he argued: 'The chiefs of these estates now call themselves Rajputs; [but]... [t]heir position altogether renders their claim to be considered Rajputs extremely doubtful, ... They were no doubt all Bhuiyas originally; they certainly do not look like Rajputs.'[1]

Later British administrators and visitors like Cobden-Ramsay in early 20th century Political Agent of the region, as such certainly familiar with Bonai and the neighbouring states and also interested in the history of these tracts and the royal families—, often reproduced Dalton's views regarding

Bonai, though without the racial overtones.[2] At the same time he also proposed a very different take more generally on the past of Western Orissan ruler and summarized this perspective in the following way:

> They [the feudatory states—the author] were first inhabited by aboriginal races, chiefly Bhuiyas, Savars, Gonds and Khonds.... In course of time their hill retreats were penetrated by Aryan adventurers, who by reason of their superior prowess and intelligence, gradually overthrew the tribal Chiefs and established themselves in their place. Tradition relates how these daring interlopers, most of whom were Rajputs from the north, came to Puri on pilgrimage and remained behind to found kingdoms and dynasties.[3]

While contemporary accounts often simply allude to "[d]ivergent views [which] are available regarding the origin of ruling family"[4], it is this second narrative which is clearly exemplified, in fact dominant, in the family chronicles (*bansabali, vamsavali*) of the Bonai rulers—stressing the Rajput or Ksatriya credentials of their own clan and claiming to be 'stranger kings', that is, having come from outside of Orissa. The locally produced or reproduced texts on the 'history'[5] of the former princely state as well as royal family of Bonai, collected in this volume, all belong to this tradition. Before turning to the locally circulating family chronicles of and texts on the royal family it is necessary to briefly introduce Bonai as a feudatory state within the region and to discuss the history or 'biographies' of these texts as well as the conditions and context of their production and alteration, as far as they are known.

THE FEUDATORY STATE OF BONAI

Following Cohn's[6] famous analysis of a multi-layered and dynamic pre-colonial political structure, distinguishing between imperial, secondary/regional and local level, Bonai might be considered as a 'little kingdom'. As such, it came under the often only loose overlordship of the Mughals and their appointed governors (*subahdars*) after 1576, when the Mughals—stepwise—conquered Orissa. Subsequently they divided it into two major constituents: on the one hand the Mughalbandi or 'crown land',[7] that is, the coastal plain, and on the other hand, the so-called Garhjat or 'fortress-born'[8] states, that is, clusters of states. This distinction between Mughalbandi, i.e. areas under the more direct control of a *subahdar* at the regional centre Cuttack, and Garhjat states in the north-western (and southern) part continued and still continues to influence regional identities. Of particular importance here is the cluster around and under the Sambalpur and Patna Rajas, which also exercised a certain influence over neighbouring states in the hilly hinterland.

These states were sometimes referred to as Sambalpur tracts or Sambalpur Garhjats.[9] Though they were obliged to pay tribute to the *subahdar*, the Garhjat states under the control of little kings remained relatively independent. However, in 1751 the overlordship passed into the hands of the Marathas, namely the Bhonsle Rajas of Nagpur, and remained under their control until 1803 when the East India Company occupied the coastal belt. Though Bonai and the Sambalpur Garhjat tracts were returned to the Marathas in 1806, they came finally under British control in 1818 and were officially ceded in 1826.

Feudatory/Tributary States of Orissa (adopted from map of Central Provinces 1909)

After 1803, the East India Company entered into engagements and treaties with the chiefs, but the ultimate status of these states was determined only later on and the situation remained, particularly up to the Great Uprising in 1857/8, relatively fluid. For example, in 1849 Sambalpur that had exercised a form of overlordship over nearby kingdoms such as Bonai, was seized–

ostensibly under the Doctrine of Lapse. Yet, after the Great Uprising or so-called Mutiny, and revision of the British policy towards the native states, the boundaries of the states were more or less frozen–though in many cases they were surveyed in a more precise form only decades later.

Under colonial rule, Bonai and other Garhjat states around Sambalpur were initially administered as part of the South-Western Frontier Agency (formed in 1833), which in 1854 was transformed into the Chota Nagpur Division under a Commissioner in Ranchi. However, after 1860 only a few states such as Bonai remained under this division, while others such as neighbouring Bamra became part of the Central Provinces.

Figure 1: An old seal of Bonai with a handwritten peacock motif as symbol of the Kadamba dynasty (file dated 1899)

It was not until 1888 that the status of the so-called Tributary Mahals of Orissa was finally clarified. The High Court in Calcutta ruled that 17 states in the Orissa Division did not form part of British India—a view subsequently accepted by the Secretary of State for India.[10] Soon afterwards, in 1891, the same status was conferred to the states of the Chota Nagpur Division (Gangpur, Bonai) and new treaties (*sanads*) were issued to them as well specifying their position *vis-à-vis* the British, their powers and tribute.

In 1905, after the division of Bengal, another administrative reform was initiated and Bonai, Bamra and others were attached to the Orissa Division and thus united with the other 17 Tributary states under a Commissioner in Cuttack. While the states were under direct supervision of the Commissioner up to the reform, the office of the Political Agent was created under the Commissioner. L.E.B. Cobden-Ramsay, well known for his book *Feudatory States of Orissa*,[11] was appointed to this newly-created post in 1906 and stationed in Sambalpur to 'assist' the ruling chiefs of the 24 feudatory states which is today an integral part of the Union State of Orissa.

Cobden-Ramsay's book published in 1910, contributed to the use of the term 'feudatory state' for kingdoms such as Bonai—otherwise also labelled 'native state', 'princely state' or 'tributary state/mahal'. The central element constituting the 'feudal' relations between the states and the British crown was the payment of a tribute linked to an inferior rank. This quality was particularly stressed and expressed in the term 'tributary state', used almost interchangeably with 'feudatory state'.[12] Similarly, semantically Raja was more or less used like chief, though it was later qualified as 'ruling chief' or 'feudatory chief' to distinguish the heads of states from other title-holders, who may have headed estates rather than states.

In 1922 yet another administrative re-organization led to the formal abolition of the offices of Commissioner with regard to the states and the Political Agent was rechristened as Political Agent and Commissioner, Orissa Feudatory States and included the states of Sareikela and Kharsuan at that time as well—now a part of Jharkhand.[13] However, connections beyond Orissa did not cease, but were maintained, e.g. within a new administrative unit—the Eastern States Agency—formed in 1935 along with the states in present-day Chhattisgarh and Jharkhand and elsewhere.

Following Independence, kingship was formally abolished and the state of Bonai merged with the province of Orissa in January 1948. Moreover, the remaining privileges and apanages (privy purse) were abolished in 1972 and the ruling families derecognized, yet the royal families such as in Bonai remain actively involved in a range of activities in their former realms—notably during the major festivals such as Cheitra Parba and Dussehra.

Figure 2: Late Sri Kadamba Kesari Chandra Deo, the last Raja of Bonai to be recognized as head of the royal family by the Indian government (Courtesy the royal family of Bonai, © Uwe Skoda)

Figure 3: Late Sri Kadamba Kesari Chandra Deo, Rajasahib of Bonai, 2009
(© Uwe Skoda)

TRACING THE HISTORY OF THE 'HISTORIES' *OR* TEXTS IN TIME

The number of indigenous texts dealing with the past of Bonai and to some extent circulating in the area, e.g. by borrowing, clearly indicates a vivid interest in the past and perhaps on the side of Brahmin or priestly families as well as other families loyal to the Raja a perceived responsibility for 'record-keeping'.[14] However, the origin of many of these—often handwritten or rather hand-copied—chronicles introduced here cannot be traced precisely to one author, but is rather a collective endeavour and remains to some extent obscure.

If people are asked about the sources on the local history of Bonai, they often refer to a text or texts known as the *Kadamba Gatha* (Story of the Kadambas). Some hold the belief that there have been authoritative palm manuscripts with this name long ago but when asked about its whereabouts they often lament—particularly the family of the former royal priests (*rajpurohit*)—that 'university people'[15] once came to Bonai and took away all the documents, which have never been returned to the rightful owners.[16] Still others claim that the 'original' *Kadamba Gatha* is kept in the Sub-Collectors' Office (the former Diwan's Office). However, archival research in this office did not lead to the discovery of any such text, and the same people so convinced about the existence of the text in that office later added regretfully, that the text had presumably been stolen from there. Thus, it turned out relatively quickly that there was no 'master copy' as such, if indeed there had even been any such single authoritative source in Bonai.

However, an Oriya text (i.e. in Oriya language and script) was kept by the late Raja, Sri Kadamba Kesari Chandra Deo, belonging to the Kadamba dynasty. It is often commonly identified as *Kadamba Gatha*, though it has no title and the late Raja Sahib often argued it should appropriately be titled as *Bansabali of Bonai Rajfamily* or 'Chronicles of the Royal Family of Bonai'—*bansabali*, being an Oriya term lexically clearly linked to *vamshavali*, which is used elsewhere in India. Like *vamsha*, *bansa* refers to 'bamboo or cane, where the joints of the stem are suggestive of generational growth'[17]—the composite term *vamshavali* being used not only for royal dynasties and might be literally translated as 'paths of succession'.[18]

The handwritten text which the Raja owns, is pinned on an re-used calendar, is not very old, perhaps just about 20 years or even less. Going by the handwriting it seems to have been written at different times. For example, a paragraph on the death of the Rani or Queen in 2002 appears to be a supplementary, and has been included only recently. It also indicates that the

Figure 4: Narayan Sathua with his Bansabali of Bonai Rajfamily on a re-used calendar, 2007 (© Uwe Skoda)

chronicles are a living tradition rather than an affair of the past—despite the abolition of kingship decades ago.

This text owned by the Raja is included here as Chapter II in its English translation and as Chapter III in the Oriya original. The ruling family acknowledges and more or less authorizes these chronicles as 'official' history of their family and state, though the late Raja contended that the text is not always complete and occasionally he narrated some additional elements. *Bansabali of Bonai Rajfamily* does not refer to a single, uniform text, but rather a corpus of individual texts and might more appropriately be called a 'local archive'. As such, it contains legends (*kimbadanti*) of various gods and goddesses of the kingdom—partly in verse form—but also various fragments of dubious origin, for example a short passage on Lord Jagannath but without any heading and not linked to any other part of the compilation. Most importantly, the text also includes a clearly marked part titled *Bonai Rajbansa Madla*[19] or 'Chronicle of the Bonai Royal Family/Clan' which narrates explicitly the past of the ruling family. Thus, in combining texts with different styles and characteristics into a whole, in its compilation-like structure, this text from Bonai resembles earlier Orissan texts such as the *Madala Panji* in Puri (Kulke 2001 [1987]b: 163), while it differs considerably in terms of content, i.e. apart from the chronicles of the royal family one finds in Bonai primarily legends of different deities, while in Puri the temple records form the major part within the *Madala Panji*.

A second identical copy of the *Bansabali of Bonai Rajfamily* is owned by the Sathua family, a *sonari* or goldsmith family, staying adjacent to the old fort, though not in the innermost part, and being loyal to the Raja. As the late Raja acknowledged, both copies were written—or perhaps better reproduced or duplicated, at least partly—by hand by Narayan Sathua, head of the Sathua family. They contain a short text almost at the end of the collection titled *Sathua Bansa Madla*, in which the link between the royal family and the Sathua family is explained. According to it, a merchant (Bania) family was brought to the kingdom, where they started to produce sacred threads made of gold to be handed over to the Raja during the annual installation rites. The king, being pleased with their work, then assigned the title *Sathua* to them or 'those staying with (*sath*) him'. Moreover, as Narayan Sathua explains, this *madla* has been composed by him, based on older palm manuscripts, and was apparently added to the royal chronicles later, indicating also the creative element in reproducing texts such as royal chronicles.[20]

How did Narayan Sathua get hold of the chronicles? He offered the following explanation:

In the olden days it was difficult to bring anything from *Rajbati* [palace]. Once upon a time I was eating *gram* [a kind of tiffin] from a *chanabala* (gram seller). After eating I saw that on the paper the *madla* of the Raja was written. I told the gram seller to give me the paper. But he told that the paper had already been used. I knew that all the documents were in possession of a Bhitiria [servant allowed into the inner quarters–author], Bansidhar Senapati.[21] One day he begged me for four hundred rupees in loan. At that time I told him I will give you the money but you have to give all the documents of king that you have kept. I will return them to you after reading. He gave me all the documents of the king's *madla*. Then I went to a constable to write it. He and his three friends copied all the things in one night. For which I gave them four kilogram of sweets. On the next day I returned all the documents to him.

In this way he acquired and preserved palace documents investing his own money. He presumed that the papers on the history of the ruling family were written by the former Rajpurohit (royal priest) Gopinath Mishra. However, when asked about the origin of some of the smaller fragments in the volume such as the already mentioned few lines on Lord Jagannath (see page 73 in this volume) he exclaimed:

I did not write the text. I did not know about the text also. Now I am seeing it when you show it to me. This is an incident as in the case of Balaram Das when he was writing the *Gitagovinda*. In a passage, where he had to describe Radha he did not know what to write. His wife's name was also Radha. So there he left the pen and paper and went to take his bath. After that he took his food. He came back and saw that whatever he had to write had already been written. Like that this incident had happened.

Thus, when confronted with the fragment on Lord Jagannath he argued that he had never seen that passage before and it was a divine intervention or rather revelation–a revealed text rather than a remembered one. Leaving aside the origin of this fragment, the late Raja ascribed the *Bansabali of Bonai Rajfamily* in his possession unambiguously and directly to Gopinath Mishra, who he believed used earlier texts to compile it. This opinion is substantiated in another text written by Gopinath Mishra's son, late Surendranath Mishra, added here as an appendix. Surendranath Mishra's nephew, Jagdish Mishra owns this text, titled *Chapter XIV*, thus, referring again to a compilation named *Kadamba Gatha* his uncle apparently once had in his possession. *Chapter XIV* contains primarily the history and genealogy of his own family and was therefore withheld by the family, while the main text was handed over faithfully to the 'university people'. The title of this *Chapter*

Figure 5: Surendranath Mishra, son of Rajpurohit Gopinath Mishra, undated photograph, adapted from *Journal of Kalinga Historical Research Society*, vol. 11, no. 1, June 1947

XIV differs from the subtitles of the version kept by the Raja and the Sathua, which suggests that those versions were not identical.

Coming back to the question of authorship, *Chapter XIV* indicates the existence of earlier texts as well. According to Surendranath Mishra, the writing of chronicles started several generations ago and is linked to the Satpathy family, a Brahmin family from Sambalpur that had married into the Rajpurohit (Mishra) family. Here the writing of chronicles, of a *Kadamba Gatha*, is related particularly to one ancestor, Damodar Satpathy, but it is also mentioned that the previous palm manuscripts (*pothi*) were destroyed by a fire in the Jagannath temple. In passing, it might be mentioned that one can observe a similar creative 'mixing' of previous sources and texts in other more recent texts. For example, Purna Chandra Mishra, who, being related to the Rajpurohit family of Bonai, wrote in 1993 a text titled *History of the Royal Clan* (in Oriya). He stated explicitly in the beginning of the text that Kumari Dibya Manjari Deo, daughter of Sri Chinmaya Kumar, had copied the text from *Rajbati* (palace) and added whatever he had heard from his father's elder brother, Jadumani Mishra.[22]

Moreover, Surendranath Mishra himself further contributed to the writing of chronicles and in addition to the just mentioned appendix in 1967 he wrote another text under the title *Kadamba Gatha* while he was a headmaster in Sundargarh and also belonged to the O.E.S. (Orissa Educational Service). He claims in the introduction to the text that it is actually a synopsis of his father's notes. Thus, it is shorter than the *Bansabali* text and was written exclusively in English, but does not differ substantially from it in terms of the content. Accordingly, Gopinath Mishra wrote a *Kadamba Gatha* in 1914 in verse form. In 1948 this book written by his father was sent to Cuttack for publication,[23] but a published version was never sent back. The loss is linked by Surendranath Mishra to the political turmoil in the post-merger era (Kharswan and Saraikela agitation). In line with this, he also remarked in *Chapter XIV* that he owns a *Kadamba Gatha* written by his father Gopinath Mishra in 1949, i.e. written immediately after it must have dawned upon him that the previous version sent for publication was somehow lost in the process. Though no copy of Gopinath Mishra's text could be located in Bonai itself, Kailash Chandra Dash, teaching history at the Evening College in the nearby steel city of Rourkela between 1980 and 1992 and thus familiar with the region, collected a *Kadamba Gatha* signed by Gopinath Mishra (cantos 1-10) and contributed it to this volume. It is mentioned in this text, included here as Chapter IV (English translation) and Chapter V (Oriya), that it has been copied by Gangadhar Rout belonging to Baleswar district with the assistance of Kabi Pradhan in 1939. Therefore one might presume that this text is a version of the *Kadamba Gatha* sent for publication, but nothing more is known about Gangadhar Rout and his involvement in the production of the royal chronicles. However, the text written by Madan Mohan Mishra, Rajpurohit of the Keonjhar royal family, included here as Chapter VI, documents that we may also encounter other texts outside of Bonai, for example from neighbouring Keonjhar, which may actually predate this text. It is possible that such older texts which Madan Mohan Mishra refers to and includes parts from a Sanskrit text, may have actually informed the text written by Gangadhar Rout or other authors.

Coming back to Surendranath Mishra, while his relatives believe that the English version of *Kadamba Gatha* he wrote, included here as Chapter VII, was submitted as an MA thesis in history at the Sambalpur University, established in 1967 just a few months before this text was written, the author himself mentions that it was written specifically for the university museum and indeed a copy of it is preserved in the archive of the university's history department.[24] The foundation of the Sambalpur University is therefore linked by local interlocutors to the loss of chronicles, but also—simultaneously—to the production and preservation of histories.[25]

Considering the timing of the later version one may argue, as Sammadar (1998) has, while writing on the *Jungle Mahal* Jambani,[26] that the production

Figure 6: Jagdish Mishra, descendant of the Rajpurohit family of Bonai, 2006 (© Uwe Skoda)

of the texts during the twilight of the royal regime and afterwards bears testimony to a certain melancholy and are also conscious attempts by the authors—in case of Jambani also a Rajpurohit and a former estate official—'...to tell the world that they too were somebodies in the past; that the power structure ... included them; and this was a small attempt to repay the bounty bestowed upon them by the raja' (Ibid.: 31).

Indeed, this might have been a motif for rewriting the *Kadamba Gatha* in 1949 and perhaps even more so for the late twentieth-century handwritten copies of Narayan Sathua, who apparently took over the role of royal record-keeper after the Rajpurohit family had discontinued this duty, i.e. after the death of Surendranath Mishra. However, there were certainly other factors which led to the (re-)composition of the texts. The university has already been mentioned as a recent influence and the interest of outside researchers, notably Germans since the first Orissa Research Projects in the late 1960s, might be mentioned here as well—both of which does not exclude the possibility of a certain nostalgia. More significantly perhaps, *Chapter XIV* compiled by Surendranath Mishra highlights another significant external factor leading to the intricacies of the production or at least a certain rewriting of the chronicles. It states:

> In the year 1914 as per the directions of the British Government, the Bihar Government had asked some questions to the then king of Bonai Sri Dharanidhar Indra Deo Dev about his genealogy. The Raja Saheb at that time told Gopinath Purohit, father of the compiler, to give an explanatory note along with the copy of the Madla. The Bonai Madla and the history of Kadamba dynasty was submitted to the Government along with the explanatory notes.

This statement suggests that the chronicles as such were not 'invented' and were not just written in response to the 'West' and its project of history construction—the text genre itself clearly predates British paramountcy.[27] But it shows that certain alterations or rather explanations were required *vis-à-vis* the colonial power. Apart from the internal motives to document and rescue the past, for the colonial administration local and regional histories became mosaic stones of the wider colonial project of generating knowledge about the subjects through various 'investigative modalities'[28] of which the 'historiographic modality' was seen as 'most complex, pervasive and powerful' (ibid.). '... knowledge of the history and practices of Indian states was seen as the most valuable form of knowledge on which to build the colonial state' (Cohn 1997: 5).

The influence of colonial centres demanding and collecting information from subordinated positions within an imperial hierarchy is also visible in a letter written by C.E. Buckland, Chief Secretary to the Government of Bengal to the Commissioner of Chota Nagpur on 15 May 1901, as part of a file of the Political Department titled *Preparation of Brief Histories of Native States, 1901-02*. It states

> The Lieutenant-Governor considers it desirable that the brief history of each of the Tributary and Political States of Chota Nagpur required by the Government of India should be prepared by you, kept up to date in your office annually and submitted to this Government not later than the 1st May of each year.
> (Archive of the Commissioner, Ranchi, Collection X, File 51)

The Commissioner in turn asked all the Rajas under his jurisdiction for their 'histories' as described by Surendranath Mishra. A sample attached to the letter of Buckland demonstrated the style of a 'brief history' as expected by the Government of Bengal, who 'desired' rather a synopsis of the history of the political situation and of the royal family than an elaborate chronology of events. By setting certain norms to which the subjects had to adapt to and to comply with the colonial overlords shaped the representation of historical or mythical events. However, while in some cases, e.g. in these 'brief histories' mythical narratives were simply reproduced in a positivistic manner by the colonial authorities themselves, in other cases colonial officers were critical of the historicity or factuality of the supposed 'histories' of the native states.[29] In any case colonial authorities initiated comprehensive collections of data, producing their own archives such as the famous Mackenzie Collection (Kulke 2001 [1987]b: 166). In Orissa, in 1910 (reprint 1982), the former Political Agent of Sambalpur, L.E.B. Cobden-Ramsay compiled and published the first printed volume of histories of all Orissan princely families titled *Feudatory States of Orissa* enabling a direct comparison of their family chronicles or *vamsavalis*. In Cobden-Ramsay's volume, however, he offers a short family history of Bonai deviating considerably from the above-listed 'native' sources. He does not mention the origin of his information, but he was certainly familiar with Bonai, touring the area personally.[30] So it is difficult to pass over this discrepancy.

Moreover, under the aegis of the colonial administration trying to establish the rule of law 'genealogies (*vamshavalis*) systematically collected by settlement and revenue officials, now became the basis of authenticating rights to property' as Kasturi (2002: 2)[31] remarks. The influence of a new legalism is noticeable in case of still another text dealing with the history of the family of one of the Jagirdars or Zamindars under the Bonai Raja (not included in this volume). Contesting the authority of the Raja and offering a radically deviating account of the Bonai history, this text written for a local court modelled along British lines documents perhaps most visibly a certain penetrating force of the British rule in terms of courts or more generally of outside factors in formulating the chronicles—an influence which exists to a larger or lesser degree in all texts introduced here as well as for other *vamsavalis* (Kulke 2001 [1987]a: 141).

CONCLUSION

Thus, venturing deeper into the history of Bonai one encounters a variety of texts with their own object biographies. These documents have been produced, modified, (re-)compiled or perhaps even fabricated under specific historic circumstances. The writing and re-writing has been stimulated by various internal and external factors. Research scholars searching for texts are one factor, while the production and modification of 'chronicles' was encouraged, even demanded, by the paramount power in its endeavour to generate knowledge. They were also used and instrumentalized in the legal system established by a colonial administration and have probably always been 'legal charters'[32] to authorize kings, who in a double-edged process authorized certain texts, however, contested they may be, which in turn narrated the kings' rightful succession in an illustrious family. As such the chronicles record power configurations as well as family histories. Yet, it is important to note that these texts such as the *madlas* from Bonai were not just invented, but rather earlier texts were extended and adapted to new purposes. The text genre of chronicles linked to the Puranic tradition certainly predates colonial rule—the famous *Madala Panji* might also be mentioned in this regard—though all texts included in this volume can only be traced to the colonial era.

With reference to genealogies in the Puranic tradition Romila Thapar once argued: 'They are rarely, if ever, faithful records of the past reality but they can be memories of social relations.'[33] Whether or not the texts are always factually correct cannot be decided here and is not the purpose of this volume. Rather, as Thapar reminds us, there is surplus of evidence, i.e. the narratives go beyond a pure description of the line of succession. Instead, the chronicles of Bonai also offer rich material on the complex relationships between overlords and 'little kings', who in turn were overlords themselves in a multi-layered politico-religious system. The texts illustrate the relations between Gajapati rulers, Bonai Rajas and Bhuiyan chiefs, to name a few. At times, the chronicles hint at instances of contestation or dependency. Those texts introduced here relate the kingdom of Bonai to a variety of centres, for example Puri, indicating a multi-centred configuration, as well as to a several religious traditions underlining an eclectic and accommodative approach of the Bonai Rajas *vis-à-vis* the divine sphere.

Though the intention of this volume is to introduce and preserve texts on the history of Bonai, not to analyse them in detail, one may note in passing that the texts also describe processes of state formation and centralization —a plurality of chiefs is replaced by a single Raja and the area unified as a realm. In this sense one might interpret the texts also as a reflection on the transition from a clan-based to a caste-based society, as Thapar suggested.[34] At the same time, the texts demonstrate the importance of autochthonous communities and what I prefer to call 'authority of the soil' represented by 'original settlers' *vis-à-vis* the 'stranger king'. However, going beyond the texts one easily notes that these written sources are only part of a larger cultural memory. The chronicles correspond with—reflect and were probably determined by—the wider socio-religious configuration of the kingdom. This entanglement is or at least used to be clearly visible in the rituals of investiture every new Raja had to undergo or is recognizable in the ritual routine in major temples in Bonai such as the Lord Baneshwar temple that is, by and large, in the hands of the Bhuiyan community. It was their chief, as the chronicles state, who allied with the first Raja and enabled him to conquer the realm—the central point of commencement for the kingdom of Bonai.

NOTES

1. Dalton 1865: 1-2.
2. For example, W.W. Hunter 1877, *A Statistical Account of Bengal*, Vol. XVII *Singhbhum District, Tributary States of Chuta Nagpur, Manbhum*, London: Trubner; R.V. Russell 1916, *The Tribes and Castes of the Central Provinces of India*, Vol. II, London: Macmillan [E-block 2007: http://www.gutenberg.org/files/22010/22010-h/22010-h.htm#d0e83541.
3. Cobden-Ramsay 1982 [1910]: 22.
4. See http://orissa.gov.in/e-magazine/Orissareview/2010/December/engpdf/189-195.pdf - accessed 26/01/2013.
5. 'History' is used here in a very wide sense, i.e. as 'indigenous discourse about the past' (Dirks 1989: 58), not in a more narrow 'Western' sense of 'history', which itself is first and foremost a particular 'culturally constructed practice' (Hirsch/Steward 2005: 267) and 'cannot be assumed to exist as a mode of knowledge outside the West' (ibid: 265). Though the concept of history varies in the 'West' itself, as Hirsch and Steward

acknowledge, the authors question specifically common assumptions in European historiography on a possible separation of the past from the present. However, in other cultures not just the past and present, but also the future might be implicating each other or may be fused intrinsically. As such, the past-present-future relations themselves have to be investigated as cultural forms.

6. Cohn 2001 [1962].
7. Mubayi 2005.
8. Ibid.
9. Cobden-Ramsay 1982 [1910]: 28.
10. Ibid.: 27.
11. Cobden-Ramsay 1982 [1910].
12. States such as Sareikela exempted from paying tributes were classified as 'Political States'.
13. On the administrative reforms and classifications see Aitchison, C.U. 1930.
14. To mention a few other texts that deal with the history of Bonai and circulate locally or are known by locals and could not be included here: An unpublished text has been written by Purna Chandra Mishra titled *History of the Royal Clan* (in Oriya), written in 1993. Its content is very similar to the text the Raja owns and therefore it has not been included here (see below). Another example is a short text by G.N. Dandia titled *Bonai State* which gives an overview over some aspects of the royal chronicles (published in a souvenir under the title *Banashri* on the occasion of the Diamond Jubilee of the Raja Dharanidhar High School). Moreover, some people refer to the census literature, e.g. the *Orissa District Gazetteers*, ed. N. Senapati and D.C. Kuanr, Sundargarh, 1971 [1975]. Or people may also refer to P.K. Sahu's *Oriya Itihas*, Cuttack: Nalanda, 1988. All these texts discuss the history of Bonai and of the ruling family to some degree and may have mutually influenced each other to some extent.
15. Sometimes the name Dr. N.K. Naik is mentioned too—perhaps referring to the founding father of the History Department at the Sambalpur University.
16. The Late Raja, Sri Kadamba Kesari Chandra Deo, remembers that people from the newly-established university came to the palace and asked for permission to take away a portrait of his father, the last ruling chief, to be exhibited in the museum of the History Department. Permission was granted and the portrait is still displayed in the museum.
17. Thapar 2000 [1991]: 712.
18. Thapar 2000 [1992]: 790.

19. Kulke (2001 [1987]: 154ff) reviews various explanations of the term *madla* or *madala*, which he links to *mudala* (sealed with a ring) indicating royal orders or to drum (*madala*) because the palm-leaf manuscripts were tied in big bundles looking like drums. Kulke favours the latter explanation. Referring to the *Madala Panji* of Puri, Kulke argues that *madala* denotes the whole corpus of temple records and not only the family chronicles (*vamshavali* or *rajbhog*). Here, however, *madla* specifically designates the family chronicle, while *gatha* is used as term for the whole compilation.
20. In an interview he described the history of the text in the following way: Once upon a time a professor of Sambalpur University came and took all the documents and palm leaves. But a patch of palm leaves was left which was the *madla of sathua* family. And a quarrel was going on in between our Sathua families. So at the end my aunt (*kaki*) threw the patch of palm leaves into the river. When we asked about the palm leaves she told us everything. When I went to take bath I found the palm leaves in the river and collected them. From that palm leaves I wrote the *madla of Sathua*.
21. Bansidhar Senapati was a trusted servant of the last ruler, Raja Dharanidhar Indra Deo, who was also seen as his 'pet servant'.
22. The text is very similar to the one owned by the Raja and therefore has not been included in this volume.
23. In the text it is mentioned that the book was sent to Saraswat Press in Cuttack, but I was unable to trace any publishing house by that name in Cuttack.
24. It is not very likely that S.N. Mishra submitted the chapter as an M.A. thesis—first because of his own statement and second in an article for the *Journal of the Kalinga Historical Research Society*, vol. II, no. I, June 1947, he was already introduced as an M.A.
25. For the historical documents preserved in Sambalpur see *Descriptive Catalogue of the Palm Leaf Manuscripts*, ed. P.K. Mishra, University Museum, Dept. of History, Sambalpur University, 1985.
26. Situated further east of Bonai in present-day West Bengal bordering Jharkhand.
27. The texts from Puri appear to date back to 1600 (Kulke 2001 [1987] b: 170), while south Indian *vamshavalis* are known from the eighteenth century (Dirks 1989: 55ff).
28. Cohn (1997: 5).
29. For Bonai see, e.g. Dalton (1865: 6) or Cobden-Ramsay (1982 [1910]: 144).
30. In his version Cobden-Ramsay (1982 [1910]: 143ff) argues that the family came from Ceylon (Sri Lanka), but 'the founder of the family was abandoned by his mother under a *kadamba* (...) tree' (143). The child

was rescued by a peacock. Thus, Cobden-Ramsay's sketchy account contains central elements of the other narratives described in detail below, but there is no story of conquest, which is replaced by the seemingly helpless infant absent in any other narrative. This is surprising because Cobden-Ramsay had visited Bonai at least twice before the book was published as his tour reports to Bonai in 1904 and 1907 indicate.

31. With reference to Rajput families in present-day Uttar Pradesh.
32. Thapar (2000 [1991]: 710).
33. Thapar (2000 [1991]: 709).
34. Thapar (2000 [1992]: 783).

REFERENCES

Aitchison, C.U. (1930), *A Collection of Treaties, Engagements and Sanads*, Calcutta: Government of India.

Cobden-Ramsay, L.E.B. (1982) [1910], *Feudatory States of Orissa*, Calcutta: Firma KLM Private Limited.

Cohn, B.S. (2001) [1962], 'Political Systems in Eighteenth-Century India: The Banares Region', in: Cohn, *An Anthropologist among the Historians and other Essays*, pp. 483-99.

—— (1997) 'Colonialism and its Forms of Knowledge', *The British in India*, Delhi: Oxford University Press.

Dalton, E.T. (1865), 'Notes of a Tour made in 1863-64 in the Tributary Mehals under the Commissioner of Chota-Nagpore, Bonai, Gangbore, Odeypore and Sirgooja', *Journal of the Asiatic Society of Bengal*, 34 (2), pp. 1-31.

Dirks, N.B. (1989), *The Hollow Crown: Ethnohistory of an Indian Kingdom*, Bombay: Orient Longman.

Hirsch, E. and C. Steward (2005), 'Introduction: Ethnographies of Historicity', *History and Anthropology*, 16, 3, September 2005, pp. 261-74.

Kulke, H. (2001) [1976], 'Ksatriyaization and Social Change: A Study in the Orissan Setting', in: H. Kulke, *Kings and Cults: State Formation and Legitimation in India and Southeast Asia*, New Delhi: Manohar, pp. 82-92.

—— (2001) [1987], 'The Chronicles and the Temple Records of the Madala Panji: A Reassessment of the Evidence', in: Kulke, *Kings and Cults:* pp. 137-58.

Kasturi, M. (2002), *Embattled Identities: Rajput Lineage and the Colonial State in Nineteenth-Century North India*, New Delhi: Oxford University Press.

Mubayi, Y. (2005), *Altar of Power: The Temple and the State in the Land of Jagannatha, Sixteenth to Nineteenth Centuries*, Delhi: Manohar.

Samaddar, R. (1998), *Memory, Identity, Power: Politics in the Jungle Mahals 1890-1950*, Chennai: Orient Longman.

Schnepel, B. (2001), Kings and Rebel Kings: Rituals of Incorporation and Dissent in South Orissa, in: H. Kulke and B. Schnepal (eds.), *Jagannath Revisited*, New Delhi: Manohar, pp. 271-96.

Singh Deo, J.B. (2004), *800 years of Singha Dynasty: 800 years of Singh Bhum: 'Singha Bhumi', 800 years of Land of Lions*, privately published commemorative souvenir.

Skoda, U. (2005), *The Aghrias: A Peasant Caste on a Tribal Frontier*, New Delhi: Manohar.

Stein, B. (1975), 'The State and the Agrarian Order in Medieval South Asia: A Historiographical Critique', in: B. Stein, *Essays on South India*, Hawaii: University Press of Hawaii, pp. 64-91.

Tambiah, S.J. (1985a), 'The Galactic Polity in Southeast Asia', in: S.J. Tambiah, *Culture, Thought, and Social Action*, Cambridge: Harvard University Press, pp. 252-86.

——, (1985b), 'A Reformulation of Geertz's Conception of the Theatre State', in: Tambiah, *Culture, Thought and Social Action*, pp. 316-38.

Thapar, R. (2000) [1991], 'Genealogical Patterns of Perception of the Past', in ibid., *Cultural Pasts*, New Delhi: Oxford University Press, pp. 709-53.

——, (2000) [1992], 'Clan, Caste and Origin Myths in Early India', in ibid., *Cultural Pasts*, New Delhi: Oxfod University Press, pp. 782-96.

CHAPTER II

Bansabali of Bonai Rajfamily (English Translation)

Om Namah Shivaya

SHIVA TANDABA (DANCE)

Small drum rings *dibi dibi*, mind and spirit, mind and spirit are pleased.
O' Lord Shiva, clotted hair looks beautiful on your head and swiftly flowing river Ganga is present there.
The moon looks like a beautiful crown on your head and the external scarf is present there.
O' Lord Shiva, small drum rings *dibi dibi*, mind and spirit, mind and spirit are pleased.
Ashes covered on your body and tiger skin on your waist also looks beautiful and the *rudraksha*[1] are present.
A small water pot and a trident are in your hands.
In your other hand fearlessness is present, in one hand the seeds of bead tree are present.
O' Shiva small drum rings, mind and spirit, mind and spirit are pleased.
At the feet of your carrier Brusabha.
Small drum rings *dibi dibi*, mind and spirit, mind and spirit are pleased.
In the east some gods are present, in the west Kartikeshwar is present.
In the south Ganesh is present and looks beautiful, on the north Goddess Parbati is present.
Small drum rings *dibi dibi*, mind and spirit, mind and spirit are pleased.
In the east a tank looks beautiful, in the west river Brahmani is present.
On the northern side river Brahmani is flowing speedily, in the south the image of Morning Queen beautifully standing.
Small drum rings *dibi dibi*, mind and spirit, mind and spirit are pleased.
The king of rocks is present and carrying the residence of Harihar.[2]
Praying under the feet of Shiva, small drum rings *dibi dibi*.

BONAI HISTORY (ITIHAS)

Prayer of Baneshwar

O' Baba Baneshwar take away my sorrows and sufferings.

I am praying under your feet, be kind to me.
Sronita Nagar of the State was at the last point.
Here Banasur had lived.
By seeing the devotion of Banasur, Kasi Biswanath came and halted at Bonaigada and he was called Baneshwar.[3]
Banasur propagated Baneshwar as a famous God.
The village named Deogaon is His place of stay.
Banasur has constructed a temple.
In the front He is sitting on His carrier Brusabha.
And his eternal beauty has spread in the 14 worlds.
There the king's palace is situated.
In the north there is standing the temple of Kumari Devi.
All by serving Her getting relief from all dangers.
O' Baba Baneshwar take away my sorrows and sufferings.
The servant Harihar is narrating from the palm-leaf scriptures.
Taking shelter under the feet of Baneshwar.
Accept my prayer O' five-faced God Baneshwar.
By drowning in an ocean of sorrows and sufferings I am perplexed.
Whether you keep me or not I am an orphan under you.
Accept me O' inhabitant of the cremation ground, O' Digambar.
You always hold a trident which looks beautiful.
By concentrating under your feet, the writer Dharanidhar is writing.
Writer Haricharan Deo

GENESIS OF BANESHWAR

Previously, Bonai state was known as Sronita Nagar and ruled by Banasur. His mother was....[4] Everyday Banasur used to go to Kashi to worship Lord Shiva. One day his mother told him, 'It gives me pain that everyday you are going to Kashi to worship Lord Shiva. From tomorrow try to please Lord Shiva and bring him to our Home. I am blessing you.' The next day Banasur went to Kashi and worshipped Lord Shiva for few days. Finally Lord Shiva was pleased by him and told Banasur, 'What do you want?'. Banasur replied, 'I have been asked by my mother to please you through constant worshipping, and you appeared. It's my cordial request that you please come to my state.' Lord Shiva told him, 'I will go, but there is a condition, you start walking, while walking as soon as you look back at me, I will stay there.' Banasur asked, 'How do I know that you are coming behind me?' Lord Shiva told, 'I will go sitting on the Brushaba and a bell around its neck will be ringing. From the ringing of Brushaba's bell you will know.' Banasur agreed to it. Lord Shiva told, 'You can start walking',

Banasur started walking and Lord Shiva was coming behind him. After some time Banasur reached the banks of river Brahmani, and Lord Shiva knew he had come to the area of Banasur. The Brahmani river was flowing northwards and Lord Shiva thought, it's the northern Ganga and a good place for him. With an intention to stay there, he stopped Brushaba and subsequently its bell did not ring. Banasur looked back as he could not hear the sound of the bell anymore. He suspected, Lord Shiva was not coming behind him. When he looked back, he saw that Lord Shiva was standing there. Lord Shiva said, 'Being pleased with your sincere worship I came to your state but I will not move further as you did not keep our agreement. You have to make a temple for me within a night. I will reside here.' Banasur applied all his power to pull the God to take him to his home, but he failed. Then a temple was made there and Lord Shiva worshipped. At that time the entrance gate had not been made and everyone worshipped there. According to the name of Banasur, Sronita Nagar was named Bonai. And Lord Shiva was also named as Baneshwar according to the name of Banasur. This power (*shakti*) is the joint idol of Lord Shiva and Parbati and the Linga is directed towards nether world (*patalagami*). This type of Linga is a rare one, and is not seen commonly. This was told by Banasur.

ASTASHAMBHU (EIGHT TYPES OF LORD SHIVA)

Type	Place
Baneshwar	Deogaon
Negnalishwar	Koida
Jataleshwar	Gugua
Bakuleshwar	Near to Rajbati (palace)
Khireshwar	Gugua
Jhadeshwar	Tendara
Sapneshwar	Bonaikala
Kupeshwar	Patna, cursed (*abhisakta*) temple Jugeswara

PRADHAN DEBI (MAIN DEITIES)

1. Kumari–Main deity of Raja Saheb (King)
2. Khanda Pat–Main deity of Saantaa at Ladam Village
3. Andhaari–Deity of Mohapatra
4. Balanipat–Main deity of Danda Pata
5. Kanta Debi–Deity of Bonaigarh King
6. Chandi–Deity of Kalei Leader/Sardar
7. Basuli–Deity of Bonai king
8. Rambha Debi (in Barkot)–After a war between the Bonai king and Deogarh

king, the latter occupied the area up to Ambagaon Siaanjula and Rambha Debi was left there and is worshipped by the king of Deogarh.

WORK OF THE GODDESS

1. After killing Mahisasura, Mahamaya[5] took the shape of Astashambhu (eight types of Lord Shiva) and pleased the Goddesses in eight types of replicas.
2. When Khireswava uttered Wah! Baneshwar emerged there.
3. Khireswava cooled down her hunger by offering her milk.[6]
4. As the hair was spread (*mukula*), he got it confined and tied up, so he is called Jatalaswara.[7]
5. Nengeleswara–After getting him dressed, he named as Nengeleswara.[8]
6. Jhadeswara–As blood and dust spread over her body, which had been cleaned up (*jhadiba*) and so named as Jhadeswara.
7. Sapneswara–The goddesses could see their war in the dream (*swapna*) so they could cool down the anger of Debta who are called Sapneswara.
8. Kupeswara–As she had an angry/furious look (*kopadrusti*) she planned how to cool down the anger. As she pleased him, she is named as Kupeswara.

LEGEND OF KUMARI[9] (*KUMARI ONKA KIMBADANTI*)

It is known that Kumari Debi was the age-old goddess of the fort (Gada Debi) at the time of Banasur's ruling. The evident Kumari Debi is worshipped as Astashambhu. She takes care of the state's well-being. Once, a Brahmachari[10] came here. At that time Bonai was full of dense forests. He stayed at Kumari Debi's place to worship her. He had a student (*shishya*) with him. He sent the student to fetch water from the river and himself went to the village to beg for alms. After returning he saw that the water was there but the boy was missing. The Brahmachari searched everywhere, but did not find the boy. Then he saw a pair of footprints in front of the Goddess. He thought that the Goddess had eaten his student. He angrily threw the full plate with food offerings (*jou*) on the face of Kumari Debi and her face has been hidden ever since. From that day onwards the Goddess has been worshipped in that form. She is popularly known as Kumari Debi. Kumari Debi has got three names: (1) Kumari (2) Shunya Kumari[11] and (3) Adbhuta Kumari[12]. She is worshipped in these three names, three times. Everyday she is worshipped as Kumari. At the time of drought, she is worshipped as Shunya Kumari and called Chandi. When there is an epidemic like chickenpox, smallpox, etc., milk cake (*chena*), sweet drinks (*pana*), hibiscus flower (*mandar phul*), a new earthen pot, incense (*jhuna*) and red clothes are offered to the Debi, and she is worshipped from all the four directions. At this time the Debi is worshipped as Adbhuta Debi. She is the popular Goddess of Bonai. If one worships her with a pure heart one becomes successful. Many people have heard the sound of a horse riding and horsewhip (*chabuk*). All who surrender to her, have their wishes fulfilled.

SURRENDERING TO MAA

Prayer (janan) *to Mother Kumari*

Oh, mother world, caretaker, presiding deity of Bonai, adorable Maa,
Mahisamardini, Danger Tarini, Giver of Boldness, Maa,
You are the caretaker of the whole world, you are the bearer of whole world, Maa,
Sankar,[13] Bhabani, Tutelary deity of Bonai, Maa,
Great danger avoiding mother having three feet and three eyes, Maa,
Tutelary deity of Bonai, Durga of the forest and Banasur Goddess,
caretaker of the fort, you are the mother of the whole world, omnipresent Bonai mother, Maa,
I surrender at your feet, fulfil my wishes, Harihar, Maa.

LEGEND OF KUPESHWAR

Kupeswar is the glory (*kirti*) of the Sarangi *bansa*. They were three brothers and very rich. Since the eldest brother had no children so his wife went to surrender herself to Baba Baneshwar. Baneshwar was pleased with her and asked her, 'you do not have any children'. She replied, 'You are everything, if you show mercy upon me everything is possible.' So he gave a snake baby to her through a dream. After some days she gave birth to a snake (*sapa*) son (*putra*). The snake was brought up with loving care. Everyday her mother fed her milk and the snake went out in the evenings to wander around. One day the snake child was late, so the mother told her sisters-in-law (*ja*)[14] to feed the snake with milk when he returns and went for a bath. But they wanted to kill the snake because they feared that the snake may bite any of the family members one day. So when the snake came back, one of the sisters-in-law gave him a bowl of hot milk. When the snake tasted it, the snake rejected it and never came back to their home again. His mother searched for him everywhere but unable to find him she was inconsolable. A few days later the Sarangi brothers separated and divided the family property among themselves. The snake should have got a share too, but since it had gone away, it did not receive any share. His mother felt sad due to this fact. However, just at the time of dividing the properties among the brothers, the snake suddenly turned up and coiled himself around the largest part of the share. The snake's portion of property was thus given to the person who had taken care of it. The snake then went away but came later to his parents in a dream. The snake said as they had given hot milk angrily (*kopare*) to him, so he had left but his portion of property should not belong to anybody but rather a temple should be built upon it. So a temple was built here and the snake was worshipped here in form of a stone idol. The temple was inaugurated by the king himself and every necessary arrangement was made for the temple. Till now the snake is worshipped here in the name of Kupeswar, as the snake had been given hot milk in anger (*kopare*). Some property is being kept inside the temple premises where at noon time sunlight will fall and it will be used by Kupeshwar in future.

Till now the snake can be seen in the temple and on his head there is a mark of hot milk. That is why before entering the temple one should clap hands three times. Inside the temple toward the north side a hole is there through which the snake can come and go when it pleases.

LEGEND OF BAKULESHWAR

A *patayat* (king's second son) from the Kadamba clan (*bansa*) once went to Petapeti[15] Darah (river gorge) for hunting. While he going in the boat, it suddenly stopped in the middle of the river and refused to move in spite of all possible efforts. Rather it went round and round. The Patayat could not understand the reason for it, so a fisherman (*keuta*) dived into the water to know the reason. The fisherman saw that a *linga* was there. The *patayat* bid the fisherman to fetch it. From that day onwards the Darah earlier called Petapati Darah it is now called Deo Darah. As Debta/Dian has emerged from it the *linga* was taken and placed in the north direction and worshipped as Bakuleswara.

LEGEND OF KANT KUMARI

Once a Babaji (sage) from Keonjhar came to Sronita Nagar (Bonai). He was staying at the Baneshwar temple. He owned many things like a 'one-faced'[16] (*ekamukhi*) *rudraksha mala*,[17] a *nrushingha salagram*[18] and a *nabadurga kankana*.[19] One day the Raja's men visited Baneshwar and saw all these things. At that time *Rajabhishek*[20] was going on but the Raja did not have a *nrushingha salagram* or a *rudraksha mala* in his house. People informed the Raja that the Babaji had all these things. The Raja gave orders to bring them from the Babaji's house. When the Raja's loyal men went to get these things from the Babaji he refused to part with them but they tried to have it forcibly. The Babaji hoodwinked them saying that he would give it to them the next day and meanwhile fled the village Kansara in the same night. The next day when the Raja's people came they could not find him and started began looking for him. Finally they found him at Kansara. After killing the Babaji they took away the 'one-faced' *rudraksa, nrushingha salagram* and *nabadurga kankana.* After a few years, the place where the Babaji was killed was turned into an agricultural land and belonged to a person of the Pana caste. One day when he was ploughing the land, he could feel that an iron thing had struck against his plough. He just put it aside and continued ploughing. After ploughing for another four or five times he again faced the same problem. Finally he could see that it was something like the iron part of a husking pedal (*dhinki's sama*[21]). He took it home to use it in his husking pedal. One day the Pana having spread the paddy to dry on the threshing floor went away to take his bath. The same day a moneylender (*mahajan*) from whom he had taken a loan came to his house for his money. Not finding anybody he decided to wait. To his astonishment he noticed that as soon as birds started to peck at the paddy, a snake would came out from the *sama* and drive them away. An idea came to him to ask the Pana for the *sama*, when the Pana returned on seeing the *mahajan* he paid obeisance to him. Then both of them talked for a while about the loan. Afterwards the Pana changed his wet clothes and started grinding paddy with the help of a husking pedal. But the *mahajan* kept sitting there and said that he would not leave unless the Pana returned his money. Then the Pana winnowed the paddy and got rice from it. To the *mahajan's* surprise he got the same quantity of rice as much as he had paddy. The *mahajan* then again asked for the *sama* telling him that he will relieve the Pana from his loan if he gave it to him. So the Pana gave the *sama* to him and the *mahajan* went back home happily. The same night the *mahajan* had a dream that, if he did not return the *sama* to where it belonged his clan (*bansa*) would be wiped out. Pana also dreamed that he should give back the *sama* to the king otherwise his clan will be wiped out. That night the king also dreamed that whatever he sees the first thing in the morning, he should worship it. That night a Bhuiyan of Jala also dreamed that he should go to the king early in the morning and bring the *sama* from the Rajbati. The Bhuiyan did the same and the Raja gave it to him. The Bhuiyan kept it in Jala. After some days again the king dreamed that it (the *sama*) will be worshipped as Kanta Debi. From that day onwards Kanta Debi is visible on the day of *pratipada*.[22] She is worshipped from the second day of Aswina (September/October) to the day of full moon (*purnima*). *Chandi-patha*[23] is observed on *astami* (8th day). Buffaloes and goats are sacrificed. Before that the Bhuiyan comes and takes a handful of flowers offered to the deity (*puspanjali*) on the day of the new moon (*amabasya*). Then the goddess is taken along with her seat (*asan*) through (the villages of) Haldi Kundri,

Nuadihi, Khuntgaon, Poegaon, Jakeikala, Jamkei, Upurada to Kantajodi. On the opposite side of Singardei, in a place named Kantajodi, a ritual on a special platform (*mandali puja*) is performed for Kanta Debi. Then the Raja Saheb goes with his watchmen (*prahari*) beating the *dhol* and playing the *muhuri* to her. The Bhuiyan leaves Kanta Debi thinking that the king is coming to kill him. The Raja than asks his followers to search for the Bhuiyan and call him back, but he does not come. The Raja does not wait for him, but takes Kumari Debi and hands her over to his priest (*pujari*) with the title *Amat.*[24] This is called *kantabhet.* After finishing the Debi Puja at midnight she meets Kumari Debi and stays with her like a sister in the armoury (*khanda ghar*[25]) in a bowl filled with blood (*rakta handi*). The next day, *puja* is performed at Rajbati. The Raja takes her and worships her at his place. Afterwards she is worshipped by his kinsmen (*bhayali*) and the daughter (*jema*) and at every household, including at the Brahmins' quarter (*Brahmin sahi*). The Raja places the Debi at the big gate (*bara dwar*) towards the outer area of the fort (*bahari garh*). The next day she is worshipped in *bahari garh* and in the morning a *puja* is performed called *neem chakuli.* The person (Pana) who found the Debi, worships Kanta Debi offering *chakuli pitha* (a type of traditional rice cake) with *neem* leaves. After the *chakuli puja*, the Debi is taken to the opposite side of the river and *dasahara* begins. A grand ritual is observed on the day of the full moon (*purnima*) in every house via the villages Lalei, Tankajodi, Brahmanigaon, Amatpali, Madhypur, Kuruda, Bhogala, Kulpos and accompanied by beating of drums and playing *muhuri*, Kanta Debi is taken to her *medha.*[26] The Bhuiyan then alone goes to the *medha* and leaves the the Debi there. Since that day, the Debi has been worshipped in this manner.

Once some people from Keonjhar were sitting atop a tree to steal the Debi. They had seen the place where the Bhuiyan had kept the Debi. But when they tried to take away the Debi from the *medha*, they all died beneath a *mahua* tree. When the Bhuiyan went to offer *puspanjali* to the Debi on the day of *amabasya*, the Debi was found missing. He was very worried and prayed to the Debi. She told him, 'I am beneath a *mahua* tree. I was stolen by some people. You will worship me from the day of *dwitiya* (the second day of the month).' From that day onwards, after he had retrieved the Debi from beneath the *mahua* tree the Bhuiyan performed *puja* on the day of *dwitiya*. The Raja got the information that the Debi was coming late. From then onwards the Raja appointed the *pradhans* of 16 villages for the security of the Debi and gave the *pradhans* cloths as rewards. To this day 16 *pradhans* of the Debi meet the Raja before they come out on the day of *astami*. Beside this, they also offer agricultural produce, fruits and sacrificed *prasad* as gift (*bheti*) to the Raja. The Raja in turn offers them cooking items. 108 people also perform *Chandi-patha* from the next day (*pratipada*) of Bhadraba Purnami for 15 days. On the day of *pratipada, belabarni* is observed. The second day (*dwitiya*) is called *hatipanchami*[27] also known as *gajasasti*[28] and *aswasasti*[29]. On the next day, arms and ammunitions are worshipped at the *khanda ghar* and Brahmins are fed (*bhojana*). When Kanta Debi is taken to the opposite side of the river, *dasahara parba* is observed. Now the groups (*dala*) of Saanta, Dandapata and Mohapatra come to the Rajbati. The Rajbati group is called the Raja's group. Soldiers belonging to Baharigarh Badadwara Sahi, Patadwara and other groups also join them. The Raja goes to the *dasahara parba* sitting on a silver sedan (*tamajan*) and a sword. Besides the Raja, Tikayat, Patayat, Rajkumar and Kumar also go, sitting atop an elephant on a silver palanquin (*palanki*). The British police escort them in front and from behind the Raja's group. All of them head for the *dasahara parba*. At the *dasahara* field, wrestling, *kasrat* (exercise) and archery contests are held among the different groups of soldiers. At the end, the Raja distributes prizes. On his return from the *dasahara* field, the Raja is welcomed back with dance and song and is worshipped (*bandapana*) with incense at every square. Returning to the Rajbati the soldiers from different places are given a big feast (*bhoji*).

Note: Some time back, as the Debi's idol got damaged, it was repaired on the advise of Anuruddha Sathua with the help of Ananta Sahu, Gobardhan and Narayan Sathua. It was repaired with copper. Again at the time of Raja Sri Kadamba Kesari Chandra Deo, as the previous copper work was not so strong, he gave permission to repair again with better material. It was done on 5 October 1992 at Bakuleswara Mandap by five persons, viz., Murali, Kedar, Gobardhan, Narayan and Gangadhar.

MADLA[30] OF SINGARDEI[31]

The *chaitra parba* started during the time of the 48th King Sri Bhikari Deo Chandra Deb. He started this *parba* by bringing the idol of Basudi[32] from the Nath[33] house in Gamlei. The king had a daughter. On the last day of *chaitra parba*, in the morning when she was combing her hair, the maidservants (*dasi*) happened to see her face and were shocked to see three eyes on her in the mirror. They told this stange phenomenon to the queen. The queen asked her daughter: 'You are putting on make-up, are you going somewhere?' She answered, 'yes, am going on a journey.' On that day at 2 am she just vanished. A search party was sent for her. At last she was spotted sitting at on the eastern side of a mountain. From that day onwards she was worshipped there as a Debi. As she had gone there donning make-up, the mountain is called Singardei mountain, and the Goddess Singardei. Whoever worships her is said to attain success. Once the *amat*[33] after finishing his *puja* had left behind his pot (*lota*) for worshipping her. When he went back to fetch it, he was amazed to see the Debi had taken the form of a tiger and was devouring the *prasad/bhoga*. The Goddess told *amat*: 'I am sparing you as you are the *pujari*. If it had been someone else, I would not have left him alive. I am throwing this *lota*. Wherever the *lota* falls, you will worship me there.' From that day the place where the *lota* fell is worshipped. Till date a day before *chaitra parba* people go there to worship her, beating the drum (*dhol*) and playing the *muhuri* to worship her. It's the Debi's order.

MADLA OF JAGANNATH (BUDHA GOSEI[34])

The 48th king, Sri Bhikari Deo Deb, established the temple of Lord Jagannath and it was he who started the car festival. During those days the Rajbati houses were very close to one another. The Debta (Lord Jagannath) was kept inside the *dhabaghar*.[35] However, once when it had caught fire, a Brahmin, Laxman Mishra by name, moved Lord Jagannath 100 feet away. Afterwards two small idols of Balabhadra and Subhadra were added beside him. The car festival started during the period of King Dharanidhar. Another three idols of the three Lords (Jagannath, Balabhadra and Subhadra) were made. Dharanidher thought of conversing the old idols in the water. But the Raja had a dream that night not to immerse the idol of Lord Jagannath in the water, but rather he should worship it as Budha Gosei, and offer rice, *kalam saga*,[36] and *biridali*[37] as *bhoga*. From that day onwards, Budha Gosei is worshipped. As the two other idols of Balabhadra and Subhadra had got damaged, they were immersed in the water. At that time the car festival was observed with three carts of Lord Jagannath, Balabhadra and Subhadra. It is said that Laxman Mishra was very strong and could was easily take out one of the wheels of cart to take bath sitting on it. He is even said to press mustard seeds over his palm and extract the oil out of it and massage it on his body. Once he bent a tamarind tree[38] and gave the tamarind leaves to the goats to eat. Another time a *malla* (wrestler) came and told him: 'Arrange another *malla*, I want to wrestle'. Laxman Mishra just pulled down a hanging branch of a tree and gave it to the *malla* to hold and went away telling him he will fetch another *malla*. When the *malla* let go off the branch, it went up 10 *hath*[39] and the *malla* fell down. Feeling extremely ashamed, he went way. He (Laxman Mishra) had so much strength. He was also engaged in the salt business. Once, observing that it was about to rain and all the salt sacks were lying on the veranda, he told his son: 'to bring the bags in'. His son immediately went to fetch some labourers for this work. Meanwhile the rain had already started. He (Laxman Mishra) was suffering from high fever at the time and his hands were trembling. Yet he carried all the salt bags inside and kept them in the corridor with the help of his bare teeth. When his son came back, he asked his father: 'who had brought these bags in the corridor' his father replied: 'I have brought them in. For this little work, if you depend on labourers, what will you do in life?' When he died, he was taken to the riverside to be cremated. His daughter Sushila Mishra returning from Indrapur, saw that her father's urine was kept in a bowl in the house. Seeing the bowl she knew that her father was alive. She immediately ran to the funeral site (riverside) and reached before the fire had been hit to burn the dead body. She shouted: 'Don't light the fire, he is still alive'. A medicine was poured through his nose and he got up. He lived for another 12 years after that. Being very pleased with his work the Bonai king donated the Sautipali village to him.

ASADHA RATHJATRA (JUNE-JULY CAR FESTIVAL)

Quarrel (Kali) between Laxmi and Narayan

Om. Jaganahaya Namah
(Salute to Lord Jagannath)

Dasi
(Maidservant of Laxmi)

Dasi is telling O' mother, hear me
your husband the head of the gods has returned back.
The car (*rath*) is standing on the main gate (*singhadwar*)
O' mother, because of the huge gathering of devotees the road is not visible.
Now you hear the sound of the conch and great round drum (*nisan*) it sounds loudly.

Laxmi

O' Dasi, when the god of gods (Jagannath) has come
you organize my festival in town.
In each and every ward, O' Dasi
lanes of the locality are decorated by fixing bunches of pearls.
When there is moon, heat and fan[40]
and incense must have been arranged in all the areas,
and the god (Jagannath) will come;
close the doors of the temple.
Whatever sorrows he gave me
O' Dasi, ever if He is the god,
how I will allow Him to come.

Let the husband's elder brother (*dedsasur*) enter into the house,
but both the brother and sister (*bhai bhauni*) stay outside the main gate.
O' Dasi, if they will stay outside then only they will realize what happiness they have enjoyed in the Gundicha Jatra (i.e. car festival).

Jagannath The husband of Laxmi, Nagarabara
knowing her thoughts, with a smiling face he was saying,
O' Dasi open the door,
what did I say that you are behaving in this way?[41]
Which thing did you come to know that you are making such a scene,
because you know everything,
what more we will tell you?

Dasi Dasi is telling of Padmanava,[42] please hear,
if we leave the door what benefit you will get.
O' god (Prabhu) what more work you have got now in the main temple,
when you have left Laxmi, O' mighty hand (Jagannath) now you have come near.

Jagannath God is now telling that in olden days King Indradyumna had requested me and taken confirmed words from me when she knows about the things, she gets up, Gundicha Rani three idols came.
O' Dasi we came back very soon,
O' Dasi we uplifted the Chandalas.
When we went for the good of our devotees,
so in the world people came to know about it.

Dasi Then why you have not taken our beloved wife Laxmi along with you,
when she is our beloved half life partner (*ardhanga nari*)?
If Kamalini (Laxmi) would have gone with you in Gundicha Jatra then what loss it would have been?

Jagannath On such festival only the gods go.
In the procession there is a huge crowd
and along with me, my elder brother Halapani (Balabhadra) is going,
so, O' Dasi, I have not taken Kamalini (Laxmi) along with me.

Dasi

Brahma and all the gods are the sons of Laxmi,
she is Jagatmata, the mother of the entire creation.
So in her going there is no bar for Her,
but definitely you are disinterested in Kamala (Laxmi)
so you left Her.
Whatever you will say that cannot convince Laxmi.

Jagannath

Gundicha House is not our permanent place of stay,
wherever Kamala (Laxmi) is present my mind is there.
She is my life's most lovable wife,
I am god (*thakur*), she is goddess (*thakurani*).

Laxmi

O' my lord you told rightly,
how well you know me, you have been exposed now.
Whatever *bhog-prasad* you have given to Laxmi,
you have given low quality of rice (dalua rice) and green leaves to eat.
O' god (Prabhu) the happiness given by you
became famous in the entire world.
You are having 52 crore store houses
and god Kubera (god of wealth) is our orderly servant.
Astha Nidhi (eight valuable things) are in your hands
and whatever you will say that cannot be believed.
O' Dasi, whatever was there in the 52 crore store houses
you have carried away
along with her flat stone, pestle stone, broom stick and the winnowing fan.
He has carried it to the store house.
O' god (Prabhu) it is shameful to say
that what you, Devaraj (king of gods) have done to me.

Jagannath

The god is telling, you are meandering around by saying so many unnecessary things
and you are not paying attention to our problem.
Now see that the dark cloud has overshadowed everything
and there will be continuous rainfall.
By the rain water my body will get wet
but our anger has not cooled down.
Sri Nilamber (Balabhadra) has been allowed to enter inside the temple
but you have kept us outside the boundary.

O' Dasi open the door,
why are you reluctant to open the door.
We have brought one silk saree (Chitrameghi Pata)[43]
for Laxmi whose father (*tata*) is the King Ratnakara.

Laxmi

The moon (*sudhakara*) is my younger brother,
Brahmand (creator of the entire universe) is now telling in this way to convince me in his favour.
Dresses of gods were not available to Him,
so you take back this 'Chitrameghi Pata' and give it to your loving sister.

Jagannath

God Himself who has lotus-like eyes is defeated before a young maiden,
Sri Bidyachuta applied his wisdom.
He gave some bribe to the Dasi and said
O' Dasi you go and tell Kamala in the heavenly forest.
On being bribed, the Dasi opened the door immediately.
The God of love (Kamadeva) gives a side long glance through the corner of his eyes.
Sudha (honey) is present everywhere,
the sound of the conch is heard because Laxmi and Narayan both will be united.
Both enter into the room situated deep inside the temple.
They prepared many things.
They sat there and laughed.
Goddess Laxmi Devi massaged the feet of God Jagannath.
And under these feet of the god, the writer Brahmana Biswamber is begging for shelter.

MADLA OF CHANDI DEBI

It was the reign of the 49th King Raja Pitambar Indra Deb Deo. It was many years since Chandi Debi was placed near the Brahmani River side. Chandi is the chief Debi of the Brahmins. Raja Pitambar renamed Deogaon as Taankajoda revenue village (*mauja*) and brought 16 Brahmin households there, from somewhere else. Among them, the Raja selected one as the head, honouring him as *sardar* (leader) and also appointing him as Gountia (headman) with the responsibility of worshipping Chandi Debi. From that day onwards the *sardar* started worshipping the Debi. The latter was pleased with him and his economic and social status increased. They were close to the Bonaigarh Rajbati. Everyday he worshipped Chandi Debi and only then partook his food. Chandi Debi was so pleased and blessed him that she gave him the boon to cross the river by sitting on a plate. Seeing this the other Brahmins got jealous and complained to the Raja and against the *sardar*. They warned the Raja that some day or the other the *sardar* would harm him because he has brought the Debi under his control by offering her liquor. The Raja did not believe it as he was a supreme (*srestha*) Brahmin. The Brahmins then told the Raja to call upon him and check. Next day when the *sardar* was taking the *puja* items to the Debi, the Raja wanted to check the *puja* items. The *sardar* said, 'Be quick as the *puja* time is getting delayed'. He was bringing liquor from the liquor man's (*sundhi's*) house. The Raja asked: 'What are you taking in that *lota*?' The Brahmin said: 'It's milk, sir'. The Raja told him to pour it into another pot. The Brahmin poured it, praying to the Debi. The Raja and the other members saw that it was milk. The Raja then ordered that the milk be boiled. When it was done cream floated over the milk. Then he ordered to make out of it curd, and told the *sardar* to see that it has turned to curd. He then told the *sardar* that he wanted to a visit Chandi Debi along with him. Next day was the *navanna*.[44] Accordingly, the next morning the Raja went to Chandi Debi with the *sardar*. Reaching the river side he could not see any boat there. It was the month of *bhadraba* and the water level was very high. The Raja asked the *sardar* how to cross the river. The *sardar* prayed to the Chandi Debi and clapped his hands three times and automatically a boat came to the river side. Again the Raja questioned that there was no ferryman. The *sardar* told him 'Don't be frightened, sit in the boat. Ma Chandi will take us to the opposite side, as we are going to her place, she will take the responsibility of our journey.' After the Raja and the *sardar* were sitting in the boat, it reached the opposite side by itself. The Raja was pleased as he watched his *puja* for Chandi Debi and his doubt over the *sardar* was dissolved and he believed in Chandi Ma. Again the boat came to its previous place on its own, i.e. to the Rajbati side. This *ghat* is called Ranisala ghat. The boat stopped there, the Raja worshipped the boat and then the boat again went to the opposite side. Till now, on the day of *navanna*, *puja* is performed on that *ghat* called the chandi boat (*danga*) *puja*.[45] If anything goes wrong with the rituals then the boat circles around at the middle of the river and comes back to the river side. After praying to Chandi Debi, again the boat starts its journey back. Till now nothing has gone wrong with that boat, neither has it faced any danger. It's a belief that if one watches from the Patatanga Ghat (on the opposite side) it looks like the shape of a woman with a *mukut* (crown) over her head and a *kalasi* (auspicious pitcher) in her hand. Approaching nearer, she hides herself and is only seen as a rounded rock. Till now in front of

Chandi Debi a sign of Kalapahada (Black Mountain) is seen.

It's an old tale,
Wah! Ramchandi Wah!
Seating Kalapahada outside, you have gone to fetch water.

MADLA OF BONAI KINGDOM

The former name of Bonaigarh was Sronita Nagar. Pratap Deo who had come from the Singhal island was its first king. The state to which he belonged was Udepur and his caste was Kshatriya. Raja Pratap Deo came with his seven brothers from Singhal to visit Lord Jagannatha. Among the seven brothers, Pratap Deo, Bir Pratap Deo and Bhagirathi Deo were of the same parents (*sahodara*) while Mitrabhanu, Udebhanu, Chitrabhanu and Bruhatbhanu were their cousins (*sathi bhai* [46]). They took one year to reach Puri. At that time the king of Puri was Gajapati. When they reached Atharanala they came to know that the pilgrims have to pay some *tikas* (tax) to visit Lord Jagannath. The seven brothers said: 'We have neither ever paid any *tikas* to any *badshah* nor have we offered any *salam*, now what do we do? Let us introduce ourselves to Raja Gajapati. If he denies we would enter forcibly.' Having decided this the seven brothers introduced themselves to the 'Tax Collector'. But he denied them permission unless they gave *tikas*, as it was the king's order. The seven brothers then threatened that they would enter forcibly if they were denied permission. Listening to this the 'Tax Collector' gave this message to the king. The Raja told if they haven't bowed down before anyone and want to go forcibly then let them go. Immediately the Raja kept sharp-edged *karata* (saw[47]) on the way to Atharanala. And then the seven brothers were told to move if they wanted to go forcibly. Listening to this the four brothers angrily ran with their horses and died by being beheaded by the *karata*. And when the remaining three brothers ran with their horses on that way, the king's followers stopped them and sent message to the king. The Raja came to the spot and saw the four dead bodies and allowed the remaining three brothers to visit without *tikas*. The three brothers then went to Cuttack and stayed there for a few days. Mitrabhanu and Udebhanu went to Singhbhum via Jajpur while Pratap Deo came to Bonai via Kapilash and Malyagiri.

At that time Bonai was a dense jungle. First Pratap Deo came to Singhjoda and stayed there changing its name to Kadambadiha. At that time Kolha, Bhuiyan, Keuta and other Adibasi people were staying at Bonai. Among them, the Bhuiyans were the supreme (*srestha*) group enjoying the *jamindari* (landlordship). After staying there for a few days, Pratap Deo came to know that this state belonged to Banasur and so he worshipped Shiva on the banks of the Brahmani River. According to the name of Banasur, Shiva was named as Baneshwar. Baneshwar also blessed the *debta's* devotees. Hearing this Pratap Deo went to the Brahmani River with a person and took his bath and visited Baneshwar. After constantly visiting for same days the *jamindars* there came to know of it. Those *jamindars* were Mahabira,[48] Bira[49] and Hamira.[50] It is said that these three *jamindars* were a part of Banasur (demon). Mahabira was at Satkota, which is 1 mile away from Baneshwar, whereas Bira was at Tasipara. Apart from that, Necha Keuta was at Keut Marani and Leda Kamar at Sundhikona. All of them gathered at Kamar's house and had a discussion that a stranger (*videshi*) was motivating the people. How to kill him? The next day all of them lay in wait of him armed with weapons. Early next morning when Pratap Deo was returning from Baneshwar he saw them and was surprised as he had never seen them before. He wondered whether they were waiting to kill him? Thinking this he entered the jungle. On the other hand, the people waiting for him were wondering why Pratap Deo did not come? Mahabira said, he might have heard our voice and entered the jungle. Then Necha Keuta climbed on a tree and saw that Pratap Deo was moving towards the northern side. Immediately he shouted to the other to follow Pratap Deo. Realising that he was being chased Pratap Deo looked around for a safe hiding place. Then he saw a hollow tree (*gacha khola*). He prayed to Baneshwar and entered into the hollow tree. A peacock was sitting atop the tree. It wiped out the footprints of Pratap Deo with its tail and again sat on the tree. When the *jamindars* reached there they couldn't find Pratap Deo anywhere. Mahabira told Lecha[51] and Leja[52] to keep a watch around the temple, instructed him to wait there and kill him if he came there. The others then left the place. Pratap Deo heard and saw everything through a hole in the tree and the whole day he did not come out from there out of fear. That night Baneshwar appeared in his dream and gave him the order 'Pratap Deo, I make you the king of Sronita Nagar. You will enjoy the kingship without any hindrance'. The Raja asked: 'How can I be the king?' Baneshwar said: 'Tomorrow morning whosoever you meet in the temple, keep him with you to kill those people. Being the king of this place you have to worship the tutelary deity (*ista debi*). The Debi will order you what to do in your dream.' The Raja made a *danda pranam*[53] and came out from the hollow of the tree. He spent the entire night beneath the tree and went for bathing early next morning. Meanwhile Kalai of Kalaipasi dreamed to send Lechada of his house to the temple early in the morning. That night Kalai Kisan called Lechada and told him to visit the temple. When Lechada was crossing the river, he saw Pratap Deo taking his bath. The Raja seeing Lechada recalled his dream. He asked about Lechada's caste (*jati*) and home (*ghar*) and also asked who were the rulers of his locality. Lechada said, 'Hamira, Mahabir, Bira, Lecha Keut, Leja Kamar and Kahiru, these six people, sir'. Then Raja told Lechada about the dream. The Raja asked Lechada how to kill them?. He replied that these people were staying at different places so it was difficult to kill them together. 'We have to kill them one by one', he said. Pratap Deo promised to make him a *jamindar* when he would be king. Pleased, Lechada told him, 'we will kill them tomorrow'. Discussing this, they both reached Baneshwar and went to Pratap Deo's residence. Next day, both went to Keut Marani and killed the Keut. When Lechada called Keut, he came out of his home and told Pratap Deo, 'Yesterday you slipped away, today Kuaari has brought you here'. No sooner had he completed this sentence, Pratap Deo shot an arrow at him. While dying Keut said, 'Though Baneshwar has made you the king, you will worship me only otherwise you will get harmed'. The Raja said, 'I will worship you at my home. But you had mentioned, Kuaari, where is she?' The Lecha said, 'She is at the northern side of your house, worship the *ista debi* Kuaari, her name is Kuaari, Shunya Kuaari and Adbhuta Kuaari.' After listening to all this, the Raja chopped off his head with the sword. From that day onward Keut has been worshipped as Keut Deo.

Now they went towards Sundhikona. Leja Kamar was returning from his bath. Lechada indicated to Pratap Deo that this was Leja. Immediately Pratap Deo shot him dead with an arrow. Raja and Lechada went to the river side. Lechada went to Mahabira's house and called Mahabira. When he came out of his house immediately Pratap Deo shot him with an arrow. Lying wounded Mahabira said, 'Whosoever will kill me, will be the king here. He will have to worship me, or else his clan will vanish'. Pratap Deo said 'I will worship you.' Mahabira's dead body was burnt on the eastern side of his home and there he was worshipped. The duo now went to Kantsara. At that time Kaheru Rana was digging the earth. They buried him at the place where he was digging. He was worshipped at that place. Then they went to Satakuta and killed Bira. He was worshipped at that place as Goda Debi. Then they went to Kashipada and killed Hamira. While he was dying Hamira cursed him: 'Whoever kills me, any member of his clan who will come to this village will be *aputritka*'.[54] Hearing this Pratap Deo became a little bit upset. Next day, Kalei Kisan came and on hearing how Pratap Deo had vanquished his enemies uttered 'well done'. He then gathered all the people to make Pratap Deo the king. Pratap Deo's *abhishek* (anointment) was performed. A *chhatra* (umbrella) was made and offered to Baneshwar. Raja Pratap Deo made Lechada, the 'Samanta'. Since then there have been a succession of kings, viz.:

1. Raja Pratap Indra Deo Deb.
2. Dinamani Deo Chandra Deb Raja.
3. Harichandra Indradev Deo Raja.
4. Madhusudam Gobind Deo.
5. Krutibas Deo Chandra Deb Raja.
6. Patrumenta Deo Gobinda Deb Raja.
7. Sri Mukund Deo Indra Deb Raja.
8. Srinidhara Deo Chandra Deb Raja.
9. Srinibas Deo Gobind Deb Raja. This Raja had no children, so his brother became the king.
10. Dambarudhar Deo Indra Deo Raja.
11. Baneshwar Deo Indra Dev Raja.
12. Sri Nilakantha Deo Gobind Deb Raja.
13. Sri Narayan Deo Indra Deb Raja.
14. Hrusikesh Deo Chandra Deb Raja.
15. Sri Jadumani Deo Gobind Deb Raja. He got married in Mayurbhanj, i.e. Mayurbhanj Raja's daughter.
16. Sri Sirapani Deo Indra Deb Raja. Married in Patna,[55] left Singhjoda and made his state at Gharbuda.
17. Sri Mukund Deo Chandra Deb Raja. He married in Singhbhum.
18. Sri Bikram Deo Gobinda Deb Raja. Got married in Mayurbhanj, but he had no son, so his brother became the next Raja.
19. Sri Kampal Deo Indra Deb Raja. Married in Singhbhum.
20. Sri Biranchi Deo Chandra Deb Raja. Married in Patna.
21. Sri Madhab Deo Gobinda Deb Raja. Married in Mayurbhanj, left Gharbuda and built his fort at Bonaigarh.
22. Sri Basudeb Deb Indra Deo. This King married in Patna. He left Gharbuda and stayed at Bonaigarh.
23. Sri Mahendra Deo Chandra Deb Raja. Married in Singhbhum.
24. Sri Gadadhar Deo Gobinda Deo Raja. Married in Mayurbhanj.
25. Sri Makardwaj Deo Indra Deo. Married in Singhbhum and constructed the Kumari temple.
26. Sri Paramanand Deo Chandra Deb Raja. Married in Patna.
27. Sri Giridhari Pani Deo Gobinda Deo Debraj. Married in Mayurbhanj. As this King had no son he made his brother's son the Raja.
28. Sri Purusottam Deo Indra Deb Raja. Married in Bamanda,[65] he made arrangement of the Pujari as well as the *bhoga* for Baneshwar.
29. Sri Ugrapratap Deo Chandra Deo Raja. Married in Nagpur.
30. Sri Chitabhanu Deo Gobind Deo Raja. Married in Patna.
31. Sri Padmanar Deo Indra Deo Raja. Married in Singhbum.
32. Sri Trilochan Deo Chandra Deo Raja. Married in Singhbhum.
33. Sri Indra Pratap Indra Deo Raja. Married in Bamanda, from the 32nd King Gobinda Deo left Patna.

34. Sri Kadam Keshari Chandra Deb Raja. Married in Mayurbhanj and brought the Nath family from Angul.
35. Purundar Deo Indra Deb Raja. Married in Nagpur.
36. Sri Jadunath Deo Indra Deb Raja Married in Mayurbhanj. He brought Srikara Mishra from Purusottam.[57]
37. Sri Ramachandra Deo Chandra Deb Raja. Married in Singhbhum.
38. Sri Udit Narayan Chandra Deb Deo Raja. Married in Keonjhar. His elder brother (Ugra Pratap) wanted to get *abhishek* at Keonjhar. But Samanta family (*ghar*) and other gentlemen denied this, and without heeding them he went to Keonjhar. So Udit Narayan became the king. Ugra Pratap stayed at Talcher.
39. Kalia Chandra Deo Indra Deo Raja. Married in Patna. In this period conflict arouse between Bamanda and Keonjhar.
40. Sri Bir Kishor Deo Chandradeb. Married in Singhbhum.
41. Sri Balunkeswar Deo Indra Deb Raja. Married in Mayurbhanj.
42. Sri Baneshwar Deo Chandra Deb. Married in Bamanda and went to Bamanda with Samanta family and stayed at his brother's (*bhai*) place. From Bamanda he went to Samanta family (*ghar*) and returned at night. His concubine's (*rakhita*) son went to Athmallik and became king there. His name was Banamali.
43. Sri Gobinda Chandra Indra Deb Raja. Married in Bamanda.
44. Sri Narasingh Deo Tikayat. Married in Saranda, Bihar.
45. His Son Gopinath Chandra Deo. Married in Keonjhar.
46. Sri Ramahari Deo Indra Deo. Married in Bamanda. He brought the Dandpat from Budha Sambar.
47. Sri Raghuraj Deo Chandra Deb Raja. Married in Singhbhum.
48. Sri Harinarayan Deo Raja. Married in Sonepur.
49. Sri Bhikari Deo Indra Deo Raja. Married in Patna and made the idol of Lord Jagannath and started the Rath Jatra.
50. Sri Pitambara Deo Indra Deo Raja. Married in Mayurbhanj. Pitambara renamed Deogaon as Taankojoda village as a full name and brought 16 Brahmin families and kept them there. He brought Mahapatra from *Brahmani paat* and learned *akhada* and gave him (Mahapatra) 12 villages and made him the Mahapatra.
51. Sri Bhagirathi Deo (Tikayat) married in Patna.
52. His son Sri Raghunath Deo Chandra Deo Raja married in Keonjhar and renamed Patna (old name) giving it the name Raghunathpur (new name) and made the Kupeswar temple.
53. Sri Shiv Narayan Deo Indra Deb Raja. Married in Sonepur. Made the Gopal idol (*jiu*), installed Andhari Debi. Shiv Narayanpur was ruled by Brahmins. He repaired Baneshwar and Sapneswara temples. Ghusura Hanuman temple was constructed by him.
54. Sri Chandrasekher Deo Indra Deo Raja. Married in Keonjhar. As he was *unmada*,[58] Rani Padmabati ruled the state along with the British govern-

ment. San-Rani (younger queen) Swapna Debi was the daughter of her *sahi* (hamlet) (i.e. of the Raja of Keonjhar). And her son was Sridhar Deo.

55. Sridhar Deo Indra Deb Raja. Married in Sareikela. He remarried to a Bhayadi's (relative) daughter of Anandpur Jamidar clan (*bansa*) of Singhbhum. He had three sons: Nilambara, Biswambara and Harekrushna. Kaleipasi Jamindar Krushna Samanta unnecessarily rebelled against him out of jealousy. British government's police quelled the rebellion finally. The rebellion caused huge losses to the king as well as his subjects. Finally the rebels were arrested and imprisoned. In his period a *Bhuianmeli* (Bhuiyan gathering) took place at Keonjhar. With the help of the British soldiers he extended his state (*rajya*) and received the title Raja Bahadur from the British government.
    Dhananjaya Bhanja was the king of Keonjhar. During his reign, *nalakathi*[59] arrangement was done. The two Gand Jamindars rebelled against this arrangement and the Commissioner had to come and sort it out. The king was very wealthy. In his period one *pacca* house (*ghar*) and eight schools were built. According to tradition, the Gamardiha revenue village (*mauja*) was gifted to Mukul Purohit. The king increased the respect (*marjada*) of the royal clan (*rajbansa*) greatly with his deeds.
56. Sri Nilambar Deo Indra Raja married in Mayurbhanj. He had three other queens. Two were the daughters of Banka *jamindar* of Sareikela and another was Dusani *jamindar's* daughter. He had four sons: Dharanidhar, Hirabraja Dhar, Jadumani (Rairakhol Raja), and Harischandra Deo. During his ruling *prajas* were happy and it was during his reign that the first wealth house (*dhana ghar*) was established. Concerning this state (*atarastate*), land deeds (*patta*) of two forests (*jungle*) were given to British companies. This king had the same interest for earning wealth as well as religious work. He made two Brushababas out of a marble stone brought by his father and donated it to Baneshwar. In his period the Gopaljiu temple was reconstructed and since the idol (*murti*) was broken, he replaced it with another idol.
57. Sri Daranidhar Deo Indra Deo Raja married in Bamanda. As he was very young at the time of his father's death, *anawadis*[60] ruling took place. In the year 1913 he took charge of his state. During his period Jagannath house (*ghar*) was broken and reconstructed. The Raja also constructed the *goura gabind mathi*. In his period, a Kadamba Kshatriya (Pitambara Deo on 15 January 1943) was hanged. His queen Rani Amarabati built the Jagmohan temple. As this king had no son, he adopted Hirabraja Dhar Deo's son. Rani Amarabati died of a fever when she went to visit the Kurupam state in the year 1919. The Raja had a mistress (*rakhita rani*). Once he went to Puri with her and remained there purchasing a house and did not come back to Bonai again. In 1947 the Congress government took away the state. After one year, i.e. in 1948, Raja Dharanidhar died at Puri. After him his adopted son became the king.

58. Kadamba Keshari Chandra Deb Deo Raja married in Bastar. He had three sons 1. Kiran Kishor (Tikayat), 2. a middle son who died shortly after birth,[61] 3. Bir Kishor. The middle son Pateda had died on the day of *akshayatrutiya*.[62] On 20 April 1971 (in the month of Chaitra) at 10 am his elder son Tikayat Kiran Kishor died. During this king's period the front gate of the Baneshwar temple was reconstructed and the Kuaari temple was made into a concrete (*pacca*) one. Also, a change was made in the manner of worship of Kanta Debi. Instead of worshipping her in every household, it was done at a *mandali* (pandal). So *amat* was denied performing the *puja*. For their convenience the king made a committee. The *amat* could not be convinced and he handed over his resignation to the king. In it he mentioned, he will not do any work of the king or any god's or goddesses' *puja*. When his descendants were asked they also declined. Finally Sri Nilagiri's son belonging to Deogaon agreed to do *puja* and so the king tied a *siripa* (turban) around his head and made him *amat*. Since then he performed the *pujas* for all gods and goddesses. Later, *amat's* descendants performed the *pujas* and are doing so till now. This king gifted some silver items got made by Raja Dharanidhar to the Debottara Committee. The present Debottara authority now owns them. The list of things include:[63]

1. Big size cobra	1 piece, 8 kg and 50 g
2. Middle size cobra	3 piece (a) 3 kg and 300 g; (b) 3 kg and 550 g; (c) 3 kg and 25 g
3. Small cobra	(a) 575 g; (b) 625 g
4. *Chhatra*	1 piece, 5 kg and 770g
5. *Lota*	1 piece (baruaa) 750 g
6. Platform plate	8 piece, 2 kg and 750 g
7. Kumbha	4 piece, 1 kg and 125 g
8. Gomukhi	3 piece, 320 g
	Total 32 kg and 640 g

[in continuation of the Rajbansa Madla–the authors] The king of Bonai, Kadamba Kishore Chandra Deo's Rani (queen) Geeta Kumari Devi, expired at 4:30 at Rajkumar College, which is located at Raipur in the State of Chhattisgarh on 20 December (Pausa) 2002 (Friday). At that time she had completed 55 years of her marital life. Her age at that time was 72 years.

NRUSINGHA PURANA

Ratnakara III (Occan)
(Detailed position of the child in the mother's womb)
Sesha Narasingha Janma (birth)

Along with Ananta (Seshadev), the biggest endless hooded snake on whose body Lord Vishnu is sleeping permanently, so He is called 'Ananta Sai'. He is growing in the mother's womb by staying in the left side skilfully.

In this way the days passed by and nine months were completed. Seshadev (the Ananta) could not tolerate the labour pain anymore.

He told Vishnu, O' master, O' mahaprabhu hear me, let us go quickly now and finish our delivery.

Sri Hari (Vishnu) told why you are so impatient. As long as ten months are not completed the body will not be strong.

If the child is born in seven months, the body will not be strong. If the child is born in eight months then the child will never survive.

If the child is born in nine months then the mother will get much pain. If the child is born in ten months then everything will be light and easier.

Seshadev told, when you are giving me orders, now hear, I will tell about the labour pain of a mother.

When the mother gets labour pain in her womb, I will tell you Sir, before you O' Bhabagrahi (addressing to Lord Vishnu).

When a mother and father get united in sexual intercourse a new life enters through the semen.

That forms the body by entering into the mother's womb. From the first day there is a reflection of water.

On the 5th day it forms a body of blood and looks red in colour. From that stage it grows gradually.

On the 10th day it looks like the jujube berry (*badari*). On the 15th day its shape is like an egg.

On the 30th day the head is formed. On 40 (fourty) days the feet are seen.

In 60 (sixty) days both the hands are seen. Again eyes, nose and ears are formed.

After 65 (sixty-five) days the mouth is seen.

In 70 (seventy) days the anus is opened.

In 89 (eighty-nine) days the fingers are completely formed. In 80 (eighty) days the skin of the body with hair looks squeezed.

In 90 (ninety) days the nails are formed. In 100 (one hundred) days head is lifted upwards.

On the 5th month the dazzling of seven metals are visible, bone, flesh, marrow, fat, skin, blood and semen.

In the 6th month the five elements enter in these seven levels and the nature shows its working by staying in the heart.

In $5^1/_2$ months the child feels hungry and thirsty and in the 6th month the heart starts functioning.

Due to hunger and thirst the soul is perturbed. Knowing this God meets at once.

He brings a fan thus fitting it in the house of the soul and constructs it carefully.

He says this fanning will drive out the hunger, thirst and disease.

Your vein is connected to your navel cord and by the wind of the fanning let your eyes be open.

From the mother's stomach the rice juice will ooze and by eating that you will be satisfied.

By telling this God vanished. By the touch of that wind the doors will be opened.

When the doors are opened the ring worms will enter into the mother's womb through the nose and ears.

After seven month again the mother gets pain when the hands and feet are tied up together.

Due to the darkness in the womb the fetus becomes confused, but by the blessing of God, again the joining is opened.

The child lies in the mother's womb like a prisoner. How can I describe the sorrows and suffering felt by the child in the mother's womb?

Now when the mother eats any hot food at that time the child gets pain. Again when the mother eats any sour food, raw food, bitter food or chilly food then child gets pain and is perturbed.

How can I tell about the punishment of the eighth month. The child is frightened knowing about the womb.

When the mother walks at that time the child thinks that he may die. But when the mother sleeps quietly on the mattress, at that time the child is anxious.

And at the time the child says, the mother is dead, and the child says, how can I be born.

Like this the child is in distress in the mother's womb, being restless and closes its eyes.

Lying in the midst of the foul smell of pus, blood and saliva where it is covered with urine and excreta. The child is fully covered in that uneasy atmosphere.

The bad smell enters into its nostrils. And the child cries sitting in distress.

So his mind is not stable, tears flow continuously from the eyes of the child, and he calls God crying in the mother's womb.

By knowing the child's cry God covers the body of the child with a net.

At that time God gives the knowledge of Brahman to the child and tells the child to recite the name of Hari so that he will be released.

By hearing these words from the mouth of God and after getting the knowledge of Brahman the child starts reciting the name of God.

With the concentration in mind the child calls God and says 'O, Prabhu, Narahari release me.

O' Prabhu Narayana, I am taking shelter under your feet, so you relieve me from this Hell.

The mother's womb is a very dark place, so, O' Padmanaba, if I stay here I cannot get liberation.

O' four-handed Prabhu you relieve me from the pains of womb. O' Bhabagrahi (God).

If I am released from this then I will worship you and recite your name by staying under your feet, and I shall not fall once again in this danger.'

In this way after getting the knowledge of Brahman the child completes nine months and enters the tenth month.

Again in that tenth month the mother gets pain and she is not able to move freely because of her heavy stomach.

So she prays to Goddess Durga and to Sri Hari and she says, O' Prabhu please help me to overcome this pain.

After praying like this, mother calls to Jagannath. Then Gobinda is pleased and helps her.

Prabhu Bhabagrahi orders the soothing air to enter into the mother's womb.

When the child gets up quickly and moves around and pushes, it hurts.

By the blessing of Gobinda, the pain of the womb is driven out and from that stage the way out from the womb is visible to the child.

The child gives pressure with his head and comes out of the mother's womb through a passage from the vagina.

After falling on the ground, the attachment of the living world attracts, so the child cries loudly uttering 'kuan', 'kuan'.

In this way Vishnu tells in front of the younger brother that a child in the mother's womb gets such type of pains.

Everyone is born in this way, so O' my Lord I elaborately described it to you.

Then Prabhu said, O' Ananta, listen: Why should we annoyed for such a simple matter?

If we see the birth of a child from the mother's womb as a bad thing then how can we be full of happiness in this world?

The people of the whole world understand that we are present in all the living beings as *atma* (soul) and show themselves as *atma* when the child is born from the mother's womb.

We, Narahari, being present everywhere in this world and if we dislike the birth then how can we be born.

We are present in all *atmas* but the people of this world are unable to recognize us.

All the labour pain which is told now, no doubt it is troublesome but I have told you, so that you may understand it.

If a bad man comes in contact with a bad woman then his semen bears all troubles.

Those who are cruel, malicious, dishonest, wicked, hypocritical, deceitful, adulterous, etc.–lower caste persons (*chandala*),

Vicious, rough, violent, wicked person, sinful person, great sinners and all criminals.

If they insert their semen in the womb of a woman, she has to bear the sorrow in her womb for this act.

When the semen of a person who has a good soul enters into the womb of a woman then the woman does not get much labour pain.

Absolute Brahman (Parama Brahma) and we are the creator of the entire universe (*Brahmanda*) and in the womb how will Bidhata (The God) give us pain (labour pain) to our mother?

Now nine months are complete and the tenth month has reached so let us go out said both the brothers happily.[64]

By telling this god himself got ready for his birth, by holding the sign of *sankha* (conch), *chakra* (wheel), *gada* (mace or club) and *padma* (lotus) in his four hands.

Both the brothers talked in the mother's womb and prepared themselves for the birth which took place smoothly.

When the delivery time was very near, Queen Bhagabati was unable to sit quietly as her stomach felt may heavy.

When she felt the labour pain in the womb, Deba Narayan could know that and so He made himself lighter so that his mother would get relief.

When unlimited worlds are hidden in the body of God there is nobody on this earth to hold Him, i.e. the weight of the entire world.

But the daughter of the king is most lucky as she was able to hold the God in her womb. Since God has no birth, He is also called Chakrapani (Vishnu).

And, that mother is the first power (Adishakti), so that she can bear God in Her womb.

When the 10th month was completed both the brothers were keen to be born.

By the strength of the mind, labour pain came. There was labour pain repeatedly on the lunar day, i.e. on the 14th day of the light fortnight of Baisakha month (Chaturdasi).[65]

At this auspicious moment a star named 'Swati' was seen on a zodiac sign call 'Tula-chandra'. That auspicious time was named 'Toutila'.

At home it was 7.24 am (GMT) and the sun was entering into the zodiacal sign of 'Singha'. The planet 'Bruhaspati' (Jupiter) was in the second position and in the sixth position was the planet 'Sani' (Saturn).

In the third position the moon is seen and the son of Bhrugu (Venus) was busy in his works. In such a holy moment there is repeated labour pain.

All the maidservants (i.e. *dhai, poili, paribari*), etc., were engaged in the services of the mother.

After this the sons were born from the mother's womb and seeing it, the *paribaries* (servants) went and informed the king about this fact.

The *paribaries* told the king 'O' Probhu the queen has given birth to a son who is looks like Sri Hari himself'.

Sri Hari has taken birth by holding 18 signs and in four hands holding *sankha, chakra, gada* and *padma.* On his body we have seen the sign of Sribatsa[66] though we only saw him for a moment.

If you see he might look like your son. But to us he looks like Vishnu.

He has taken the incarnation having one lakh of qualities. As soon as we saw him our eyes were fully satisfied.

While the maidservant (*dasi*) was telling this to the king another one came running and informed the king:

'The queen is again having labour pain.'

The king said, go immediately to her. I know that another son will be born.

Tonight I have seen a dream that two sons will be born from the womb of the queen.

You see, that fact is now going to be proved; when there is labour pain it means another son will be born.

While the king was talking, another son was born and the maidservant (*poili*) came running to inform the king.

She said, it is definitely 'Ananta' as he looks exactly like him and how will I describe his qualities.

On hearing this king Krushnaballav was very happy and gifted a lot of much wealth to the *dhai* (midwife).

He orders to celebrate this occasion with great pomp throughout the state. Everywhere people played on musical instruments like conch, flute, etc., and were dancing and singing.

The drums were played in eighteen different styles and there were twelve kinds of clapping, the ladies were singing songs and gave out the 'hulhuli' sound with their tongue.

They entered the different places of the state on the way, in the market and some snatched away the thin, fine dress of others jokingly and enjoyed.

The market and the roads reverberated with dancing and singing.

When it became dark in each and every house there were rows of lamps/torches were lit up.

The night looked like day, and the moon seemed invisible. Groups of stars were seen in the sky.

All were talking about the two sons born in the king's house and that were actually Ananta and Bhabagrahi.

Both the sons will kill all the demons and liberate the world.

Some say Hari and Hara are born and they look beautiful, being the sons of King Krishanaballav.

People talked to each other and then the *dhai* went to dress up the two boys.

They cut the navel cord in the confinement room (*antudi*) and bathed them in scented water.

The *dhai* made the two sons sleep on a bed covered with silk bedsheets.

The colour of their bodies was white and their bodies were dazzling as lightning in the sky.

On the waist a thin yellow cloth was tied which looked very beautiful. People became fascinated by seeing at this beautiful sight.

The signs of *sankha*, *chakra*, *gada* and *padma* were dazzling. The four-handed appearance was looking like a pillar of pearl.

Both lips and the eyes were shining. The sign of Vishnu blossomed in the heart's place.

Under the waist line was tied a thread of eight gems which looked beautiful. On the shoulders the golden sacred thread (*paita*) was looking beautiful.

In order to attract the mind of the people of the whole world Hari was showing various kinds of appearances from time to time.

He was looking beautiful like the blue clouds and in this way god shines this light.

The four arms were hanging up to the thighs. The cow feet sign was seen on His body and was dazzling.

The earrings of gems looked beautiful in both ears, and the mark of sandalwood paste (*chandan*) on the forehead looked like the moon.

The yellow coloured cloth made the waist look beautiful like the dazzling light of lightning among black clouds.

The curly hair and the crown on the head looked beautiful like the light of seven planets.

The sign of Vishnu on his body was like the dazzling of thousands of 'Kaustubha'[67] gems and thousands of suns.

Different kinds of flower garlands hanging on his body looked beautiful.

On the hands there were rings of gold, on the arms there were armlets and bracelets, all of gold. On his waist a string of golden bells was hanging, and producing a sweet sound.

The rings on both the feet looked beautiful. The whole of *Brahmanda* was extremely pleased to see him. His body looked beautiful with all the ornaments.

His body looked like one crore of Indian cupids. The people of Badrika State were happy looking at Him.

Sixty-four thousand girls came to the place daily and all sat near Him (Vishnu), and worshipped His feet.

The ladies of the *Brahmanda* gave out 'hulhuli' sounds with their tongue. Eight maidservants holding fly brush in their hands were engaged in fanning Him.

Eight maidservants held an umbrella on his (Vishnu) head and people took the dust of his feet and smeared it on their bodies.

The mother Bhagabati was very happy to see her two sons. All her sorrows were already driven out and her eyes became very clear.

The Brahmins came and chanted the *mantras* near him and Gods from heaven showered flowers upon him.

King Krishnaballav searched for one auspicious moment to see his sons.

He took with him different coloured flowers in a golden pot to welcome them.

Conch players with two pairs of conches proceeded ahead of him by blowing conches and behind them were repeatedly Brahmins reciting *slokas* from the Vedas,

Following them were pairs of flute players along with the bards (*bhat*) singing songs in praise of the kings two sons.

The king appeared like this before his sons and saw that his two sons were sleeping.

Holding a *sankha*, *chakra*, *gada* and *padma* in the four hands along with Ananta, He was sleeping.

Seeing this, the king was overjoyed and thought to himself that it could only be Govinda and no one else.

Due to his devotion the eyes of the king filled up with tears and again he looked at them intently.

Seeing Sri Hari in him he was amazed and prostrated himself on the ground and saluted Him at his feet.

Then he stood up and said, O' my 'Swami' (Lord) you are the 'Brahmarasi' (Vishnu). In order to save the pious men you have taken birth in this world.

When Bidhata (Lord) does not know your glory and its limitation and myself being a man (a mute in the universe) how can I serve you O Sripati?

You have taken incarnation and came to the earth for the well-being of mankind and you have taken your birth in my house holding a most beautiful body.

With which water shall I wash your feet, since river Ganga flows from your feet?

With which of flowers shall I adorn your hair and worship you whose beloved is the Thakurani of Brindaban?

How shall I worship you whose wife is Sri Mahalaxmi?

By reciting which *mantra* shall I see you, whose wife is Sharada poetess? What seat shall I give you to sit, whose devotee is Ananta and who is sleeping in the 'Ananta Sajjya' (bed) permanently?

With which scent will I spray you, whose body is adorned with the 'Bada Singhar'[68] dress?

What clothes shall I give you to wear, under whose waist a yellow loin-cloth is always tied?

With which of gems can I decorate your entire body, who has 52 crore store houses filled with gems?

When the eighteen signs are on his lotus-like feet, being an ordinary man how can I think of describing you.

I am fortunate that I could see you today, the *sankha*, *chakra*, *gada* and *padma* in your four hands.

'O' 'Prabhu', O' Kamalakanta! I am asking for shelter under you today. Today I saw you and my eyes fill with satisfaction.

Because I am having you in my house, innumerable gods are coming to my abode to have a *darshan* of you.

In order to see Him with my own eyes, I am serving you by the strength I get from yoga knowledge.

Krishnaballava fell on the lotus-like feet of Vishnu and prayed to Him with folded hands.

On seeing the intense devotion of His father, Narayan thought in his mind that he could recognize my qualities.

He will recognize me this way, so what should I appear like?

He thought in his mind to give an illusionary covering (*maya potala*) to his father (Ballava).

When the power of Maya covered Ballava
he at once thought of Govinda as his son.

Then he took Him from the mattress and held Him in his hands by considering him as his son. Then he took his son and put him on the lap of his beloved wife and told her to hold her son.

He ordered the *dasis* to look after his son and after that went back.

After this O' Narada, hear now the voice of Brahma and Rudra (Mahadev) and come serving under the feet of Vishnu.

God Varuna (God of rain), Chandra (Moon), Surya (Sun God) came along with Kubera (God of wealth), Pawana (God of wind), Yama (God of death), Agni (God of fire),

Basuki (God King of serpents), and the Guards of ten directions,

all other Gods, Gandharva Bidyadhar (the demi-god) sat there and organized a meeting.

The Kinnaries (demi-goddesses), Appasari (heavenly nymphs) groups and other bards of Heaven, forefathers along with the Dharma Debata (the God of dharma) gathered there.

Then came the sages, named Agashi, Pulasthya, Jawali, Janaka.

Then came Kapila, Goutam, Karma Risi, Mandakarna, Marichi, Pulaha, Kratu, etc., all those who are devoted to penance or meditation.

Then came Basistha, Sanaka Muni (Sage), Kapila, Balmiki, Panchasikha Durbasa, etc.

Then came Rushya Srunga having the power of Bibhandaka and Attatriteya, Angirasa, Bharadwaj, Jaimini, Ultanga,

Then came Katyayana, Parasara, Lomasa, Chayabana, Galaba, Ramancha and Muni Baisampayana.

Krupajala, Sundana, Gargya, Bedagarva, Kapila, Dadhichi, Kalinjana, Bamadeva.

Angira, Lomas, Byasa, Parasara Muni, Baruni. Then came Satyananda there having all learned personalities.

Then came Astabakra, Balasilya, Bedu and Uttumga, Maitriya, Sukramuni, Bhrugu, Sarabhanga.

Pippalatana, Bihanga Muni, Duttatriteya and other sages gathered in Badrika town.

Narada, Sananda, Parananda, Satyananda all sage groups came and joined along with Prajapati (king).

All goddesses joined and showered flowers while Paramesti was coming towards the God.

Parbati, Jagatdhatri, Gayatri, Savitri, Kinnari (demi-goddesses), Appasari (nymphs) were escorted by Sachi Padmaretri.

All the wives of sages (Risi Patnies) led by Ganga met Him directly.

Some sang songs and some gave out the 'hulhuli' sounds with their tongue, some worshipped, and some came dancing and dancing swaying their bodies from this side to that side.

Some uttered 'Hari Hari' and some uttered 'Balarama'. Some uttered 'Krushna, Krushna' and some uttered 'Ghanashyama'.

Some uttered 'Jagannath' and some uttered 'Sri Pati'. Some uttered 'Bhagwan' and some uttered 'Jagajyoti'.

Some praised Badrikapura which is looking beautiful like a second Baikuntha (the abode of Vishnu).

When leaving Baikuntha, Sri Hari was present there, so all the Gods were coming there leaving all the holy places (*tirtha*).

All were paying salute under the feet of Sri Hari and the devotees were serving under the lotus feet of Govinda.

The idol which never appeared came and appeared there, so prominently. It was Narayana Himself who is the inhabitant of the milk ocean (*khira samudra*).

He has come to Badrika Dham. O' this is the land, place and village of this King who is worthy to be praised.

O' see in the heart of Vishnu Kamalini (Goddess Laxmi) has reached. Sarada and Mata Thakurani are serving there.

Mahaprabhu is sleeping on the 'Anantasajjya' and he is looking as if he is sitting on a throne of pearl.

In the earlier days what we had seen in Baikuntha now we see that in Badrika Dham.

Also the eighteen signs are seen on his body–the *sankha, chakra, gada, padma, kodanda* (bow), and *kulisa* (thunderbolt),

Dhwaja (flag), *bajra* (lightning), *saranga* (moon), *kharga* (sword), *musala* (club), *jumba* (yawn), *gopuspada* (cowfeet), *sayaka* (arrow), *ankusa* (goad[69]), *langala* (plough).

And also flute (*tabaru*) and trap (*pasa*). These 18 signs are visible to the gods only and not to human beings.

The gods by seeing these signs stood up and prayed with folded hands and said, 'We saw Vishnu in Baikuntha and came back'.

In order to save his devotees Vishnu himself took such an appearance (form), and the man who sees this will be freed from all his sins.

We saw the *srimukha* (face of god) and all our sorrows and suffering have been driven out. And by looking at *padmamukha* (the lotus-like face of Vishnu) we got the holy directions for our soul.

Your devotees are roaming in the forest of white water lilies and in that forest your face is like the autumnal moon.

At the end of the day Nath (Vishnu) took up this incarnation. In that water lily forest our friendship with god will blossom.

By looking at your eighteen signs we took shelter beneath your feet.

By holding a club, plough, sword and lightning in your hand you save your devotees O' Nath by killing the demons.

By keeping your eighteen signs in mind all your devotees are running to Baikuntha in order to see you and a salute your feet.

Under your lotus feet the whole world is liberated. The going of Brahman is your unity.

'Kaustubha Mani'[70] is seen on your chest and by seeing it, we the gods are saved.

Your name and heroic flag is holy for the *mela*. And that flag is seen for us only.

The bird 'Pakhiraj', who is your chariot, is the carrier of Brahman-semen, which is most active.

Crores of worlds are all in your womb. So the holy bird is able to carry your heavy weight.

So long as the world is there you will kill and drive out the demons by sitting on 'Garuda' *bahana* (chariot).

The Krishnaballav king is most fortunate because you took your birth from the womb of his wife.

For four birth cycles he will be your father. By telling this Bidhata is praising him.

Now we know that surely the demons will die because you have already taken up your incarnation.

The demons have already enjoyed 20 *jugas* (ages) and their time will be over since they will be killed by the God (Vishnu).

You are Antaryami because you know everyone's mind and thoughts so definitely those who are fortunate will worship you.

The man who has earned much wealth, if he does not give alms then he is called a poor man.

If you earn money and if you do not do good works in the name of Dharma then Narahari cannot be with you, because Hari is always present on the side of Dharma.

In whose house Laxmi Narayana is present he is known as a fortunate man in the world.

The Gods prayed to God to save the earth.

And after saying that they went back.

Brahma climbed up to the hill of 'Swarapadapa' and reached Jasabantipur.

After Brahma left all other gods went to their respective places,

The writer is telling that I am Bipra Pitambara and I am taking shelter under the feet of 'Gobinda'.

CONVERSATION BETWEEN SRI LAXMI AND SRI JAGANNATH

Dasi[71]

Dasi says O' Mother!
You have entered, Debaraya,
The cart is ready in front of the Lion's Gate (*Singha Dwara*)
The crowd is so big that the road cannot be seen
The beating of the drum (*nisan*) is very loud (1)

Listen to the sound of the conch (*sankha*)
Raja Gajapati is in the gathering
Horses, elephants, pedestrians (*padati*) are innumerable
Rythms of metal instruments (*kahala, kardala, kansala*)[72]
Kettledrum and flute (*bheri mahuri*) is heard everywhere (2)

Cool moonlight is everywhere
White *chhati*[73] is overhead.

Laxmi

Laxmi says 'Alo Dasi' you go:
Close the Bajra Kilani door[74]
The husband's elder brother (*dedhasura*) enters the house.
Let the block-faced[75] be outside the door
Close the Bajra Kilani door (3)

Dasi gets this order.

Jagannath

Nagabara[76] knowing the feeling of Laxmi
he tells smilingly
'Alo' Paribari[77] open the door!
For what reason you are angry?
What more should we tell? (4)

You are Lo sajana.[78]

Dasi

Dasi is telling 'Aho' Padmanabha[79]
Leaving the door, what's your benefit?
What work is there in the big temple (*badadeula*)?
Mahabahu (big shouldered), you left and have come again.

You are Laxmi's husband, you should be ashamed. (5)

Now Debaraja.

Jagannath	Prabhu (god) is telling, Lo, leave these things She is higher than all *priyabatis* (loving ladies) Do you know, the gem worn on the head of a girl is her wealth Who has the intellect to win the world? (6)

See my body, without Kamala (Laxmi).

Dasi	It's known, even if you do not say To loose the way in Bali town (*nagar*) Isn't it your Gundicha[80] house Where you have girls dancing and singing Tears are rolling down (7)

Frustrated Puri.

Jagannath	Alo, it is hard to convince you! You tell big things. Is Gundicha house a permanent place? Wherever Kamala (Laxmi) is, there is our mind. We both are Thakur, Thakurani (God, Goddess) (8)

Wow, darling.

Dasi	Nagarabara, tell me the truth! Your talk is very sweet. Your heart is most cruel. You are a merciless man You left without judging any fault. (9)

Oh Rajkumari!

Jagannath	Ancient Raja Indradyumna Took a vow from us. With Gundicha Rani's blessing We three sat on the cart. Killed the sinful (*papi*), the fallen (*chandal*), the outcasets (*patita*). (10)

Returned in a hurry.

Dasi	When you went with your devotees Gundicha was heard in the world

Why didn't you take her with you?
She is a faithful wife
Would your Gundicha tour have gone wrong, (11)

with Kamalini (Laxmi)?

Jagannath

In festivals Debatas (Gods) are present.
There is a mad rush.
The elder two were with me.
So we did not take Debi Kamalini (Laxmi)
She is a daughter-in-law of this clan, a daughter of this ocean (12)

It would not be right.

Dasi

Debatas (Lord) like Indra, Brahma?
Laxmi is the ultimate mother of everyone
This thing is agreed upon everywhere.
You abandoned Kamala (Laxmi)
You only tell sweet and clever things. (13)

Jagannath

It is difficult to convince women.
The more you try to convince them, the more they disagree.
Look, clouds have come up.
It is raining heavily.
Still your anger is not cooling down. (14)

I am already wet.

Dasi

Go back, Deva Chakradhara (Jagannath)
You stayed permanently in Bali Nagar
You both stayed with Subhadra.
Everyday you are with a new girl.
Now your sister (*bhauni*) has become the wife. (15)

You should be ashamed.

Jagannath

Subhadra is our younger sister.
We took her with us because of the festival
We have never stayed separated.
Where Rama Krushna is, there is Subhadra.
One soul, separate bodies.
Acquiring, knowing nothing. (16)

Dasi

Tell me some good things, Gosai (Jagannath)

I will make you speechless
The *bhoga* you have given to Laxmi.
Dalua[81] rice with *kalamba* saga.[82]
It became famous in the three worlds
How much affection you have (towards Laxmi). (17)

Jagannath

Your stock (*bhandara*) is of 52 crore
Kubera Debta (Lord of Wealth) is the *parichara* (caretaker)
Eight types of wealth (*astanidhi*) are in his hand.
And you are blaming me!
Kotiswara[83] is born a beggar (*daridra*). (18)

Dasi

You took it with you the 52 crore stock
Leaving here the *sila silapua* (a pestle stone and a slap stone for grinding).
Chhanchuni *kula*,[84] you are telling her a stock holder!
What you did, Debadhi Raja (Raja of Rajas)
Do you not feel ashamed, telling these? (19)

Jagannath

You are prolonging the argument.
You are not considering our heart's pain.
Sri Nilambara (Balabhadra) went inside.
But you have kept me outside.
I have brought paintings of cloud. (20)

Open the door

Dasi

Whoever is Ratnakara[85] is Tata[86]
Sudhakara (nectar) himself is the younger brother (*kanista bhrata*)
Brahmandanatha,[87] when his mind is pleased.

Give it to the new (*naba*) loving sister (*bhagni*). (21)

Return it.

Jagannath

Oh! Girls having lotus eyes. You seen to be having bright minds.
Gave wealth as bribe to the *dasis*.
Talking to Kamala, sweet words
The *dasis* opened the door for getting the bribe.
Sri Chakadola (Jagannath) entered inside.

Saw Kamala, saw one other, and were overwhelmed with happiness.
Sri Duitiari (Jagannath) inhaled her head on his lap.
Prabhu Jagannath smiles, and says,
Have mercy and listen to me! Mother of the world, wake up quickly.
We will talk sitting in the palanquin. (22)

Let's go!

Laxmi

Well said Debadhiraj.
Laxmi's husband, are you ashamed?
You have brought your loving sister
and talking alone to her very sweetly.
Why do you hide your face in shame.
It is a matter of happiness. (23)

Stirija

You are a fool, you could not get me after convincing.
Subhadra is your sister-in-law.
Welcome her with sweet words.
Praise my close friend (*sakhi*). (24)

She will be pleased.

Laxmi

Kamala looked with happy eyes.
With a light smile she held her hands.
Took her and made her sit in the palanquin.
Talking sarcastically she forgot the sorrow of separation, and became happy.
All mankind (*manaba*), demons (*danaba*) and gods (*debta*) discuss among themselves.
All who were present were allowed to go back to their own places.
'I completed the purification work by burning incense, etc.
As Karuna Nidhi (Jagannath) will sleep.'
Jagannath spent many nights happily
talking to Kamala (Laxmi).
When Jagannath and Laxmi went to see the sun in a chariot
at first only the wheels of the car was visible to the sun.
As flowers wait for the big black bee (*bhramura*),

like the *Chatak* (a bird) is looking for rain to come.
Likewise when a lover is away from home,
when Laxmi and Narayan (Jagannath) met
together they become very happy,
Beneath Radha Krushna's both feet,
sinners surrender themselves.
What Bipru[88] Maheswara wished,
those powerful things they can do,
to release us from the sins and fears of death. (25)

MADLA OF SATHUA CLAN

Deogarh Raja Saheb had brought Srikant Sathua from the South Gate (*dwar*) of Puri. Bamanda kept the merchant (Bania), giving the title Kinda Gauntia. Later as his daughter (*jhio*) and daughter-in-law (*bhuasuni*) were seen in bad eyes,[89] he did not stay there and smashed a stone there saying no Bania will stay in Bamanda. He went towards Bonai via Barkot. At that time Bonai's Raja sent people to ask us, seeing that we have come here. Then they asked about our clan and said 'Raja is calling you'. They told (immigrant): 'One Raja brought us and wanted to torture us, that's why we came here within a night. This is also a Raja like that', he said 'we will not listen to him' and they came back. Raja send the *paik chara*[90] and they brought them to the Raja. We felt sad, so he told 'One Raja has done a mistake that does not mean that every Raja will do the same mistake'. 'Do not be angry with me. I will keep you in my presence and will do all the necessary arrangements. You are my *sathi* (friend) and you stay with me, so your title will be Sathua. My state is Bonaigarh and your *garh* (fort) becomes Baharigarh. As you have come from a pleasant place and also from outside (*baharu*) I'm giving you the name *baharighar*.' And also after giving the land, from that day he has to take care of our well-being. At that time there was *nuakhai* festival. He called us and said: 'Tomorrow is Nuakhai—wont you observe it?' We said 'We do not have anything, how will we eat *nua* (new rice)'. The Raja said 'In our state whatever you get from anyone, you just start *nuakhai*. If anyone has complaints he should come to us and I will take care of it'. We started *nuakhai* that night. We woke up at 4 a.m., stole paddy from paddy fields, arranged *guda* (molasses), ghee, etc., caught hold of things whatever we got from whomever. While fetching water from the river, a snake was there raising its *phana*[91] at the *ghat* which was made in our name. We returned back from there and went there again with a sword, rice (*naibaidya*), incense sticks (*dhupa*) and offering of *harida* and worshipped the snake. It went down into the water. We had to cut the water by the sword, then we took water and came. We were near to Kurei *patra* (leaves). When we wanted to bring it, the snake was there too. When we went near the tree, it left the place and went away. As we are of Nagesra *gotra*, we worshipped it and started eating the *nua* and started worshipping the *Ista Debi* Kuaari and within that night we finished our *nuakhai*. Then early next morning we went to the Raja to offer him obeisance. He said: 'You ate *nuakhai* earlier'. We have eaten bowing down (praying) to Kuaari *Ista Debi*, so the Raja said 'I had asked you to do so. Hence you need not feel guilty. You are telling that you have seen a cobra at the time of fetching water. Cobra is the carrier of Baneshwar. So you have made Kuaari as your *ista debi*. May your *nuakhai* be successful.' We never give *nuakhai* to married daughters (*bibahela jio*) or to any relatives. We eat it early in the morning, and is immediately afterward float the *patri* (the leaf bowl to eat *nua*) in the river. From that day we stayed with the title (*upadhi*) *Sathuaa* at Baharigarh. The Raja said: 'You will give me a golden sacred thread on my *abhishek*.' We asked: 'From where will we get the gold?' 'I will tell the Brahmins. Brahmins will collect money (*chandas*) and will give the money to you. With that money you will make the golden thread.' It is given to the Raja on Pous Purnima. From that day Raja started to give people one by one and they stayed with us. From that day the hamlet started.

[ON JAGANNATH][92]

That day tears rolled down from the eyes of hundreds of devotees with thoughts of great joy and respect. On this day, as per the humble request of the poet Balaram Das, Jagannath left the big chariot of Badadanda and came to the Baliratha.[93] He became tired and stopped. That day he was unable to carry the power of Orissa as per the devotee Salbegar. But he has the capacity to do many things. That is why he is known as *danarakshaka* (keeper of gifts).

Above all he does not make a distinction between any castes. He does not have much desire for good food. Here the banner of secularism always flies. All religion means the same to him. All have the right to take *prasad*. This is proved in *Laxmi Purana*. Here the importance of *mahaprasad* is fully accepted.

Dibakara Das says about the writings of Jagannath as thus:

The offering intended for a deity
That will be offered by Baladeva
Jagannath will be well pleased
It is thought to be tasted by God
The *mahaprasad* gets finished.

Sri Jagannath is a dazzling representative of Srikshetra's and a holistic independent controller of the equality of all religions. He is a constant source of friendship and kindness. That is why he is known as a person who stands for a united nation. We are under such a *debta* having a great arm of care and protection. Each person of Orissa should feel proud that s/he is born in such a holy land like Orissa.

TRADITION OF GADAJATA BONAI AND SOME BRIGHT CHAPTERS IN ITS HISTORY

The following narration aims to give us a glance of how, after Independence, the foundation stone for the propagation of education was laid in Gadajata Bonai.

Generally it has been seen that in many Gadajatas (states) Rajas tortured their subjects (*praja*) through the system of forced labour (*bheti begari*), of which there are many instances. But there were some states where the Rajas have worked hard for their subjects' overall development and welfare, for instance, Bamanda's Raja Sir Basudev Sudhal Deb and his son Raja Sachidananda Tribhuban Deb. For their good work for their state they were praised by the British government of that time (*tadanintana*) and people still remember them. In Bonai Gadajata too, propagation of the education did not go neglected.

When the neighbouring Bamanda was so developed in education, literature, science, society, agriculture, trade, economics, etc., it was natural that there will be an influence on Bonai Gadajata too. More so because Bonai's Rajas generally maintained a good relation with the Rajas of Gadajatas like Bamanda, Pallahada, Kalahandi, Dhenkanal, etc.

Several steps were taken for the propagation of education in Bonai generally from 1853 onwards. During that time Raja Shiv Narayan Indra Deo sent Bhagirathi Purohit, etc., to Varanasi to study how to propagate education in Bonai.

In later years, Raja Dayanidhi Chandra Deo made a *chou padhi*[94] close to the Bonai Rajbati realizing the importance of education. Where poetry, astronomy and ayurveda were taught. The Raja brought a Pandit from Puri to teach these subjects. People like Sri Keshaba Patra, Chamrudhara Mishra and Damodara Pujahari studied there.

At the time of the reign of Raja Nilambara Chandra Deo, i.e. in 1897, the *chou padhi* was shut down and was replaced by a discussion hall (*sabha*). Here well-known poets and critics like Janardan Padhi, *Kumara Sambhaba*; Bidyadhana Jena; the author of *Batis Singhasan's*, Jadu Phatkar, the author of *Banua sastra* and poetry analyst Jaydeb Satpathy attended, communicated and propagated knowledge discussion in the state. Raja Nilambara Deo himself authored a humourous book *Kalanidhi Gitikabya*. Raja Sachidananda of the neighbouring state Bamanda also left his mark of knowledge and plight by making primary education compulsory in 1909 and arrangement was made to construct an upper primary school for both boys and girls in every village having more than 50 residents. Like this steps had been taken to construct a modern school in Bonai state in 1902. In that year it was finalized to construct the Bonai Rajbati School. On 20 December 1902, Sri Madhusudhan Panda and Sri Godadhar Panigrahi of Sambalpur joined as Head Pandit and second Head Pandit respectively. Nilamani Baidya, Kalakara Dash, Banchhanidhi Behere, Pitambara Sahu were among the first students of this school. The development of education for women was also encouraged. As a result, many girls came forward to take admission in that school. Brajabala Debi and seven other girls joined the school in 1908 (15-12-1908). Later on (dated 8-3-1910) this school was converted to an Upper Primary school. With the passing of time, the strength of the school increased, as shown below:

Date	Boys	Girls	Total
08-03-1910	50	2	52
21-08-1911	49	4	53
11-12-1912	54	10	64
09-04-1913	65	11	76
24-01-1914	75	15	90
01-10-1915	105	18	124

The above table shows that with the passage of time, in Bonai, awareness towards education increased. In 1914, as in Rajbati School, the education level increased from 2 to 3: Ramakrushna Nath was appointed as the head teacher, Brudabana Panda as assistant teacher and Baneam Nath as monitor.

As Bamanda Raja Sachidananda Tribhuban Deb had done for the propagation of education, similarly in Bonai. Raja Sri Dharanidhar Chandra Deo Deb followed the same pattern and gained the goodwill of the people and remained in their memory for all times to come.

Raja Dharanidhar was coronated in 1901 and immediately took steps for the quick development and propagation of education. With his effort, between 1907 and 1913, nine primary schools were constructed in Bonaigarh, Tumkala, Sharadhapur, Jungala, Bijakuli, Banki, Kaleiposh, Kuliposh and Tendara. The school at Kaleiposh was the first to be established in Kudeikala where Sri Anenda Mahanta (Mundagaam) was a teacher.

In these schools, primary importance was given to the teaching of Mathematics and Literature as is clearly evident from the school agency's inspector A.G. Deefhe's inspection report dated 20 March 1911. In his views, 'the teachers should pay special attention to the subjects of Reading, Dictation, Writing and Arithmetic and should give their pupils a very careful and thorough[95] grounding in them'.[96] Arrangements were made to keep one teacher from Cuttack or Puri district in every primary school to teach Literature. So Sri Debanath Kar from Mula Basanta village (a coastal area) came to Bonai. It's known from instructor A.G. Hapip's report that at that time in Bonai one instructor pandit, 17 teachers and 2 monitors were appointed. In 1916, the number of schools started increasing: 17 primary schools were established in Lahunipada, Kenabheta, Satkuta, Ghosra and other places. Out of those, there upper primary school started at Bonaigarh, Jungala and Lahunipada. In that year an inspector's post was created in Bonai and Sri Biseswara Bhanja was appointed as its inspector.

20-26 JUNE 1993s PRAJATANTRA SAPTAHIKI (ONE WEEKLY EDITION)[97]

Sri Mandira Womb house (main house) repairing. 28 (*anka*) Sri Bira Kesheri Deb (Puri Gajapati) third floor 28 March 1993 on the time of repairing the following persons Sri Damedeva Mohapatra, Bandhu Mohapatra from Bonai, it has been writing. Lime plastering they had done (must be the persons belongs to Bonai, involved in the repairing).

NOTES

1. *Rudraksha* (literally 'Rudra-eyed') = a broad-leaved tree. Its seeds are used for prayer beads and for bead chains (*mala*).
2. Vishnu and Shiva.
3. Apparently Banasura in line 6 and Baneshwar in line 7 have been mixed.
4. Space is left in the original—apparently to fill in the name later.
5. Goddess Durga.
6. *Khir* = Milk.
7. *Jatadari* = who has matted hair on the head; *jateshwara* = plaited hair.
8. *Nagala* = Naked.
9. *Kumari* = virgin.
10. *Brahmacharya*.
11. *Shunya* = nil, zero, emptiness, void?
12. *Adbhuta* = strange (not related to *bhut*).
13. Lord Shiva.
14. Husband's younger brother's wife.
15. Literally: up to the stomach/waist.
16. Engraved with faces on one side of the bead.
17. A necklace in which the beads are made of the seeds of a big wild tree.

18. Round pebbles found in the bed of Gandaki River and worshipped as Vishnu.
19. A bracelet in the name of Goddess Durga or 'Nine Durgas'.
20. Investiture of a new king–the Rajkumar taking oath as Raja.
21. *Sama* = iron part of a husking pedal/*dhinki*.
22. The first day of a lunar fortnight.
23. A sacred scripture read for Goddess Chandi.
24. *Amat* = non-Brahmanical priest in Bonai belonging to the Sudh community.
25. *Khanda* = sword; *ghar* = house, room. Here the armoury.
26. A platform used as a seat for an idol.
27. *Hati* = elephant; *panchami* = fifth. Probably the day to worship the royal elephants.
28. *Gaja* = elephant.
29. *Aswa* = horse.
30. *Madla* = see the discussion on the term in the introduction.
31. The name *Singar* might be derived from *shrungar* = toilet in the sense of make-up.
32. Probably a spelling mistake since the Goddess is usually referred to as Basuli.
33. A renowned Brahmin family in Bonai.
34. Budha Gosain = 'Old Master'.
35. Roof spaces/'upstairs' in a mud house.
36. A type of edible leaves.
37. A type of pulse.
38. Rather a branch of the tamarind tree.
39. 1 *hath* = 18 inch.
40. Made of the lower portion of a cow tail or bunch of which fruits grow (coconut/date palm).
41. *Håta* = cunning, jest–in the sense of a sarcastic remark.
42. Referring to Jagannath. Padma = lotus.
43. *Chitra* = picture, *megha* = cloud, *pata* = raw silk. Referring to a silk saree on which clouds are printed/woven.
44. Festival when rice of the new paddy is consumed.
45. *Danga* = boat.
46. *Sathi* = friend, but *sathi bhai* here probably as friend brothers in the sense of cousin brothers.
47. Big sword, literally = saw.
48. *Mahabira* = great hero.
49. *Bira* = hero.
50. *Hamira* = proud person, in the negative sense = bastard.
51. Since Lecha had not been mentioned before, it might be Necha here?
52. Since Leja has not been mentioned before, it might be Leda here?
53. *Pranam* with spreading the hands and legs on the ground (falling prostate).

54. *Aputrika* = without any son.
55. Patna may refer to various places here. Very likely it might be Patna State (present Bolangir district of Orissa) rather then Patna in present Bihar or the market area of Bonaigarh which is known as Patna too.
56. Another spelling for the neighbouring state of Bamra.
57. Possibly referring to Puri.
58. Mental imbalance.
59. *Nala* = pipe, as used for measurement.
60. Probably here 'Court of Ward'.
61. The middle son, Tribikram Keshor Deo, died due to meningitis at the age of 6 months.
62. The third day of the lunar fortnight.
63. The list refers to a donation of the Raja to the Baneshwar temple.
64. Let us take up our birth.
65. Roughly March-April.
66. The curly hair which is on the chest of Vishnu.
67. Gem worn by Vishnu on his chest.
68. Literally: 'great dress'.
69. Instrument used by Mahouts to control elephants.
70. A gem worn on the chest of Vishnu.
71. Maidservant.
72. Various musical instruments. *Kahali* = indigenous trumpet, *kansala* = cimbel, *kardala* = probably brass/bell metal instrument.
73. *Chhati* = mushroom. Possibly a writing mistake and it should be *chatri* = umbrella.
74. The main door of a temple *Bajra* = thunder; *kilani* = nail.
75. Probably a term for Jagannath.
76. Jagannath – literally *nagar* = town, *bara* = husband.
77. Female head of the family.
78. One who knows everything.
79. Jagannath.
80. Mother's (younger) sister (*mausi*) of Lord Jagannath.
81. A variety of paddy.
82. A type of edible leaves.
83. Perhaps Laxmi.
84. Winnowing fan.
85. *Ratnakara* = Ocean.
86. *Tata* = Father, revered person.
87. Lord of the Universe – presumably referring to Vishnu.
88. In the text Bipru is written meaning priest/Brahmin. However, given the text it might be a spelling mistake and it should be Bishnu (Vishnu) instead.
89. People were talking in a derogatory way.
90. Foot = soldiers or infantry.

91. The expanded hood of a snake.
92. There is no headline in the original text. It appears to be a fragment only. Possibly from a newspaper article.
93. *Bali* = sand, *rath* = car.
94. A village school.
95. *Through* in the original, but probably a spelling mistake.
96. Written in English in the Oriya text.
97. A fragment – probably from the weekly journal *Prajatantra Saptahiki*. The reason for the inclusion of this fragment remains obscure.

CHAPTER III

ଓଁ ନମଃ ଶିବାୟ

-ଶିବ ତାଣ୍ଡବ-

ଡିବି ଡିବି ଡମ୍ବରୁ ବାଜେ, ମନ ଚିତ ମନଚିତ ରଞ୍ଜେ
ହେ ଶିବ ଜଟା ମସ୍ତକେ ସାଜେ ଗଙ୍ଗା ପ୍ରଖର ବିରାଜେ

ଶଶାଙ୍କ ଶେଖର ସାଜେ ଉତ୍ତରୀ ଅନନ୍ତ ବିରାଜେ
ହେ ଶିବ ଡିବିଡିବି ଡମ୍ବରୁ ବାଜେ ମନ ଚିତ ମନ ଚିତ ରଞ୍ଜେ

ବିଭୁତି ଭୂଷଣ ସାଜେ କୋଟିରେ ବ୍ୟାଘ୍ର ଚର୍ମ ସାଜେ ରୁଦ୍ରାକ୍ଷ
ବିରାଜେ
କମଣ୍ଡଳୁ ହସ୍ତେ ତ୍ରିଶୁଳ କରେ ବିରାଜେ

ଅନ୍ୟ ହସ୍ତେ ଅଭୟ ବିରାଜେ ଏକ ହସ୍ତେ ରୁଦ୍ରାକ୍ଷର ବିଜେ
ହେ ଶିବ ଡିବିଡିବି ଡମ୍ବରୁ ବାଜେ ମନ ଚିତ ମନ ଚିତ ରଞ୍ଜେ

ପୟରେ କଠଉ ବିରାଜେ ବୃଷଭ ବାହାନ ସାଜେ
ଡିବି ଡିବି ଡମ୍ବରୁ ବାଜେ ମନ ଚିତ ମନ ଚିତ ରଞ୍ଜେ

ପୂର୍ବେ କେତେଦେବ ବିଜେ ପଶ୍ଚିମେ କାର୍ତ୍ତିକେଶ୍ୱର ବିଜେ
ଦକ୍ଷିଣ ଗଣେଶ ସାଜେ ଉତ୍ତର ପାର୍ବତୀ ଦେବୀ ବିଜେ

ଡିବିଡିବି ଡମ୍ବରୁ ବାଜେ ପାନ ଚିତ ମନ ଚିତ ରଞ୍ଜେ
ପୂର୍ବେ ପୁଷ୍କରିଣୀ ସାଜେ ପଶ୍ଚିମେ ବ୍ରାହ୍ମଣୀ ବିରାଜେ

ଉତ୍ତର ବ୍ରାହ୍ମଣୀ ପ୍ରଖର ରାଜେ ଦକ୍ଷିଣେ ଉଷା ମେଢ଼ ସାଜେ
ଡିବିଡିବି ଡମ୍ବରୁ ବାଜେ ମନ ଚିତ ମନ ଚିତ ରଞ୍ଜେ

ପଥର ଘରିଆ ବିରାଜେ ବହେବାସ ହରିହର
ଧାଇ ଶିବ ପୟର ଡିବିଡିବି ଡମ୍ବରୁ ବାଜେ ।

ବଣାଇଁ ଇତିହାସ

-ବାଣେଶ୍ୱର ଜଣାଣ-

ଆହେ ବାବା ବାଣେଶ୍ୱର ମୋ ଦୁଃଖ ହର ।
ତବ ପଦେ ଜଣାଉଛି ସୁଦୟା କର
ଆଦ୍ୟେ ଶ୍ରୋଣିତ ନଗର ଥିଲା ରାଜ୍ୟର
ଏଣେ ବାସ କରିଥିଲା ବାଣା ଅସୁର
ବାଣାସୁର ଭକ୍ତି ଦେଖି କାଶି ବିଶ୍ୱନାଥ ଆସି
ବଣାଇଁଗଡରେ ହେଲେଟି ସ୍ଥିର, ନାମ ହେଲା ବାଣାସୁର
ବାଣ ସର୍ଗ ବାଣେଶ୍ୱର ପ୍ରସିଦ୍ଧ ଦେବତା ବୋଲି କଲା ପ୍ରଚାର
ଦେଓଗାଁ ବୋଲିଣ ଗ୍ରାମ ଏଥିପରେ ନିଜଗ୍ରାମ
ଦେଉଳ ତୋଳାଇ ଅଛି ବାଣା ଅସୁର,
ସମ୍ମୁଖେ ବୃଷ ବାହାନ ତଦପରେ ଆରୋହଣ
ଚତୁର୍ଦ୍ଦଶ ଭୂବନରେ ଶୋଭା ପ୍ରକାଶ,
ତହିଁ ଅଛି ରାଜାଙ୍କ ନଗର
ଉତ୍ତରେ ଅଛି କୁମାରୀ ଦେବୀଙ୍କ ମନ୍ଦିର
ସର୍ବଜନ ତାଙ୍କୁ ସେବି ନାନା ବିପତ୍ତିରୁ ପାଉଛନ୍ତି ଉଦ୍ଧାର
ଆହେ ବାବା ବାଣେଶ୍ୱର ମୋ ଦୁଃଖ ହର,
କହେ ଦାଶ ହରିହର ତାଳପତ୍ରରୁ ବାହାର
ଶରଣ ନେଉଛି ବାଣେଶ୍ୱର ଦାୟର,

ଘେନ ଏହି ଜଣାଣ ପଂଚାନନ ହେ ବାଣେଶ୍ୱର
ପଡି ଭବସାଗରେ ଦୁଃଖଭରେ ହେଲି କାତର,
ରଖ ନ ରଖ ନାଥ ମୁଁ ଅନାଥ ତବ କିଂକର
ଘେନ ଶ୍ୱସାନ ବାସୀ ହେ ପିଉସୀ ଦିଗାମ୍ବର
ଖଣ୍ଡତ୍ରିଶୁଳ କରେ ନିରନ୍ତର ଶୋଭା ପଖର
ଲେଖେ ଧରଣୀଧର ଧିଆଇ ତବ ପୟର ।

-ବାଣେଶ୍ୱରଙ୍କ ଉତ୍ପତ୍ତି-

ପୂର୍ବେ ବଣାଇଁ ରାଜ୍ୟ ଥିଲା ଶ୍ରୋଣିତ ନଗର । ଏଠାରେ ବାଣା ଅସୁର ରାଜତ୍ୱ କରୁଥିଲା । ଦିନେ ତାଙ୍କର ମାଆ କହିଲେ, ତୁ ପ୍ରତ୍ୟେକ ଦିନ ଯାଇ ଶିବ ପୂଜା କରି ଆସିବାଟା ମତେ ମହାକଷ୍ଟ ଲାଗୁଛି । ତୁ କାଲିଠୁଁ ଶିବଙ୍କୁ ପ୍ରସନ୍ନ କରି ଆମ ଘରକୁ ଆଣିବୁ । ମୁଁ ତୋତେ ଆଶିର୍ବାଦ ଦେଉଛି । ତା ଆରଦିନ ବାଣାସୁର କାଶୀଧାମକୁ ଗଲେ । ନିର୍ଦ୍ଧିଷ୍ଟ କେତେଦିନ ଶିବଙ୍କୁ ପୂଜା କଲେ । ଶିବ ତାଙ୍କ ଠାରେ ପ୍ରଶନ୍ନ ହେଲେ ଓ କହିଲେ କହ ବାଣାସୁର ତୁ କଣ ଚାହୁଁ ବାଣାସୁର କହିଲେ ମୋ ମାଆଙ୍କର ଆଦେଶରେ ଭକ୍ତି କରି ମୁଁ ଆପଣଙ୍କୁ ପାଇଛି ମୋର ଅନୁରୋଧ ଆପଣ ମୋ ରାଜ୍ୟକୁ ଯିବେ । ଶିବ ତାଙ୍କୁ କହିଲେ, ମୁଁ ଯିବି କିନ୍ତୁ ଗୋଟିଏ ସର୍ତରୋ ତୁ ଚାଲ, ତୁ ଯାଉଥିବୁ ମୋତେ ତୁ ଯେଉଁଠାରେ ପଛକରି ଅନାଇବୁ ମୁଁ ସେଇଠି ରହିବି । ବାଣାସୁର କହିଲା, ଆପଣ ପଛପଟେ ଆସୁଛନ୍ତି ବୋଲି ମୁଁ କିପରି ଜାଣିବି । ଶିବ କହିଲେ ମୁଁ ବୃଷର ଉପରେ ବିଜେ କରି ଯିବି । ହେଲେ ବୃଷର ଘଂଟି ବାଜୁଥିବ ବାଜୁଥିବ ତୁ ସେଇଟା ଅନୁମାନ କରିବୁ । ବାଣାସୁର ତାହା ରାଜି ହେଲା । ଶିବ କହିଲେ ତୁ ଚାଲ । ବାଣାସୁର ଆସୁଅଛି ତା ପଛରେ ଶିବ ଆସୁଛନ୍ତି । କିଛି ସମୟପରେ ବାଣାସୁର ବ୍ରାହ୍ମଣୀ କୂଳରେ

ପ୍ରବେଶ ହେଲା । ବ୍ରାହ୍ମଣୀ କୂଳକୁ ବାଣାସୁର ଆସିଗଲା । ଶିବ ଜାଣିଲେ ମୁଁ ତ ତାର ଗଡକୁ ଆସିଗଲି, ବ୍ରାହ୍ମଣୀ ଉତ୍ତର ବାହିନୀ ହୋଇଛି । ମନରେ ଭାବିଲେ ଏ ତ ଉତ୍ତର ବାହିନୀ ଗଙ୍ଗା । ଏଣୁ ଏହା ମୋର ଉତ୍ତମ ସ୍ଥାନ । ଏଣୁ ସେଠି ରହିବା ଉଦ୍ଦେଶ୍ୟରେ ବୃଷଭ ସେଠାରେ ଠିଆ ହେଲେ, ଘଂଟି ବାଜିଲା ନାହିଁ । କିଛି କ୍ଷଣ ଘଂଟି ଶବ୍ଦ ନ ଶୁଣିବାରୁ ବାଣାସୁର ପଛକୁ ଚାହିଁଲା । କାରଣ ଶିବ ଆସୁ ନାହାନ୍ତି ବୋଲି ତାର ସନ୍ଦେହ ହେଲା । ସେ ଦେଖିଲା ଶିବ ସେଠାରେ ଉଭା ହୋଇଛନ୍ତି । ଶିବ କହିଲେ ତୋ ଭକ୍ତିରେ ମୁଁ ତୋ ରାଜ୍ୟକୁ ଆସିଲି, ମୁଁ ଏଠାରୁ ଆଉ ଯିବି ନାହିଁ, କାରଣ ତୁ ତୋର ସର୍ତ ଭଙ୍ଗ କଲୁ । ତୁ ଗୋଟିଏ ରାତ୍ର ମଧ୍ୟରେ ମୋର ମନ୍ଦିର ନିର୍ମାଣ କର, ମୁଁ ଏଇଠି ରହିବି। ବାଣାସୁର ଗୃହକୁ ନେବା ପାଇଁ ଶକ୍ତି ଉଠାଇବାକୁ ବଳ ଲଗାଇଲା, କିନ୍ତୁ ପାରିଲା ନାହିଁ । ତାପରେ ସେଠାରେ ମନ୍ଦିର ନିର୍ମାଣ ହେଲା, ଶିବପୂଜା ପାଇଲେ । ତାଙ୍କର ମୁଖଶାଳା ସେତେବେଳେ ନଥିଲା । ଜଣେ ଜଣେ ଯାଇ ଶିବଙ୍କୁ ପୂଜା କରୁଥିଲେ । ବାଣାସୁର ନାମ ଅନୁସାରେ ଶୋଣିତ ନଗର ହେଲା ବଣାଇଁ ।ଶିବମଧ ବାଣାସୁରଙ୍କ ନାମ ଅନୁସାରେ ବାଣେଶ୍ୱର ହେଲେ । ଏ ଶକ୍ତି ଶିବପାର୍ବତୀଙ୍କର ଯୁଗଳ ମୂର୍ତୀ ଲିଙ୍ଗ ପାତାଳଗାମୀ ।ଚଉଦ ଭୂବନ ମଧ୍ୟରେ ଏପରି ଲିଙ୍ଗ ଦେଖାଯିବ ନାହିଁ, ବାଣାସୁର କଥିତ ।

ଅଷ୍ଟଶମ୍ଭୁ

୧- ବାଣେଶ୍ୱର - ଦେଓଗାଁ

୨- ନେଇଙ୍ଗଲିଶ୍ୱର - କୋଇଡା

୩- ଜଟେଲେଶ୍ୱର - ଗୁଗୁଆ

୪- ବକୁଳେଶ୍ୱର - ରାଜବାଟୀ ପାଖ

୫- କ୍ଷୀରେଶ୍ୱର - ଗୁଗୁଆ
୬- ଝାଡେଶ୍ୱର - ଟେଣ୍ଡରା
୭- ସପ୍ନେଶ୍ୱର - ବନେଇ କଲା
୮ - କୂପେଶ୍ୱର - ପାଟଣା, ଅଭିଶାପ୍ତ ମନ୍ଦିର ଯୁଗେଶ୍ୱର

ପ୍ରଧାନ ଦେବୀ

୧- କୁମାରୀ- ରାଜା ସାହେବଙ୍କର ପ୍ରଧାନ ଦେବୀ
୨ - ଖଣ୍ଡାପାଟ - ସାଆନ୍ତଙ୍କର ପ୍ରଧାନ ଦେବୀ (ଲଡାମ ଠାରେ)
୩ - ଅନ୍ଧାରୀ - ମହାପାତ୍ରଙ୍କର ଦେବୀ
୪ - ବଲାଣୀପାଟ - ଦଣ୍ଡପାଟଙ୍କ ପ୍ରଧାନ ଦେବୀ
୫ - କନ୍ତଦେବୀ - ବଣାଇଁଗଡ ରାଜା ସାହେବଙ୍କ ଦେବୀ
୬- ଚଣ୍ଡୀ - ଲଲେଇର ସର୍ଦ୍ଦାରଙ୍କ ଦେବୀ
୭ - ବାସୁଲୀ - ବଣାଇଁ ରାଜା ସାହେବଙ୍କ ଦେବୀ
୮ - ରମ୍ଭାଦେବୀ - ବଣାଁଇ ରାଜା ଓ ଦେବଗଡ ରାଜାଙ୍କ ମଧ୍ୟରେ ଯୁଦ୍ଧ ହେବାରୁ ଆମ୍ବଗାଁ ସିଆଁଳୁଳ ପାଖରୁ ସେ ଦଖଲ କରିନେଲେ । ସେଠାରେ ରମ୍ଭାଦେବୀ ରତି କଲେ । ସେଠାରେ ଦେବଗଡ ରାଜା ପୂଜା କରନ୍ତି ।

ଦେବୀଙ୍କ କାର୍ଯ୍ୟ

୧- ମହିଷାସୁରକୁ ବଧ କରିସାରିଲାପରେ ମହାମାୟା ଏହି ଅଷ୍ଟଶମ୍ଭୁ ରୂପଧରି ଆଠ ପ୍ରକାରର ଦେବୀଙ୍କୁ ଶାନ୍ତି କରିଥିଲେ ।
୨ - ବାଃ କହିବାରୁ ବାଣେଶ୍ୱର ସେଠାରେ ଉତ୍‌ପତି ହେଲେ ।
୩ - କ୍ଷୁଧାରେ କ୍ଷୀରେଶ୍ୱର ତାଙ୍କୁ କ୍ଷୀର ଦେଇ ଶାନ୍ତି କଲା ।
୪ - କେଶ ମୁକୁଳା ଥିବାରୁ ତାଙ୍କୁ ଏକତ୍ରିତକରି ବାନ୍ଧି ଦେବାରୁ ତାଙ୍କ ନାମ ଜଟଳେଶ୍ୱର ହେଲା ।

୫ - ନେଙ୍ଗେଳେଶ୍ୱର - ତାଙ୍କୁ ବସ୍ତ୍ର ପରିଧାନ କରିଲା ପରେ ତାଙ୍କ ନାମ ହେଲା ନେଙ୍ଗେଳେଶ୍ୱର ।

୬ - ଝାଡେଶ୍ୱର - ତାଙ୍କ ଦେହରେ ରକ୍ତ ଲାଗିଥିଲା ଏବଂ ଧୂଳି ସବୁ ଝାଡିଦେବାରୁ ତାଙ୍କ ନାମ ହେଲା ଝାଡେଶ୍ୱର ।

୭- ସପ୍ନେଶ୍ୱର ଦେବୀ ସପ୍ନ ମାଧମରେ ନିଜ ଯୁଦ୍ଧ କଥା ଦେଖି ଦେବତା ମାନଙ୍କର କ୍ରୋଧ ଶାନ୍ତି କରିଥିବାରୁ ସପ୍ନେଶ୍ୱର ହେଲେ ।

୮ - କୋପେଶ୍ୱର - ତାଙ୍କର କୋପଦୃଷ୍ଟି ଥିବାରୁ ତାଙ୍କୁ କିପରି ଭାବରେ ସନ୍ତୁଷ୍ଟ କରିପାରିଲେ ସେ ସନ୍ତୁଷ୍ଟ ହେବେ । ତାଙ୍କର ସେହି କୋପ ଶାନ୍ତି କରିବାରୁ ତାଙ୍କୁ କୋପେଶ୍ୱର କୁହାଗଲା ।

ପୁରୀ

ଜୁନ୍ - ୨୦-୨୬-୧୯୯୩ ର ପ୍ରଜାତନ୍ତ୍ର ସାପ୍ତାହିକ ଶ୍ରୀମନ୍ଦିର ଗର୍ଭଗୃହ ମରାମତି ୨୮ଅଙ୍କ ଶ୍ରୀ ବୀରକେଶର ଦେବ (ପୁରୀ ଗଜପତି) ତୃତୀୟ ମହଲା ୨୮ମାର୍ଚ୍ଚ ୧୯୯୩ ମରାମତି କରିଥିବା ସମୟରେ ନିମ୍ନଲିଖିତ ବ୍ୟକ୍ତ ଶ୍ରୀ ଦାମଦର ମହାପାତ୍ର,ବିନ୍ଦୁ ମହାପାତ୍ର ବଣାଇଁର ବୋଲି ଲେଖାଅଛି । ତୁମ୍ଭି ପ୍ଲାଷ୍ଟରିଙ୍ଗ କରିଥିଲେ ।

କୁମାରୀଙ୍କ କିମ୍ବଦନ୍ତି

ଜଣାଯାଏ କୁମାରୀ ଦେବୀ ବାଣାସୁର ଥିବା ଅମଳର ଗଡଦେବୀ । ପ୍ରତ୍ୟକ୍ଷ କୁମାରୀ ଦେବୀ ଅଷ୍ଟଶମ୍ଭୁରେ ପୂଜିତ । ସେ ସମସ୍ତ ଭଲମନ୍ଦ ବୁଝନ୍ତି । ଥରେ ଜଣେ ବ୍ରହ୍ମଚାରୀ ଆସି ଥିଲେ । ସେତେବେଳେ ବଣାଇଁ ଘୋର ଜଙ୍ଗଲରେ ପରିପୂର୍ଣ୍ଣ ଥିଲା। ସେତେବେଳେ ସେ କୁମାରୀ ମନ୍ଦିରରେ ପୂଜା କରିବା ପାଇଁ

ମାଙ୍କ ପାଖରେ ରହିଲେ । ତାଙ୍କ ପାଖରେ ଜଣେ ଶିଷ୍ୟ ଥିଲେ । ଶିଷ୍ୟକୁ ପାଣି ପାଇଁ ନଦୀକୁ ପଠାଇ, ନିଜେ ଭିକ୍ଷା ଗ୍ରହଣ ପାଇଁ ଗ୍ରାମକୁ ଗଲେ । ଫେରି ଆସି ଦେଖିଲେ ଯେ ପାଣି ଅଛି ଶିଷ୍ୟ ନାହିଁ । ବ୍ରହ୍ମଚାରୀ ଜଣକ ଚାରିଆଡେ ଖୋଜିଲେ, କିନ୍ତୁ ଶିଷ୍ୟକୁ ପାଇଲେ ନାହିଁ । କିନ୍ତୁ ଦେଖିଲେ ଦେବୀଙ୍କ ସମ୍ମୁଖରେ ଦୁଇଟି ପାଦଚିହ୍ନ ଦେଖାଯାଉଛି । ସେ ଭାବିଲେ ଦେବୀ ଶିଷ୍ୟକୁ ଖାଇ ଦେଇଛି । ବ୍ରହ୍ମଚାରୀ ଉତ୍ୟକ୍ତ ହୋଇ ଚଣ୍ଡି ସମ୍ପୁଟ କରି ନଉପୂର୍ଣ୍ଣ ଥାଳି ଦେବୀଙ୍କ ମୁହଁରେ ମାରିଲେ । ଦେବୀଙ୍କର ମୁହଁ ବନ୍ଦ ହୋଇଗଲା, ସେହିଦିନଠାରୁ ମା ସେହି ରୂପରେ ପୂଜା ପାଉଛନ୍ତି, ସେ କୁଆଁରୀ ଦେବୀ ନାମରେ ବିଖ୍ୟାତ । କୁମାରୀଙ୍କର ତିନୋଟି ନାମ । ୧- କୁମାରି ୨- ଶୂନ୍ୟକୁମାରୀ ୩- ଅଦ୍ଭୁତ କୁମାରୀ । ଏହି ତିନି ନାମରେ ପୂଜା ହୁଏ ତିନି ସମୟରେ । ପ୍ରତ୍ୟେକ ଦୈନିକ ସେ କୁମାରୀ ନାମରେ ପୂଜା ହୁଅନ୍ତି । ଯେତେବେଳେ ବର୍ଷା ହୁଏ ନାହିଁ ସେତେବେଳେ ଶୂନ୍ୟ କୁମାରୀ ନାମରେ ଲୋକେ ପୂଜା କରନ୍ତି ଓ ଚଣ୍ଡି ସମ୍ପୁଟ କରନ୍ତି । ଯେତେବେଳେ ପ୍ରଚୁର ଭାବରେ ସଂକ୍ରାମକ ରୋଗ ଯଥାଃ- ହଇଜା, ବସନ୍ତ ଇତ୍ୟାଦି ହୁଏ ଚାରି ଦିଗକୁ ଛେନାପଣା,ମନ୍ଦାରମାଳ, ନୂଆହାଣ୍ଡି ଓ ଲାଲବସ୍ତ୍ର, ଝୁଣା ଦେଇ ଚାରିଦିଗରୁ ପୂଜା କରନ୍ତି । ଅନେକ ଥରେ ରୋଗରୁ ମୁକ୍ତି ପାଇଛନ୍ତି । ବଣାଇଁର ଇଏ ପ୍ରସିଦ୍ଧ ଦେବୀ, ତାଙ୍କୁ ସିଦ୍ଧ ମନରେ ପୂଜିଲେ ଫଳ ଦିଅନ୍ତି । ଅନେକ ଲୋକ ଘୋଡାରେ ଯିବାରୁ ଶବ୍ଦ,ଚାବୁକର ଶବ୍ଦ ମଧ୍ୟ ଶୁଣିଛନ୍ତି । ଏ ମାଙ୍କର ଶରଣ ଗଲେ ସେ ସମସ୍ତଙ୍କର ମନସ୍କାମନା ପୂରଣ କରନ୍ତି । ଜୟ ମା ଶରଣଂ

ମା କୁମାରୀଙ୍କ ଜଣାଣ

ଜୟ ମା ଭବାନୀ ବଣାଇଁ ମଣ୍ଡିନୀ ଅପର ଧାରିଣୀ ମାଁ

ମହିଁସା ମର୍ଦ୍ଦିନୀ ବିପଦ ତାରିଣୀ ଅଭୟ ଦାୟିନୀ ମାଁ
ଜଗତ ଧାରିଣୀ ତୁହିମା ଜନନୀ ରାଜେ ରାଜେଶ୍ୱରୀ ମାଁ
ସଂକର ଭବାନୀ ବଣାଇଁ ଇଷ୍ଟଦେବୀ ମହେରୀ ମାଁ
ମହାଆପଦ ବାରିଣୀ ତ୍ରିପଦ ଧାରିଣୀ ତ୍ରିନେତ୍ର ଧାରିଣୀ ମାଁ
ବଣାଇଁ ଇଷ୍ଟଦେବୀ ବାଣାଦୁର୍ଗ ବାସିନୀ ବାଣାସୁର ଦେବୀ
ଗଡ ରକ୍ଷଣୀ ତୁହିମା ଭବାନୀ ସର୍ବାବାସି ବଣାଇଁ ମାଁ
ତୋ ପାଦେ ଶରଣ, ତୋ ପାଦେ ଶରଣ ମାଗିଣ ଲେଖେ ହରିହର ମାଁ

କୃପେଶ୍ୱରଙ୍କ କିମ୍ବଦନ୍ତୀ

କୃପେଶ୍ୱର ଷଡଙ୍ଗୀ ବଂଶର କୀର୍ତୀ ।ସେମାନେ ବହୁତ ଧନବାନ ଥିଲେ, ସେମାନେ ତିନିଭାଇ । ବଡଭାଇର କୌଣସି ସନ୍ତାନ ନାହିଁ । ତାଙ୍କ ସ୍ତ୍ରୀ ଯାଇ ବାବା ବାଣେଶ୍ୱରଙ୍କ ନିକଟରେ ଧାରଣା ଦେଲେ । ବାଣେଶ୍ୱର ତାଙ୍କଠାରେ ପ୍ରସନ୍ନ ହେଲେ ଓ କହିଲେ ତୋର ଗର୍ଭରେ କୌଣସି ସନ୍ତାନ ନାହିଁ । ଷଡଙ୍ଗୀ କହିଲେ ତୁମେ ଅକନେ କର୍ମଦାୟକ, ତେଣୁ ତୁମେ ଦୟା କଲେ ସବୁ ହେବ । ତେଣୁ ତାଙ୍କୁ ଏକ ସର୍ପପୂତ୍ର ସପ୍ନରେ ଦାନ କଲେ । କିଛିଦିନ ପରେ ଷଡଙ୍ଗୀ ପରିବାରରେ ଏକ ସର୍ପପୁତ୍ର ଜାତ ହେଲା । ସେହି ସର୍ପକୁ ଷଡଙ୍ଗୀ ପରିବାର ଲାଳନ ପାଳନ କଲେ, ତାଙ୍କ ମା ସର୍ପକୁ ସବୁଦିନେ ଗୋରସ ଖାଇବାକୁ ଦେଇ ପ୍ରତିପାଳନ କରନ୍ତି । ସର୍ପ ବାହାରକୁ ବୁଲିବାକୁ ଯାଏ । ଦିନେ ସର୍ପର ଖାଇବା ସମୟ ଡେରି ହେବାରୁ ଷଡଙ୍ଗୀ ତାଙ୍କର ଜାମାତାଙ୍କୁ କହିଲେ, ସର୍ପଆସିଲେ ଗୋରସ ଖାଇବାକୁ ଦେଇଦେବା ମୁଁ ଗାଧୋଇ ଯାଉଛି, କିନ୍ତୁ ଜା ମାନେ ତାକୁ ମାରିଦେବାକୁ ଚାହୁଁଥିଲେ । କାରଣ ସେ ପରିବାରରେ ରହନ୍ତିମାନେ କେତେବେଳେ କାହାକୁ କାମୁଡି ପକାଇବ, ତେଣୁ

ଯେତେବେଳେ ସର୍ପଆସିଲା ଜ୍ଞା ଏକ ପାତ୍ରରେ ଗରମ କ୍ଷୀର ଆଣି ନାଗକୁ ଦେଲା । ନାମ ମୁହଁ ମାରି ଚାଲିଗଲା ଓ ପୁନର୍ବାର ଆସିଲା ନାହିଁ ।ତାଙ୍କ ମା ନାଗକୁ ବହୁତ ଖୋଜିଲେ କିନ୍ତୁ ତାଙ୍କୁ ପାଇଲେ ନାହିଁ । ମା ନାଗକୁ ହରାଇ ଥିବାରୁ ବହୁତ କାନ୍ଦିଲେ । କିଛିଦିନ ପରେ ଷଡଙ୍ଗୀ ପରିବାରର ଭାଇମାନଙ୍କ ମଧ୍ୟରେ ଭାଗବ । ହେଲା । ସର୍ପ ଏକ ଭାଗ ପାଇବା କଥା, କିନ୍ତୁ ସର୍ପ ପଳାଇଛି ଭାବି ତାଙ୍କୁ କିଛି ଭାଗ ଦିଆଯାଇ ନଥିଲା । ଏହାପାଇଁ ତାଙ୍କ ମା ବହୁତ ଦୁଃଖ ପ୍ରକାଶ କଲେ । କିଛିଦିନ ଅନ୍ତେ ସେମାନଙ୍କର ଭାଇଭାଗ ହେଲା । କିନ୍ତୁ ସେହି ଭାଗ ସମୟରେ ସର୍ପ ଆସି ପହଂଚିଲା, ସେମାନେ ଆଶ୍ଚର୍ଯ୍ୟ ହେଲେ ଯେଉଁଟି ବଡ ଭାଗ ଥିଲେ ସର୍ପଟି ସେଠି କୁଣ୍ଡଳୀ ମାରି ରହିଲା, ତେଣୁ ସେ ଭାଗଟା ସର୍ପକୁ ଯିଏ ପ୍ରତିପାଳନ କରିଥିଲା ତାଙ୍କୁ ଦେଲେ । ସର୍ପ ପଳାଇ ଗଲା ଓ ରାତିରେ ସପ୍ନ ହେଲା ଏମାନେ ମୋତେ କୋପରେ ଗରମ ଗୋରସ ଦେଲେ । ମୋ ଭାଗ ସମ୍ପତିରେ ଗୋଟିଏ ମନ୍ଦିର ନିର୍ମାଣ କରାଅ ଓ ମନ୍ଦିର ନିର୍ମିତ ହେଲା । ନାଗ ପାଷାଣ ହୋଇ ସେଠାରେ ପୂଜିତ ହେଲେ, ରାଜାଙ୍କ ଦ୍ୱାରା ମନ୍ଦିର ପ୍ରତିଷ୍ଠା କରାଗଲା । ମନ୍ଦିର ପରିଚାଳନା ପାଇଁ ସୁବନ୍ଦୋବସ୍ତ କରାଗଲା । ଏବେ ମଧ୍ୟ ନାଗ କୂପେଶ୍ୱର ନାମରେ ସେଠାରେ ପୂଜା ପାଉଛନ୍ତି । କାରଣ ତାଙ୍କୁ କୋପ କରି ତାତିଲା ଗୋରସ ଦିଆଯାଇଥିଲା । ମନ୍ଦିରର ଦଧିନଭୁତି ନଥିବ, ମଧ୍ୟାହ୍ନ ସମୟର ସୂର୍ଯ୍ୟ କିରଣ ଯେଉଁଠି ପଡିବ ସେହିଠାରେ କିଛି ସମ୍ପତି ରଖାଯାଇଛି, ଯାହାକି ଭବିଷ୍ୟତରେ କୂପେଶ୍ୱରଙ୍କ କାର୍ଯ୍ୟରେ ଆସିପାରେ । ଏବେମଧ୍ୟ ସେହି ନାଗ ମନ୍ଦିରରେ ଦେଖିବାକୁ ମିଳେ । ଆଉ ତାଙ୍କ ମୁଣ୍ଡରେ ଗରମ ଗୋରସର ଦାଗ ଦେଖିବାକୁ ମିଳେ । ତେଣୁ ମନ୍ଦିରରେ ପ୍ରବେଶ କରିବା ପୂର୍ବରୁ ତିନିଥର କରତାଳି ଦେବାକୁ ପଡେ, ମନ୍ଦିରର ଭିତରପାଖ

ଉତ୍ତର ଦିଗକୁ ଏକ ରନ୍ଧ୍ର ଅଛି ଯେଉଁ ରନ୍ଧ୍ରରେ ସେ ଯିବା ଆସିବା କରନ୍ତି ।

ବକୂଳେଶ୍ୱରଙ୍କ କିମ୍ବଦନ୍ତୀ

କଦମ୍ବ ବଂଶର ଜଣେ ପଂଚାୟତ, ପେଟାପେଟ[୧] ଦରହକୁ ଶିକାର ଉଦ୍ଦେଶ୍ୟରେ ଯାଇଥିଲେ । ନୌବିହାର ସମୟରେ ନଦୀର ମଧ୍ୟଭାଗରେ ନୌକା ସ୍ଥିର ହୋଇଯାଏ । ଯେତେ ଚେଷ୍ଟା କଲେ ମଧ୍ୟ ଆଗକୁ ଯାଏ ନାହିଁ । ବରଂ ସେଠାରେ ଚକ୍ରାକାରରେ ଘୂରିବୁଲେ । ଏହି କାରଣ ହେତୁ ପଟାୟତ ଡଙ୍ଗା କାହିଁକି ବୁଲୁଛି ବୋଲି କହିବାରୁ କେଉଟ ପାଣିଭିତରେ ବୁଡିଲା । କେଉଁଟ ହାତମାରି ଜାଣିଲା ସେଠାରେ ଗୋଟିଏ ଲିଙ୍ଗ ଅଛି । ତାପରେ ପଟାୟତ ତାକୁ ଆଣିବାକୁ କହିଲା ଓ ଝରା ତାହା ଆଣିଲା । ସେହିଦିନଠାରୁ ସେହି ଦରହର ନାମ ଦେଓଦରହ ହେଲା । ଲିଙ୍ଗକୁ ଆଣି ତାଙ୍କ ଉତ୍ତର ପାର୍ଶ୍ୱରେ ସ୍ଥାପନ କଲେ । ସେ ବକୁଳେଶ୍ୱର ନାମରେ ବିଖ୍ୟାତ । ତାଙ୍କୁ ସମସ୍ତେ ପୂଜାକରି ବର ପାଉଛନ୍ତି ।

କନ୍ତକୁମାରୀଙ୍କ କିମ୍ବଦନ୍ତୀ

କେନ୍ଦୁଝରରୁ ଜଣେ ବାବାଜୀ ଶୋଣିତ ନଗର(ବଣାଇଁ)କୁ ଆସିଥିଲେ, ସେ ବାଣେଶ୍ୱର ମନ୍ଦିରରେ ପହଂଚିଲେ । ତାଙ୍କ ପାଖରେ ଅନେକ ଜିନିଷ ଥିଲା । ସେଗୁଡିକ ମଧ୍ୟରେ ଏକମୁଖୀ ରୁଦ୍ରାକ୍ଷ, ନୃସିଂହ ଶାଳଗ୍ରାମ ଓ ନବଦୁର୍ଗା କଙ୍କଣ ଥିଲା । ଦିନେ

---

[୧] ପେଟାପେଟି ଦରହ – ଏହା ଏକ ପ୍ରାଚୀନ ନାମ । ଏବେ ତାର ନାମ ପରିବର୍ତ୍ତନ କରି ଦେଉଦରହ ରଖାଯାଇଛି, ଦେବତା ଅର୍ଥାତ ଦିଅଁ ବାହାରିବାରୁ ତାର ନାଁ ଦିଆଗଲା ଦେଉଦରହ ।

ରାଜାଙ୍କର ଲୋକ ବାଣେଶ୍ୱରଙ୍କୁ ଦର୍ଶନ କରିବାକୁ ଯାଇଏସବୁ ଦେଖିଲେ ।ସେତେବେଳେ ବଣାଇଁରେ (ଶ୍ରୋଣିତ ନଗର) ରାଜାଭିଷେକ ହେଲା । କିନ୍ତୁ ସେତେବେଳେ ରାଜାଘରେ ନୃସିଂହ ଶାଳଗ୍ରାମ କିମ୍ବା ରୁଦ୍ରାକ୍ଷର ମାନେ ନଥିଲା । ବାବାଜୀଙ୍କର ଏହିସବୁ ଜିନିଷକୁ ଦେଖି ରାଜାଙ୍କର ଲୋକମାନେ ରାଜାଙ୍କୁ କହିଲେ । ରାଜା ତାହା ମାଗି ଆଣିବାକୁ ଆଦେଶ ଦେଲେ । ତାଙ୍କର ବିଶିଷ୍ଟ ଲୋକ ବାବାଜୀ ପାଖରୁ ସେସବୁ ଆଣିବାକୁ ଗଲେ । କିନ୍ତୁ ସେମାନଙ୍କୁ କାଲି ଦେବି ବୋଲି ଠକି ବାବାଜୀ ସେହିଦିନ ରାତ୍ରିରେ ହିଁ କଂସରା ଦେଇ ପଳାଇଗଲେ । ରାଜାଘର ଲୋକ ଆସି ଦେଖିଲେ ବାବାଜୀ ନାହିଁ । ଫଳରେ ସେମାନେ ତାଙ୍କୁ ଖୋଜିବାକୁ ଗଲେ । କଂସରାରେ ବାବାଜୀଙ୍କୁ ଭେଟିଲେ । ତାପରେ ବାବାଜୀଙ୍କୁ ମାରି ଏକମୁଖୀ ରୁଦ୍ରାକ୍ଷ, ନୃସିଂହ ଶାଳଗ୍ରାମ, ନବଦୁର୍ଗା କଙ୍କଣ ଆଣିଲେ । କିଛି କାଳପରେ ବାବାଜୀ ମରିଥିବା ସ୍ଥାନ ଏକ ଜମିରେ ପରିଣତ ହେଲା । ତାହା ଏକ ପ୍ରାଣର ଜମିଥିଲା । ଦିନେ ପାଣ ହଳ କରୁ କରୁ ତାଂକର ଲଙ୍ଗଳର ଲୁହାରେ କିଛି ଲୁହା ଆକାରର ଏକ ପଦାର୍ଥ ଲାଗିଲା । ତାକୁ ପା ଣରେ ଆଡ କରି ହଳ କରିଲା । ଏପରି ଚାରିପା ଥର ହଳ କରନ୍ତେ ତାହା ପୁଣି ଲାଗିଲା । ଶେଷରେ ଦେଖିଲା ଏହି ଲାଗିଥିବା ଲୁହା ଖଣ୍ଡକ ଢେଙ୍କି ସମାପରି । ସେ ଭାବିଲା ଏହାକୁ ନେଇ ସମା କରିବି । ସେ ଦିଗକୁ ନେଇ ଢେଙ୍କିରେ ଲଗାଇଲା । ଦିନେ ପାଣ ଧାନ ଶୁଖାଇ ଗାଧୋଇ ଯାଇଥିଲା । ସେହିଦିନ ସେ ଯେଉଁ ମହାଜନ ଠାରୁ ଟଙ୍କା କରଜ କରିଥିଲା ସେ ପହଂଚିଲା । ଦେଖିଲା ପାଣଘରେ କେହି ନାହାନ୍ତି । ମହାଜନ ଦେଖିଲା ଯେ ଧାନ ଖାଉଥିବା ଚଢ଼େଇ ମାନଙ୍କୁ ସୀମାପାଖରୁ ଏକ ସର୍ପ ଆସି ଘଉଡେଉଛି । ମହାଜନ ଆଶ୍ଚର୍ଯ୍ୟ ହୋଇଗଲା । ସେ ଭାବିଲା ପାଣଠାରୁ ଏହା ମାଗିନେବ । ପାଣ ଆସି ଘରେ ପହଂଚିଲା । ମହାଜନଙ୍କୁ ଦେଖି ପାଣ ନମସ୍କାର କଲା ।

ତା'ପରେ ସେମାନେ ଟଙ୍କା କରଜ ବିଷୟରେ କିଛି କଥାବାର୍ତ୍ତା ହେଲେ, ତା ପରେ ପାଣ କପଡା ବଦଳି ଧାନକୁଟିଲା । ମହାଜନ ସେହିଠାରେ ହିଁ ବସିଥିଲା । ତୁ ପଇସା ନଦେଲେ ମୁଁ ଯିବିନାହିଁ ବୋଲି ମହାଜନ କହୁଥାଏ । ତାପରେ ପାଣ ଧାନକୁ ପାଛୋଟି ଚାଉଳ ବାହାର କଲା । ଯେତିକି ଧାନକୁ ସେତିକି ଚାଉଳ । ଏହା ଦେଖି ମହାଜନ ଆହୁରି ଆଶ୍ଚର୍ଯ୍ୟ ହୋଇଗଲା । ମହାଜନ କରଜ କଟିଯିବା କଥା କହି ପାଣକୁ ଢେଙ୍କି ସମାଟି ମାଗିଲା । ପାଣ ସମାଟିକୁ ମହାଜନକୁ ଦେଲା । ସାହୁକାର ବା ମହାଜନ ସମାଟିକୁ ନେଇ ଖୁସିରେ ଘରକୁ ଫେରିଲା । ରାତ୍ରିରେ ମହାଜନକୁ ସ୍ୱପ୍ନହେଲା ଯେ, ତୁ ମୋତେ ଯେଉଁଠାରୁ ଆଣିଛୁ ମୋତେ ନେଇ ସେହି ପାଣ ଘରେ ଛାଡିଦେଇ ଆସ, ନହେଲେ ତୋର ବଂଶ ନାଶ କରିବି । ପାଣକୁ ମଧ୍ୟ ସ୍ୱପ୍ନ ହେଲା ଯେ ତୁ ମୋତେ ନେଇ ରାଜାଙ୍କୁ ଦେବୁ ନହେଲେ ତୋର ବଂଶ ନାଶ ହେବ । ରାଜାଙ୍କୁ ମଧ୍ୟ ସେହି ରାତ୍ରିରେ ସ୍ୱପ୍ନ ହୋଇଥାଏ ଯେ, ତୁ ଯାହାକୁ ସକାଳୁ ଦେଖିବୁ ତାକୁ ପୂଜା କରିବୁ । ସେହି ରାତ୍ରିରେ ଜଲର ଏକ ଭୂୟାଁକୁ ସ୍ୱପ୍ନ ହେଲା ଯେ, ତୁ ସକାଳ ନ ହେଉଣୁ ଘରୁ ବାହାରି ରାଜବାଟୀକୁ ଯିବୁ, ରାଜାଙ୍କଠାରୁ ମୋତେ ଆଣିବୁ, ଭୂୟାଁ ସେଇଆ କଲା । ରାଜା ତାହାଙ୍କୁ ସମର୍ପଣ କଲେ । ଭୂୟାଁ ନେଇ ତାଙ୍କୁ ଜଲରେ ରଖିଲା । କିଛିଦିନପରେ ରାଜାଙ୍କୁ ସ୍ୱପ୍ନ ହେଲା ଯେସେ କନ୍ତଦେବୀ ନାମରେ ପୂଜା ପାଇବେ । ସେହିଦିନଠାରୁ କନ୍ତଦେବୀ ପ୍ରତିପଦା ଦିନ ବାହାରନ୍ତି । ସେ ଆଶ୍ୱିନ ଦ୍ୱୀତୀୟା ଦିନଠାରୁ ପୂର୍ଣ୍ଣିମା ପର୍ଯ୍ୟନ୍ତ ପୂଜା ପାଆନ୍ତି । ଚଣ୍ଡିପାଠ ହୁଏ, ଅଷ୍ଟମୀ ଦିନ ମହାପୂଜା ହୁଏ । ବୋଦା ଓ ପାଢ ବଳି ପଡେ । ତା'ଆଗରୁ ଭୂୟାଁ ଆସି ଅମାବାସ୍ୟା ଦିନ ପୁଷ୍ପା ଳୀ ନେଇଥାଏ । ତା'ପରେ ଦେବୀ ନିଜ ଆସନରେ ହଳଦୀକୁନ୍ଦର, ନୂଆଡିହି, ଖୁ ଗାଁ, ପୋଲଗାଁ,ଜକୈକଲା, ଜମକେଇ, ଉପୁରଡା ଦେଇ କନ୍ତଯୋଡିକୁ ଆସନ୍ତି ।

ସିଙ୍ଗାରଦେଇଙ୍କର ମଧସ୍ଥଳୀ କନ୍ତଯୋଡିକୁ ଆସନ୍ତି । ସିଙ୍ଗାରଦେଇଙ୍କର ମଧସ୍ଥଳୀ କନ୍ତଯୋଡି ଠାରେ କନ୍ତଦେବୀଙ୍କର ଏକ ମଣ୍ଡଳୀ ପୂଜା ହୁଏ । ରାଜା ସାହେବ ସନ୍ଧ୍ୟାରେ ଯେତେବେଳେ ତାଙ୍କ ପ୍ରହରୀ ମାନଙ୍କୁ ଧରି, ଢୋଲ, ମହୁରୀ, ବଜାଇ କନ୍ତଦେବୀଙ୍କୁ ଆଣି ଯାଆନ୍ତି ସେତେବେଳେ ମୋତେ ରାଜା ମାରିବାକୁ ଆସୁଛନ୍ତି ବୋଲି ଭାବି ଭୂୟାଁ ଦେବୀଙ୍କୁ ଛାଡି ପଳାଇଯାଏ । ତା'ପରେ ରାଜା ନିଜଲୋକଙ୍କ ହାତରେ ଭୂୟାଁଙ୍କୁ ଡକାଇ ପଠାନ୍ତି, କିନ୍ତୁ ଭୂୟାଁ ଆସେ ନାହିଁ । କିନ୍ତୁ ରାଜା ଅପେକ୍ଷା ନକରି କୁଆଁରୀ ଦେବୀଙ୍କ ପୂଜାରୀ ଆମାତଙ୍କ ହାତରେ ଦେବୀଙ୍କୁ ନେଲେ ।ଏହାକୁ କନ୍ତହେଟ କୁହାଯାଏ । ତା'ପରେ ସେଇଠୁ ଦେବୀ ପୂଜା ସାରି ରାତ୍ରି ବାରଟା ସମୟରେ ଭଉଣୀ ହିସାବରେ କୁଆଁରୀ ଦେବୀଙ୍କ ସଙ୍ଗରେ ସାକ୍ଷାତ ହୋଇ ଖଣ୍ଡାଘରେ ରାତ୍ରିବାରଟାରେ ରକ୍ତହାଣ୍ଡିରେ ରହନ୍ତି । ତା'ପରଦିନ ରାଜବାଟୀରେ ପୂଜା ହୁଏ । ରାଜାତାଙ୍କୁ ନେଇ ତାଙ୍କ ନଗରୀରେ ପୂଜା କରନ୍ତି । ତାଙ୍କ ଭାୟାଳି, ଜେମା ପ୍ରତ୍ୟେକ ଘରେ ପୂଜା ହୋଇ ସାରିଲାପରେ ବ୍ରାହ୍ମଣ ସାହି ପୂଜା ସାରି ବାହାରିପଡି ବଡଦ୍ୱାରରେ ରାଜା ଦେବୀଙ୍କୁ ସମର୍ପଣ କରନ୍ତି । ଆଉଦିନ ବାହାରିଗଡ ପୂଜା ହୋଇ ସକାଳୁ ନିମଚକୁଳି ବୋଲି ଏକ ପୂଜା ହୁଏ । ଯୋଉ ଲୋକ (ପାଣ) କନ୍ତଦେବୀଙ୍କୁ ପାଇଥିଲା ସେ କନ୍ତଦେବୀଙ୍କୁ ନିମପତ୍ରରେ ଚକୁଳିପିଠାରେ ପୂଜା କରନ୍ତି । ନିମଚକୁଳି ପୂଜାପରେ ଦେବୀ ନଦୀ ସେପାର ଗଲେ ଦଶହରା ହୁଏ । ଲଲେଇ, ଟାଙ୍କଯୋଡା, ବ୍ରାହ୍ମଣ ଗାଁ, ଆମାତପାଲି, ମଧୁପୁର, କୁରୁଡା, ଭୋଗଲା, କୁଳିପୋଷ, ଦେଇ ପୂର୍ଣ୍ଣିମାଦିନ ତାଙ୍କ ଘରେ ବଡ ପୂଜା ହୁଏ । ଢୋଲ ମହୁରୀ ବଜାଇ କନ୍ତଦେବୀଙ୍କୁ ତାଙ୍କ ମେଢ଼କୁ ନିଆଯାଏ । ତା'ପରେ ଭୂୟାଁ ଏକୁଟିଆ ହୋଇ ଦେବୀଙ୍କୁ ମେଢରେ ଛାଡିଆସେ । ପୂର୍ବାନୁକ୍ରମେ ଦେବୀ ଏହିପରି ପୂଜା ହୋଇ ଆସୁଛନ୍ତି । ମଝିରେ ଥରେ

କେଉଁଝରର କେତେଲୋକ ସେହି ଦେବୀଙ୍କୁ ଚୋରି କରିବାପାଇଁ ଗଛ ଉପରେ ଛକି ରହିଥିଲେ । ଯେତେବେଳେ ଭୂୟାଁ ଦେବୀଙ୍କୁ ଏକୁଟିଆ ନେଇ ଛାଡିଆସେ ତାହା ସେମାନେ ଦେଖିଥିଲେ । ସେମାନେ ଦେବୀଙ୍କ ମେଢ ପର୍ଯ୍ୟନ୍ତ ଯାଇ ଦେବୀଙ୍କୁ ଚୋରିକରି ନେଇଯିବା ସମୟରେ ଗୋଟିଏ ମହୁଲ ଗଛ ମୂଳରେ ମରିଯାଇଥିଲେ । ତତ୍‌ପରେ ଭୂୟାଁ ଯେତେବେଳେ ଆମାବାସ୍ୟା ଦିନ ମହାପୁରୁଙ୍କୁ ପୁଷ୍ପା ଲୀଞ୍ଜଲି ଦେଇ ପୂଜା କରିବାକୁ ଯାଏ ସେତେବେଳେ ଦେବୀ ସେଠାରେ ନଥିଲେ । ସେ ଭାରୀ ବିସ୍ମିତ ହୋଇ ଦେବୀଙ୍କୁ ସ୍ମରଣ କଲା । ଦେବୀମାଁ ହୁକୁମ ଦେଲେ ମୁଁ ମହୁଲ ଗଛମୂଳେ ଅଛି, ମୋତେ ଛୋରି କରି ନେଇଯାଉଥିଲେ । ତୁ ସେହି ଯାଗାରୁ ଦ୍ୱିତୀୟା ଦିନ ପୂଜା କରିବୁ । ସେହିଦିନଠାରୁ ମହୁଲ ଗଛ ମୂଳରୁ ଦେବୀଙ୍କୁ ଯାଇ ଭୂୟାଁ ଦ୍ୱିତୀୟା ଦିନଠାରୁ ପୂଜା କରେ । ଦେବୀଙ୍କ ବାହାରିବା ଡେରି ହୋଇଥିବା କଥା ରାଜା ଶୁଣିଲେ । ସେହି ଦିନଠାରୁ ରାଜା ଷୋହଳ ପ୍ରଧାନ ଦେବାତାଙ୍କୁ ରକ୍ଷା କରିବେ ବୋଲି ଷୋହଳଟା ଗାଁ ର ପ୍ରଧାନ ମାନଙ୍କୁପ୍ରଧାନ ଉପାଧି ଦେଇ ଶିରପା କଲେ । ଏବେ ସୁଦ୍ଧା ଷୋହଳ ପ୍ରଧାନେ ଦେବୀ ବାହାରିବା ଅଷ୍ଟମୀ ଦିନ ପହଂଚିବା ଆଗରୁ ରାଜାଙ୍କୁ ଭେଟ କରନ୍ତି । ତାଙ୍କର କୃଷି ଜାତୀୟ ଫସଲ, ଫଳମୂଳ ତାରତା ବଳି ମଧ୍ୟ ରାଜାଙ୍କୁ ଭେଟି ଦିଅନ୍ତି । ରାଜା ସେମାନଙ୍କୁ ସେହିଦିନ ରୋଷେଇ ଛାଡି ଦିଅନ୍ତି । ଭାଦ୍ରବ ପୂର୍ଣ୍ଣମୀ ପରଦିନ ପ୍ରତିପଦା ଦିନଠାରୁ ପନ୍ଦରଦିନ ପର୍ଯ୍ୟନ୍ତ ୧୦୮ଲୋକ ଚଣ୍ଡିପାଠ କରନ୍ତି । ପ୍ରତିପଦା ଦିନ ବେଲବର୍ଣ୍ଣୀ ହୁଏ । ଦ୍ୱିତୀୟା ଦିନକୁ ହାତୀ ପଂଚମୀ କହନ୍ତି । ହାତୀ ପଂଚମୀକୁ ଗଜଷଷ୍ଠୀ ମଧ୍ୟ କୁହାଯାଏ । ଅଶ୍ୱଷଷ୍ଠୀ ମଧ୍ୟ କୁହାଯାଏ । ତା'ପରଦିନ ରାଜାଙ୍କର ସମସ୍ତ ଅସ୍ତ୍ରଶସ୍ତ୍ର ଖଣ୍ଡାଘରେ ପୂଜା ହୁଏ । ବ୍ରାହ୍ମଣମାନଙ୍କ ଭୂରିଭୋଜନ ଦିଆଯାଏ । ତା'ପରେ ଦଶହରା ଦିନ କନ୍ତଦେବୀ ଆରପାରକୁ ଗଲାବେଳେ ଦଶହରା ପର୍ବ ଆରମ୍ଭ ହୁଏ ।

ସେତେବେଳେ ସାଆନ୍ତ, ଦଣ୍ଡପାଟ ଓ ମହାପାତ୍ର ତିନିଟି ଦଳ ଆସନ୍ତି ରାଜବାଟୀକୁ । ଜରେଇକଳାର ଦଳକୁ ରାଜାଙ୍କ ଦଳ ବୋଲି କୁହାଯାଏ । ବାହାରିଗଡ ବଡଦ୍ୱାର ସାହିର ସୈନ୍ୟ, ପଟାଦ୍ୱାରର ସୈନ୍ୟ ଓ ଅନ୍ୟାନ୍ୟ ଦଳ ସବୁ ଆସନ୍ତି, ରାଜା ରୂପାର ତାମଯାନରେ ଦଶହରାକୁ ଖଣ୍ଡାଧରି ବାହାରନ୍ତି, ରାଜାଙ୍କ ପଛକୁ ଟିକାୟତ, ପଟାୟତ, ରାଜକୁମାର ଓ କୁମାର ମାନେ ହାତୀ ଉପରେ ସୁସଜ୍ଜିତ ରୂପା ପାଲିଙ୍କି ରେ ବସି ଦଶହରା ପର୍ବକୁ ଯାଆନ୍ତି । ଏହି ପର୍ବକୁ ଯିବା ସମୟରେ ତତ୍‌କାଳିନ ବ୍ରିଟିଶ୍ ପୋଲିସ ତାଙ୍କ ଆଗରେ ଏବଂ ପଛରେ ସମତଳରେ ଗମନ କରନ୍ତି। ଦଶହରା ପଡିଆରେ ରାଜାଙ୍କ ସହିତ ଯାଇଥିବାସୈନ୍ୟ ସାମନ୍ତ,କୁସ୍ତିକସରତ ଲକ୍ଷଭେଦୀ ଆଦି କରନ୍ତି ଓ ଖେଳ ଶେଷରେ ତାଙ୍କୁ କିଛି ପୁରସ୍କାର ଦିଆଯାଏ । ଫେରିଲା ବେଳେ ସମସ୍ତ ଛକ ଜାଗା ମାନଙ୍କରେ ବିଭିନ୍ନ ପ୍ରକାର ନୃତ୍ୟଗୀତ କରି ରାଜାଙ୍କୁ ବନ୍ଦାପନା କରିଥାନ୍ତି । ରାଜବାଟୀରେ ପହଂଚିବା ପରେ ବିଭିନ୍ନ ସ୍ଥାନରୁ ଆସିଥିବା ସୈନ୍ୟମାନଙ୍କୁ ଭୋଜି ଭାତରେ ଆପ୍ୟାୟିତ କରନ୍ତି । ମଝିରେ ଦେବତା କ୍ଷୟ ଦେଖା ଯିବାରୁ ମଝିଆ ବାଲୁ ମମ୍ମତ କର୍ମେ ମଝିଆ ବାଲୁ ରହିଥିବା ଜାଗାରେ ଅନୁରୁଦ୍ଧ ସାଥୁଆର ପରାମର୍ଶ କର୍ମେ ଅନନ୍ତ ସାହୁ, ଗଙ୍ଗା, ଗୋବର୍ଦ୍ଧନ ନାରାୟଣ ସାଥୁଆ ଥାଇ ମୂର୍ତିଟି ସୂରବାବୁ ଥାଇ ମୂର୍ତିଟି ତମ୍ଭାରେ ବନ୍ଧା ହୋଇଥିଲା । ଶ୍ରୀ କଦମ୍ବ କେଶରୀ ଚନ୍ଦ୍ରଦେଓ ଦେବଙ୍କ ସମୟରେ ପୂର୍ବ ବନ୍ଧା ପାତଳା ଥିବାରୁ ଦେବୀ ମଜବୁତ୍ ନରହିବାରୁ ମଜବୁତ୍ କରି ବାନ୍ଧିବାକୁ ରାଜା ଅନୁମତି ଦେଲେ । ଏହା ବକଳଶ୍ୱେର ମଣ୍ଡପରେ ୧୦ ମାସ ୫ ତାରିଖ ୧୯୯୨ ମସିହାରେ ବନ୍ଧା ହେଲା । ଏହା ମୂରଲୀ, କେଦାର, ଗୋବର୍ଦ୍ଧନ, ନାରାୟଣ, ଗଙ୍ଗାଧର ୫ଜଣ ମିଶି ବାନ୍ଧିଥିଲେ ।

ସିଙ୍ଗାରଦେଇଙ୍କ ମାଦଳା

୪୮ତମ ରାଜା ଶ୍ରୀ ଭିକାରୀ ଦେଓ ଚନ୍ଦ୍ରଦେବଙ୍କ ସମୟରେ ଚୈତ୍ର ପର୍ବ ଆରମ୍ଭ ହୋଇଥିଲା । ସେ ସମଲେଇ ନାଥ ଘରୁ ବୁସୁକି ମୂର୍ତୀ ଆଣି ଏହି ପର୍ବ ଆରମ୍ଭ କରିଥିଲେ । ସେହି ସମୟରେ ତାଙ୍କର ଏକ ଝିଅ ଥିଲେ । ଚୈତ୍ର ପର୍ବ ଶେଷଦିନ ସକାଳୁ ସେ ମୁଣ୍ଡ କୁଣ୍ଡାଉଥିଲେ । ଦାସୀମାନେ ଆଇନାରେ ଦେଖିଲେ ତାଙ୍କର ତିନୋଟି ଆଖି ଦେଖାଯାଉଛି । ସେମାନେ ରାଣୀଙ୍କୁ ଏ କଥା କହିଲେ । ରାଣୀ ଏ ସବୁ ଦେଖୀ ଜେମାଙ୍କୁ ପଚାରିଲେ, ମା ତୁମେ ସିଙ୍ଗାର ହେଉଛ, କୁଆଡେ ଯିବ? ଜେମା କହିଲେ ମୁଁ ଯାତ୍ରା କରିବାକୁ ଯିବି । ସେହିଦିନ ରାତ୍ରି ଦୁଇଟାରେ କୁଆଡେ ଅନ୍ତର୍ଦ୍ଧାନ ହୋଇଗଲେ । ରାଜା ଘରଲୋକେ ସବୁ ଖୋଜାଖୋଜି କରିବାରୁ ଦେଖାଗଲା ଉଆସର ପୂର୍ବ ପଟେ ଥିବା ପାହାଡରେ ଜେମା ବିଜେ ହୋଇଛନ୍ତି । ସେହି ଦିନୁ ସେଠାରେ ଦେବୀ ରୂପରେ ପୂଜା ପାଇଲେ । ସିଙ୍ଗାର କରି ଯାଇଥିବା ହେତୁ ସେହି ପାହାଡର ନାମ ସିଙ୍ଗାର ଦେଇ ପାହାଡ ଅଟେ । ଦେବୀଙ୍କର ନାମ ମଧ୍ୟ ସିଙ୍ଗାର ଦେଇ । ତାଙ୍କୁ ସମସ୍ତେ ପୂଜା କରି ନିଜର ଫଳ ପାଆନ୍ତି, ଥରେ ଅମାନ୍ତ ପୂଜା ସାରି ତାର ପୂଜା କରା ଲୋଟାଟି ଆଣିବାକୁ ଗଲା, ଦେଖିଲା ଦେବୀ ବାଘରୂପରେ ଉଭା ହୋଇ ଭୋଗ ସେବନ କରୁଛନ୍ତି । ଦେବୀ ଅମାନ୍ତଙ୍କୁ କହିଲେ ଯେ ସେ ପୂଜାରୀ ହୋଇଥିବାରୁ ଦେବୀ ତାଙ୍କୁ ଛାଡି ଦେଲେ, ଆଉ କେହି ହୋଇଥିଲେ ସେ ବଂଚିନଥାନ୍ତା । ଏ ଲୋଟାଟା ମୁଁ ପୋଫାଡି ଦେଉଛି, ଯେଉଁଠି ପଡିବ ତୁ ସେଇଠାରେ ମୋତେ ପୂଜା କରିବୁ, ସେହିଦିନଠାରୁ ସେହି ଲୋଟା ପାଖରେ ପୂଜା ହୁଏ । ଆଜିଯାଏ ମଧ୍ୟ ଚୈତ୍ର ପର୍ବର ଦିନେ ଆଗରୁ ଲୋକମାନେ ସେଠାକୁ

ଢୋଲମହୁରୀ ବଜାଇ ପୂଜା କରିବାକୁ ଯାଆନ୍ତି, ଏହା ଦେବୀଙ୍କ ଆଜ୍ଞା ।

ଜଗନ୍ନାଥଙ୍କ ମାଦଳା
(ବୁଢ଼ା ଗୋସେଇଁ)

୪୮ତମ ରାଜା ଶ୍ରୀ ଭିକାରୀ ଦେଓ ଦେବ ଜଗନ୍ନାଥ ପ୍ରତିଷ୍ଠା କରି ରଥଯାତ୍ରା କରିଥିଲେ । ସେତେବେଳେ ରାଜବାଟୀରେ ଘରଗୁଡିକ ଲଗାଲଗି ହୋଇ ରହିଥିଲା । ସେ ମାଟିର ଢବା ଘରେ ଦେବତାଙ୍କୁ ରଖିଥିଲେ । ନିଆଁ ଲାଗିବାରୁ ଲକ୍ଷ୍ମଣ ମିଶ୍ର ନାମକ ଜଣେ ବ୍ରାହ୍ମଣ ଜଗନ୍ନାଥଙ୍କୁ ନେଇ ଶହେ କଦମ୍ ଦୂରକୁ ନେଇଯାଇଥିଲେ । ତା'ପରେ ଛୋଟ ମୂର୍ତ୍ତି ଦୁଇଟି ତିଆରି ହେଲା, ରାଜା ଧରଣୀଧରଙ୍କ ସମୟରେ ରଥଯାତ୍ରା ହେଲା । ତିନି ମୂର୍ତ୍ତି ତିଆରି କଲେ । ସେ ପୁରୁଣା ମୂର୍ତ୍ତିଙ୍କୁ ଭସାଇ ଦେବାର ମନବୃତି ଥିଲା । କିନ୍ତୁ ରାଜାଙ୍କୁ ରାତ୍ରିରେ ସପ୍ନ ହେଲା ଯେ, ମୁଁ ବୁଢ଼ା ଗୋସେଇଁ ରୂପରେ ପୂଜା ପାଇବି । ମୋତେ ବଗଡା ଅନ୍ନ, କଳମ ଶାଗ, ବିରିଡାଲି ଭୋଗଦେବ । ସେହି ମୂର୍ତ୍ତି ସେହିଦିନୁ ରହିଲେ, ବୁଢ଼ା ଗୋସେଇଁ ଆଜି ପର୍ଯ୍ୟନ୍ତ ପୂଜା ପାଉଛନ୍ତି । ଛୋଟ ମୂର୍ତ୍ତି ଦୁଇଟା ଖରାପ ହୋଇଯିବାରୁ ଭସାଇ ଦିଆଗଲା । ସେତେବେଳେ ତିନିଟା ରଥ ଚାଲୁଥିଲା । ଲକ୍ଷ୍ମଣ ମିଶ୍ର ପରି ବଳବାନ ଥିଲେ । ତାଙ୍କୁ କହନ୍ତି ଯେ ଗୋଟିଏ ରଥର ଚକ ଖୋଲି ତା'ଉପରେ ବସି ସେ ପ୍ରତ୍ୟେକ ଦିନ ଗାଧୋଉ ଥିଲେ । ହାତରେ ସୋରିଷ ଦଳି ଯେଉଁ ତେଲ ବାହାରେ ତାକୁ ଲଗାଉଥିଲେ । ଥରେ ସେ ତେନ୍ତୁଳି ଗଛ ଓହଳାଇ ଛେଳି ମାନଙ୍କୁ ତେନ୍ତୁଳି ପତ୍ର ଦେଉଥାଆନ୍ତି । ଜଣେ ମାଲ ଆସି ତାଙ୍କୁ କହିଲା ମୋତେ ମାଲ ଦିଅ, ମୁଁ ଲଢେଇ କରିବି । କିନ୍ତୁ ଲକ୍ଷ୍ମଣ ମିଶ୍ର ମାଲକୁ ଓହଳିଥିବା ଡାଳ ମାଲ -ଯିଏ କୁସ୍ତି କରେ, ତାକୁ

ଧରାଇ ମିଛଟାରେ ମାଲକୁ ଡାକିଦେବି କହି ପଳାଇଗଲେ । ମାଲ ଡାଳଟିକୁ ଛାଡିବାରୁ ଡାଳଟି ଦଶହାତ ଉପରକୁ ଉଠିଗଲା ମାଲ ପଡିଗଲା । ଲଜ୍ଜା ପାଇ ମାଲ ପଳାଇଗଲା । ତାଙ୍କ ଦେହରେ ଏପରି ବଳ ଥିଲା । ସେ ଲୁଣ ବେପାର ମଧ୍ୟ କରୁଥିଲେ । ତାଙ୍କ ଘରର ଦୁଆରରେ ସବୁ ଲୁଣ ବସ୍ତା ଥିଲା । ତାଙ୍କ ପୁଅକୁ ଡାକି କହିଲେ ବର୍ଷା ଆସୁଛି ଲୁଣବସ୍ତା ସବୁ ବାରଣ୍ଡାକୁ ଉଠାଇଦିଅ । ତାଙ୍କ ପୁଅ ଲୋକ ଖୋଜି ଯିବାରେ ବର୍ଷା ଆସିଗଲା । ଲକ୍ଷ୍ମଣ ମିଶ୍ର ଜ୍ୱରରେ କମ୍ପୁଥିଲେ ଓ ହାତ ମଧ୍ୟ ଥରୁଥିଲା । ହେଲେ ମଧ୍ୟ ସେ ନିଜ ଦାନ୍ତରେ ଲୁଣବସ୍ତାକୁ ଧରି ବାରଣ୍ଡା ଉପରେ ରଖି ଦେଲେ । ପୁଅ ଆସି ଦେଖନ୍ତି ତ ଲୁଣବସ୍ତା ଦୁଆରେ ନାହିଁ । ତାଙ୍କ ପୁଅ ତାଙ୍କୁ ପଚାରିବାରୁ ଏ ଲୁଣବସ୍ତା ଉପରକୁ କିଏ ଉଠାଇଲା ତାଙ୍କ ବାପା ଉତ୍ତର ଦେଇଥିଲେ ଏ ସାମାନ୍ୟ କଥାପାଇଁ ଯଦି ମୂଲିଆ ଦରକାର ହୁଏ ତୁମେ କଣ କାମ କରିବ । ସେ ଯେତେବେଳେ ମୃତ୍ୟୁବରଣ କଲେ ତାଙ୍କୁ ନଦୀଘାଟକୁ ନେଇଥାଆନ୍ତି । ତାଙ୍କ ଝିଅ ସୁଶୀଳା ମିଶ୍ର ଇନ୍ଦରପୁର ଠାରୁ ଆସି ଦେଖିଲେ ଯେ ତାଙ୍କ ବାପାଙ୍କର ପରିଶ୍ରା ଏକ ପାତ୍ରରେ ଅଛି । ପରିଶ୍ରା ଦେଖି ସେ ଜାଣିପାରିଲେ ଯେ ବାପା ମରି ନାହାନ୍ତି,ସେ ସଙ୍ଗେ ସଙ୍ଗେ ଶବଘାଟକୁ ଯାଇ ଶବକୁ ଅଗ୍ନିଦାହ କରିବା ଆଗରୁ ସେଠାରେ ପହଂଚିଲେ । କହିଲେ ବାପାଙ୍କୁ ଦାହ କରନାହିଁ । ବାପା ଜୀବିତ ଅଛନ୍ତ, ତାଙ୍କ ବ୍ରହ୍ମରନ୍ଧ୍ରରେ କଣ ଔଷଧ ଫୋଡା କରି ଦେଇ ଦେବାରୁ ସେ ସଚେତ ହୋଇଗଲେ । ସେ ଆଉ ବାର ବର୍ଷ ବଂଚିଲେ । ବଣାଇ ରାଜା ସାହେବ ତାଙ୍କ କାର୍ଯ୍ୟରେ ସନ୍ତୁଷ୍ଟ ହୋଇ ସାଉଁଟି ପାଲି ଗ୍ରାମ ଦାନ ଦେଲେ, ସେହି ଦିନଠାରୁ ବୁଢା ଗୋସେଇଁ ଆଜି ପର୍ଯ୍ୟନ୍ତ ଅଛନ୍ତି ।

ଆଷାଢ଼ ରଥ ଯାତ୍ର

ଲକ୍ଷ୍ମୀ ନାରାୟଣ କଳି

ଓଁ ଜଗନ୍ନାଥାୟ ନମଃ

ଦାସୀଃ-ଦାସୀ ବୋଲୁଛନ୍ତି ଶୁଣଗୋ ମାଏ
ବିଜେ କଲେ ତୁମ ଦେବାଧି ରାୟେ
ସିଂହଦ୍ୱାରେ ରହିଅଛି ରଥ
ମାଏ ଗୋ ଜନଗହଳେ ନ ଦିଶଇ ପଥ,
ଶଙ୍ଖ ଧ୍ୱନି ଶୁଣ ଅତି ଉତ୍‌କଟେ ବାଜଇ ନିଷାଣ

ଲକ୍ଷ୍ମୀଃ - ଅଇଲେ ଯେବେଲୋ ଦେବାଧି ଦେବ
ନଗରେ ମୋର କରାଅ ଉତ୍‌ସବ
ପୁରେ ପୁରେ ମଣ୍ଡ ଜନେ କରି ଦାସୀଲୋ
ମୁକୁତା ଲମ୍ବାଅ କେରି କି କେରି ।
ଚନ୍ଦ୍ରା ତପଟାଣ ଚାମର ଲଗାଅ ତଥି ପାଖେଣ
ଧୂପର ବିଧିଲୋ ଭିଆଇଥିବ
ପ୍ରଭୂ ବିଜେ ଜାଣି କବାଟ ଦେବ ।
ଆମ୍ଭକୁ ଯାହା ଦେଇଗଲେ ଦୁଃଖ
ଦାସୀଲୋ ପ୍ରଭୂ ହୋଇଲେ ଆସିବେ କେମନ୍ତ
ଆସି ଦେଢଶୁର ପଶନ୍ତୁ ଘରେ
ଭାଇ ଭଉଣୀ ଥାନ୍ତୁ ସିଂହଦ୍ୱାରେ ।
ଚିନ୍ତିବେ ବାହାରେ ଦାସୀଲୋ ସୁଖ ମିଳିବ ଗୁଣ୍ଡିଚା ଯାତ୍ରାରେ

ଜଗନ୍ନାଥଃ- ନାଗର ବର ଲକ୍ଷ୍ମୀ ଭାବ ଜାଣି
ଦରହାସେ କରୁଅଛନ୍ତି ବାଣୀ
ଆଲୋ ପରିବାରି ଫେଡ କବାଟ
କେଉଁ କଥାକୁ ଲୋ କରୁଛ ହଟ ।

କେଉଁକଥା ଜାଣି ଲଗାଅ ନାଟଲୋ ସୁଜାଣ ତୁମ୍ଭେ
ଅଧିକ କି ଆଉ କହିବୁ ଆମ୍ଭେ

ଦାସୀ:- ଦାସୀ ବୋଲୁଛନ୍ତି ଶୁଣ ପଦ୍ମଲାଭ
ଦ୍ୱାର ଛାଡିଲେ କିସ ତୁମ୍ଭ ଲାଭ
ବଡ ଦେଉଳେ କି କାର୍ଯ୍ୟ ଆଉ
ପ୍ରଭୁହେ ତେଜି ବିଜେ କଲ ମହାବାହୁ ।

ଜଗନ୍ନାଥ:- ପ୍ରଭୁ ବୋଲନ୍ତି ଯେ ପୂର୍ବ କୋଳେ ରାଜା ଇନ୍ଦ୍ରଦ୍ୟୁମ୍ନ
କରାଇଥିଲା ସତ୍ୟବନେ
ଗୁଣ୍ଡିଚାରାଣୀ ଭକ୍ତିଭାବ ଜାଣି
ବିଜେ କଲୁ ରଥେ ମୁରତି ତିନି
ଦାସୀଲୋ ଆଇଲୁ ତୁରିତେ
ଦାସୀଲୋ ତାରିଲୁ ଚଣ୍ଡାଳ ପତିତେ,
ବିଜେ କଲ ଯେବେ ଭକ୍ତଙ୍କ ହିତେ ।
ଗୁଣ୍ଡିଚା ବୋଲି ଶୁଭିଲା ଜଗତେ ।

ଦାସୀ:- ସଙ୍ଗତେ ନ ନେଲ କି ଗୁଣ ଧରି
ସେତ ପ୍ରିୟବତୀ ଅର୍ଦ୍ଧାଙ୍ଗ ନାରୀ
ଗଲେ କମଳିନୀ ଗୁଣ୍ଡିଚା ଯାତ୍ରା କି ହୁଅନ୍ତା ହାନୀ

ଜଗନ୍ନାଥ:- ଯାତ୍ରା ଉଛବେ ଦେବଗଣେ ଯାନ୍ତି,
ଗହଳ ପଟୁଆରୀ ଯନ୍ତାପନ୍ତି
ସଙ୍ଗତେ ଜ୍ୟେଷ୍ଠ ଭାଇ ହଳପାଣି
ଦାସୀଲୋ ତେଣୁ ନ ନେଲୁ ସଙ୍ଗେ କମଳିନୀ

ଦାସୀ:- ବ୍ରହ୍ମା ଆଦି କରି ଯେତେ ଦେବତା

ପରମ ଲକ୍ଷ୍ମୀ ଯେ ସବୁରି ମାତା
ଏ କଥାରେ ନାହିଁ କିଛି ବିରୋଧ
ନିଶ୍ଚୟ ଛାଡିଲ କମଳା ସଧ
କେତେ ଚଳୁରାଇ ପ୍ରଭୁହେ ବଂଚିବା କଥା କୁହ ବଂଚାଇ

ଜଗନ୍ନାଥଃ- ଗୁଣିଚା ଘରକି ସର୍ବଦା ସ୍ଥାନ
ଯହିଁ କମଳା ତହିଁ ଆମ୍ଭ ମନ
ସେ ପ୍ରାଣର ପ୍ରିୟା
ଆମ୍ଭେ ଠାକୁର, ଠାକୁରାଣୀ ଶ୍ରୀୟା

ଲକ୍ଷ୍ମୀଃ- ଉତ୍‌ତମ କଥା କହିଲ ଗୋସାଇଁ
ଜାଣିବା ପଣ କି ଚିହ୍ନା ନଯାଇ
ଲକ୍ଷ୍ମୀକୁ ଯାହା ଦେଇଗଲ ଭୋଗ
ଡାଲୁଆ ଅନ୍ନକୁ କଳମ ଶାଗ
ପ୍ରଭୁହେ ତୁମ୍ଭ ସୁଖ ଏତେ
ବିଖ୍ୟାତ ହୋଇଲା ସାଗ ଜଗତେ,
ବାଉନ କୋଟି ଯେ ନିଜ ଭଣ୍ଡାର
କୁବେର ଦେବତା ଯା ପରିଚାରୀ
ଅଷ୍ଟନିଧି ଅଛି ଯାହାର ହାତେ
ତୁମ୍ଭେ କହିଲେ କି ଯଦି ପରତେ
ଦାସୀଲୋ ବାଉନ କୋଟି ଯେ ଭଣ୍ଡାର ଯେତେ
ବୁହାଇ ନେଲ ଯେ ଆପଣା ସଙ୍ଗତେ,
ଶୀଳ, ଶୀଳପଡା, ଛଂଚୁଣୀ, କୁଲା
ଭଣ୍ଡାର ଘରିଆ ବୁହାଇ ନେଲା ।
ପ୍ରଭୁହେ କହିବାକୁ ଲାଜ
ଯେମନ୍ତ କରିଗଲ ଦେବରାଜ

ଜଗନ୍ନାଥଃ- ବେଳକୁ ବଳଲୋ ବଢାଅ ଲତା
ମନେ ନ ଘେନ ଆମ୍ଭର କଥା,
ଦେଖ ଘୋଟିଅଛି ଏ କଳା ମେଘ
ଅକ୍ଷୁନ୍ନ ଧାରା ବରଷିବ ଜଳ,
ତିନ୍ତିବ ଶ୍ରୀଅଙ୍ଗ ଏ କେତେ
ଶାନ୍ତି ନୁହେଁ ତୁମ୍ଭ ରାଗ
ଭିତରକୁ ଗଲେ ଶ୍ରୀନିଳାମ୍ବର
ଆମ୍ଭକୁ ରଖିଛ ବେଢା ବାହାର ।
ଦାସୀ ବୋଲନ୍ତି ଲୋ ଫେଡ କବାଟ
କେଉଁ କଥାକୁଲୋ କରିଛ ହଟ ।
ଆଣିଛୁ ଆମ୍ଭେ ଚିତ୍ରମେଘୀ ପାଟ
ରତ୍ନାକର ରାଜା ଯାହାର ତାତ

ଲକ୍ଷ୍ମୀଃ- ସଙ୍ଗ ସୁଧାକର କନିଷ୍ଠ ଭ୍ରାତ
ବ୍ରହ୍ମାଣ ପତି କି ଲୋଭିବାକୁ
ଦେବାଙ୍ଗ ବସନ ନମିଳେ ତାଙ୍କୁ,
ବାହୁଡାଇ ନିଅ ନବ ଅନୁରାଗୀ ଭଗିନୀକୁ ଦିଅ ।
ଜଗନ୍ନାଥଃ- ଯୁବତୀରେ ହାରି ପଙ୍କଜ ନେତ୍ର
ବୁଦ୍ଧି ଏ ରଚିଲେ ଶ୍ରୀବିଦ୍ୟଚ୍ୟୁତ,
ଦାସୀଙ୍କୁ କିଛି ଲାଂଚ ଦେଇ ଧନ
ଦାସୀଲୋ କମଳାଙ୍କୁ କହ ଦିବ୍ୟବନେ
ଦାସୀ ଲାଂଚ ପାଇ
ଫେଡି ଦେଲେ ବେଗେ କବାଟ ଯାଇ,
ଶୀରେ ଅନଙ୍ଗ ଅପାଙ୍ଗରେ ଦୃଷ୍ଟି
ମଣୁ ଅଛନ୍ତି ସୁଧା ସମ ଦୃଷ୍ଟି
ଶୁଭେ ଶଙ୍ଖଧ୍ୱନୀ ଲକ୍ଷ୍ମୀ ନାରାୟଣ ଭେଟି ବେନି ।
ଭିତରକୁ ଗଲେ ଶ୍ରୀଚକାଡୋଳା

ଦେଖି ଆଗେ ଉଭା ହେଲେ କମଳା,
ଶୀରେ ଅନଙ୍ଗ ଆପାଙ୍ଗରେ ଦୃଷ୍ଟି
ମଣୁ ଅଛନ୍ତି ସଦା ସମବୃଷ୍ଟି।
ଶୁଭେ ହରି ଧ୍ୱନୀ ଲକ୍ଷ୍ମୀ ନାରାୟଣ ଏ ଭେଟ ବେନି ।
ଭିତର ପୁରେ ପ୍ରବେଶିଲେ ଯାଇ
ମୋର ହିଁ ଯୋଗାଡ କଲେ ତିଆର
ହାସ୍ୟରସେ ବସି,
ଭଗବାନଙ୍କ ଲକ୍ଷ୍ମୀଦେବୀ ଚାପିଲେ ପୟର
ସେ ଚରଣ ଯୋଗେ ବିପ୍ର ବିଶ୍ୱମ୍ଭର ଶରଣ ମାଗେ ।

-ସମାପ୍ତ-

ଚଣ୍ଡୀଦେବୀଙ୍କ ମାଦଳା

୪୯ତମ ରାଜା ପିତାମ୍ବର ଇନ୍ଦ୍ର ଦେବ ଦେଓଙ୍କ ସମୟର କଥା । ଚଣ୍ଡୀଦେବୀ ବ୍ରାହ୍ମଣୀ ନଦୀ କୂଳରେ ବହୁ ଆଗରୁ ଥିଲେ । ଚଣ୍ଡୀ ହେଉଛନ୍ତି ବ୍ରାହ୍ମଣ ମାନଙ୍କ ଶ୍ରେଷ୍ଠଦେବୀ ।ଦେଓଗାଁ ପ୍ରତି ବଦଳରେ ଟାଙ୍କଯୋଡା ମୌଜାକୁ ରାଜା ପିତାମ୍ବର ପୁରା ନାମ ଦେଇ ଷୋଳ ଘର ବ୍ରାହ୍ମଣ ଆଣି ରଖିଲେ ।ତାଙ୍କ ମଧ୍ୟରୁ ଜଣକୁ ମୁଖ୍ୟକରି ସର୍ଦ୍ଧାର ପଦଦେଇ ତାଙ୍କୁ ଗ୍ରାମର ଗଉଁତିଆ କଲେ ଓ ପୂଜା କରିବା ନିମନ୍ତେ ସେ ଦେବୀଙ୍କୁ ଜିମା ଦେଲେ । ସେହି ଦିନଠାରୁ ସେ ଦେବୀଙ୍କୁ ପୂଜାକରି ସର୍ଦ୍ଧାର ତାଙ୍କୁ ପ୍ରସନ୍ନ କଲେ । ତାଙ୍କର ଧନଧାନ୍ୟ ଓ ପ୍ରାଧାନ୍ୟ ବୃଦ୍ଧି ହେଲା । ବଣାଁଇଗଡ ରାଜାବାଟୀ ପାଖରେ ସେମାନେ ଥିଲେ । ସେ ସବୁଦିନେ ଚଣ୍ଡିଦେବୀଙ୍କୁ ପୂଜା କରିଯାଆନ୍ତି । ପୂଜା କରିସାରିଲା ପରେ ସେ ଅନ୍ନ, ଜଳ ସ୍ପର୍ଶ କରନ୍ତି ।ସେ ଏପରି ଭାବରେ ଦେବୀଙ୍କୁ ପ୍ରସନ୍ନ କଲେ ଯେ ପାଣି ଉପରେ ଥାଳିଟିଏ ରଖି ମଧ୍ୟ ତା'ଉପରେ ସେ

ବସି ଯିବା ଆସିବା କରିପାରୁଥିଲେ । ତାଙ୍କର ପ୍ରଭାବ ଦେଖି ଅନ୍ୟ ବ୍ରାହ୍ମଣ ମାନେ ସବୁ ରାଜାଙ୍କୁ ଆପତି ଜଣାଇଲେ, କହିଲେ ଯେ ସର୍ଦ୍ଧାର ଦିନେ ନା ଦିନେ ଆପଣଙ୍କର ଅମଙ୍ଗଳ କରିପାରନ୍ତି ।ସେ ମଦ ଦେଇ ଦେବୀଙ୍କୁ ବଶୀଭୁତ କରିଛନ୍ତି । ରାଜା ବିଶ୍ୱାସ କଲେ ନାହିଁ ଯେହେତୁ ସେ ହେଉଛନ୍ତି ଜଣେ ଶ୍ରେଷ୍ଠ ବ୍ରାହ୍ମଣ । ବ୍ରାହ୍ମଣମାନେ କହିଲେ ଆପଣମାନେ ସର୍ଦ୍ଧାରଙ୍କୁ ଡାକି ପରୀକ୍ଷା କରନ୍ତୁ, ସେ ତାପରଦିନ ପୂଜା ସାମଗ୍ରୀ ଧରି ଯିବା ସମୟରେ ତାଙ୍କୁ ଡାକି ପରୀକ୍ଷା କରିବାକୁ ଚାହିଁଲେ । ସେ କହିଲେ କଣ କହୁଛନ୍ତି କୁହନ୍ତୁ ପୂଜାର ସମୟ ହୋଇଗଲାଣି । ସେ ଶୁଣ୍ଡୀଘରୁ ମଦ ନେଇ ଯାଉଥିଲେ, ରାଜା କହିଲେ ଲୋଟାରେ କଣ ନେଇ ଯାଉଛ ? ବ୍ରାହ୍ମଣ କହିଲେ ମୁଁ କ୍ଷୀର ଦେଇ ଯାଉଛି । ରାଜା ଦେଖିବା ପାଇଁ ଗୋଟିଏ ପାତ୍ରରେ ଢାଳିଲେ । ବ୍ରାହ୍ମଣ ମାଙ୍କୁ କାରଣ ଦେଇ ଢାଳିଲେ । ରାଜା ଓ ଉପସ୍ଥିତ ମଣ୍ଡଳୀ ତାଙ୍କୁ କ୍ଷୀର ଦେଖିଲେ । ତତ୍‌କ୍ଷଣାତ୍ ତାଙ୍କୁ ସିଝେଇବାକୁ କହିଲେ । କ୍ଷୀର ରେ ସର ପଡିଲା। ରାଜା କହିଲେ ଏ କ୍ଷୀରକୁ ଦହି ବସାହେବ,ତୁମେ କାଲି ଆସି ଦେଖିବ ଓ ମୁଁ ତୁମ ସହିତ ମାଙ୍କୁ ଦର୍ଶନ କରିବାପାଇଁ ଯିବି,ତାପର ଦନି ନବାନ୍ନ ସମୟ ଥାଏ । ରାଜା ତାପରଦିନ ସର୍ଦ୍ଧାରଙ୍କ ସହିତ ବାହାରିଲେ ଚଣ୍ଡିଦେବୀଙ୍କୁ ଦର୍ଶନ କରିବାକୁ, ନଦୀକୂଳରେ ଉପସ୍ଥିତ ହୋଇ ଦେଖିଲେ ଯେ ଡଙ୍ଗାନାହିଁ । ଭାଦ୍ରବ ମାସ ନଦୀ ବଢିଛି,ରାଜା-ସର୍ଦ୍ଧାରଙ୍କୁ କହିଲେ ଯିବା କେମିତି ? ସର୍ଦ୍ଧାର ମାଙ୍କ ନା ଧରି ତିନିଟା ତାଳି ମାରିଲେ । ଡଙ୍ଗା ଆପେ କୂଳରେ ଆସି ଲାଗିଗଲା, ସେଠାରେ କେହିହେଲେ ନଥିଲେ । ରାଜା କହିଲେ ଡଙ୍ଗା ଚଳାଇବା ପାଇଁ କେହି ନାହାନ୍ତି, କେମିତି ଯିବା ? ସର୍ଦ୍ଧାର କହିଲେ ମା'ହିଁ ଆମ୍ଭକୁ ନେବେ । ଡଙ୍ଗାରେ ବସନ୍ତୁ କିଛି ଭୟ କରନ୍ତୁ ନାହିଁ । ଡଙ୍ଗାର ଦାୟୀ ଚଣ୍ଡୀମା ଜାଣନ୍ତି । ସେ ଆମ୍ଭଙ୍କୁ ନେଇଯିବେ । ରାଜା ଓ ସର୍ଦ୍ଧାର ବସିବା ପରେ ଡଙ୍ଗା ଆପେ

ଯାଇ ଆର କୂଳରେ ଲାଗିଗଲା । ରାଜା ସନ୍ତୋଷ ହୋଇ ତାଙ୍କର ପୂଜା ଦେଖିଲେ । ତାଙ୍କର ଅବିଶ୍ୱାସ ଦୂର ହୋଇଗଲା । ମାଙ୍କ ପ୍ରତି ପୂର୍ଣ୍ଣ ବିଶ୍ୱାସ କଲେ, ସେ ଡଙ୍ଗା ପୁଣି ଆସି ରାଜବାଟୀ ପାଖଲେ ଲାଗିଲା । ସେହି ଘାଟର ନାଁ ରାଣିଶାଳ ଘାଟ । ଡଙ୍ଗା ସେହିଠାରେ ରହିଲା । ରାଜା ତାକୁ ପୂଜା କଲେ । ତା'ପରେ ଡଙ୍ଗା ପୁଣି ଆରକୂଳକୁ ଚାଲିଗଲା । ଏବେ ସୁଦ୍ଧା ରାଜାଙ୍କ ନବାନ୍ନ ପୂଜାଦିନ ଚଣ୍ଡୀଡଙ୍ଗା ବୋଲି ସେହି ଘାଟରେ ପୂଜା ହୁଏ ଓ ଡଙ୍ଗା ଆସି ପୂଜା ହୁଏ, ଯଦି ଡଙ୍ଗାର କିଛି ବିଘ୍ନ ହୁଏ ତା ହେଲେ ଡଙ୍ଗା ମଝିନଦୀରେ ଘୂରିବୁଲେ ଓ ପୁଣି କୂଳକୁ ଆସି ଲାଗିଯାଏ ।ପୁଣି ମାନସିକ କରି ଡଙ୍ଗା ସେହି ଘାଟରେ ଚାଲେ । ଏବେ ସୁଦ୍ଧା ସେହି ଡଙ୍ଗାର କୌଣସି ବିପଦ ଆସିନାହିଁ ପଟାଟାଙ୍ଗର ଘାଟରେ ଦେଖିଲେ ଗୋଟିଏ ସ୍ତ୍ରୀ ଆକୃତି କଳସୀ ଧରିଥିବାର, ମୁକୁଟ ସହ ଦେଖାଯାଏ । ପାଖକୁ ଗଲେ ସେ ଗୁପ୍ତ ହୋଇଯାଆନ୍ତି । କେବଳ ଗୋଟିଏ ଗୋଲାକାର ପଥର ଧରି ଦେଖାଯାଏ । ଏବେ ମଧ୍ୟ କଳାପାହାଡର ଚିହ୍ନ ଅଛି । ତାଙ୍କ ସାମ୍ନାରେ

ପ୍ରାଚୀନ ରୁଢ଼ି ଅଛି ଯେ, :-
" ଭାଳା ରାମଚଣ୍ଡୀ ଭାଳାରେ
କଳାପାହାଡକୁ ଦୁଆରେ ବସାଇ
ଭାଳା ପାଣି ଆଣି ଗଲାରେ

ବଣାଇଁ ରାଜବଂଶ ମାଦଳା

ବଣାଇଁଗଡର ପୂର୍ବନାମ ଶ୍ରୋଣିତ ନଗର ଥିଲା । ଏଠାରେ ପ୍ରଥମେ ପ୍ରତାପ ଦେଓ ରାଜା ହେଲେ, ସେ ସିଂହଳ ଦ୍ୱୀପରୁ ଆସିଥିଲେ । ରାଜ୍ୟର ନାମ ଉଦେପୁର ଜାତି କ୍ଷତ୍ରୀୟ । ରାଜା ପ୍ରତାପ ଦେଓ ସାତ ଭାଇ ସହ ସିଂହଳରୁ ଶ୍ରୀ ଜଗନ୍ନଥଙ୍କୁ ଦର୍ଶନ କରିବାକୁ ଆସିଥିଲେ । ଏମାନେ ହେଲେ ପ୍ରତାପ ଦେଓ, ବୀର

ପ୍ରତାପ ଦେଓ, ଭରା ପ୍ରତାପ ଦେଓ । ଏ ତିନିଜଣ ସହୋଦର ଭାଇ । ଅନ୍ୟ ଚାରିଜଣ ମିତ୍ରଭାନୁ, ଉଦେଭାନୁ, ଚିତ୍ରଭାନୁ ଓ ବୃହତଭାନୁ । ଏମାନେ ସାଥିଭାଇ । ନିଜ ଦେଶରୁ ଏମାନେ ଏକ ବର୍ଷରେ ପୁରୀରେ ପହଂଚି ଥିଲେ । ସେତେବେଳେ ପୁରୀରେ ଗଜପତି ରାଜା ଥିଲେ । ଏ ସାତଭାଇ ପୁରୀ ଅଠରନଳାରେ ଆସି ପହଂଚିଲେ, ଶୁଣିଲେ ଯାତ୍ରୀମାନେ ମହାସୁଲ ବା ଟିକସ ଦେଇ ଜଗନ୍ନାଥ ଦର୍ଶନ କରୁଛନ୍ତି । ସାତଭାଇ ବିଚାର କଲେ ଆମ୍ଭେମାନେ କୌଣସି ବାଦଶାହଙ୍କୁ ଟିକସ ଦେଇ ନାହିଁ କି ସଲାମୀ କରିନାହୁଁ, ଏବେ କିପରି ହେବ? ଚାଲ ଗଜପତିଙ୍କୁ ଆମ୍ଭର ପରିଚୟ ଦେବା । ଯଦି ଆବମାନନା କରନ୍ତି ଜୋର୍ କରି ପ୍ରବେଶ କରିବା । ଏପରି ବିଚାର କରି ସାତଭାଇ ଟିକସ ଆଦାୟକାରୀ ମାନଙ୍କୁ ନିଜର ପରିଚୟ ଦେଲେ । କିନ୍ତୁ ସେମାନେ କହିଲେ ବିନା ଟିକଟରେ ଆମ୍ଭେ କାହାରିକୁ ଛାଡିବୁ ନାହିଁ । ରାଜାଙ୍କ ଆଦେଶ ନାହିଁ । ଏହା ଶୁଣି ସାତଭାଇ କହିଲେ ଛାଡି ନଦେଲେ ଜବରଦସ୍ତ ପଶିବୁ । ଏହା ଶୁଣି ଟିକସ ଆଦାୟକାରୀମାନେ ରାଜାଙ୍କୁ କହିଲେ । ରାଜା କହିଲେ ସେମାନେ ଯଦି କାହାରିକୁ ମୁଣ୍ଡ ନୁଆଁଇ ନାହାନ୍ତି ତେବେ ଜବରଦସ୍ତି ଯିବେ ଯଦି ଯାଆନ୍ତୁ ଏବଂ ରାଜା ଅଠରନଳା ରାସ୍ତାରେ ତୀକ୍ଷ୍ଣ ଧାର କରତ ବସାଇଦେଲେ ଏବଂ ସାତଭାଇଙ୍କୁ କହିଲେ ଜବରଦସ୍ତି ଯିବ ଯଦି ଯାଅ । ଏହାଶୁଣି ସେମାନଙ୍କ ମଧ୍ୟରୁ ଚାରିଭାଇ ରାଗରେ ଘୋଡା ଦୌଡାଇ ଦେଲେ ଏବଂ କରତରେ ପଡି ପ୍ରାଣ ହରାଇଲେ । ବାକି ତିନିଜଣ ଘୋଡା ଦୌଡାଇବା ସମୟରେ ରାଜାଙ୍କ ଲୋକ ସେମାନଙ୍କୁ ଅଟକାଇଲେ ଏବଂ ରାଜାଙ୍କୁ ଖବର ଦେଲେ । ରାଜା ଆସି ଚାରି ଭାଇଙ୍କ ମୃତ ଶରୀର ଦେଖିଲେ ଏବଂ ଜୀବିତ ତିନି ଭାଇଙ୍କୁ ବିନା ଟିକସରେ ଦର୍ଶନ କରିପାରିବେ ବୋଲି ଆଦେଶ ଦେଲେ । ତାପରେ ତିନିଭାଇ କଟକ ଗଲେ ଓ ସେଠାରେ କିଛି

ଦିନ ରହି ଚିତ୍ରଭାନୁ ଓ ଉଦେଭାନୁ ଯାଜପୁର ଦେଇ ସିଂହଭୁମ ଗଲେ । ପ୍ରତାପ ଦେଓ କପିଳାସ, ମାଲ୍ୟଗିରି ଦେଇ ବଣାଇଁ ଆସିଲେ । ସେତେବେଳେ ବଣାଇଁ ଜଙ୍ଗଲରେ ପରିପୂର୍ଣ୍ଣ ଥିଲା । ପ୍ରଥମେ ପ୍ରତାପ ଦେଓ ଆସି ସିଂଜୋଡାରେ ପହଂଚିଲେ ଓ ସେଠାରେ ରହି ତାର ନାମ କଦମ୍ବ ଡିହ ନାମ ଦେଲେ । ସେ ସମୟରେ ବଣାଇଁରେ କୋହ୍ଲ, ଭୂୟାଁମାନେ ଏମାନଙ୍କ ମଧ୍ୟରେ ଶ୍ରେଷ୍ଠ ଥିଲେ ଓ ସେମାନେ ଜମିଦାରୀ କରୁଥିଲେ । କିଛିଦିନ ରହିବା ପରେ ପ୍ରତାପ ଦେଓ ଶୁଣିବାକୁ ପାଇଲେ ଯେ ଏ ରାଜ୍ୟ ବାଣାସୁରର ଓ ସେ ବ୍ରାହ୍ମଣୀନଦୀ କୂଳରେ ଶିବଙ୍କୁ ରଖି ପୂଜା କରୁଛି । ବାଣାସୁରର ନାମ ଅନୁସାରେ ଶିବଙ୍କର ନାମ ବାଣେଶ୍ୱର ଥିଲା, ବାଣେଶ୍ୱର ପ୍ରତ୍ୟକ୍ଷ ଦେବତା ଭକ୍ତଙ୍କୁ ବର ମଧ ଦିଅନ୍ତି । ଏହାଶୁଣି ବାଣେଶ୍ୱର ଦର୍ଶନରେ ଜଣେ ଲୋକ ସାଙ୍ଗରେ ପ୍ରତାପ ଦେଓ ଆସିଲେ ଓ ବ୍ରାହ୍ମଣୀ ନଦୀରେ ସ୍ନାନକରି ବାଣେଶ୍ୱର ଦର୍ଶନ କଲେ । ଏହିପରି କିଛି ଦିନ ଦର୍ଶନ କରିବାପରେ ଏକଥା ଜମିଦାର ମାନେ ଜାଣିଲେ । ଏସବୁ ଜମିଦାର ମାନେ ହେଲେ ମହାବୀରା, ବୀରା, ହମିରା ଏ ତିନିଜଣ ବାଣାସୁରର ଅଂଶ ବୋଲି କୁହାଯାଏ । ମହାବୀରା ବାଣେଶ୍ୱରଙ୍କଠାରୁ ଏକମାଇଲ ଦୂର ସାତକୋଟାରେ, ବୀରା ତାସିପଡା ରେ ଥିଲେ । ଏହା ଛଡା ନେଚ କେଉଟ କେଉଟମାରଣୀରେ, ଲେଦ କମାର ଶୁଣ୍ଡୀ କୋଣରେ ଥିଲେ । ଏମାନେ ସମସ୍ତେ କମାର ଘରେ ଠୁଳ ହୋଇ ବିଚାର କଲେ ଯେ ଗୋଟିଏ ବିଦେଶୀ ଆସି ଲୋକମାନଙ୍କୁ ମତାଉଛି । ତାକୁ କିପରି ମାରିବା । ଏପରି ବିଚାର କରି ଆରଦିନ ସମସ୍ତେ ରାସ୍ତାରେ ହାତହତିଆର ଧରି ଜଗିଲେ । ସେଦିନ ଭୋର ସକାଳୁ ପ୍ରତାପ ଦେଓ ଦର୍ଶନ କରି ଆସିବା ସମୟରେ ଏମାନଙ୍କୁ ଦେଖି ଚିନ୍ତାକଲେ ଯେ କେବେ ତ ଏମାନଙ୍କୁ ଦେଖାନାହିଁ । ଆଜି କିପରି ଅଛନ୍ତି ମୋତେ ମାରିବାକୁ ଅଛନ୍ତି କି ? ଏହା ଭାବି ସେ ଜଙ୍ଗଲ

ଭିତରକୁ ପଶିଗଲେ । ଏଣେ ଏମାନେ ଭାବୁଛନ୍ତି ବିଦେଶୀ କାହିଁକି ଆସିଲା ନାହିଁ, ମହାବୀରା କହିଲା ଆମର ପାଟିଶୁଣି ବୋଧହୁଏ ସେ ଜଙ୍ଗଲ ଆଡେ ପଳାଇଲା । ଏହାଶୁଣି ନେଟ କେଉଟ ଗୋଟିଏ ଗଛ ଉପରେ ଚଢି ଦେଖିଲା ପ୍ରତାପ ଦେଓ ଉତ୍ତର ପଟେ ଯାଉଛନ୍ତି । ତତ୍‌କ୍ଷଣ ଡାକପକାଇ ପଛରେ ଗୋଡାଇଲେ । ଏହା ଜାଣିପାରି ପ୍ରାଣବଂଚାଇବା ପାଇଁ ପ୍ରତାପ ଦେଓ ଏପଟ ସେପଟ ଦେଖିଲେ, ତାଙ୍କ ନଜରରେ ଏକ ଖୋଳଥିବା ଗଛ ପଡିଲା । ସେ ବାଣେଶ୍ୱରଙ୍କୁ ଧ୍ୟାନକରି ସେହି କୋରଡରେ ପଶିଗଲେ । ସେ ଗଛରେ ଗୋଟିଏ ମୟୁର ବସିଥିଲା । ସେ ପ୍ରତାପ ଦେଓଙ୍କ ପାଦଚିହ୍ନକୁ ପୁଛରେ ଲିଭାଇଦେଲା ଓ ପୁଣିଥରେ ଗଛରେ ବସିଲା । ଜମିଦାରମାନେ ସେଠାରେ ପହଂଚି ଦେଖିଲେ କେହି କୁଆଡେ ନାହାନ୍ତି । ଖୋଜା ଖୋଜି କଲେ ପାଇଲେ ନାହିଁ । ମହାବୀରା କହିଲା ଲେଡ ଓ ଲେଜ ମନ୍ଦିର ଚାରିପାଖ ଜଗିରହନ୍ତୁ । ନପାଇଲେ ଏଠାରେ ଜଗରହନ୍ତୁ, ଆସିଲେ ମାରିବେ । ଏହା କହି ସମସ୍ତେ ସେଠାରୁ ପଳାଇଗଲେ । ପ୍ରତାପ ଦେଓ ସେଠାରେ ରହି ସବୁ ଦେଖିଲେ ଓ ଭୟରେ ସେଠାରୁ ସେଦିନ ବାହାରିଲେ ନାହିଁ । ସେହିଦିନ ରାତ୍ରିରେ ବାଣେଶ୍ୱରଙ୍କ ଆଜ୍ଞା ହେଲା ଯେ, ପ୍ରତାପ ଦେଓ ଆମ୍ଭେ ତୁମ୍ଭଙ୍କୁ ଶ୍ରୋଣିତ ନଗରର ରାଜା କଲୁ । ତୁମ୍ଭେ ନିଷ୍କ କ ଭାବେ ରାଜ୍ୟ ଭୋଗ କର । ରାଜା ପଚାରିଲେ ମୁଁ କିପରି ରାଜା ହେବି? ବାଣେଶ୍ୱର କହିଲେ କାଲି ପ୍ରଭାତରୁ ମନ୍ଦିରରେ ଯାହାକୁ ଦେଖିବ ତାକୁ ସାଙ୍ଗରେ ରଖି ଏମାନଙ୍କୁ ମାରିବ । ରାଜା ହୋଇ ଏଠାକାର ଅଷ୍ଟଦେବୀଙ୍କୁ ପୂଜା ଦେବୁ । ଦେବୀ ତୁମକୁ ସପ୍ନାଦେଶ କରିବେ । ରାଜା ଦଣ୍ଡ ପ୍ରଣାମ କରି କୋରଡରୁ ବାହାରିଲେ । ସେହି ଗଛ ମୂଳରେ ରାତି ପୁହାଇ ପ୍ରଭାତରୁ ସ୍ନାନ କରିଗଲେ । ଠିକ୍ ସମୟରେ କଲେଇ ପଷି କଲେ କୁ ସପ୍ନାଦେଶ ହେଲା, ତୋ ଘରେ ଥିବା ଲେଚଡାକୁ ବଡି ସକାଳୁ ମନ୍ଦିରକୁ

ପଠାଇବୁ, କଲେଇ କିଷାନ ସେହି ରାତ୍ରିରେ ଲେଚଡାକୁ ଡାକି କହିଲା ତୁ ଦେଉଳକୁ ଯାଆ ଦର୍ଶନ କରି ଆସିବୁ । ଏହା ଶୁଣି ଲେଚଡା ଦର୍ଶନ କରିବାକୁ ଗଲା । ନଦୀପାର ହେବା ସମୟରେ ଦେଖିଲା ପ୍ରତାପ ଦେଓ ସ୍ନାନ କରୁଛନ୍ତି । ରାଜା ଲେଚଡାର ଜାତିଘର ପଚାରିଲେ ।ତା ଛଡା ଏଠାର ଶାସକ ଲୋକ କିଏ ଅଛି ପଚାରିଲେ । ଲେଚଡା କହିଲା ହମିରା, ମହାବୀରା, ବୀରା, ଲେଚ କେଉଟ, ଲେଜ କମାର ଓ କହରୁ କମାର ଏ ଛଅ ଜଣଙ୍କ ଆଜ୍ଞା ଏଠାରେ ଚାଲୁଅଛି । ତା'ପରେ ରାଜା ଲେଚିଡାକୁ ସପ୍ନାଦେଶ କଥା କହିଲେ । ରାଜା କହିଲେ ଲେଚଡାକୁ କିପରି ମାରିବା । ଲେଚଡା କହିଲା ଏମାନେ ଅଲଗା ଅଲଗା ଜାଗାରେ ରହୁଛନ୍ତି ଏମାନଙ୍କୁ ଏକାଠି ମାରିବା କଷ୍ଟକର, ଏଣୁ ଏମାନଙ୍କର ଅଜଣାରେ ଏମାନଙ୍କୁ ମାରିବା । ପ୍ରତାପ ଦେଓ କହିଲେ ମୁଁ ରାଜା ହେଲେ ତୋତେ ଜମିଦାର କରିବି । ଲେଚଡା କହିଲା କାଲି ମାରିବା । ଏପରି କଥାହୋଇ ବାଣେଶ୍ୱରକୁ ଦର୍ଶନକରି ପ୍ରତାପ ଦେଓ ଥିବା ଘରକୁ ଫେରିଲେ । ଆରଦିନ ଦୁହେଁ କେଉଟ ମାରଣୀ ଯାଇ କେଉଟକୁ ମାରିଲେ । ଲେଚଡା କେଉଟକୁ ଡାକିବାରୁ ସେ ଘରୁ ବାହାରି ଆସି ପ୍ରତାପ ଦେଓଙ୍କୁ କହିଲା, କାଲି ପଲାଇଥିଲୁ ଆଜି କୁଆଁରୀ ତୋତେ ଆଣି ଦେଇଛି । ଆଣି ଦେଇଛି କହୁକହୁ ପ୍ରତାପ ଦେଓ ତୀର ମାରିଲେ, ମୃତ୍ୟୁ ସମୟରେ କେଉଟ କହିଲା ବାଣେଶ୍ୱର ତୋତେ ରାଜା କଲେ ମୋତେ ପୂଜା କରିବୁ ନହେଲେ କଷ୍ଟପାଇବୁ । ରାଜା କହିଲେ ମୋ ଘରେ ତୋତେ ପୂଜା ଦେବି ବାକି କୁଆଁରୀ ବୋଲି କହିଲୁ ଯେ ସେ କେଉଁଠି ଅଛନ୍ତି । ଲେଚ କହିଲା ଯେ ଗୃହର ଉତ୍ତରରେ । ଇଷ୍ଟଦେବୀ କୁଆଁରୀକୁ ପୂଜା କରିବୁ ତା ନାଁ ହେଲା କୁଆଁରୀ, ଶୂନ୍ୟ ଖଣ୍ଡାରେ ତା ମୁଣ୍ଡ କାଟି ଦେଲେ । ସେହିଦିନୁ କେଉଟ କେଉଟ ଦେଓ ନାମରେ ପୂଜା ହୋଇ ଆସୁଛି । ସେଠାରୁ ଶୁଣ୍ଠିକୋଣକୁ ଗଲେ । ଦେଖିଲେ

ଲେଜ କମାର ସ୍ନାନ କରି ଫେରୁଛି । ଲେଟଡା ଚିହ୍ନାଇ ଦେଲା । ପ୍ରତାପ ଦେଓ ସଙ୍ଗେ ସଙ୍ଗେ ତୀର ମାରିଲେ । ତୀର ବାଜିବାରୁ ଲେଜ କମାର ମଲା । ରାଜା ଓ ଲେଚଡା ନଦୀ କୂଳକୁ ଗଲେ । ଲେଚଡା ମହାବୀରା ଘରକୁଯାଇ ମହାବୀରାକୁ ଡାକିବାରୁ ସେ ଘରୁ ବାହାରି ଆସିଲା । ପ୍ରତାପ ଦେଓ ସଙ୍ଗେ ସଙ୍ଗେ ତାକୁ ତୀର ମାରିଲେ । ତୀର ବାଜିବାରୁ ମହାବୀରା କହିଲା ମୋତେ ଯିଏ ମାରିବ ସେ ଏଠାର ରାଜା ହେବ । ମୋତେ ପୂଜା କରିବ ନହେଲେ ତାର ବଂଶ ନାଶ ହେବ । ପ୍ରତାପ ଦେଓ କହିଲେ ମୁଁ ତୋତେ ଏଠାରେ ପୂଜା କରିବି ।ମହାବିରାର ଶବକୁ ତା ଘରର ପୂର୍ବପଟେ ପୋଡିଦେଲେ ଏବଂ ସେ ସେଠାରେ ପୂଜା ପାଇଲେ, ତାପରେ କନ୍ତସରା ଗଲେ । କଇରୁ ରଣା ସେତେବେଳେ ମାଟି ଖୋଳୁଥାଏ । ତାକୁ ସେଇ ମାଟି ଖୋଳା ଜାଗାରେ ପୋତି ପକାଇଲେ, ସେହିଠାରେ ସେ ପୂଜାପାଏ । ତାପରେ ସାତକୁଟା ଯାଇ ବୀରାକୁ ମାରିଲେ । ସେ ସେଠାରେ ଗଡଦେବୀ ନାମରେ ପୂଜାପାଏ । ସେଠାରୁ କାଶୀପଡା ଯାଇ ହମିରାକୁ ମାରିଲେ, ହମିରା ମଲାବେଳେ ଅଭିଶାପ ଦେଲେ ମୋତେ ଯିଏ ମାରିଲା ତା ବଂଶରେ ଯିଏ ଏ ଗାଁକୁ ଆସିବ ସେ ଅପୁତ୍ରିକ ହେବ । ପ୍ରତାପ ଦେଓ ଏହା ଶୁଣି ମନଦୁଃଖ କଲେ । ପରଦିନ କଲେଇ କିଷାନ ଆସିଲା ଏବଂ ସବୁଶୁଣି କହିଲା ଭଲ ହେଲ, ପ୍ରତାପ ଦେଓଙ୍କୁ ରାଜା କରିବାପାଇଁ ସବୁ ଲୋକଙ୍କୁ ରୁଣ୍ଡକଲା । ପ୍ରତାପ ଦେଓଙ୍କ ଅଭିଷେକ କରାଗଲା । ଛତ୍ର ଗୋଟିଏ ବନାଇ ବାଣେଶ୍ୱରଙ୍କୁ ଚଢାଗଲା । ରାଜା ପ୍ରତାପ ଦେଓ ଲେଚଡାକୁ ସାମନ୍ତ କଲେ, ସେଦିନୁ ଆଜି ପର୍ଯ୍ୟନ୍ତ ଅନେକ ଜଣ ରାଜା ହେଲେଣି ସେମାନେ ହେଲେ –

୧- ରାଜା ପ୍ରତାପ ଇନ୍ଦ୍ର ଦେଓ ଦେବ

୨- ଦିନମଣି ଦେଓ ଚନ୍ଦ୍ର ଦେବ ରାଜା

୩- ହରିଚନ୍ଦ୍ର ଇନ୍ଦ୍ରଦେବ ଦେଓ ରାଜା

୪- ମଧୁସୂଦନ ଗୋବିନ୍ଦ ଦେଓ ରାଜା

୫- କୃତିବାସ ଦେଓ ଚନ୍ଦ୍ର ଦେବ ରାଜା

୬- ପଦ୍ମନାଭ ଦେଓ ଗୋବିନ୍ଦ ଦେବ ରାଜା

୭- ଶ୍ରୀ ମୁକୁନ୍ଦ ଦେଓ ଇନ୍ଦ୍ର ଦେବ ରାଜା

୮- ଶ୍ରୀଧର ଦେଓ ଚନ୍ଦ୍ର ଦେବ ରାଜା

୯- ଶ୍ରୀ ନିବାସ ଦେଓ ଗୋବିନ୍ଦ ଦେବ ରାଜା ଏହି ରାଜା ଅପୁତ୍ରିକ ଥିବାରୁ ତାଙ୍କ ଭାଇ ରାଜା ହେଲେ ।

୧୦- ଡମ୍ବରୁ ଧର ଦେଓ ଇନ୍ଦ୍ର ଦେଓ ରାଜା

୧୧- ବାଣେଶ୍ୱର ଦେଓ ଇନ୍ଦ୍ର ଦେବ ରାଜା

୧୨- ଶ୍ରୀ ନୀଳକଣ୍ଠ ଦେଓ ଗୋବିନ୍ଦ ଦେବ ରାଜା

୧୩- ଶ୍ରୀ ନାରାୟଣ ଦେଓ ଇନ୍ଦ୍ର ଦେବ ରାଜା

୧୪- ହୃଷିକେଶ ଦେଓ ଇନ୍ଦ୍ର ଦେବ ରାଜା

୧୫- ଶ୍ରୀ ଯଦୁମଣୀ ଦେଓ ଗୋବିନ୍ଦ ଦେବ ରାଜା ମୟୁରଭଞ୍ଜରେ ବିବାହ କରିଥିଲେ ।

୧୬- ଶ୍ରୀ ଶିରପାଣି ଦେଓ ଇନ୍ଦ୍ରଦେବ ରାଜପାଟଣା ରେ ବିବାହ କରିଥିଲେ ଓ ସିଂକୋତା ଛାଡି ଘରବୁଡାରେ ଗଡ କରିଥିଲେ

୧୭- ଶ୍ରୀ ମୁକୁନ୍ଦ ଦେଓ ଚନ୍ଦ୍ରଦେବ ରାଜା ସିଂହଭୂମି ରେ ବିବାହ କରିଥିଲେ ।

୧୮- ଶ୍ରୀ ବିକ୍ରମ ଦେଓ ଗୋବିନ୍ଦ ଦେବ ରାଜା ମୟୁରଭଞ୍ଜରେ ବିବାହ କଲେ କିନ୍ତୁ ଅପୁତ୍ରିକ ଥିବାରୁ ତାଙ୍କର ଭାଇ ରାଜା ହେଲେ ।

୧୯- ଶ୍ରୀ କାମପାଳ ଦେଓ ଇନ୍ଦ୍ର ଦେବ ରାଜା ବିଂଭୂମିରେ ବିବାହ କରିଥିଲେ ।

୨୦- ଶ୍ରୀ ବିରଂଚି ଦେଓ ଇନ୍ଦ୍ର ଦେବ ରାଜା ପାଟଣାରେ ବାହା ହୋଇଥିଲେ ।

୨୧-ଶ୍ରୀ ମାଧବ ଦେଓ ଗୋବିନ୍ଦ ଦେବ ରାଜା ମୟୁରଭଞ୍ଜରେ ବିବାହ କଲେ ଓ ଘରବୁଡା ଛାଡି ବଣାଇଁଗଡରେ ଗଡ ବନାଇଲେ ।

୨୨-ଶ୍ରୀ ବାସୁଦେବ ଦେଓ ଇନ୍ଦ୍ର ଦେଓ ଏହି ରାଜା ପାଟଣାରେ ବିବାହ କରିଥିଲେ । ଏହି ରାଜା ଘରବୁଡା ତ୍ୟାଗ କରି ବଣାଇଁରେ ଆସି ରହିଲେ ।

୨୩-ଶ୍ରୀ ମହେନ୍ଦ୍ର ଦେଓ ଚନ୍ଦ୍ରଦେବ ରାଜା ସିଂହଭୂମିରେ ବାହା ହୋଇଥିଲେ ।

୨୪-ଶ୍ରୀ ଗଦାଧର ଦେଓ ଗୋବିନ୍ଦ ଦେଓ ରାଜା ମୟୁରଭଞ୍ଜରେ ବାହାହେଲେ ।

୨୫-ଶ୍ରୀ ମକରଧ୍ୱଜ ଦେଓ ଇନ୍ଦ୍ରଦେଓ ସିଂହଭୂମିରେ ବାହା ହେଲେ ଓ କୁମାରୀ ମନ୍ଦିର ପ୍ରତିଷ୍ଠା କଲେ ।

୨୬- ଶ୍ରୀ ପରମାନନ୍ଦ ଦେଓ ଚନ୍ଦ୍ର ଦେବ ରାଜା ପାଟଣାରେ ବିବାହ କରିଥିଲେ ।

୨୭- ଶ୍ରୀ ଗିରିଧାରୀ ପାଣି ଦେଓ ଗୋବିନ୍ଦ ଦେଓ ଦେବରାଜ ମୟୁରଭଞ୍ଜରେ ବିବାହ କରିଥିଲେ । ଏହାଙ୍କ ପୁତ୍ର ନଥିବାରୁ ଭାଇର ପୁଅକୁ ରାଜା କରାଇଲେ ।

୨୮-ଶ୍ରୀ ପୁରୁଷୋତମ ଦେଓ ଇନ୍ଦ୍ର ଦେବ ରାଜା ବାମଣ୍ଡାରେ ବିବାହ କଲେ ଓ ବାଣେଶ୍ୱରଙ୍କ ଭୋଗ ଓ ପୂଜକ ବନ୍ଦୋବସ୍ତ କଲେ ।

୨୯-ଶ୍ରୀ ଉଗ୍ର ପ୍ରତାପ ଦେଓ ଚନ୍ଦ୍ର ଦେଓ ରାଜା ନାଗପୁରରୁ ବିବାହ କଲେ ।

୩୦-ଶ୍ରୀ ଚିତ୍ରଭାନୁ ଦେଓ ଗୋବିନ୍ଦ ଦେଓ ରାଜା ପାଟଣାରୁ ବିବାହ କଲେ ।

୩୧-ଶ୍ରୀ ପଦ୍ମନାଭ ଦେଓ ଇନ୍ଦ୍ର ଦେଓ ରାଜା ସିଂହଭୂମିରୁ ବିବାହ କଲେ ।

୩୨-ଶ୍ରୀ ତ୍ରିଲୋଚନ ଦେଓ ଚନ୍ଦ୍ର ଦେଓ ରାଜା ବାମଣ୍ଡାରୁ ବିବାହ କଲେ ।

୩୩-ଶ୍ରୀ ଇନ୍ଦ୍ର ପ୍ରତାପ ଇନ୍ଦ୍ର ଦେଓ ରାଜା ବାମଣ୍ଡାରୁ ବିବାହ କଲେ ଓ ଏହି ୩୨ତମ ରାଜାଙ୍କ ଠାରୁ ଗୋବିନ୍ଦ ଦେଓ ପାଟଣା ଛାଡିଲେ ।

୩୪-ଶ୍ରୀ କଦମ୍ବ କେଶରୀ ଚନ୍ଦ୍ର ଦେବ ରାଜା ମୟୁରଭଞ୍ଜରୁ ବିବାହ କଲେ ଓ ଅନୁଗୁଳରୁ ନାଥ ଘରକୁ ଆଣିଲେ ।

୩୫-ପୁରୁନ୍ଦର ଦେଓ ଇନ୍ଦ୍ରଦେବ ରାଜା ନାଗପୁରରୁ ବିବାହ କଲେ ।

୩୬- ଶ୍ରୀ ଯଦୁନାଥ ଦେଓ ଇନ୍ଦ୍ର ଦେବ ମୟୁରଭଞ୍ଜରୁ ବିବାହ କଲେ । ଶ୍ରୀକର ମିତ୍ରଙ୍କୁ ପୁରୁଷୋତମ ରୁ ଆଣିଲେ ।

୩୭-ଶ୍ରୀ ରାମଚନ୍ଦ୍ର ଦେଓ ଚନ୍ଦ୍ର ଦେବ ରାଜା ସିଂହଭୂମିରୁ ବିବାହ କଲେ ।

୩୮-ଶ୍ରୀ ଉଦିତ ନାରାୟଣ ଚନ୍ଦ୍ର ଦେବ ଦେଓ ରାଜା କେନ୍ଦୁଝରରୁ ବିବାହ କଲେ ଏହାଙ୍କ ବଡଭାଇ ଉଗ୍ର ପ୍ରତାପ କେଉଁଝରରେ ଅଭିଷେକ ହେବାକୁ ଚାହିଁଲେ । କିନ୍ତୁ ସାମନ୍ତ ଘର ଓ ଭଦ୍ରଲୋକମାନେ ମନା କଲେ କିନ୍ତୁ ନମାନି କେଉଁଝର ଚାଲିଗଲେ । ଏଣୁ ଉଦିତ ନାରାୟଣ ରାଜା ହେଲେ । ଉଗ୍ର ପ୍ରତାପ ତାଳଚେରରେ ରାଜା ହେଲେ ।

୩୯-କାଳିଆ ଚନ୍ଦ୍ର ଦେଓ ଇନ୍ଦ୍ର ଦେଓ ରାଜା ପାଟଣାରେ ବିହାହ କରିଥିଲେ । ଏହାଙ୍କ ସମୟରେ ବାମଣ୍ଡା ଓ କେନ୍ଦୁଝର ମଧ୍ୟରେ ବିବାଦ ହେଲା ।

୪୦-ଶ୍ରୀ ବୀରକିଶୋର ଦେଓ ଚନ୍ଦ୍ର ଦେବ ସିଂହଭୂମିରେ ବିବାହ କଲେ ।

୪୧-ଶ୍ରୀ ବାଲୁକେଶ୍ୱର ଦେଓ ଇନ୍ଦ୍ର ଦେବ ରାଜା ମୟୁରଭଞ୍ଜରେ ବିବାହ କଲେ ।

୪୨-ଶ୍ରୀ ବାଣେଶ୍ୱର ଦେଓ ଚନ୍ଦ୍ରଦେବ ରାଜ୍ୟ ବାମଣ୍ଡାରେ ବିବାହ କଲେ ଓ ସାମନ୍ତ ଘର ସାଙ୍ଗେ ଲାଗି ବାମଣ୍ଡାରେ ଭାଇର

ପୁରରେ ରହିଲେ ବାମଣ୍ଡାରୁ ସାମନ୍ତଘର ଯାଇ ରାତିରେ ଆଣିଲେ । ସେ ଆସିବା ସମୟରେ ତାଙ୍କ ରକ୍ଷୀତାର ପୁଅ ପଳାଇଯାଇ ଆଠମଲ୍ଲିକରେ ରାଜା ହେଲେ । ତାଙ୍କ ନାମ ବନମାଳୀ ଥିଲା ।

୪୩-ଶ୍ରୀ ଗୋବିନ୍ଦ ଦେଓ ଇନ୍ଦ୍ର ଦେବ ରାଜା ବାମଣ୍ଡାରୁ ବିବାହ କଲେ

୪୪-ଶ୍ରୀ ନରସିଂହ ଦେଓ ଟିକାୟତ ବିହାର ସାରଣ୍ଡାରେ ବିବାହ କଲେ ।

୪୫- ତାଙ୍କ ପୁଅ ଗୋପୀନାଥ ଚନ୍ଦ୍ର ଦେଓ ରାଜା କେଉଁଝରରେ ବିବାହ କଲେ

୪୬-ଶ୍ରୀ ରାମହରି ଦେଓ ଇନ୍ଦ୍ର ଦେବ ରାଜା ବାମଣ୍ଡାରେ ବିବାହ କଲେ । ସେ ବୁଢ଼ା ସମ୍ବରରୁ ଆଣି ଦଣ୍ଡପାଟ କଲେ ।

୪୭-ଶ୍ରୀ ରଘୁରାଜ ଦେଓ ଚନ୍ଦ୍ର ଦେବ ରାଜା ସିଂହଭୂମିରେ ବିବାହ କଲେ

୪୮-ଶ୍ରୀ ହରିନାରାୟଣ ଦେଓ ରାଜା ସୋନପୁରରୁ ବିବାହ କଲେ

୪୯-ଭିକାରୀ ଦେଓ ଇନ୍ଦ୍ର ଦେଓ ରାଜା ପାଟଣାରେ ବିବାହ କଲେ ଓ ଜଗନ୍ନାଥ ମହାପ୍ରଭୁଙ୍କୁ ତିଆରି କରାଇ ରଥଯାତ୍ରା କଲେ ।

୫୦-ଶ୍ରୀ ପିତାମ୍ବର ଦେଓ ଇନ୍ଦ୍ର ଦେଓ ରାଜା ମୟୂରଭଞ୍ଜରେ ବିବାହ କଲେ । ଦେଓଙ୍କାଁ ପ୍ରତିବଦଳରେ ଟାଙ୍କଯୋଡା ମୌଜାକୁ ପିତାମ୍ବର ପୁରାନାମ ଦେଇ ଷୋହଳ ଘର ବ୍ରାହ୍ମଣ ଆଣି ରଖିଲେ । ବ୍ରାହ୍ମଣୀପାଟରୁ ମହାପାତ୍ର ଘରକୁ ଆଣି ଆଖଡା ଶିଖିଲେ ଓ ବାରଖଣ୍ଡ ଗାଁ ଦେଇ ମହାପାତ୍ର କଲେ

୫୧-ଶ୍ରୀ ଭାଗିରଥି ଦେଓ (ଟିକାୟତ) ପାଟଣାରେ ବିବାହ କଲେ

୫୨-ତାଙ୍କ ପୁଅ ଶ୍ରୀ ରଘୁନାଥ ଦେଓ ଚନ୍ଦ୍ର ଦେଓ ପୂଜା କେନ୍ଦୁଝରରେ ବିବାହ କଲେ ଓ ରଘୁନାଥପୁର ନାମ ଦେଇ ପାଟଣା ବସାଇଲେ ଏବଂ କୂପେଶ୍ୱର ମନ୍ଦିର ନିର୍ମାଣ କଲେ ।

୫୩-ଶ୍ରୀ ଶିବ ନାରାୟଣ ଦେଓ ଇନ୍ଦ୍ର ଦେବ ରାଜା ସୋନପୁରରୁ ବିବାହ କଲେ । ଗୋପାଳ ଜିଉ ତିଆରି କଲେ । ଅନ୍ଧାରୀ ଦେବୀ ପ୍ରତିଷ୍ଠା କଲେ । ଶିବନାରାୟଣ ପୁରକୁ ବ୍ରାହ୍ମଣ ଶାସନ କଲେ । ବାଣେଶ୍ୱର ଓ ସପ୍ତେଶ୍ୱର ମନ୍ଦିର ମରାମତି ହେଲା । ଘୁଷୁରା ହନୁମାନ ମନ୍ଦିର ତିଆରି ହେଲା ।

୫୪-ଶ୍ରୀ ଚନ୍ଦ୍ରଶେଖର ଦେଓ ଇନ୍ଦ୍ର ଦେଓ ରାଜା କେନ୍ଦୁଝରରୁ ବିବାହ କଲେ, ଏହାଙ୍କ ଉନ୍ମାଦ ରୋଗ ଥିବାରୁ ବ୍ରିଟିଶ ସରକାରଙ୍କ ଦ୍ୱାରା ମିଶି ରାଣୀ ପଦ୍ମାବତୀ ରାଜ୍ୟ ଶାସନ କରୁଥିଲେ । ସାନରାଣୀ ସପ୍ନାଦେବୀ ତାଙ୍କ ସାହିର ଝିଅ ତାଙ୍କ ପୁଅ ଶ୍ରୀଧର ଦେଓ ।

୫୫-ଶ୍ରୀଧର ଦେଓ ଇନ୍ଦ୍ରଦେବ ରାଜା ସଢେଇକଳାରେ ବିବାହ କଲେ, ଦ୍ୱିତୀୟ ବିବାହ କରିଥିଲେ ସିଂହଭୂମିର ଜମିଦାର ଆନନ୍ଦପୁର ଜମିଦାର ବଂଶର ଜନୈକ ଭାୟାଜିତଙ୍କ କନ୍ୟା । ଏହାଙ୍କର ତିନିପୁତ୍ର ଥିଲେ ନିଳାମ୍ବର, ବିଶ୍ୱମ୍ବର, ହରେକୃଷ୍ଣ । ଏହାଙ୍କ ସହିତରେ କଲେପଷି ଜମିଦାର କୃଷ୍ଣ ସାମନ୍ତ ଅକାରଣ ବିଷୟାଉ ବସିଭୁତ ହୋଇ ଗୋଟିଏ ବିଦ୍ରୋହ ଘୋଷଣା କଲେ, ବିଦ୍ରୋହ ଶାନ୍ତ କରିବା ପାଇଁ ବ୍ରିଟିଶ ସରକାରଙ୍କ ପୋଲିସ ଆସିଗଲେ । ଏହି ବିଦ୍ରୋହରେ ରାଜା ଓ ପ୍ରଜାଙ୍କର ବହୁତ କ୍ଷତି ହେଲା ଶେଷରେ ବିଦ୍ରୋହୀ ଦଳ ଧରାପଡି ଜେଲ୍ ଗଲେ । ଏହାଙ୍କ ସମୟରେ କେନ୍ଦୁଝରରେ ଭୂୟାଁ ମେଳି ହୋଇଥିଲା । ଏହି ସୁଯୋଗରେ ବ୍ରିଟିସ୍ ସରକାରଙ୍କ ସୈନ୍ୟ ସାହାର୍ଯ୍ୟରେ ରାଜା ବିସ୍ତାର କଲେ ଓ ବ୍ରିଟିଶ ସରକାରଙ୍କ ଠାରୁ ରାଜା ବାହାଦୁର ଉପାଧି ପାଇଲେ । କେନ୍ଦୁଝର ରାଜା ଧନଞ୍ଜୟ ଭଞ୍ଜ ଥିଲେ ଏହାଙ୍କ ସମୟରେ ନଳକାଳ ବନ୍ଦୋବସ୍ତ ହୋଇଥିଲା । ସେହି ବନ୍ଦୋବସ୍ତକୁ ଅବମାନନା କରି ଷଣ୍ଡ ଜମିଦାର ଦୁଇଜଣ ବିଦ୍ରୋହ କରିଥିଲେ । କମିଶନର ଆସି ନିଷ୍ପତି କରିଥିଲେ । ଏ ରାଜା ଅତ୍ୟନ୍ତ ଦାନଶୀଳ ଥିଲେ । ଏହାଙ୍କ ସମୟରେ ଗୋଟିଏ

ପକ୍କା ଘର ଓ ଆଠୋଟି ସ୍କୁଲ ତିଆରି ହୋଇଥିଲା । ପ୍ରାଚୀନ ନିୟମ ଅନୁସାରେ ଗମାର ସିଂହ ମୌଜା ମୁକୁଳ ପୁରୋହିତଙ୍କୁ ଦିଆଗଲା ।ଏ ରାଜା ରାଜାବଂଶର ମର୍ଯ୍ୟାଦା ନିଭାଇ ଥିଲେ ।

୫୬-ଶ୍ରୀ ନିଳାମ୍ବର ଦେଓ ଇନ୍ଦ୍ରଦେବ ରାଜା ମୟୁରଭଞ୍ଜ ରେ ବିବାହ କଲେ । ଏହାଙ୍କ ଆଉ ତିନିଜଣ ରାଣୀ ଥିଲେ । ଦୁଇଜଣ ସଢେଇକଳା ବାଙ୍କ ସାହି ଜମିଦାରଙ୍କ କନ୍ୟା ଏବଂ ଆଉ ଜଣେ ଦୁରାନୀ ଜମିଦାରଙ୍କ କନ୍ୟା । ଏହାଙ୍କ ଚୋରୋଟି ପୁତ୍ର ଥିଲେ: ୧- ଧରଣୀଧର ୨- ହୀରାବ୍ରଜ ଧର ୩- ଯଦୁମଣୀ (ରେଢାଖୋଳ ରାଜା) ୪-ହରିଶ୍ଚନ୍ଦ୍ର ଦେଓ । ଏହାଙ୍କ ଶାଶନରେ ପ୍ରଜା ଅସନ୍ତୁଷ୍ଟ ନଥିଲେ । ଏହାଙ୍କ ସମୟରେ ପ୍ରଥମେ ଧନାଗାରର ସୁତ୍ରପାତ ହୋଇଥିଲା । ଅତ୍ର ଷ୍ଟେଟ ର ଦୁଇଟି ଜଙ୍ଗଲର ପଟ୍ଟା ବ୍ରିଟିଶ କମ୍ପାନିକୁ ଦିଆଗଲା । ଏ ରାଜା ଧନ ଅର୍ଜନରେ ଯେତିକି ଆଗ୍ରହୀ ଥିଲେ, ଧର୍ମ କାର୍ଯ୍ୟରେ ମଧ୍ୟ ସେତିକି ଦୃଢ ଥିଲେ, ପିତାଙ୍କ ଦ୍ୱାରା ଆନୀତ ଗୋଟିଏ ମାର୍ବଲ ପ୍ରସ୍ତରରେ ଦୁଇଟି ବୃଷଭ ବନାଇ ବାଣେଶ୍ୱରଙ୍କୁ ଅର୍ପଣ କରିଥିଲେ । ଏହାଙ୍କ ସମୟରେ ଗୋପାଳ ଜିଉ ମନ୍ଦିର ପୁନଃ ନିର୍ମାଣ ହୋଇଥିଲା । ଏବଂ ମୂର୍ତୀ ଭାଙ୍ଗୀ ଯାଇଥିବାରୁ ଏକ ନୂତନ ମୂର୍ତୀ କ୍ରୟକରି ପ୍ରତିଷ୍ଠା କଲେ ।

୫୭- ଶ୍ରୀ ଧରଣୀଧର ଦେଓ ଇନ୍ଦ୍ର ଦେବ ରାଜା ବାମଣ୍ଡାରେ ବିବାହ କରିଥିଲେ । ପିତାଙ୍କ ମୃତ୍ୟୁ ବେଳକୁ ଅଳ୍ପ ବୟସ ହୋଇଥିବାରୁ ଅଣଓ୍ୱାଡିସ ଶାସନ ହୋଇଥିଲା । ୧୯୧୩ ମେ ମାସରେ ଶାସନଭାର ଗ୍ରହଣ କରିଥିଲେ । ଏହାଙ୍କ ସମୟରେ ଜଗନ୍ନାଥ ବିଗ୍ରହ ସବୁ ଭାଙ୍ଗି ଯାଇଥିବାରୁ ନୂତନ ତିଆରି ହେଲା ଏରାଜା ଗୌର ଗୋବିନ୍ଦ ମଠ ତିଆରି କରିଥିଲେ । ଏହାଙ୍କ ସମୟରେ ଜଣେ କନ୍ଧ ବଂଶୀୟ କ୍ଷତ୍ରିୟଙ୍କୁ ଫାଶୀ ଦିଆଯାଇଥିଲା (୧୫-୧-୧୯୪୩ ମସିହାରେ ପୀତାମ୍ବର ଦେଓ ଙ୍କୁ)ଏରାଜା ରାଣୀ ଅମରାବଣ ଜଗମୋହନ ମନ୍ଦିର ନିର୍ମାଣ କରାଇ ଥିଲେ ।

ଏହାଙ୍କ ପୁତ୍ର ନଥିବାରୁ ଜୀରାବ୍ରଜଧର ଦେଓ ଙ୍କ ପୁତ୍ରକୁ ପୋଷ୍ୟ ପୁତ୍ର କରିଥିଲେ । ରାଣୀ ଅମରାବତୀ କୁରୁପଣା ରାଜ୍ୟକୁ ଭ୍ରମଣ କରିଯାଇଥିବା ବେଳେ ସେଠାରେ ଜ୍ୱର ରୋଗରେ ପୀଡିତ ହୋଇ ୧୯୧୯ ନର ମୃତ୍ୟୁ ବରଣ କଲେ । ଏ ରାଜାଙ୍କର ଜଣେ ରକ୍ଷୀତା ରାଣୀ ଥିଲେ । ତାଙ୍କ ସହିତ ପୁରୀ ଦର୍ଶନ କରିବାକୁ ଯାଇ ଫେରିଲେ ନାହିଁ । ୧୯୪୭ ମସିହାରେ କଂଗ୍ରେସ ସରକାର ରାଜ୍ୟ ଛଡାଇ ନେଲେ, ତାର ଏକବର୍ଷ ପରେ ୧୯୪୮ ମସିହାରେ ରାଜା ଧରଣୀଧର ପୁରୀ ଧାମରେ ଦେହତ୍ୟାଗ କଲେ । ତାଙ୍କରପୋଷ୍ୟପୁତ୍ର ରାଜା ହେଲେ ।

୫୮-କଦମ୍ବ କେଶରୀ ଚନ୍ଦ୍ର ଦେବ ଦେଓ ରାଜା ବସ୍ତର ରେ ବିବାହ କରିଥିଲେ । ଏହାଙ୍କର ତିନିପୁତ୍ର ଥିଲେ-୧- କିରଣ କିଶୋର (ଟିକାୟତ) ୨- ମଧ୍ୟମ ପୁତ୍ରର ମୃତ୍ୟୁ ୩- ବୀରକିଶୋର । ଅକ୍ଷୟ ତୃତୀୟା ଦିନ ମଧ୍ୟମ ପୁତ୍ର ପଟେଡଙ୍କର ମୃତ୍ୟୁ ହେଲା । ୧୯୭୧ ମସିହା ଏପ୍ରିଲ ମାସ ୨୦ତାରିଖ (ଚୈତ୍ର ମାସରେ)୧୦ ଘଣ୍ଟିକା ସମୟରେ ଜ୍ୟେଷ୍ଠପୁତ୍ର ଟିକାୟତ କିରଣ କିଶୋରଙ୍କର ମୃତ୍ୟୁ ହୋଇଥିଲା । ଏ ରାଜାଙ୍କ ସମୟରେ ବାଣେଶ୍ୱର ମନ୍ଦିରର ମୁଖଶାଳା ପୁନଃ ନିର୍ମାଣ ହେଲା ଓ କୁଆଁରୀ ମନ୍ଦିରପକ୍କା ଘର ହେଲା । ଏ ରାଜାଙ୍କ ସମୟରେ କନ୍ତଦେବୀଙ୍କ ପୂଜା ପରିବର୍ତନ ହେଲା । ଘରେ ଘରେ ପୂଜା ହେବା ପରିବର୍ତେ ମଣ୍ଡୟୀ ପୂଜା ହେଲା । ଏଥିରେ ଅମାନ୍ତ ପୂଜା କରିବାକୁ ମନା କଲା । ତଦ୍ୱାରା କିଛି, ଦିନି ଦେହୁରୀମାନେ ପୂଜା କଲେ । ରାଜା ଏହାର ସୁବିଧା ପାଇଁ ଗୋଟିଏ କମିଟି ଗଠନ କରିଥିଲେ । ଅମାନ୍ତକୁ ବହୁତ ବୁଝାଗଲା ।କିନ୍ତୁ ସେ ନମାନି ରାଜାଙ୍କୁ ଇସ୍ତାଫା ପତ୍ର ଦେଲା । ସେଠାରେ ସେ ଲେଖିଥିଲା ଯେ ରାଜାଙ୍କର କୌଣସି କାମ ଓ ଦେବାଦେବୀ ପୂଜା କରିବ ନାହିଁ । ତାପରେ ତାଙ୍କର ବଂଶଜ ମାନଙ୍କୁ ମଧ୍ୟ ପଚରା ଯିବାରୁ ସେମାନେ ନାରାଜ ହେଲେ । ତେଣୁ ରାଜା

ଦେଓଗାଁ ଶ୍ରୀ ନୀଳଗୀରିଙ୍କ ପୁରା ପୂଜା କରିବାପାଇଁ ପ୍ରସ୍ତୁତ ହେବାରୁ ତାକୁ ଶିରୀପା ବାନ୍ଧି ଅମାନ୍ତ କଲେ ଏବଂ ସେ ସମସ୍ତ ଦେବାଦେବୀ ପୂଜା କରିଆସୁଛନ୍ତି । ପରେ ପୁଣି ଅମାନ୍ତଙ୍କର ବଂଶଧର ପୁଜା କଲେ । ଏବଂ ଏବେ ମଧ୍ୟ ପୂଜା କରୁଛନ୍ତି । ରାଜା ଧରଣୀଧରଙ୍କ ଦ୍ୱାରା ତିଆରି ହୋଇଥିବା କେତେକ ରୌପ୍ୟ ନିର୍ମିତ ସାମଗ୍ରୀ, ଏହି ରାଜା ଦେବୋର କମିଟିକୁ ଦାନ କଲେ । ମସିହାରେ ତତ୍କାଳିନ ଦେବୋର ଅଧିକାରୀ ସେଗୁଡିକୁ ଗ୍ରହଣ କଲେ ।

<u>ସାମଗ୍ରୀର ତାଲିକା:-</u>

୧- ବଡନାଗ - ୧ଟି -		୮ କି.ଗ୍ରା.	୫୦ ଗ୍ରାମ
୨- ମଧ୍ୟମ ନାଗ ତିନୋଟି - ୩ଟି			
	କ)	୩ କି.ଗ୍ରା.	୩୦୦ ଗ୍ରାମ
	ଖ)	୩ କି.ଗ୍ରା	୫୫୦ ଗ୍ରାମ
	ଗ)	୩ କି.ଗ୍ରା	୨୫ ଗ୍ରାମ
୩-ଛୋଟ ନାଗ ଦୁଇଟି -	କ)		୨୫୫ ଗ୍ରାମ
	ଖ)		୬୨୫ ଗ୍ରାମ
୪- ଛତ୍ର ୧ଟି-		୫ କି.ଗ୍ରା	୭୭୦ ଗ୍ରାମ
୫- ଲୋଟା ୧ଟି (ବରୁଆ)			୭୫୦ ଗ୍ରାମ
୬- ପ୍ଲାଟଫର୍ମ ପ୍ଲେଟ ୮ଟି		୨ କି.ଗ୍ରା	୭୫୦ ଗ୍ରାମ
୭- କୁମ୍ଭ ଚାରୋଟି		୧ କି.ଗ୍ରା	୧୨୫ ଗ୍ରାମ
୮- ଗୋମୁଣୀ ତିନୋଟି			୩୨୦ ଗ୍ରାମ

ମୋଟ - ୩୨ କି.ଗ୍ରା ୬୪୦ ଗ୍ରାମ

ବଣାଇଁ ରାଜବଂଶ ମାଦଳା

ବଣାଁଇ ରାଜା କଦମ୍ବ କିଶୋର ଚନ୍ଦ୍ର ଦେଓ ଦେଉ ଙ୍କ ରାଣୀ ଗୀତାକୁମାରୀ ଦେବୀ ୨୦ ଡିସେମ୍ବର (ପୌଷ) ୨୦୦୨ ଶୁକ୍ରବାର ରେ ଛତିଶଗଡ ରାଜ୍ୟରେ ଅବସ୍ଥିତ ରାୟପୁର ର ରାଜକୁମାର ଦେହତ୍ୟାଗ କଲେ । ସେତେବେଳକୁ ତାଙ୍କର ବିବାହର ୫୫ବର୍ଷ ହୋଇଥିଲା ଓ ତାଙ୍କୁ ୭୨ ବର୍ଷ ହୋଇଥିଲା ।

ତୃତୀୟ ରତ୍ନାକର

ନୃସିଂହନାଥ ପୁରାଣ

ବାଳକ ମାତୃଗର୍ଭର କଥା (ଶେଷ ନୃସିଂହ ଜନ୍ମ)

ଅନନ୍ତଙ୍କୁ ସଙ୍ଗେ ଘେନି ସେ ଅନନ୍ତଶାୟୀ
ବଢନ୍ତି ମାତାଗର୍ଭରେ ବାମେ ଦକ୍ଷେ ରହି ।

ଏମନ୍ତେ ସେ ଦିନୁଦିନ ହୋନ୍ତେ ନବମାସ
ଗର୍ଭର କଷ୍ଟକୁ ସହି ନ ପାରିଲେ ଶେଷ ।

ବିଷ୍ଣୁଙ୍କୁ ବୋଇଲେ ସାମୀ ଶୁଣ ମହାପ୍ରଭୁ
ଶୀଘ୍ର ହୋଇ ଚାଲ ଏବେ ଜନମିବା ଗର୍ଭୁ ।

ଶ୍ରୀହର ବୋଇଲେ କିପାଁ ଆତୁର ଯେ ହୁଅ
ଦଶମାସ ନହୋଇଲେ ଟାଣ ନୋହେ ଦେହ ।

ସପ୍ତମାସେ ଜନମିଲେ ଟାଣ ନୋହେ ଦେହୀ
ଆଠରେ ଜନ୍ମିଲେ ପୁତ୍ର କେବେ ନ ବଞ୍ଚଇ ।

ନବମରେ ଉପୁଜିଲେ ମାତା ପାଏ କ୍ଳେଶ

ଦଶମେ ଜନ୍ମିଲେ ସବୁ କଥାକୁ ଉଶ୍ୱାସ ।

ଶେଷଦେବ ବୋଇଲେ ଏ ଆଜ୍ଞା ଯେବେହେଲା
କହିବି ଗର୍ଭର କଷ୍ଟ ଶୁଣ ଏବେ ଭଲା ।

ଜନନୀ ଉଦରେ ଯେତେ ଯେତେ କଷ୍ଟ ପାଇ
ଛାମୁରେ କହୁଛି ତାହା ଶୁଣ ଭାବଗ୍ରାହୀ ।

ଯେତେବେଳେ ମାତା ପିତା ହୋନ୍ତି ଏକଠାବ
ସେ ବୀର୍ଯ୍ୟର ମଧ୍ୟରେ ଯେ ପଶେ ଯାଇ ଜୀବ ।

ମାତାର ଗର୍ଭରେ ପଡି ଧରେ ଦେହ କାନ୍ତି
ପ୍ରଥମ ଦିନୁ ହୁଅଇ ଜଳବିନ୍ଦୁ ଜ୍ୟୋତି ।

ପଂଚମ ଦିନରେ ହୋଏ ରକ୍ ବର୍ଣ୍ଣ କାୟେ
ସେହିଠାରୁ କ୍ରମେ କ୍ରମେ ହୋଇ ବୃଦ୍ଧି ପାଏ ।

ବଦରି ଫଳର ପ୍ରାୟେ ଦିଶେ ଦିନ ଦଶେ
ଅଣ୍ଡାର ଆକାର ହୁଏ ପନ୍ଦର ଦିବସେ ।

ତିରିଶ ଦିନ ପ୍ରକାଶ ହୁଏ ମଥା ଆସି
ଚାଳିଶ ଦିନରେ ଯାଇ ଚରଣ ପ୍ରକାଶି ।

ଷାଠିଏ ଦିନ ପ୍ରକାଶ ପୁଣି ବେନି ଭୁଜ
ଆବର ଚକ୍ଷୁ ନାସିକା ହୁଏ କର୍ଣ୍ଣ ଭୁଜ ।
ପଂଚଷଠି ଦିନରେ ଯେ ହୁଏ ତୁଣ୍ଡ ଗୋଟି

ସତୁରି ଦିନରେ ଯେ ମଳହାର ଯାଏ ଫାଟି ।

ଅଣାଅଶି ଦିନରେ ଯେ ଅଙ୍ଗୁଳିର ସଞ୍ଚା
ଅଶୀ ଦିନରେ ଦିଶଇ ଲୋମ ଚର୍ମ ଲୋଚା ।

ନଉ ଦିନରେ ଯେ ପୁଣି ହୋଇ ନଖମାନ
ବସାଇ ଉର୍ଦ୍ଧମୁଖରେ ବିଂଶଶତେ ଦିନ ।

ପଂଚମାସରେ ବସଇ ସପ୍ତଧାତୁ ତେଜ
ଅସ୍ଥିମାଂସ ମଜ୍ଜା ମେଦ ଚର୍ମ ରକ୍ ବୀର୍ଯ୍ୟ ।

ଏସାତ ପୁରରେ ମଧ୍ୟେ ପ ଭୂତ ଯାଇ
ପ୍ରକୃତି ପ୍ରକାଶେ ଷଢ଼ମାସେ ହୃଦେ ରହି ।

ପଂଚମାସ ପକ୍ଷକରେ ଲାଗେ କ୍ଷୁଧା ତୃଷା
ଷଢମାସରେ କରଇ ହୃଦେ ଆସି ବସ ।

କ୍ଷୁଧା ତୃଷା ଲାଗି ଆତ୍ମା ହୁଅଇ ବିକଳ
ତାହା ଜାଣିଣ ବିଧାତା ମିଳନ୍ତି ତତ୍କାଳ ।

ସୋହଂ ହଂସ ପବନର ବିଞ୍ଚଣାଟି ଆଣି
ଜୀବ ଆତ୍ମା ଘରଠାରେ ଖଞ୍ଜନ୍ତି ନିର୍ମାଣି ।

ବୋଲନ୍ତି ଏହୁ ଆଲଟେ ହୁଏ ବିଞ୍ଚା ବିଞ୍ଚି
କ୍ଷୁଧା ତୃଷା ରୋଗ ତୋତେ ନ ଲାଗିବ କିଛି ।
ନାଭିକି ଜଡି ଲାଗିଛି ତୋର ନାଡୀଗୋଟି

ବିଞ୍ଛ ଏହି ପବନରେ ଚକ୍ଷୁ ଯାଉ ଫାଟି ।

ଜନନୀ ଉଦରୁ ରନ୍ଧ୍ରେ ଅନ୍ନରସ
ମରିବ ଖାଇ ହୋଇବୁ ଜାଣ ତୁହି ତୋଷ ।

ଏମନ୍ତେ କହି ହୁଅନ୍ତେ ବିଧି ଅନ୍ତର୍ଦ୍ଧାନ
ସେହି ପବନ ବାଜିଣ ଫିଟେ ଦ୍ୱାରମାନ ।

ଦ୍ୱାର ଫିଟନ୍ତେ ପ୍ରବେଶ ହୋଇ କୃମିମାନେ
ମାତାର ଗର୍ଭେ ପଶନ୍ତି ବୁଲି ନାସା କର୍ଣ୍ଣେ ।

ସପତମ ମାସ ହେଲେ ଲଭେ ପୁଣି କଷ୍ଟ
କର ଚରଣକୁ ଛନ୍ଦି ହୁଏ ଛଟପଟ ।

ଗର୍ଭର ଅନ୍ଧାକାରରେ ପଡିହୋଏ ଘଣ୍ଟି
ଦଇବଯୋଗେ ବନ୍ଧନ ପୁଣି ଯାଏ ଫିଟି ।

ବନ୍ଦୀପରାୟେ ହୋଇଣ ପଡିଥାଏ ଗର୍ଭେ
ତହିଁର ଦୁଃଖ କହିବି କିସ ପୁଣି ଏବେ ।

ଜନନୀ କରଇ ଯେତେ ଦ୍ରବ୍ୟ ବସି ଗ୍ରାସ
ତପତ ଆହାର ଲାଗି ଶିଶୁ କରେ ତ୍ରାସ ।

ଆମ୍ବିଳ କଷା ଆବର ତିକ୍ ରାଗ ଦ୍ରବ୍ୟ
ତହିଁରେ କେତେ ବିକଳ ହୁଏ ଜାଣ ଜୀବ ।
ଅଷ୍ଟମାସର ଯେ ଦଣ୍ଡ କି କହିବି ପୁଣି

ତରଛ ସେ ହେଉଥାଏ ଗର୍ଭକଥା ଜାଣି ।

ଯେତେବେଳେ ମାତା ତାର କରଇ ଗମନ
ବ୍ୟର୍ଥେ ପଡି ମଲି ଭାଳଇ ନନ୍ଦନ ।

ଜନନୀ ଶୁଅଇ ଶେଯେ ପୁଣି ଯେତେବେଳେ
ମହା ଆକୁଳ ହୋଇଣ ଶିଶୁ ପୁଣି ଭାଳେ ।

ବୋଲଇ ମାତା ମୋହର ଗଲା ପରା ମରି
କି ରୂପେ ଆଉ ଜନ୍ମିବି ମୁହିଁ ଦେହ ଧରି ।

ଏରୂପେ ଗର୍ଭେ ଆକୁଳ ହୁଅନ୍ତେ ସେ ବଳା
ନିର୍ଜୀବ ପ୍ରାୟ ହୋଇଣ ବୁଜେ ଚକ୍ଷୁଡୋଳା ।

ସେ ଦୁର୍ଗନ୍ଧ ପୂଯ ରକ୍ ଲାଳମଧ୍ୟେ ପଡି
ଆମିଷ ଯେ ମଳମୂତ୍ର ହୋଇଥାଏ ଜଡି ।

ମନରେ ଆକୁଳ ହୋଇ କାନ୍ଦେ ଶିଶୁ ବସି
ଲୋତକ ଧାରା ନେତ୍ରରୁ ବହେ ଅନର୍ଗଳ ।

ବିଧାତାଙ୍କୁ ଚିନ୍ତାକରି କାନ୍ଦେ ଗର୍ଭେ ବାଳ
ବାଳକ ରୋଦନ ଜାଣି ହୃଦେ ଦେବବର ।

ଜାଲ ଗୋଟିଏ ବେଢ଼ାନ୍ତି ଆଣି ଦେହେ ତାର

ବ୍ରହ୍ମଜ୍ଞାନକୁ ଯେ କହି ଦିଅନ୍ତି ସମ୍ମୁଖେ ।

ବୋଲନ୍ତି ତରିବୁ ଯେବେ ଭଜ ହରି ମୁଖେ

ବିଧାତା ମୁଖରୁ ଏହିପରି ବାକ୍ୟ ଶୁଣି
ଜ୍ଞାନକୁ ପାଇ ବାଳକ ଭଜେ ଚକ୍ରପାଣି

ପରମ ପୁରୁଷକୁ ସେ ଭଜେ ଧ୍ୟାନ କରି ।
ବୋଲଇ ମୋତେ ଉଦ୍ଧାର ପ୍ରଭୁ ନରହରି

ଆହେ ପ୍ରଭୁ ନାରାୟଣ ନର୍କ ଉଦ୍ଧାରଣ ।
ରଖ ଶ୍ରୀଚରଣ ତଳେ ପଶିଲି ଶରଣ

ମହାଘୋର ଅନ୍ଧକାର ଅଟେ ମାତାଗର୍ଭ ।
ଏଥିରେ ରହିଲେ ମୋକ୍ଷ ନାହିଁ ପଦ୍ମନାଭ

ଆହେ ଚତୁର୍ଭୁଜ ପ୍ରଭୁ ମୋତେ କର ତ୍ରାହି
ଉଦ୍ଧାର ଏ ଗର୍ଭେ ଯାତନାରୁ ଭାବଗ୍ରାହୀ

ଏଥୁପାରି ହେଲେ ଭଜିବିମୁଁ ତୁମ୍ଭ ପାଦ
ଆଉ ବେଳେ ନପଡିବି ଏ ଘୋର ପ୍ରମାଦେ

ଏହିରୁପେ ଚିହ୍ନିଜ୍ଞାନ ଧରେ ବାଳଶିଷି
ନବମାସ ପୂରି ଦଶମାସ ହୁଏ ଆସି

ସେ ଦଶମାସରେ ପୁଣି ମାତା ପାଏ କଷ୍ଟ ।
ଉଠି ଚଳି ନପାରଇ ଚଡଚଡ ପେଟ
ଦୁର୍ଗାଙ୍କୁ ସୁମରି ସେହୁ ସୁମରେ ଶ୍ରୀହରି ।

ବୋଲଇ ଏଥୁ କରିବେ ପ୍ରଭୁ ମୋତେ ପାରି

ଏମନ୍ତ ଭଜନ୍ତେ ମାତା ପୁତ୍ର ଜଗନ୍ନାଥ ।
ସେଠାରୁ ଗୋବିନ୍ଦ ପୁଣି ହନ୍ତି ସାହାପକ୍ଷ

ପବନରୁ କହିଦ୍ୟନ୍ତି ପ୍ରଭୁ ଭାବଗ୍ରାହୀ ।
ପ୍ରଭୁ ଆଜ୍ଞାରେ ସୁତିକାବାୟୁ ଚଳିଯାଇ

ଜନନୀ ଗର୍ଭରେ ଶୂଳ ମାରନ୍ତେ ଯେ ପେଲି ।
ସେହି ଠାବରୁ ଟଂଚଳେ ଉଠେ ଶିଶୁ ବୁଲି

ଗୋବିନ୍ଦର କଟାକ୍ଷରୁ ଫିଟେ ଗର୍ଭ କଷ୍ଟ ।
ସେହି ଠାବରୁ ଶିଶୁକୁ ଦିଶେ ଗର୍ଭ ବାଟ

ଅଧୋମୁଖରେ ପଡିଣ ପେଲେ ମୁଣ୍ଡିଆଇଁ ।
ମାତା ଭଗଦ୍ୱାରୁ ଖସି ଭୂମିରେ ପଡଇ

ଭୂମିରେ ପଡନ୍ତେ ଆସି ଆକର୍ଷଇ ମୋହ ।
କୂଆଁ କୂଆଁ ବୋଲି ରଡି ଛାଡେ ବାଳପୁଅ

ଏ ରୂପେ କହନ୍ତି ବିଷ୍ଣୁ ଆଗେ ସାନଭାଇ
ଗର୍ଭରେ ଜାଣ ଜୀବଟି ଏତେ କଷ୍ଟ ପାଇ

ସବୁରି ଜନମପନ୍ଥା ଏସନକ ବାଣୀ
ତେଣୁ ଛାମୁରେ କହିଲି ଏହା ପରିମାଣି
ପ୍ରଭୁ ବୋଇଲେକ ତେବେ ଶୁଣହେ ଅନନ୍ତ

ଏଛାର କଥାକୁ ଆମ୍ଭେ ହେବା କି ବିରକ୍

ଆମ୍ଭେ ଯେବେ ଗର୍ଭକଥା ଘେନିବାଟି ମନ୍ଦ
ସଂସାରେ ହେବାଟି ଆମ୍ଭେ କେହ୍ନେ ପୂର୍ଣ୍ଣାନନ୍ଦ

ବୁଝିଲେ ସଂସାରେ ଆମ୍ଭେସିନା ସର୍ବଜୀବ
ଆତ୍ମାରୂପରେ ପ୍ରକାଶି ଜନ୍ମି ମାତାଗର୍ଭ

ଆମ୍ଭେ ନରହରି ଥାଉଁ ସଂସାରେ ତପୂରି
ଆମ୍ଭେ ବିକାର ଘେନିଲେ ଜନ୍ମିବା କି କରି

ସବୁ ଆତ୍ମା ଆମ୍ଭେ ଜାଣ ବୁଝିଲେ ପ୍ରମାଣ
ସଂସାର ଆମ୍ଭଙ୍କୁ ଯେ ନ ଚିହ୍ନେ ମୂର୍ଖଜନ

କହିଲ ଗର୍ଭର କଷ୍ଟ ଯେତେ ତୁମ୍ଭେ ଆଜ
ଲଭନ୍ତି ସେ କ୍ଳେଶ ଯହୁଁ କହିବା ତା ବୁଝ

କୁଯୋନିକୁ କୁ ଇନ୍ଦ୍ରିୟ ଦ୍ୟନ୍ତି ଯେତେ ଲୋକ
ତାହାଙ୍କ ବୀର୍ଯ୍ୟଟି ଲଭେ ସବୁ କଷ୍ଟଯାକ

ହିଂସ୍ରକ କୁଟିଳ ଯେହୁ ଦାମ୍ଭିକ ବିଟାଳ
କପଟି ଲମ୍ପଟି ଆଦି ଅଜ୍ଞାନ ଚଣ୍ଡାଳ

ତାମସିକ କର୍କଶ ଯେ ସାହସୀ ଦୁର୍ଭାଷୀ
ପାପି ମହାପାପୀ ଯେତେ ଆବର ଯେ ଦୋଷୀ

ଏହି ଲୋକମାନଙ୍କର ରଜ ବୀର୍ଯ୍ୟ ଯେତେ
ଜଠରେ ପଡିଣ ଦୁଃଖ ଲଭେ ଗର୍ଭଗତେ

ଯେବେ ବନ୍ତତ ପୂଣ୍ୟାତ୍ମା ପୁରୁଷର ରହି
ସେମାନେ ଗର୍ଭର ଦୁଃଖ ନ ପାଆନ୍ତି କେହି

ଆମ୍ଭେ ପରଂବ୍ରହ୍ମ ବ୍ରହ୍ମାଣ୍ଡର ସୃଷ୍ଟିକର୍ତା
ଆମ୍ଭଙ୍କୁ ଗର୍ଭରେ କଷ୍ଟଦେବ କି ବିଧାତା

ଏବେ ନବ ପୂରି ଦଶମାସ ହେଲା କାଳ
ଚାଲ ଆହେ ସୁଖେ ଏବେ ଯିବା ବେନିବାଳ

ଏତେକ ବୋଲି ଜନ୍ମକୁ ହେଲେ ସାମୀ ସଜ
ସଙ୍ଖ ଚକ୍ର ଗଦା ପଦ୍ମ ଧରି ଚରୁର୍ଭୁଜ

ମାତାଗର୍ଭେ କାଥାବାର୍ତା ହୋଇ ବେନିଭାଇ
ଜନ୍ମ ସଂଚାରକୁ ସଜ ହୋଇଲେକ ତହିଁ

ଏଥୁ ଅନନ୍ତରେ ପୁଣ ଭଗବତୀ ରାଣୀ
ପ୍ରସବବେଳେ ହୁଅନ୍ତେ ଉଠେ ପେଟ ଟାଣି

ଗର୍ଭ ବଥାନ୍ତେ ଚିନ୍ତିଲେ ଦେବୀ ନାରାୟଣ
ଗର୍ଭେ ଥାଇ ପ୍ରଭୁ ହେଲେ ଉଶ୍ୱାସ ଯେ ପୁଣ

ଅଶେଷ ପୃଥ୍ୱୀ ଅଛନ୍ତି ଯାର ଗର୍ଭଗତେ
ତଳ ଅଛି ସେ ଭାରା ସହିବାକୁ ଏ ଜଗତେ

ଧନ୍ୟ ସେହି ଭାଗବନ୍ତ ରାଜାର ବୁଲଣୀ
ଅଯୋନିଜନ୍ମା ଧଇଲେ ଗର୍ଭେ ଚକ୍ରପାଣି

ପ୍ରତ୍ୟକ୍ଷରେ ଆଦୀଶକ୍ତି ଅଟେ ସେହି ମାତା
ତେଣୁ ଧଇଲେ ସେ ଗର୍ଭଗତେ ସୃଷ୍ଟିକର୍ତା

ସମ୍ପୁର୍ଣ୍ଣ ଦଶମାସଟି ହେଲା ଯେତେବେଳେ
ଜନ୍ମ ସଂଚାରକୁ ମନ କଲ ଆଦିମୂଳେ

ପବନ ବଳରେ ଶୂନ୍ୟ ଆସିଲା ଆକର୍ଷି
ବୈଶାଖ ଶୁକ୍ଳପକ୍ଷ ତିଥି ଚତୁର୍ଦ୍ଦଶୀ

ସ୍ୱାତୀ ନାମେ ନକ୍ଷତ୍ର ସେ ତୁଳାଚନ୍ଦ୍ର ଭୋଗ
ତୌତିଳ ନାମେ କରଣ ସୌଭାଗ୍ୟ ଯେ ଯୋଗ

ବେଳ ଊନବିଂଶ ଦଣ୍ଡେ ସିଂହଲଗ୍ନ ଗୃହେ
ଦ୍ୱିତୀୟରେ ବୃହସ୍ପତି ଷଷ୍ଟେ ଶନି ରହେ

ତୃତୀୟରେ ସୁଧାକର କର୍ମେ ଭୃଗୁନାନ
ଏମନ୍ତ ବେଳରେ ଶୂଳ ଆସେ ଘନଘନ

ଧାଇ ପରିବାରୀ ଜନେ ପୋଇଲୀ ସନ୍ଧେହେ
ଯେଝାରୁପେ ସେବି ଲାଗିଛନ୍ତି ଦେହେ ଦେହେ

ଏଥି ଉତ୍ତାରେ ଯେ ପୁତ୍ରେ ଗର୍ଭୁ ଅବତରୀ
ଦେଖି ରାଜାଙ୍କୁ କହିଲେ ଯାଇ ପରିବାରୀ

ଭୋ ପ୍ରଭୁ ରାଣୀଙ୍କର ଯେ ପୁତ୍ର ହେଲା ଜାତ
ପ୍ରତ୍ୟକ୍ଷେ ଦିଶନ୍ତି ସେହି ଶ୍ରୀହରି ସଂଜାତ

ଅଷ୍ଟାଦଶ ଚିହ୍ନ ଘେନି ଜନ୍ମିଛନ୍ତି ହରି
କରେ ଦିଶେ ଶଙ୍ଖ ଚକ୍ର ଗଦା ପଦ୍ମଚାରି

ହୃଦକମଳେ ଶ୍ରୀବତ୍ସ ଚିହ୍ନ ଅଛି ବସି
ନିମିଷେ ଦେଖି କହୁଛି ସିନା ଆମ୍ଭେ ଆସି

ତୁମ୍ଭଙ୍କୁ ଅବି ଦିଶିବେ ସେହୁ ପୁତ୍ରପ୍ରାୟ
ଆମ୍ଭଙ୍କୁ ହେଲେ ସାକ୍ଷାତେ ଦିଶି ବିଷ୍ଣୁମୟ

ଅଛନ୍ତି ଲକ୍ଷେ ଲକ୍ଷଣ ଘେନ ଅବତରି
ଦେଖିବା ମାତ୍ରେ ଆମ୍ଭର ନେତ୍ର ଗଲା ପୁରି

ଏତେ ବୋଲି ଦାସୀ କହୁଁ କହୁଁ ରାଜା ଆଗେ
ଆଉ ଜଣେ ଧାଇ ଯାଇ କହିଲାକ ବେଗେ

ବୋଇଲା ରାଣୀର ପୁଣି ବଥାଉଛି ପେଟ
ଏହିରୂପେ ମହାଦେଇ ପାଉଛନ୍ତି କଷ୍ଟ

ନୃପତି ବୋଇଲେ ଆଲ ସେବ ଯାଇ ତୁମ୍ଭେ
ଆବର ପୁତ୍ରେକ ଜାତ ହେବ ଜାଣୁ ଆମ୍ଭେ

ସପନେ ଗୋଟିଏ ଦେଖିଅଛୁଁ ଆଜ ରାତ୍ରେ
ମହାଦେଇଙ୍କ ଗର୍ଭରୁ ଜାତ ବେନି ପୁତ୍ରେ

ସେ କଥା ଗୋଟି ଘଟିଲା ଦେଖଏବେ ଆସି
ଗର୍ଭଯେବେ ଟାଣୁଅଛି ଜାତହେବ ଶିଷି

ଏହି ରୂପେ କଥା ହେଉଁ ପୁତ୍ର ଜାତ ହେଲା
ତାହା ଦେଖି ପାଇଲିଏ ଧାଇଁଣ ଆସିଲା

ରାଜା ଛାମୁରେ କହିଲା ଯାଇ କରଯୋଡି
ବୋଲେ ଆଉ ପୁତ୍ରଦେବ ଜନ୍ମିଲେ ବାହୁଡି

ନିଶ୍ଚେ ଅନନ୍ତ ଜନ୍ମିଲା ପ୍ରାୟେ ସେହି ଦିଶେ
ସେ ପୁତ୍ର ଗୁଣ କହିବି କିସ ତୁମ୍ଭ ପାଶେ

ଶୁଣିଣ କୃଷ୍ଣବଲ୍ଲଭ ସନ୍ତୋଷ ହୋଇଲେ
ବହୁତ ଯେ ଧନଦ୍ରବ୍ୟ ଧାଇ କରେ ଦେଲେ

ରାଜ୍ୟ ଯାକ ଯେ ଉତ୍ସବ କଲେ ଅପ୍ରମିତ
ବଜାଇଣ ଶଙ୍ଖ ଭେରୀ କଲେ ନୃତ୍ୟ ଗୀତ

ଅଠର ବର୍ଣ୍ଣରେ ବାଦ୍ୟ ବାର ବର୍ଣ୍ଣେ ତାଳି
ସ୍ତ୍ରୀରୀଏ ଗୀତ ଗାଇଣ ଦେଲେ ହୁଳହୁଳି

ଠାବେ ଠାବେ ପଶି ଜ୍ଜର କଲେ ରାଜ୍ୟ ଦେଶ
କେହୁ ଛଡାଇ କାହାର ନେଲେ ଝୀନବାସ

ହାଟ ଜ୍ଜର ବାଟ ଜ୍ଜର ଠୋଣ୍ଡ ଜ୍ଜର କଲେ
ପହରେ ପର୍ଯ୍ୟନ୍ତେ ଦେଶେ ହେମାଳିୟା ହେଲେ

ଏରୂପେ ଆସି ହୁଅନ୍ତେ ରାତ୍ର ବେନି ଘଡି
ସମସ୍ତ ଘରେ ଲାଗିଲା ଦୀପ ଯେ ଦିହୁଡି

ଦିନ ପ୍ରାୟ ହେଲା ନିଶି ଲୁଚିଲେଟି ଚନ୍ଦ୍ର
ପୁଞ୍ଜି ପୁଞ୍ଜି ହୋଇ କେହୁ ହ୍ୱନ୍ତି ବୃନ୍ଦ ବୃନ୍ଦ

ବୋଲନ୍ତି ଜନ୍ମିଲେ ରାଜାଘରେ ପୁତ୍ର ଦୁଇ
ପ୍ରତ୍ୟକ୍ଷେ ଦିଶନ୍ତି ସେ ଅନନ୍ତ ଭାବଗ୍ରାହୀ

ପୃଥ୍ୱି ଯାକକୁ କାରଣ ବିନିପୁଅ ହେବେ
ଦୁଷ୍ଟ କ୍ଷୟକରି ଧରାଭାର ଉଶ୍ୱାସିବେ

କେ ବୋଲଇ ହରି ହର ଜନମିଲେ ଆସି
ସେ ରୂପେ ଦିଶନ୍ତି କୃଷ୍ଣବଲ୍ଲଭର ଶିଷି

ଏତେକ ବୋଲିଣ ଲୋକେ ହ୍ୱନ୍ତି କୁହାକୁହି
ଏଥୀଉତ୍‌ତାରେ ପୁତ୍ରଙ୍କୁ ସଜାଡିଲେ ଧାଇ

ଅନ୍ତୁଡି ଲଗାଇ ନାଭି କାଟି କଲେ ଭଜ
ଚତୁଃସମ ଗୋଳି ସ୍ନାନ କଲେ ଦେବରାଜ

ଦେବାଙ୍ଗ ପାଟ ବସନ ଛନ୍ତିଶର୍ଯ୍ୟ ପାଡି
ତହିଁପରେ ଶୁଆଇଲେ ଧାଇ ପୁତ୍ର ଯୋଡି

ଶୁକ୍ଳ ଜିମୁତେ ପରାୟେ ଦିଶେ ଦେହକାନ୍ତି
ବଳୟ ମଣି ରତନ ଦେହେ ଝଟକନ୍ତି

କଟୀତଟେ ଝୀନ ପୀତବସ୍ତ୍ର ଗୋଟି ଶୋହେ
ସେ ସୁନ୍ଦର ରୂପଗୋଟି ଜଗଜ୍ଜନ ମୋହେ

ଦିଶଇ ଶଙ୍ଖ ଚକ୍ର ଯେ ଗଦା ପଦ୍ମ ତେଜ
ମର୍କତର ସ୍ତମ୍ଭ ପ୍ରାୟେ ଦିଶେ ଚତୁର୍ଭୁଜ

ଅଧର ଦିଶଇ ରଙ୍ଗ ନେତ୍ର ଦିଶେ ରଙ୍ଗ
ଶ୍ରୀବତ୍ସର ଚିହ୍ନ ଫୁଟି ଦିଶେ ହୃଦଭାଗ

କଟିତଟେ ବିରାଜଇ ଅଷ୍ଟରତ୍ନ ସୂତା
କନ୍ଧରେ ଦିଶଇ ଫୁଟି ସୁବର୍ଣ୍ଣ ପଇତା

ଜଗଜ୍ଜନ ଚିତ୍ତେ ମୋହିବାର ପାଇଁ ହରି
କ୍ଷଣକେ ଦେଖାନ୍ତି ଆନ ଆନ ରୂପ ଧରି

ନୀଳଜୀମୁତ ଲୋସନେ ଦିଶେ ଶୋଭାବନ
ସେହିରୂପେ ଜ୍ୟୋତି ପ୍ରକାଶନ୍ତି ଭଗବାନ

ଜାନୁପରିଯନ୍ତେ ଲମ୍ବମାନ ଚାରିଭୁଜ
ଗୋଷ୍ପଦର ଚିହ୍ନ ଫୁଟି ଦିଶେ ମହାତେଜ

ମର୍କତ କୁଣ୍ଡଳ ବେନି ଶ୍ରବଣରେ ଶୋହେ
କପୋଳେ ଚନ୍ଦନ ବିନ୍ଦୁ ଦିଶେ ଚନ୍ଦ୍ର ପ୍ରାୟେ

କଳାମେଘେ ଦିଶେ ଯେହ୍ନେ ବିଜୁଳିର ଜ୍ୟୋତି
ଓତସନ ଦିଶଇ କଟିତଟେ ପୀତ ଧୋଭିତି

କୁଟିଳ କେଶେ ଅଳକୋପନ୍ତି ଦିଶେ ଶୋଭା
ଶିରରେ ମୁକୁଟ ଶୋହେ ସପ୍ତଗ୍ରହ ପ୍ରଭା

ଶ୍ରୀବସ୍ଥର ଚିହ୍ନ ଯାହା ଦିଶେ ଦେହମାଝେ
କୌସ୍ତୁଭ ମଣି ସହସ୍ର ସୂର୍ଯ୍ୟତେଜ ଗଞ୍ଜେ

ଯାବତ କୁସୁମ ଯାକେ ମାଳ ମାଳ ହୋଇ
ଶ୍ରୀଅଙ୍ଗରେ ଲମ୍ବିବାରୁ ସୁନ୍ଦର ଦିଶଇ

ଶ୍ରୀ ଭୁଜରେ ବିଦମୁଦି ବାହୁଟି କଙ୍କଣ
ଆରେ ସୁନା ଘାଗୁଡି ବାଜେ ରୁଣ ଝୁଣ

ଦେନି ପାଦରେ ମୁଦ୍ରିକା ବ୍ରହ୍ମାଣ୍ଡକୁ ମୋହେ
ନାନାଦି ସଜ ଲାଗି ଶ୍ରୀଅଙ୍ଗ ଶୋଭାପାଏ

କୋଟି କନ୍ଦର୍ପର ପ୍ରାୟେ ଦିଶେ ଦେହକାନ୍ତି
ବଦରିକାଦେଶ ଲୋକେଦେଖି ତୋଷ ହୋନ୍ତି

ଚୌଷଠି ସହସ୍ର କନ୍ୟା ନିତ୍ୟସ୍ଥଳେ ଆସି
ସ୍ତୁତି କରନ୍ତି ବିଷ୍ଣୁଙ୍କ ପାଦେ ସର୍ବେ ବସି ।

ବ୍ରହ୍ମାଣ୍ଡର ସ୍ତିରୀମାନେ ଦ୍ୟନ୍ତି ହୁଳହୁଳି
ଚାମର ଢ଼ାଳନ୍ତି ଅଷ୍ଟସଖି କରେ ତୋଳି

ଆବର ଟେକିଲେ ଅଷ୍ଟସଖା କରେ ଛତ୍ର
ବିଷ୍ଣୁ ପାଦଧୂଳି ବୋଲି ହୁଅନ୍ତି କେ ଗାତ୍ର

ଭଗବତି ମାଏ ବେନି ପୁତ୍ରସୁଖ ଦେଖି
କ୍ଲେଶ ଦୂରେ ଏଡି କଲେ ନିର୍ମଳ ଯେ ଆଖି

ବ୍ରାହ୍ମଣମାନେ ପଢନ୍ତି ଆସି ମନ୍ତ୍ର ଭାଗ
କୁସୁମ ବୃଷ୍ଟି କରନ୍ତି ଦେବେ ଥାଇ ସର୍ଗ

ଏଥୁଅନ୍ତେ କୃଷ୍ଣବଲ୍ଲଭ ଯେ ମହୀପାଳ
ପୁତ୍ର ଦେଖିବାକୁ ଖୋଜିଲେକ ଅନୁକୂଳ

ଯାବତ ବର୍ଣ୍ଣର ପୁଷ୍ପ ସର୍ଣ୍ଣ ପାତ୍ରେ ଘେନି
ଶ୍ରୀବନ୍ଦାଣ ଦୁର୍ବାକ୍ଷତ ଦେଖା ଦରଶନୀ

ଆଗରେ ବାଜଇ ଯୋଡା ଶଙ୍ଖ ଘନ ଘନ
ବ୍ରାହ୍ମଣେ ବେଦ ପଢିଣ କହନ୍ତି ବନେ

ଭାଟ କୟେବାର ଗୀତ ଗାନ୍ତି ଡୁହା ପାଡି
ଆଗରେ ବୀର କାହାଳୀ ବାଜେ ଯୋଡି ଯୋଡି

ଏମନ୍ତେ ରାଜା ମିଳିଲେ ଧରି ଦୁର୍ବାକ୍ଷତ
ଦେଖିଲେ ଶୋଇ ଅଛନ୍ତି ଶେଯେ ବେନିସୂତ

ଶଙ୍ଖ ଚକ୍ର ଗଦା ପଦ୍ମ ଚତୁର୍ଭୁଜ ହୋଇ
ଅନନ୍ତଙ୍କୁ ସଙ୍ଗେ ଘେନି ଛନ୍ତି ନିଦ୍ରାଯାଇ

ଦେଖିଣ ରାଜାର ଚିତ୍ତ ହୋଇଲା ଆନନ୍ଦ
ମନେ ବିଚାରନ୍ତି ଏହୁ ସାକ୍ଷାତେ ଗୋବିନ୍ଦ

ଭକ୍ତିଭାବ ହେତୁ ଅଶ୍ରୁଜଳେ ବୁଡିଗଲେ
ବେନି ନେତ୍ର ଫେଡି ପୁଣ ନିରେଖି ଚାହିଁଲେ

ଶ୍ରୀହରି ରୂପ ଦେଖିଣ ଆଚମ୍ଭିତ ହୋଇ
ଜଣାନ୍ତି ଭୂମିରେ ପଡି ପାଦତଳେ ଶୋଇ

ଉଠି ବୋଇଲେ ହେ ସ୍ୱାମି ତୁମ୍ଭେ ବ୍ରହ୍ମରାଶି
ସାଧୁ ତାରିବାକୁ ଜନ୍ମହେଲେ ମଞ୍ଚେ ଆସି

ଯାହା ମହିମାର ଅନ୍ତ ବିଧାତା ନ ପାନ୍ତି
ମୁହିଁତ ମାନବ କିସ ସେବିବି ଶ୍ରୀପତି

ତୁମ୍ଭେ ବା ଆସିଲ ପ୍ରାଣୀହିତେ ଅବତରି
ଜନ୍ମିଲ ମୋହର ଘରେ ଦିବ୍ୟ ତନୁ ଧରି

ଧୋଇବି କେବଣ ଅମ୍ବୁ ଧରି ପାଦ ତୋର
ଯାହାର ପାଦପଦ୍ମରୁ ବହେ ଗଙ୍ଗାନୀର

କି କୁସୁମ ଦେଇ ଗଭା କରିବି ମଣ୍ଡଣି
ପାର ପ୍ରିୟବତୀ ବୃନ୍ଦାବନ ଠାକୁରାଣୀ

କେଉଁ ଉପଚାର ବାଢ଼ି କରିବି ବା ପୂଜା
ଯାହାର ଶ୍ରୀ ମହାଲକ୍ଷ୍ମୀ ଅଟନ୍ତି ଭାରିଜା

କି ମନ୍ତ୍ର ପଢ଼ି କରିବି ତବ ଦରଶନ
ଯାହାର ଅଟେ ସାରଦା ପତ୍ନୀ କବିରତ୍ନ

କେବଣ ଆସନ ଦେଇ ବସାଇବି ତୋତେ
ଯାହାର ଭକ୍ତ ଅନନ୍ତ ଶର୍ଯ୍ୟା ନିଦ୍ରାଗତ

କରିବି କେବଣ ଗନ୍ଧ ଦେଇ ନିମନ୍ତ୍ରଣ
ବଡସିଂହାର ଦେଶ ଯା ଦୃଦରେ ଭୁଷଣ

କେବଣ ପିନ୍ଧା କରିବି କଟିତଟେ ଲାଗି
ଯାହାର ପୀତବସନ ସର୍ବଦା ନିଯୋଗୀ

କେବଣ ରତ୍ନ କରିବି ଅଙ୍ଗ ଆଭରଣ
ବାଆନକୋଟି ଭଣ୍ଡାର ଯାର ଅଛି ପୂର୍ଣ୍ଣ

ଯାର ଅଷ୍ଟାଦଶ ଚିହ୍ନ ପାଦପଦ୍ମେ ଅଛି
ମୁହିଁ ମାନବ ବର୍ଣ୍ଣିବି କିସ ତାହା ପାଂଚି

ଭାଗ୍ୟ ଥିବାରୁ ଦର୍ଶନ କଲି ମୁହିଁ ଆଜ
ଶ୍ରୀଶଙ୍ଖ ଚକ୍ର ଯେ ଗଦା ଶାର୍ଙ୍ଗ ଚତୁର୍ଭୁଜ

ଭୋ ପ୍ରଭୁ କମଳାକାନ୍ତ ଶରଣ ମୁଁ ତୋତେ
ମାନସ ପୂରାଇ ଆଜ ଦେଖିଲି ମୋ ନେତ୍ରେ

ଆପଣଙ୍କୁ ଘେନି ମୋର ପୂରେ ଦେବତାଏ
ଦର୍ଶନ କରୁଅଛନ୍ତି ଆସି ଅପ୍ରମେୟେ

ତାହାଙ୍କ ଦର୍ଶନ ପାଉଅଛି ଚର୍ମଡୋଳେ
ସେବାରେ ମନାଉଅଛି ଜ୍ଞାନ ଯୋଗବଳେ

ଏମନ୍ତେ କୃଷ୍ଣବଲ୍ଲଭ ବେନି କରୋଯୋଡି
ଶୁତିଲେ ବିଷ୍ଣୁଙ୍କ ପାଦପଦ୍ମ ତଳେ ପଡି

ପିତାର ଭକତି ପଣ ଦେଖି ନାରାୟଣ
ମନେ ପାଂଚିଲେ ଚିହ୍ନିଲେ ଏ ମୋହର ଗୁଣ
ଏରୂପେ ଚିହ୍ନିଲେ ପୁତ୍ର ମୁଁ କି ରୂପେ ହେବି

ମାୟାପଟଳ ଆସି ଲାଗୁଁ ବଲ୍ଲଭଙ୍କୁ
ତତକ୍ଷଣ ପୁତ୍ରକରି ମଣେ ଗୋବିନ୍ଦଙ୍କୁ

ଧଇଲେ ମୋର ବାଳକ ବୋଲିଶେୟୁତୋଳି
ପ୍ରିୟାର କୋଳରେ ଦେଲେ ପୁତ୍ର ଧର ବୋଲି

ଦାସୀଙ୍କ ବୋଇଲେ ସେବା କରଲୋ ପୁତ୍ରଙ୍କୁ
ଏତେ କହି ରାଜନ ଯେ ଗଲେ ଆସ୍ଥାନକୁ

ଏଥୁ ଅନନ୍ତରେ ବାଣି ଶୁଣହେ ନାରଦ
ବରୁଣ ଚନ୍ଦ୍ର ସୂର୍ଯ୍ୟ ଯେ ଦରଶନ କଲେ

କୁବେର ପବନ ଯମ ଅଗ୍ନି ଘେନି ତୁଲେ
ବାସୁକି ଯେ ନଇରତ ଦଶ ବିଶ୍ୱେଦେବା
ଗାନ୍ଧର୍ବ ବିଦ୍ୟାଧର ଯେ ବସି କଲେ ସଭା

କିନ୍ନରୀ ଅପ୍‌ସରୀ ଗଣ ଆବର ଚାରଣ
ଧର୍ମ ଦେବତାଙ୍କୁ ଆଦିକରି ପିତୃଗଣ

ଏହାଙ୍କ ପରେ ଆସିଲେ ପୁଣି ଋଷିଯାକ
ଅଗସ୍ତି ପଉଲସ୍ତି ଯେ ଜାବାଳି ଜନକ

କପିଳ ଗୌତ୍ତମ କଣ୍ୱଋଷି ମନ୍ଦକର୍ଣ୍ଣ
ମରୀଚି ପୁଲହ କ୍ରତୁ ଆଦି ତପୋଧନ

ବଶିଷ୍ଠ ସନକ ମୁନି କପିଳ ଆସୁରି
ବାଲମୀକ ପଂଚଶିଖ ଦୁର୍ବାସା ଆଚାରୀ

ଆତ୍ରେୟ ଯେ ବିଭାଣ୍ଡକ ଶକତି ଋଷ୍ୟଶୃଙ୍ଗ
ଅଙ୍ଗିରସ ଭରଦ୍ୱାଜ ଜୈମିନି ଉତ୍ତୁଙ୍ଗ

କାତ୍ୟାୟନ ପରାଶର ଲୋମଶ ଚ୍ୟବନ
ଗାଲବ ରୋମା ମୁନି ବଇଶମ୍ପାୟନ

କୃପାଜଳ ସୁନନ୍ଦନ ଗାର୍ଗ୍ୟ ବେଦଗର୍ଭ
କପିଳ ଦଧୀଚି କଳିଞ୍ଜନ ବାମଦେବ

ଅଙ୍ଗିରା ଲୋମଶ ବ୍ୟାସ ପରାଶର ମୁନି
ବାରୁଣୀ ସତ୍ୟାନନ୍ଦ ଯେ ସୁପଣ୍ଡିତ ଘେନି

ଅଷ୍ଟବକ୍ର ବାଲଖିଲ୍ୟା ବେତୁ ଯେ ଉତ୍ତୁଙ୍ଗ
ମଇତ୍ରେୟ ଶୁକ୍ରମୁନି ଭୃଗୁ ଶରଭଙ୍ଗ

ପିପ୍ପଳାୟନ ବିହଙ୍ଗ ମୁନି ଦତ୍ତା ତ୍ରେୟ
ବଦିକା ନଗ୍ରେ ମିଳିଲେ ଋଷି ଅପ୍ରମେୟ

ନାରଦ ସୁନନ୍ଦ ପରାନନ୍ଦ ସତ୍ୟନନ୍ଦ
ମିଳିଲେ ପ୍ରଜାପତିଙ୍କ ସଙ୍ଗେ ଋଷିବୃନ୍ଦ

ସମସ୍ତ ଦେବେ ମିଳିଣ କଲେ ପୁଷ୍ପବୃଷ୍ଟି
ଛାମୁରେ କହିଲେ ଆଗହୋଇ ପରମେଷ୍ଠୀ

ପାର୍ବତୀ ଜଗଦ୍ଧାତ୍ରୀ ଯେ ଗାୟତ୍ରୀ ସାବିତ୍ରୀ
କିନ୍ନରୀ ଅପ୍‌ସରୀ ଘେନି ଶଚୀ ପଦ୍ମନେତ୍ରୀ

ମିଳିଲେ ଯାବତ ଋଷିପତ୍ନୀ ଯେଝାମତେ
ମୁର୍ତ୍ତୀମତୀ ହୋଇ ଗଙ୍ଗା ମିଳିଲେ ସାକ୍ଷାତେ

କେ ଗୀତ ଗାନ୍ତି କେହି ଦ୍ୟନ୍ତି ହୁଳହୁଳି
କେହୁ ସ୍ତୁତି କରନ୍ତି ନାଚନ୍ତି ଢଳି ଢଳି

କେ ବୋଲେ ହରି ହରି କେ ବୋଲେ ବଳରାମ
କେ ବୋଲେ କୃଷ୍ଣ କୃଷ୍ଣ କେ ବୋଲେ ଘନଶ୍ୟାମ

କେ ବୋଲେ ଜଗନ୍ନାଥ କେ ବୋଲଇ ଶ୍ରୀପତି
କେ ବୋଲେ ଭଗବାନ କେ ବୋଲେ ଜଗଜ୍ୟୋତି

କେ ବୋଲଇ ଧନ୍ୟ ଧନ୍ୟ ବଦରିକାପୂର
ଦ୍ୱିତୀୟ ବୈକୁଣ୍ଠ ପ୍ରାୟ ଦିଶଇ ସୁନ୍ଦର

ବୈକୁଣ୍ଠ ତେଜି ଶ୍ରୀହରି ଯହିଁ ଅବସ୍ଥିତି
ସବୁ ତୀର୍ଥ ଘେନି ଦେବେ ଆସି ଯାଉଥାନ୍ତି

ଦରଶନ କରୁଥାନ୍ତି ଶ୍ରୀହରି ଚରଣେ
ସେବନ୍ତି ଗୋବିନ୍ଦ ପାଦପଦ୍ମେ ଭକତଗଣେ

ଅପ୍ରକଟ ମୂର୍ତୀ ହେଲେ ପ୍ରକଟ ଯେ ଆସି
ନିଶ୍ଚେ ନାରାୟଣ ଏହୁ କ୍ଷୀରାବ୍ଧିବ ବାସି

ଭଲା ବୀଜେକଲେ ଆସି ବଦରିକା ଧାମ
ଧନ୍ୟ ଏରାଜାର ଅଟେ ପୂର ଭୂମି ଗ୍ରାମ

ଦେଖ ଏହି ବିଷ୍ଣୁ ହୃଦେ ବିଜେ କମଳିନୀ
ଖଟି ଅଛନ୍ତି ଶାରଦା ମାତା ଠାକୁରାଣୀ

ରତ୍ନ ସିଂହାସନେ ଯେହ୍ନେ ଅନନ୍ତଶର୍ଯ୍ୟାରେ
ସେହିରୂପେ ମହାପ୍ରଭୁ ଦିଶନ୍ତି ସେଠାରେ

ପୂର୍ବକାଳେ ବୈକୁଣ୍ଠରେ ଦେଖିଥିଲୁଁ ଯାହା
ବଦରିକାରେ ଦେଖିଲୁ ଏବେ ଆସି ତାହା

ଆବର ଦେହେ ଦିଶୁଛି ଚିହ୍ନ ଅଷ୍ଟାଦଶ
ଶଙ୍ଖ ଚକ୍ର ଗଦା ପଦ୍ମ କୋଦଣ୍ଡ କୁଳିଶ

ଧ୍ୱଜ ବଜ୍ର ଶାରଙ୍ଗ ଯେ ଖଡଗ ମୂଷଳ
ଜମ୍ବୁ ଗୋଷ୍ପଦ ସାୟକ ଅଙ୍କୁଶ ଲାଙ୍ଗଳ

ତବଣୁ ପାଶ ଚିହ୍ନ ଏହିରୂପେ ଅଷ୍ଟାଦଶ
ଦେବଙ୍କୁ ଦିଶଇ ଏହା ମାନବେ ଅଦୃଶ୍ୟ

ଦେବେ ଯେ ଦେଖିଣ ଏହା ଉଠି କରଯୋଡି
ବୋଇଲେ ବୈକୁଣ୍ଠ ବିଷ୍ଣୁ ଦେଖିଲୁଁ ବାହୁଡି

ଭକତଙ୍କୁ ତାରିବାକୁ ଧରିଲେ ଏ ରୂପ
ଦେଖିବା ଲୋକଙ୍କୁ ଏବେ ଛାଡିଯିବ ପାପ

ଶ୍ରୀମୁଖକୁ ଚାହିଁଲେ କି ଥିବ ଆଉ ଦୁଃଖ
ପାଇଲୁଁ ଯେ ପୁଣ୍ୟଗତି ଦେଖି ପଦ୍ମମୁଖ

କୁମୁଦବନେ ପ୍ରାୟ ଯେ ତୁମ୍ଭ ଭକ୍ତଜନେ
ସେ ବନକୁ ତୁମ୍ଭ ମୁଖ ଶରଚନ୍ଦ୍ର ଜାଣ

ଦିବସ ଅନ୍ତେ ଯେ ନାଥ ହେଲେ ଅବତାର
ଫୁଟିବା କୁମୁଦବନେ ବନ୍ଧୁତ୍ୱ ଆମ୍ଭର

ଅଷ୍ଟାଦଶ ଚିହ୍ନ ତୋର ଭକ୍ତଜନ ହିତେ
ଦେଖି ନିସ୍ତରି ଶରଣ ପଶିଲୁଁ ଶୁଚିଭେ

ମୂଷଳ ଲାଙ୍ଗଳ ଖଡ୍‌ଗ ଧରି ବଜ୍ର କରେ
ଭକ୍ତକୁ ପାଳ ଭୋ ନାଥ ଦୁଷ୍ଟ ମାରିବାରେ

ଅଷ୍ଟାଦଶ ଚିହ୍ନ ଯାକ ଭକ୍ତେ ତୋର ଧାୟି
ଚଳୁଥାନ୍ତି ବୈକୁଣ୍ଠକୁ ଦରଶନ ପାଇଁ

ତୁମ୍ଭ ପାଦପଦ୍ମ ଘେନି ସଂସାର ମୁକତ
କୀଟୁ ବ୍ରହ୍ମ ଯାଏ ସବୁ ତୋହର ଏକତ୍ୱ

କୌସ୍ତୁଭ ମଣି ତୋହର ଦିଶେ ବକ୍ଷସ୍ଥଳ
ଆମ୍ଭେ ଦେବତାଏ ଦେଖି ନିସ୍ତରିଲୁଁଏ ହେଲେ

ମୋଲାକୁ ପବିତ୍ର ଏ ତୋ ନାମ ବୀରବାନା
ସେ ବାନା ପ୍ରକାଶିଅଛି ଆମ୍ଭଲାଗି ସିନା

ଆବର ବାହନ ତୋର ଯେଉଁ ପକ୍ଷୀରାଜ
କେଡେ ନିଅଳସ ଅଟେ ସେହି ବ୍ରହ୍ମବୀର୍ଯ୍ୟ

ତେଣୁ ତୁମ୍ଭର ବୋହଇ ଏଡେବଡ ଭାରା
ଯେଉଁ ଗର୍ଭେ ପୂରିଅଛି କୋଟି ବସୁନ୍ଧରା

ଗରୁଡ ଆସନ ପରେ ତୁମ୍ଭ ନିଜ କାୟେ
ନିବାରିବ କେତେ ଦୁଷ୍ଟ ପୃଥ୍ୱୀ ଥିବାଯାଏ

ଏ କୃଷ୍ଣବଲ୍ଲଭ ରାଜା କେଡେ ଭାଗ୍ୟବନ୍ତ
ତାହାଙ୍କ ପତ୍ନୀଗର୍ଭରୁ ହେଲେ ତୁମ୍ଭେ ଜାତ

ଚାରି ଜନ୍ମେ ସେହି ଏକା ହେବେ ତୁମ୍ଭ ପିତା
ଏତେ ବୋଲି ବହୁ ସ୍ତୁତି କରନ୍ତି ବିଧାତା

ଏବେ ଜାଣିଲୁଁ ମରିବ ନିଶ୍ଚେ ମୁରାସୁର
ଆପଣେ ଯେଣୁ ହେଲେଣି ଆସି ଅବତାର

ତେତେ କାଳଯାଏ ଥିଲା ଦୈତ୍ୟକୁ ଏ ଯୋଗ
କୋଡିଏ ଗଣ୍ଡା ଯୁଗ ତ ନେଲାଣି ସେ ଭୋଗ

ତୁମ୍ଭେ ଅନ୍ତର୍ଯ୍ୟାମୀ ଜାଣ ସବୁଙ୍କରି ଚି
ତୁମ୍ଭଙ୍କୁ ଭଜି ପାରନ୍ତି ନିଶ୍ଚେ ଭାଗ୍ୟବନ୍ତ

ପଦାର୍ଥ ଅର୍ଜି ନୁହଇ ଯେବେ ଦାତାଶୀଳ
ସେହିମାନଙ୍କୁ ଦରିଦ୍ର ବୋଲିଟି କେବଳ

ଧନ ଅର୍ଜିଲେଟି ଜାଣ ଧର୍ମ ଯେବେ କରି
ଧର୍ମୁର ପ୍ରାପତ ନିଶ୍ଚେଁ ହୋନ୍ତି ନରହରି

ଯାହାଙ୍କର ଘରେ ଲକ୍ଷ୍ମୀ ନାରାୟଣ ଥାନ୍ତି
ତାହାଙ୍କୁଟି ଭାଗ୍ୟବନ୍ତ ସଂସାରେ ବୋଲନ୍ତି

ପ୍ରବୋଧିଣ କହୁଅଛି ରଖ ଏ ଧରଣୀ
ଏ ରୂପେ କହିଣ ଦେବେ ହୋଇଲେ ମେଲାଣି

ସରପାଦପ ଗିରିର ଶିଖେ ଉଠିଗଲେ
ଯଶୋବନ୍ତୀ ପୂରେ ଯାଇଁ ବ୍ରହ୍ମା ବିଜେକଲେ

ବ୍ରହ୍ମା ଗଲାରୁ ଚଳିଲେ ଦେବେ ଯେଝାପୁର
ଶ୍ରୀ ଗୋବିନ୍ଦ ଶରଣ ମୁଁ ବିପ୍ର ପୀତାମ୍ବର

-ସମାପ୍ତ-

ଶ୍ରୀ ଲକ୍ଷ୍ମୀ ଓ ଶ୍ରୀ ଜଗନ୍ନାଥଙ୍କର ବଚନିକା

ଦାସୀ-ଦାସୀ ବୋଲନ୍ତି ଶୁଣ ଆଗେମାଏ ।
ବିଜେ ବଲେ ତୁମ୍ଭେ ଦେବାରାୟେ
ସିଂହଦ୍ୱାରେ ଲାଗିଅଛି ରଥ ।

ଜନ ଗହଳେ ନ ଦିଶଇ ପଥ ।
ଅତି ଉକ୍ରଟେ ବାଜଇ ନିଶାଣ
ଶଙ୍ଖ ଧ୍ୱନିଶୁଣ(୧)

ଗହଣେ ଅଛି ରାଜା ଗଜପତି ।
ଗଣି ବୋହେ ଅଶ୍ୱ ହସ୍ତୀ ପଦାତି
କାହାଳ କର୍ଦ୍ଦଳ କଂସାଳ ତାଳ ।
ଭେରୀ ମହୁରୀ ଶୁଭଇ ଚହଳ ।
ଶରଦେ ସମ୍ପୂର୍ଣ୍ଣ ଶଶାଙ୍କ ଜ୍ୟୋତି
ଶିରେ ଶ୍ୱେତ ଛାଡି ।(୨)

ଲକ୍ଷ୍ମୀ-ଲକ୍ଷ୍ମୀ ବୋଲନ୍ତି ଆଲୋ ଦାସୀ ଯାଅ ।
ବଜ୍ର କିଳଣ କବାଟ ପକାଅ ।
ଆସି ଦେଢ଼ଶୁରେ ପଶନ୍ତି ଘରେ ।
ଥାଉ କଳାମୁଖ ବେଢା ବାହାରେ ।
ବଜ୍ର କିଳଣ କବାଟ ପକାଇ ।
ଦାସୀ ଆଜ୍ଞାପାଇ (୩)

ଜଗା- ବାଗହବର ଲକ୍ଷ୍ମୀଭାବ ଜାଣି
ବରହାସରେ କହୁଛନ୍ତି ବାଣୀ ।
ଆଲୋ ପରିବାରି ଫେଡ କବାଟ ।
କେଉଁ କଥାକୁ ଲୋ ! କରିଛ ହଟ ।
ଅଧିକ କି ଆଉ କହିବୁଁ ଆମ୍ଭେ
ଲୋ ସଜାଣ ତୁମ୍ଭେ ।(୪)

ଦାସୀ- ଦାସୀ ବୋଲନ୍ତି ଆହେ ପଦ୍ମନାଭ ।

ଦ୍ୱାର ଛାଡିଲେ କିସ ତୁମ୍ଭ ଲାଭ ।
ବଡ ଦେଉଳେ କିସ କାର୍ଯ୍ୟ ଆଉ ।
ଲକ୍ଷ୍ମୀଗତି ମାନେ ପାଇବ ଲଜ୍ଜା
ଏବେ ଦେବରାଜା ।(୫)

ଜଗନ୍ନାଥ- ପ୍ରଭୁ ବୋଲନ୍ତି ଲୋ । ସେ କଥାଛାଡ
ସେତ ସବୁପ୍ରିୟ ବତୀରୁ ବଡ ।
ଜାଣୁ ଶିରୋମଣି ଯୁବତୀ ନିଧି ।
ସୃଷ୍ଟି ସୃଜିବାକୁ ଯାହାର ବୁଦ୍ଧି ।
ଦେଖ ଜ୍ୟୋତିନାଶ ଏ ମୋର ତନୁ ।
ସେ କମଳାବିନୁ (୬)

ଦାସୀ- ନ କହିଲେ କଥା ଗଲାଣି ଜଣା ।
ବାଲି ନଗରେ ବାଟ ହେଲ ବଣା ।
ଏ ତ ନୋହେ ତୁମ୍ଭ ଗୁଣ୍ଡିଚାଘର ।
ଯହିଁ ଯୁବତୀ ନୃତ୍ୟ ଗୀତ ସ୍ୱର ।
ଏ ନାରୀଙ୍କ ନେତ୍ରୁ ଝରୁଛି ବାରି ।
ବିରହିଣୀ ପୁରୀ । (୭)

ଜଗନ୍ନାଥ- ଆଲୋ ତୁମ୍ଭେ ଇତି ଅବୁଝା ଦାସୀ ।
ବଡିମା କଥା ଲୋ କହ ବିଶେଷ ।
ଗୁଣ୍ଡିଚା ଘର କି ସର୍ବଦା ସ୍ଥାନ ।
ଯହିଁ କମଳା ତହିଁ ଆମ୍ଭ ମନ ।
ଆମ୍ଭେ ଠାକୁର ଠାକୁରାଣୀ ଶ୍ରୀୟା ।
ହେ ପ୍ରାଣର ପ୍ରୀୟା (୮)

ଦାସୀ- ସତ କହିଲେ ହେ ନାଗରବର ।

ବନେ ତୁମ୍ଭର ଅତି ମଧୁର ।
ହୃଦୟ ତୁମ୍ଭର କର୍କଶ ପ୍ରାୟ ।
ପୁରୁଷ ତୁମ୍ଭେ ଅତିହିଁ ନିର୍ଦ୍ଦୟ
ଛାଡିଲେ କେଉଁ ଦୋଷ ବିଚାରି
ଏ ରାଜ କୁମାରୀ ।(୯)

ଜଗନ୍ନାଥ- ପୂର୍ବକାଳ ରାଜା ଇନ୍ଦ୍ରଦ୍ୟୁମନ ।
କରାଇଥିଲା ଲୋ ! ସତ୍ୟ ବଚନ ।
ଗୁଣ୍ଡିଚା ରାଣୀ ଭକ୍ତିଭାବ ଘେନି ।
ରଥେ ବସିଗଲୁଁ ମୁରତି ତିନି ।
ତାରିଲୁଁ ପାପୀ ଚାଣ୍ଡାଳ ପତିତ
ଅଇଲୁଁ ତୁରିତ (୧୦)

ଦାସୀ- ବିଜେ କଲ ଯେବେ ଭକ୍ତଙ୍କ ହିତେ
ଗୁଣ୍ଡିଚା ବୋଲି ଶୁଭିଲା ଜଗତେ ।
ସଙ୍ଗତେ ନ ନେଲ କି ଗୁଣ ଧରି
ସେ ତ ସଉଭାଗା ଅର୍ଦ୍ଧାଙ୍ଗ ନାରୀ ।
ଗୁଣ୍ଡିଚା ଯାତ୍ରାକି ହୁଅନ୍ତା ହାନି
ଗଲେ କମଳିନୀ (୧୧)

ଜଗନ୍ନାଥ- ଯାତ୍ରା, ଉତ୍ସବେ ଦେବଗଣେ ଥାନ୍ତି ।
ଗହଳ ପଟୁଆରେ ଯନ୍ତାଯନ୍ତୀ ।
ସଙ୍ଗତରେ ଜ୍ୟେଷ୍ଠ ଏ ହଳପାଣି ।
ତେଣୁ ନ ନେଲୁଁ ଦେବୀ କମଳିନୀ ।
କୁଳଭୁଆସୁଣୀ ସିନ୍ଧୁ ଦୁହିଣ
ଅନୁଚିତ କଥା ।(୧୨)

ଦାସୀ- ବ୍ରହ୍ମା, ଇନ୍ଦ୍ର ଆଦି ଯେତେ ଦେବତା ।
ପରମ ଲକ୍ଷ୍ମୀ ସବୁଙ୍କର ମାତା ।
ଏ କଥାରେ ଆଉ ନାହିଁ ବିରୋଧ ।
ନିଶ୍ଚୟ ତେଜିଲ କମଳା ସଧ
ଯେତେ ଚତୁରାଇ ଚତୁରେ କଥା କହୁଛ ବାଇ (୧୩)

ଜଗନ୍ନାଥ- ଯୁବତୀ ତାତି ଲୋ ! ଅତି ଅବୁଝା ।
ବୁଝାଇ କହିଲେ ଅଧିକେ ଯୁଝା ।
ଦେଖ ଘୋଟିଅଛି ଏ ମେଘମାଳା ।
ଅଛିଦ୍ର ଧାରା ବରଷଇ ଜଳ ।
ଏତେକ ଶାନ୍ତି ନୁହେଁ ତୁମ୍ଭ ରାଗ
ତିନ୍ତିଲା ଶ୍ରୀଅଙ୍ଗ(୧୪)

ଦାସୀ- ବାହୁଡି ଯାଅ ଦେବ ଚକ୍ରଧର
ଘର କରି ରହ ବାଲି ନଗର ।
ସୁଭଦ୍ରା ସଙ୍ଗତରେ ବେନି ପ୍ରାଣୀ ।
ଦିନୁ ଦିନୁ ପ୍ରୀତି ନବ ତରୁଣୀ ।
ଏବେ ହୋଇଛି ଭଉଣୀ ଭାରିଯା
ତେଜିଅଛି ଲଜ୍ଜା (୧୫)

ଜଗନ୍ନାଥ- ସୁଭଦ୍ରା ସାନ ଭଉଣୀ ଆମ୍ଭର ।
ଯାତ୍ରା ନିମନ୍ତେ ନେଲୁଁ ସଙ୍ଗରେ ।
ଯୁଗେ ଯୁଗେ ଜନ୍ମ ଅନ୍ତର ନାହିଁ ।
ଯହିଁ ରାମକୃଷ୍ଣ ସୁଭଦ୍ରା ତହିଁ ।
ଏକଇ ଆତ୍ମା ଭିନ୍ନ ଭିନ୍ନ ଦେହ

ଲୋ ନ ଜାଣି କହ (୧୬)

ଦାସୀ- ଉତ୍ତମ କଥା କହୁଛ ଗୋସାଇଁ ।
କହିବାପୁଣି ଲୁଚିହୋଇ ଯାଇ ।
ଲକ୍ଷ୍ମୀଙ୍କ ଯାହା ଦେଇଗଲ ଭୋଗ ।
ଡାଲୁଅ ଅନ୍ନକୁ କଳମ୍ବ ଶାଗ ।
ବିଖ୍ୟାତ ହୋଇଲା ତିନି ଜଗତେ
ସ୍ନେହ ତୁମ୍ଭ ଯେତେ (୧୭)

ଜଗନ୍ନାଥ- ବାବନ କୋଟି ଯେ ନିଜ ଭଣ୍ଡାର ।
କୁବେର ଦେବତା ହିଁ ପରିବାର ।
ଅଷ୍ଟନିଧି ଅଛି ଯାହାର ହସ୍ତେ ।
ତାହା କହିଲେ କି ଯିବ ପରତେ ।
ଜନ୍ମ ଦରିଦ୍ର ହୁଏ କୋଟୀଶ୍ୱର ।
କଟାକ୍ଷ ଯାହାର । (୧୮)

ଦାସୀ- ବାବନ କୋଟି ଭଣ୍ଡାର ସହିତେ ।
ଘେନାଇ ଗଲ ଆପଣା ସଙ୍ଗତେ
ଶିଳ ଶିହ୍ନିପୁଅ ଛା ୁଣୀ ବୁଲା ।
ଭଣ୍ଡାର ଅଧିକାରୀ ଚଳାଇଲା ।
ଯାହା କରିଗଲା ଦେବ ଧିରଜା
କହିବାକୁ ଲଜ୍ଜା । (୧୯)

ଜଗନ୍ନାଥ- ବେଲୁଁ ବେଲ କେବେ ବଢ଼ାଅ କଣ
ହୃଦରେ ଘେନ ଆମ୍ଭର ବ୍ୟଥା ।
ଭିତରକୁ ଗଲେ ଶ୍ରୀନୀଳାମ୍ବର

ଆମ୍ଭଙ୍କୁ ରଖିଲ ବେଢା ବାହା
ଆଣିଛୁଁ ଆମ୍ଭେ ଚିତ୍ର ମେଘିତ
ଫିଟାଅ କବାଟ । (୨୦)

ଦାସୀ- ରତ୍ନାକର ଅଟେ ଯାହାର ତାତ ।
ସ୍ୱୟଂ ସୁଧାକର କନିଷ୍ଠ ଭ୍ରାତ ।
ବ୍ରହ୍ମାଣ୍ଡନାଥ ଚିତ୍ତ ଲିଭିବାକୁ
ଦେବାଙ୍ଗ ବସନ ଅପୂର୍ବ ତାକୁ
ନବ ଅନୁରାଗୀ ଭଗ୍ନୀକୁ ଦିଅ ।
ଲେଉଟାଇ ନିଅ । (୨୧)

ଜଗନ୍ନାଥ- ଯୁବତୀଙ୍କି ହାରି ପଙ୍କଜ ନେତ୍ର ।
କଥାଏ ଦିଶିଲା ଶ୍ରିଦିବ୍ୟଚି ।
ଲାଂଚ ଦେଲେ ଦାସୀମାନଙ୍କ ଧନ ।
କମଳାଙ୍କୁ କହି ପ୍ରିୟ ବଚନ ।
ଅତିବେଗେ ଦେଲେ କବାଟଫେରି
ଦାସୀ ଲାଂଚ ପାଇ ।
ଭିତରକୁ ଗଲେ ଶ୍ରୀଚକାଡୋଳା
ଦେଖିଲ ଉଭା ହୋଇଛି କମଳା ।
ପରସ୍ପରରେ ଦେଖାଦେଖି ହେଲେ ।
ଆନନ୍ଦ ବାରି ବରଷଣ କଲେ ।
ମସ୍ତକ ସୁଘିଲେ ଶ୍ରୀଦଇଚ୍ଛାରି
କୋଳାଗ୍ରତ କରି
ଅଳପ ହସି ପ୍ରଭୁ ଜଗନ୍ନାଥ ।
ବୋଇଲେ ଶୁଣ ଗୋ ଜଗତମାତା ।
କେଉଁ କଥାକୁ କରିଅଛୁ ହଠ

ଅନୁକମ୍ପା କରି ସତ୍ୱର ଉଠ ।
ପଲ୍ୟଙ୍କପରେ ବସି କଥା ହେବା
ଚାଲ ଏବେ ଯିବା । (୨୨)

ଲକ୍ଷ୍ମୀ- ଭଲ କହିଲ ଦେବାଧିରାଜ ।
ଲକ୍ଷ୍ମୀପତି ପଦେ ପାଇଲୁ ଲାଜ ।
ନବ ଅନୁରାଗୀ ଭଗ୍ନୀକୁ ଆଣି ।
ଏକାନ୍ତ ବସି କହ ମୃଦୁ ବାଣୀ ।
କାହିଁକି ପୋତୁଛୁ ଲଜ୍ଜାରେ ମଥା ।
ଆନନ୍ଦିତ କଥା । (୨୩)

ଶ୍ରିରୀଜ- ତୁମ୍ଭେ ମୂରୁଖ । ଗୋ ସାକ୍ଷାତେବେ
ବୁଝାଇଲେ ହେଲେ କଥା ନର
ସୁଭଦ୍ରା ଅଟେ ତୁମ୍ଭର ନଣନ୍ଦ
ପ୍ରିୟ କଥାକହି କର ଆମ
ପ୍ରିୟ ସଖୀସଙ୍ଗେ ପ୍ରଂଶସା ନେ
ସେ ସନ୍ତୋଷ ହେବ(୨୪)

ଲକ୍ଷ୍ମୀ- ବକ୍ର ନୟନେ କମଳା ଚାହିଁଲେ
ଅଳ୍ପ ହାସ୍ୟ କରି ହସ୍ତ ଧଇଲେ
ପଲ୍ୟଙ୍କ ପରେ ନେଇ ବସାଇଲେ
ପରିହାସରେ ବନେ କହିଲେ
ବିଚ୍ଛେଦ ଦୁଃଖକୁ ପାସୋରି ଦେଇ
ସେ ପ୍ରଫୁଲ୍ଲ ହୋଇ
ମାନବ ଦାନବ ଦେବତା ଯେତେ ।
ମେଲାଣି ପାଇଲେ ଯେ ଯାହା ମୁଁ

ମାର୍ଜ୍ଜନା ମଣୋହି ଯେ ଧୂପ ବିଧି
ସାରି ପହଡିବେ କରୁଣା ନିଧି
ନାନ ବିନୋଦେ ବଂଚିଲେ ରଜନୀ
କମଳାଙ୍କୁ ଘେନି ।
ରଥାଙ୍ଗ ଯେହେ ରବି ଦରଶନେ
ମାର୍ତଣ୍ଡ ଦେଖିଲା ପଙ୍କଜବସନେ
ପୁଷ୍ପ ଭ୍ରମର ଜଳଦ ଚାତକ ।
ନିଜ ରମଣୀ ପ୍ରୋଷିତ ନାୟକ ।
ହରଷ ଲକ୍ଷ୍ମୀ ନାରାୟଣ ଚିତସେନ ସଙ୍ଗୀତ
ରାଧାକୃଷ୍ଣଙ୍କର ବେନି ଚରଣ
ଅଧମ ଜନ ପଶଇ ଶରଣ ।
ବିପ୍ର ମହେଶ୍ୱର ଭାବଇ ଯାହା ।
ଉଦ୍ଧରି ଧର ଶଙ୍ଖ-ଚକ୍ର-ବାହା ।
ନ ଥାଉ ଆଉ ଯମରାଜା ତ୍ରାସ
ଖଣ୍ଡ ମୋ କଲ୍ମଷ । (୨୫)

-ସମାପ୍ତ-

ସାଥୁଆ ବଂଶ ମାଦଳା

ଦେବଗଡ ରାଜାସାହେବ ପୁରୀ ଦକ୍ଷିଣ ଦ୍ୱାରରୁ ଶ୍ରୀକାନ୍ତ ସାଧୁଆକୁ ଆଣିଥିଲେ ବାମଣ୍ଡା ବଣିଆ କିଣ୍ଡା ଗାଁଉତିଆ ପଦ ଦେଇ ରଖିଥିଲେ, ପରେ ତାଙ୍କ ଝିଅ ଭୁଆସୁଣିକୁ ଖରାପ ନଜରରେ ଦେଖିବାରୁ ସେ ସେଠି ନରହି ବାମଣ୍ଡାରେ କେହି ବଣିଆ ନ ରହିବା ପାଇଁ ପଥର କଟାଡି ଦେଲେ, ବାରକୁଟ୍ ଦେଇ ବଣାଇଁ ବାଟେ ପଳାଇ ଆସିଲେ । ସେତେବେଳେ ବଣାଇଁରେ ରାଜା ପଳାଇଆସିବାର ଭାରଥୁର ଦେଖି ଆମକୁ ପଚାରିବା ପାଇଁ ଲୋକ ପଠାଇଲେ । ପଠାଇବାରୁ ଆମେ ବଂଶ ସବୁ କିଏ ଡାକୁଛି ବୋଲି

ପଚାରିଲେ । ରାଜା ଡାକୁଛନ୍ତି ବୋଲି କହିଲେ । ସେମାନେ କହିଲେ ଗୋଟେ ରାଜାତ ଆମକୁ ଆଣି ଅତ୍ୟାଚାର କରିବାକୁ ଚାହିଁଲେ । ଆମେ ସେଥିପାଇଁ ରାତି ଭିତରେ ପଳାଇ ଆସିଛୁଁ । ଏବେ ସେହି ରାଜା ଆମେ ତାଙ୍କ କଥା ଶୁଣିବୁ ନାହିଁ କହି ଚାଲି ଆସୁଥିଲେ । ରାଜାଙ୍କର ସବୁ ପାଇକଚାର ପଠାଇ ରାଜା ପାଖକୁ ଧରିନେଲେ । ଆମେ ଦୁଃଖ ପ୍ରକାଶ କରିବାରୁ ସେ କହିଲେ ଗୋଟେ ରାଜା ଭୁଲ କଲା ବୋଲି କଣ ସବୁ ରାଜା ଭୁଲ କରନ୍ତି । ତମେ ମୋତେ ରାଗ ନାହିଁ ବୋଲି ରାଜା କହିବେ ଓ ତାଙ୍କର ସୁବନ୍ଦବସ୍ତ କରିବାକୁ କହିଲେ । ମୋ ଗୋଡ ସମ୍ମୁଖରେ ରଖିବି ଓ ତୁମର ସବୁ ବନ୍ଦୋବସ୍ତ କରିଦେବି । ମୋର ସାଥି ଯୋଗୁଁ ସାଥି ହୋଇ ରହିଲି ଏଣୁ ତୁମ ସାଙ୍ଗିଆ ହେଲା ସାଥୁଆ । ମୋର ଗଡ ବଣାଇଁ ଗଡ ହେଲେ ତମ ଗଡ ବାହାରି ଗଡ । ପ୍ରଶାନ୍ତ ଜାଗା ଦେଇ ତୁମେ ବାହାରୁ ଆସିଛ ବୋଲି ବାହା ଗଡ ନାଁ ଦେଇ ରଖିଲେ ଓ ଜମି ବି ଦେଲେ । ସେହି ଦିନଠାରୁ ଆମର ଭଲ ମନ୍ଦ ବୁଝନ୍ତି । ସେ ସମୟରେ ନୂଆଁଖାଇ ହୋଇଥିଲା, ସେ ଆମକୁ ଡାକି କହିଲେ ନୂଆଁଖାଇ କାଲି ଖାଇବା ନାହିଁକି ବୋଲି ପ୍ରତିଶ୍ରୁତି ଦେଲେ, ଆମେ କହିଲୁ ଆମ ହାତରେ ତ କିଛି ନାହିଁ ନୂଆଁ କିପରି ଖାଇବୁ । ରାଜା କହିଲେ ଆମ ରାଜ୍ୟରେ ଯାହାଠି ଯେଉଁ ଜିନିଷ ପାଇବ ତୁମ ନୂଆଁଖିଆ ଆରମ୍ଭ କର । ଯେ କୌଣସି ଆପତ୍ତି କରିବେ ସେମାନେ ସବୁ ଆମ ପାଖକୁ ଆସିବେ । ମୁଁ ସେ କଥା ବୁଝିବି । ଆମେ ରାତି ଭିତରେ ନୂଆଁଖାଇ ଆରମ୍ଭ କରିଦେଲୁଁ । ଚାରି ବଜା ରାତିରୁ ଉଠି ଧାନ କିଆରିରୁ ଧାନ ଚୋରି ଆଣି ଯାବତ ବିଷୟ ସବୁ ଯାହାଠାରେ ଯାହା ଥିଲା ଗୁଡ, ଘିଅ ସବୁଧରି ସବୁ ବନ୍ଦୋବସ୍ତ କରିଲୁ ନଦୀକୁ ପାଣି ଆଣିଗଲା ସମୟରେ ଆମ ନାଁ ରେ ଯୋଉ ଘାଟ ତିଆରି ହୋଇଥିଲା ସେଠି ଗୋଟିଏ ସର୍ପ ଫେଣ ଟେକି କହିଥିଲା ସେଠାରୁ ଫେରି ଆସି ଖଣ୍ଡାଧରି ଚାଉଳ ଧୂପ

ନୈବେଦ୍ୟ ହରିଡା ଦେଇ ତାଙ୍କୁ ଆରାଧନା କଲୁଁ । ସେ ପାଣି ଭିତରକୁ ଚାଲିଗଲେ । ସେହି ଖଣ୍ଡାରେ ପାଣିକୁ କାଟିବାକୁ ପଡିଲା ତାପରେ ପାଣି ଧରି ଆସିଲୁଁ । କୁରେଇ ପତ୍ର ପାଖରେ ଥିଲା । ତାକୁ ଆଣିଲା ବେଳେ ବି ସର୍ପ ଛେକିଥିଲା । ଆମେ ଗଛ ପାଖକୁ ଯିବାବେଳେ ସେ ଛାଡି ପଳାଇଲା । ଆମେ ନାଗେସ୍ର ଗୁତ୍ର ବୋଲି ଆମେ ତାଙ୍କୁ ଆରାଧନା କରି ନୂଆଁ ଖାଇବା ଆରମ୍ଭ କଲୁଁ ଓ ଇଷ୍ଟଦେବୀ କୁଆଁରୀକୁ ପୂଜା ଆରମ୍ଭ କଲୁଁ । ରାତି ଭତରେ ଆମେ ନୂଆଁ ଖାଇ ସାରିଲୁ । ତାପରେ ଖୁବ ସକାଳୁ ରାଜାଙ୍କୁ ଯାଇ ନମସ୍କାର କଲୁଁ ସେହିଦିନଠାରୁ ରାଜା ପଚାରିଲେ ତୁମେ ଆଗରୁ ନୂଆଁ ଖାଇ ଦେଲ ? ଆମେ କୁଆଁରୀ ଇଷ୍ଟଦେବୀଙ୍କୁ ଶରଣ କରି ଖାଇଛୁ । ତେଣୁ ରାଜା କହିଲେ ମୁ ତ ତୁମକୁ କଥା ଦେଇଛି ଏଣୁ କୌଣସି ଦୋଷାବହ ନାହିଁ । ତୁମ ପାଣି ଆଣିବା ସମୟରେ ନାଗ ଦର୍ଶନ କରିଛ ବୋଲି କହୁଛ । ତେଣୁ ନାଗ ବାଣେଶ୍ୱରଙ୍କ ବାହାନ । ତେଣୁ କୁଆଁରୀକୁ ଇଷ୍ଟଦେବୀ କରିଛ । ତୁମର ନୂଆଁଖାଇ ସଫଳ ହେଉ । ଆମେ ନୂଆଁଖାଇ ବିଭାହେଲା ଝିଅ କିମ୍ବା ବନ୍ଧୁ ବାନ୍ଧବଙ୍କୁ ଦେଉନାହିଁ । ସକାଳୁ ଖାଇ ସଙ୍ଗେ ସଙ୍ଗେ ଆମେ ପତ୍ରୀ ଭସାଇ ଦେଉଁ । ସେହି ଦିନଠାରୁ ଆମେ ବାହାରି ଗଡର ସାଥୁଆ ଉପାଧିରେ ରହିଲୁଁ । ରାଜା କହିଲେ ମୋ ଅଭିଷେକରେ ସୁନା ପଇତା ଦେବ । ଆମେ କହିଲୁ ସେ ସୁନା କେଉଁଠୁ ଆସିବ । ବ୍ରାହ୍ମଣମାନଙ୍କୁ କହିଦେବି ବ୍ରାହ୍ମଣମାନେ ତାଙ୍କ ଚାନ୍ଦା ଠୁଳାଇ ପଇସା ତୁମକୁ ଦେବେ । ସେହି ପଇସାରେ ତୁମେ ସର୍ଣ୍ଣ ପଇତା ତିଆରି କରିବା ପୌଷ ପୂର୍ଣ୍ଣିମାରେ ରାଜାଙ୍କୁ ଦିଆଯାଏ, ସେହିଦିନଠାରୁ ରାଜା ଆମକୁ ଜଣେ ଜଣେ ଲୋକ ଆମ ପାଖରେ ରହିବାକୁ ଦେଲେ । ସେହି ଦିନଠାରୁ ବସ୍ତି ହେଲା ।

-ସମାପ୍ତ-

ଦୃଢ଼ିଭୁତ କରି ଶତ ଶତ ଦର୍ଶକ ଭକ୍ତଙ୍କର ନୟନରୁ ଖସି ଆସୁଥିଲା ଭକ୍ତି ଓ ଆନନ୍ଦର ଭାବଧାରାରେ ବିଜଡିତ ଅଶ୍ରୁର ପ୍ଲାବନ । ଠିକ୍ ଏହିଭଳି ଦିନେ କବି ବଳରାମ ଦାସଙ୍କର ଆକୁଳ ମିନତିରେ ଜଗନ୍ନାଥ ବଡଦାଣ୍ଡର ବଡରଥକୁ ଛାଡି ବଳରାମ ଦାସଙ୍କର ବାଲିରଥକୁ ଚାଲି ଆସିଥିଲେ । ଥକ୍କା ହୋଇ ଅଟକି ଯାଇଥିଲେ । ଭକ୍ତସାଲବେଗର ଡାକରେ ଏକଦା ଓଡିଶାର ସମସ୍ତ ଶକ୍ତି ତାଙ୍କୁ ସେଦିନ ଉଠାଇବାକୁ ଅକ୍ଷମ ହୋଇଥିଲେ । ସେ ଏମିତି କେତେ କଣ କରି ପାରନ୍ତି । ତେଣୁ ତାଙ୍କୁ କହେ ଦାନରକ୍ଷକ । ଭକ୍ତ ବତ୍ସଳ ଦ୍ରୌପଦୀ-ମୃଗୁଣୀ ଗଜ ଉଦ୍ଧାରକ ଇତ୍ୟାଦି । ସର୍ବୋପରି ନୀଳାଚଳ କ୍ଷେତ୍ରରେ ଜାତିଗତ ବାଛ ବିଚାର ନାହିଁ । ଖାଦ୍ୟରେ ଉଚ୍ଛିଷ୍ଟ ନାହିଁ । ଏଠାରେ ସର୍ବୋଧର୍ମ ସମନ୍ୱୟବାଦର ବାନା ଚିରି ଉଡ୍‌ଡୀୟମାନ ଏଠି ସମସ୍ତେ ସମାନ । ସମସ୍ତେ କୈବଲ୍ୟ ର ଅଧିକାରୀ । ଲକ୍ଷ୍ମୀ ପୁରାଣରେ ଏହାର ପ୍ରମାଣ ମିଳେ ।ଏଠାରେ କୈବଲ୍ୟ ବା ମହାପ୍ରସାଦର ପ୍ରାଧାନ୍ୟ ମଧ୍ୟ ସ୍ୱିକୃତ । ଜଗନ୍ନାଥ ଚରିତାମୃତରେ ଦିବାକର ଦାସ କହିଛନ୍ତି:-

ଯେ ଦ୍ରବ୍ୟ ଅମଣେହା ହେବ
ତା ବଳଦେବ ସମର୍ପିବ
ସେ ଦେବେ ସୁଭଦ୍ରାଙ୍କ ପାଖେ
ସେ ଦେବେ ଜଗନ୍ନାଥ ମୁଖେ ।
ଏ ଭାବେ ପ୍ରଭୁଙ୍କ ଆସଦ
ଶେଷେ ହୁଏ ମହା ପ୍ରସାଦ ।

ଶ୍ରୀ କ୍ଷେତ୍ରର ଅଖଣ୍ଡ ସ ।ଧିକାରୀ ଶ୍ରୀଜଗନ୍ନାଥ ସର୍ବଧର୍ମ ସମନ୍ୱୟ ବାଦର ଜାଜ୍ଜଲ୍ୟ ପ୍ରତିନିଧି । ସାମ୍ୟ ମୈତ୍ରୀ ଓ କରୁଣାର ସେ ଚିରନ୍ତନ ଉତ୍ସ ଏବଂ ତେଣୁ ଜାତୀୟ ସଂହତିର ଉଦ୍‌ଗାତା । ଏଭଳି ଏକ ଦେବତାର ଅସୀମ ବାହୁଛାୟା ତଳେ ଲାଳାୟିତ । ପୁଣ୍ୟଭୂମି

ଉତ୍କଳରେ ଜନ୍ମ ଦେଇଥିବାରୁ ପ୍ରତ୍ୟେକ ଉତ୍କଳୀୟ ନିଜକୁ ଧନ୍ୟ ମନେ କରିବା ଉଚିତ୍ ।

ଗଡଜାତ ବଣାଇଁ : କିମ୍ବଦନ୍ତୀ ଓ ଇତିହାସର ଉଜ୍ଜଳ କେତୋଟି ପୃଷ୍ଠା

ସାଧିନତା ପୂର୍ବବର୍ତୀ ଗଡଜାତ ବଣାଇଁରେ ଶିକ୍ଷା ପ୍ରସାରର ଭିତ୍ତିଭୂମି କିପରି ଥିଲା ସେ ବିଷୟରେ ଦୃଷ୍ଟିପାତ କରିବା ପ୍ରବନ୍ଧର ଲକ୍ଷ୍ୟ । ସାଧାରଣତଃ ଦେଖାଯାଇ ଅଛି ଯେ ଗଡଜାତ ଗୁଡିକରେ ରାଜାମାନେ ଅନେକ କ୍ଷେତ୍ରରେ ରାଜା ନିଜ ପ୍ରଜାଙ୍କୁ ଭେଟି ବେଗାରି ମାଧ୍ୟମରେ ଅତ୍ୟାଚାର କରିଥିବାର ବହୁ ଉଦାହରଣ ରହିଅଛି । କିନ୍ତୁ ଏପରି କେତେ ଗୁଡିଏ ଗଡଜାତ ଥିଲା । ଯେଉଁଠାରେକି ରାଜାମାନେ ନିଜ ପ୍ରଜାଙ୍କ ସର୍ବବିଧ ଉନ୍ନତି ପାଇଁ କାର୍ଯ୍ୟକରି କାଳଜୟୀ ଯଶ ରଖି ଯାଇଛନ୍ତି । ଉଦାହରଣ ସରୂପ ବାମଣ୍ଡାର ସନାମଧନ୍ୟ ରାଜା ସାର ବାସୁଦେବ, ସୁଢଳ ଦେବ ଓ ତାଙ୍କ ପୁତ୍ର ରାଜା ସଚ୍ଚିଦାନନ୍ଦ ତ୍ରିଭୁବନ ଦେବ । ତାଙ୍କର ଦେଶ ହିତକର କାର୍ଯ୍ୟ ପାଇଁ ସେମାନେ ତଦାନିନ୍ତନ ବ୍ରିଟିଶ ଗଭର୍ଣ୍ଣମେ ର ପ୍ରଶଂସା ଭାଜନ ହୋଇପାରିଥିଲେ ଓ ଅଦ୍ୟାପ ତାଙ୍କର ସ୍ମୃତି ଜନମାନସରେ ଉଭାସିତ । ଏ ଦୃଷ୍ଟିରୁ ବିଚାର କଲେ ବଣାଇଁ ଗଡ ଜାତରେ ଶିକ୍ଷାର ପ୍ରସାର ଦିଗରେ ସେତେଟା ଅବହେଲା ପ୍ରଦର୍ଶନ କରାଯାଇ ନଥିବାର ସୂଚନା ମିଳେ । ପଡୋଶୀ ରାଜ୍ୟ ବାମଣ୍ଡା ଯେତେବେଳେ ନିଜର ଉନ୍ନତି ଶିକ୍ଷା ସାହିତ୍ୟ ବିଜ୍ଞାନ, ସମାଜ, କୃଷି, ବାଣିଜ୍ୟ, ଅର୍ଥନୀତି ଆଦିରେ ସମୁନ୍ନତ ଥିଲା । ସେତେବେଳେ ତାର ସଭାବ ନିଶ୍ଚୟ ବଣାଇଁ ଗଡଜାତ ଉପରେ ପଡିବା ସାଭାବିକ । କାରଣ ବଣାଇଁର ରାଜାମାନେ ସାଧାରଣତଃ ବାମଣ୍ଡା, ପାଲଲହଡା, କଳାହାଣ୍ଡି, ଢେଙ୍କାନାଳ, ଆଦି ଗଡଜାତର ରାଜାମାନଙ୍କ ସହିତ ସୁସମ୍ପର୍କ ରକ୍ଷା କରୁଥିଲେ । ବଣାଇଁର ଶିକ୍ଷାର ପ୍ରସାର ପାଇଁ ସାଧାରଣତଃ ଖ୍ରୀ:ଅ ୧୮୫୩ରୁ ପଦକ୍ଷେପ

ନିଆଯାଇଥିବାର ଜଣାଯାଏ । ତତ୍କାଳିନ ରାଜା ଶିବ ନାରାୟଣ ଇନ୍ଦ୍ରଦେଓ ନିଜ ରାଜ୍ୟ ଶିବ ନାରାୟଣ ଇନ୍ଦ୍ର ଦେଓ ନିଜ ରାଜ୍ୟ ବଣାଇଁରେ ଶିକ୍ଷାର ମହତ୍ତ୍ୱ ବଢ଼ାଇବା ପାଇଁ ଭାଗିରଥୀ ପୁରୋହିତ ଆଦିଙ୍କୁ ବିଦ୍ୟା ଅଧ୍ୟୟନ ପାଇଁ ବାରଣାସୀ ପଠାଇ ଥିଲେ । ପରବର୍ତୀ କାଳରେ ରାଜା ଦୟାନିଧି ଚନ୍ଦ୍ରଦେଓ ଶିକ୍ଷାର ଗୁରୁତ୍ୱ ଉପଲବ୍ଧି କରି ବଣାଇଁ ରାଜବାଟୀ ନିକଟରେ ଏକ ଚଉପାଢୀ ସ୍ଥାପନ କରି ଥିଲେ । ସେଠାରେ କାବ୍ୟ, ଜ୍ୟୋତିଷ ଓ ଆୟୁର୍ବେଦ ଶିକ୍ଷା ଦେବାର ବ୍ୟବସ୍ଥା କରାଯାଇଥିଲା । ଏ ସମ୍ପର୍କୀୟ ଶିକ୍ଷା ଦେବାପାଇଁ ରାଜା ପଣ୍ଡିତ ପଦ୍ମନାଭ ଷଡଙ୍ଗୀଙ୍କୁ ପୁରୀରୁ ଆଣି ନିଯୁକ୍ତି ପ୍ରଦାନ କରିଥିଲେ । ଶ୍ରୀ କେଶବ ପାତ୍ର ଚମ୍ପୃଧର ମିଶ୍ର ଓ ଦାମୋଦର ପୂଜାହାରୀ ଆଦି ଛାତ୍ରଗଣ ସେଠାରେ ଅଧ୍ୟୟନ କରିଥିଲେ । ରାଜା ନିଳାମ୍ବର ଚନ୍ଦ୍ର ଦେଓଙ୍କ ଶାସନକାଳ ବେଳକୁ ଅର୍ଥାତ ୧୯୯୭ ଖ୍ରୀ:ଅ ବେଳକୁ ଉକ୍ତ ଚଉପାଢୀଟି ବନ୍ଦ ହୋଇଯାଇଥିଲା । ତେଣୁ ରାଜା ନିଳାମ୍ବର ଚନ୍ଦ୍ର ଦେଓ ସେଠାରେ ଏକ ଆଲୋଚନା ସଭା ପ୍ରତିଷ୍ଠା କରିଥିଲେ । ଏହି ଆଲୋଚନା ସଭାରେ ପଦ୍ୟ କୁମାର ସମ୍ଭବ ଲେଖକ ଜନାଦ୍ଦନ ପତି, ଗଦ୍ୟ ବତ୍ରିଶ ସିଂହାସନର ଲେଖକ ବିଦ୍ୟାଧନ ଜେନା । ବାଣୁଆ ଶାସ୍ତ୍ର ଲେଖକ ଯଦୁ ଫତ୍‌କାର ଓ କାବ୍ୟ ବିଷାରଦ ଜୟ ଦେବ ଶତ୍‌ପଥୀ ଯୋଗଦେଇ ରାଜ୍ୟରେ ଜ୍ଞାନ ଆଲୋଚନାର ବ୍ୟାପକ ପ୍ରସାର ଖଟାଇଥିଲେ ଏପରିକି ରାଜା ନିଳାମ୍ବର ଦେଓ ନିଜେ କୌତୁକ କଳାନିଧି ଗିତିବାକ୍ୟ ରଚନା କରିଛନ୍ତି ।ନିଜ ଜ୍ଞାନ ଗାରିମାର ଶ୍ରେଷ୍ଠତ୍ୱ ପ୍ରତିପାଦନ କରି ଯାଇଛନ୍ତି । ପଡୋଶୀ ରାଜ୍ୟ ବାମଣ୍ଡାରେ ରାଜା ସଚ୍ଚିଦାନନ୍ଦ ଶ୍ରୀ ୧୯୦୯ରେ ପ୍ରାଇମେରୀ ଶିକ୍ଷାକୁ ବାଧ୍ୟତାମୂଳକ କରିବାପାଇଁ ଆଇନ ପ୍ରଣୟନ କରିଥିଲେ। ସେ ଆଇନଅନୁସାରେ ୫୦ଘର ବାସିନ୍ଦାରୁ ଉର୍ଦ୍ଧ୍ୱ ବସତି ପ୍ରତି ଗ୍ରାମରେ ବାଳକ ବାଳିକା ମାନଙ୍କ ନିମନ୍ତେ ଗୋଟାଏ ଲେଖାଏଁ ଅପର

ପ୍ରାଇମେରୀ ସ୍କୁଲ ପ୍ରତିଷ୍ଠା କରିବାର ବ୍ୟବସ୍ଥା ଥିଲା (୯) ଠିକ୍ ସେହିପରି ବଣାଇଁ ରାଜ୍ୟରେ ଆଧୁନିକ ଧରଣର ସ୍କୁଲ ପ୍ରତିଷ୍ଠା କରିବାପାଇଁ ଖ୍ରୀ:୧୯୦୨ ରେ ପଦକ୍ଷେପ ନିଆଯାଇଥିଲା । ଠିକ୍ ସେହିବର୍ଷ ବଣାଇଁ ରାଜବାଟୀ ସ୍କୁଲ ପ୍ରତିଷ୍ଠା କରିବାପାଇଁ ଠିକ୍ ହେଲା । ସମ୍ବଲପୁରର ଶ୍ରୀ ମଧୁସୁଦନ ପଣ୍ଡା ହେଡ ପଣ୍ଡିତ ଓ ଶ୍ରୀ ଗଦାଧର ପାଣିଗ୍ରାହୀ ସେକେଣ୍ଡ ପଣ୍ଡିତ ଭାବରେ ଉକ୍ତ ସ୍କୁଲରେ ୧୯୦୨ ମସିହା ଡିସେମ୍ବର ୨୦ ତାରିଖରେ ଯୋଗଦାନ କଲେ । ନୀଲମଣୀ ବୈଦ୍ୟ, କଳାକାର ଦାସ, ବାଞ୍ଛାନିଧି ବେହେରା, ପିତାମ୍ବର ଦଳାଇ, ହରିହର କେଉଟ ଓ କ୍ଷେତ୍ର ମୋହନ ସାହୁ ପ୍ରଥମେ ଏ ସ୍କୁଲରେ ଭର୍ତି ହେଲେ । ଏହି ରାଜବାଟୀ ସ୍କୁଲ ଯେତେବେଲେ ବଣାଇଁରେ ଶିକ୍ଷା ପ୍ରସାରର ବତୀଘର ସଦୃଶ ଥିଲା । ନାରୀ ଶିକ୍ଷାର ଉନ୍ନତି ପାଇଁ ମଧ୍ୟ ସେତେବେଳେ ଉତ୍ସାହ ପ୍ରଦାନ କରାଯାଉଥିଲା । ଯାହା ଫଳରେ ଉକ୍ତ ସ୍କୁଲରେ ଅନେକ ବାଳିକା ମଧ୍ୟ ନାମ ଲେଖାଇ ପଢ଼ିବାକୁ ଆଗେଇ ଆସିଥିଲେ । ବ୍ରଜବାଳା ଦେବୀ ଆଦୀ ୭ଜଣ ବାଳିକା ସେହି ସ୍କୁଲରେ ୧୯୦୮ରେ (୧୫-୧୨-୧୯୦୮) ରେ ଯୋଗ ଦେଇଥିଲେ । ପରେ ପରେ ତା. ୮-୩-୧୯୧୦ ମସିହାରେ ସ୍କୁଲଟି ଉଚ୍ଚ ପ୍ରାଥମିକ ସ୍କୁଲରେ ପରିଣତ ହେଲା । ସମୟକ୍ରମେ ଉକ୍ତ ସ୍କୁଲର ଛାତ୍ରଛାତ୍ରୀ ସଂଖ୍ୟା ନିମ୍ନରେ ପ୍ରଦ ହେଲା ।

	ଛାତ୍ର	ଛାତ୍ରୀ	ମୋଟ
ତା.୮-୩-୧୯୧୦	୫୦	୨	୫୦
ତା.୨୧-୮-୧୯୧୧	୪୯	୪	୫୩
ତା.୧୧-୧୨-୧୯୧୨	୫୪	୧୦	୬୪
ତା.୯-୪-୧୯୧୩	୬୫	୧୧	୭୬
ତା.୨୪-୧-୧୯୧୪	୭୫	୧୫	୯୦
ତା.୧-୧୦-୧୯୧୫	୧୦୬	୧୮	୧୨

ଉପରୋକ୍ତ ପରିସଂଖ୍ୟାନରୁ ଜଣାଯାଏ ଯେ ସମୟାନୁକ୍ରମେ ବଣାଇଁରେ ଶିକ୍ଷା ପ୍ରତି ସଚେତନତା ବୃଦ୍ଧି ପାଇଥିଲା । ୧୯୧୪ ମସିହାରେ ରାଜବାଟୀ ସ୍କୁଲର ଶିକ୍ଷା ସଂଖ୍ୟା ୨ଜଣରୁ ୩ଜଣ କୁ ବୃଦ୍ଧି ହେବାରୁ ରାମକୃଷ୍ଣ ନାଥ ପ୍ରଧାନ ଶିକ୍ଷକ ବୃନ୍ଦାବନ ପଣ୍ଡା-ସହକାରୀ ଶିକ୍ଷକ ଓ ବାନାମ୍ବର ନାଥ ମନିଟର ଭାବେ ସ୍ଥାନିତ ହେଲେ । ବାମଣ୍ଡା ରାଜା ସଚ୍ଚିଦାନନ୍ଦ ତ୍ରିଭୁବନ ଦେଓ ଯେପରି ବାମଣ୍ଡାରେ ବ୍ୟାପକ ଭାବେ ଶିକ୍ଷାର ପ୍ରସାର କରିଥିଲେ । ବଣାଇଁରେ ରାଜା ଶ୍ରୀ ଧରଣୀଧର ଚନ୍ଦ୍ରଦେଓ ଦେବ ତଦ୍ରୂପ ବଣାଇଁରେ ଶିକ୍ଷାର ପ୍ରସାର କରି ବଣାଇଁ ବାସୀଙ୍କ ଶ୍ରଦ୍ଧାଭାଜନ ତଥା ପ୍ରାତଃ ସ୍ମରଣୀୟ ହୋଇ ପାରିଥିଲେ । ରାଜା ଧରଣୀଧର ୧୯୦୧ରେ ସିଂହାସନ ଆରୋହଣ କଲେ ଓ ସଙ୍ଗେ ସଙ୍ଗେ ଶିକ୍ଷା ପ୍ରସାର ଦୃଢ଼ ଉନ୍ନତି ପାଇଁ ସଫଳ ପଦକ୍ଷେପମାନ ଗ୍ରହଣ କଲେ । ତାଙ୍କର ପ୍ରଚେଷ୍ଟାରେ ୧୯୦୭ ମସିହାରୁ ୧୯୧୩ ମସିହା ମଧ୍ୟରେ ବଣାଇଁରେ ୯ଟି ପ୍ରାଥମିକ ସ୍କୁଲ ପ୍ରତିଷ୍ଠା ହୋଇଥିଲା । ୧- ବଣାଇଁ ଗଡ ୨- ତୁମକଲା ୩- ଶରଧାପୁର ୪- ଜାଙ୍ଗଲା ୫- ବିଜାକୁଲି ୬- ବାଙ୍କି ୭- କଲେଇପୋଷ ୮- କୁଲିପୋଷ ୯- ତେଣ୍ଡରା । କଲେଇପୋଷର ସ୍କୁଲଟି ପ୍ରଥମେ କୁଡେଇ କଳାରେ ସ୍ଥାପିତ ହୋଇଥିଲା ଓ କୁଡେଇ କଳା ସ୍କୁଲରେ ଶ୍ରୀ ଆନନ୍ଦ ମାହାନ୍ତ (ମୁଣ୍ଡାଗାଁ) ଶିକ୍ଷକ ଥିଲେ ।

ସ୍କୁଲ ଗୁଡିକରେ ଗଣିତ ଓ ଭାଷା ଶିକ୍ଷାକୁ ବିଶେଷ ଗୁରୁତ୍ୱ ଦିଆଯାଉଥିଲା । ତା.୨୦-୩-୧୯୧୧ ମସିହାରେ ତତ୍‌କାଳିକ ସ୍କୁଲ ଏଜେନ୍‌ସୀ ଇନିସ୍‌ପେକ୍ଟର ଗକ୍ସ. ଇ.ଏ. ଉରରଲଷର ଙ୍କ ଗୋଟିଏ ପରିଦର୍ଶନ ରିପୋର୍ଟରୁ ଏହା ସ୍ପଷ୍ଟ ଜଣାପଡେ ତାଙ୍କ ମତରେ the teachers should pay special attention to the subjects of Reading, Dictation, Writing and Arithmetic and should give their pupils a very careful and thorough[1] grounding in them. ଭାଷାଶିକ୍ଷା ଦେବାପାଇଁ ପ୍ରତ୍ୟେକ ପ୍ରାଇମେରୀ ସ୍କୁଲରେ ଜଣେ ଲେଖାଏଁ କଟକ ବା ପୁରୀ ଜିଲ୍ଲାର ଶିକ୍ଷକ ରଖିବାପାଇଁ ବ୍ୟବସ୍ଥା କରିଗଲା । ଏ ଦୃଷ୍ଟିକୁ ମୂଳ ବସନ୍ତ ଗ୍ରାମର ଶ୍ରୀଦେବନାଥ କର ବଣାଇଁକୁ ଆସିଥିଲେ ସେତେବେଳେ ବଣାଇଁରେ ଜଣେ ଇନିସ୍‌ପେକ୍ଟର ପଣ୍ଡିତ ୧୭ଜଣ ଶିକ୍ଷକ ଓ ଦୁଇଜଣ ମନିଟର ନିଯୁକ୍ତ ଥିବାର କଥା ସେତେବେଳର ପରିଦର୍ଶକ ଇ.ଏ ହିପ୍‌ପିଙ୍କର ବିବରଣୀରୁ ଜଣାଯାଏ, ୧୯୧୬ ମସିହାରେ ବଣାଇଁରେ ସ୍କୁଲ ସଂଖ୍ୟା ବଢ଼ିବାକୁ ଲାଗିଲା । ଲହୁଣିପଡା, କେନାଭଟା, ମାତକୁଟା, ଘୋଷରା ଆଦି ସ୍ଥାନରେ ୧୭ଟି ପ୍ରାଥମିକ ସ୍କୁଲ ସ୍ଥାପିତ ହୋଇଥିଲା ଓ ସେଥିରୁ ବଣାଇଁଗଡ ଜାଙ୍ଗଲା ତଥା ଲହୁଣିପଡାରେ ୩ଟି ଉଚ୍ଚ ପ୍ରାଥମିକ ସ୍କୁଲ ହେଲା । ସ୍କୁଲ ଗୁଡିକରେ ଆଦର୍ଶ ପାଠ୍ୟଦାନ ପ୍ରଣାଳୀ ଓ ପରିଚାଳନା ଆଦି ନିରେଖିବା ପାଇଁ ସେହି ବର୍ଷ ବଣାଇଁରେ ସ୍କୁଲ ବିଭାଗର ସବ୍‌ଇନିସ୍‌ପେକ୍ଟର ପଦସୃଷ୍ଟି କରାଯାଇ ଶ୍ରୀ ବିଶେଶ୍ୱର ଭଞ୍ଜଙ୍କୁ ପ୍ରଥମେ ନିଯୁକ୍ତି ପ୍ରଦାନ କରାଗଲା ।

–ସମାପ୍ତ–

ଜୁନ୍ ୨୦-୨୬-୧୯୯୩ ମସିହାରେ ପ୍ରଜାତନ୍ତ୍ର ସାପ୍ତାହିକି ଶ୍ରୀମନ୍ଦିର ଗର୍ଭଗୃହ ମରାମତ ୨୮ଅଙ୍କ ଶ୍ରୀ.ବିରକେଶରୀ ଦେବ(ପୁରୀଗଜପତି) ତୃତୀୟ ମହଲ ୨୮ ମାର୍ଚ୍ଚ ୧୯୯୩ ମରାମତି କରି ଥିବା ସମୟରେ ନିମ୍ନଲିଖିତ ବ୍ୟକ୍ତି ଶ୍ରୀ ଦାମଦର ମହାପାତ୍ର, ବନ୍ଧୁ ମହାପାତ୍ର ବଣାଇଁର ବୋଲି ଲେଖାଅଛି । ଚୁନ ପ୍ଲାଷ୍ଟରିଙ୍ଗ କରିଥିଲେ

[1] Though in the original, but probably a spelling mistake.

CHAPTER IV

Kadamba Gatha by Rajpurohit Gopinath Mishra (English Translation)

DEDICATION LETTER

Sri Dharanidhar Indradev, the king of Bonai Fort, the glorious sea who is worshipped by his subjects those who were well acquainted with his qualities.

The flag of Indradev engrossed with peaceful qualities is flying in the whole world. His peaceful qualities are compared with that of the qualities of the sea.

I am a very poor meaningless son, so by what wealth I will worship under your feet O' my respected king. Only I know to dedicate my devoted flowers and sandalwood filled with my love and respect in your respected name.

As I am having an invincible desire to write the chronicles of your clan (*bansabali*) so I am composing it in the form of cantos (*chanda*).

I have neither intellect nor I am highly educated so that I will satisfy you in my writings, still I have been appointed by you as the only Royal Poet, having a small house of education.

Only by dedicating in your holy name I put my devoted flowers and sandalwood paste under your respected feet.

So respectfully I pray to you in my open heart and mind to excuse me if I have committed any mistakes.

Yours faithfully,

Sd/-

Gopinath Mishra,

Rajpurohit of Bonai Raj Family.

FIRST CANTO

Musical mode (rag) 'Basanta Baradi'

Stanza 1
O, Gajanana Ganesh, the son of Lord Shiva and Parbati, the supreme felicity; you are the destroyer of obstacles, so may you always be victorious.

Stanza 2
The great Brahman, Lord Shiva has decorated your forehead with vermilion. He is eradicating all kinds of troubles of Gods, He is holding the moon on His head so He is called 'Chandra Sekhar'. May you always be victorious.

Stanza 3
The three worlds were tied in the hands of demons, so war took place between the heavenly gods and the demons. When the gods could not release the three worlds, by your intellect the God Hara [Shiva] destroyed the demons.

Stanza 4
So, the God King Shiva being overpleased with you gave a boon and you are worshipped in the entire world.

Stanza 5
You are the son of Girija [Parbati] so your place is *sataj* (flower of truth). In devotion you are a great devotee so you are always loved by your parents.

Stanza 6
You are, Chaitanya, always you concentrate your mind in devotion and reciting prayers. You are helping and saving all those who take shelter under your feet.

Stanza 7
'O' you are the ocean of kindness for all the people of this mortal world, give me shelter under your flag which is marked with kindness.

Stanza 8
Your belly is wide and is filled with knowledge; your belly is large and like fire, you are fearless.

Stanza 9
When you dance your wisps of hairs fall on your body; which represents the thirty-two qualities of fine arts. You are the lover of the Tandab dance and when you dance you are fully immersed into the dance.

Stanza 10
So, O' son of Basudeva [Shiva and Parbati], be kind on me, so that I will say the details of the Kadamba clan of Bonai State.

Stanza 11
I salute you O', the son of Panchanana and Ambika [Shiva and Parbati]. Lord Shiva is holding the moon on His head and His chariot is the bull.

Stanza 12
Being victorious, He [Lord Shiva] destroyed all traces of the darkness, Madana was his enemy.... He wears the tiger skin and his body is besmeared with ash. He is holding river [Ganga] on his matted hair.

Stanza 13
After getting a boon from Brahma, the son of the sea king Jalandhar, won all the three worlds.

Stanza 14
...by taking all the gods with you, O' god you killed him in the war and you saved the three worlds.

Stanza 15
...O', Jatadhara (Lord with the matted hair/Shiva), your three eyes are like three suns. You are Hara, the husband of Uma [Parbati]. You hold a trident and a small drum (*dambaru*).

Stanza 16
...when Daksha Prajapati, your father-in-law did not invite you to the *yagya* performed by him, an enraged Uma went to Her father's house.

Stanza 17
When Prajapati insulted his daughter Uma, the chaste lady (*sati*) jumped into the burning fire of the *yagya* and destroyed Her life.

Stanza 18
Out of anger, you cut the head of Daksha Prajapati and fixed the head of a he-goat instead and after that you became 'Sulapani' [Lord Shiva].

Stanza 19
Being angry you showed your powers to your mother-in-law; too after seeing that the entire Brahmanda [covering three worlds] worships you.

Stanza 20
Arjuna as a hunter killed a rhinoceros (*ganda*). He kept the dead rhinoceros' neck on his arrow and rotated it.

Stanza 21
Being overpleased with him you gave the imperishable quiver 'Pasupat' to him along with a boon.

Stanza 22
At the time of elopement of Usha, the daughter of Banasur, you fought against the Yadabs [descendants of Yadu dynasty] and saved Banasur.

Stanza 23
In order to destroy your sexual desire you left Kapilash, went to Kasi and settled down there and since then you are called 'Biswabasa'.

Stanza 24
In Varanasi, Banasur pleased you both husband and wife with his *tandab* dance (ecstatic dance).

Stanza 25
Being overpleased you asked Banasur, 'You have already received the boon of living in three worlds. Ask another boon.'

Stanza 26
Banasur said, 'Hear me, O' Trilochan [Shiva], if you are so pleased with 'me, then come to my house.'

Stanza 27
'I will keep you as my tutelary deity (*ishta debta*) in my house and serve you and I will be very grateful to take shelter under your feet.'

Stanza 28
Lord Shiva agreed and told Banasur that the boon has been granted and so proceed to your house, I will follow you. Keep talking to me'.

Stanza 29
'Listening to the jingling of the tinkling anklet I will follow you. So, O' Banasur, do quickly proceed.'

Stanza 30
Listening to Lord Shiva, Banasur proceeded while Lord Shiva walked behind him, carrying water.

Stanza 31
Giving out the sound of the anklet Brusabha went. In this way they arrived in Srunita Nagara.

Stanza 32
At the eastern bank of the river Brahmani that was flowing towards the north, Lord Shiva thought the that it was like Ganga water.

Stanza 33
He said that this was good solitary burial ground (i.e. on the bank of river Brahmani). Lord Shiva saw that place as a place for pilgrimage and halted there.

Stanza 34
As the sound of the bell of Brusabha ceased, Banasur looked behind to see whether Shiva was following him or not.

Stanza 35
Lord Shiva had told Banasur not to look behind. And if he did, Shiva would stay in that place.

Stanza 36
'As there is a burial ground on the bank of the river Brahmani this place is peaceful, we are happy here.'

Stanza 37
'I will stay here ... and I will be known by your name, as Baneswar.'

Stanza 38
Those who will worship me by uttering your name, will reap the fruits of eight kinds of wealth and will stay in my house.

Stanza 39
So, Banasur, now you go to my house. In this way Shiva convinced Banasur and sent him back.

Stanza 40
Owing to the devotion of Banasur, Shiva halted in that place of Bonai State, which later on became famous in the whole world as a place of pilgrimage.

Stanza 41
In this way Baneswar stayed in Bonai fort (*durga*) ... so the kings of Bonai, of each generation worshipped Baneswar, who always saved them.

Stanza 42
O' Gangadhar, O' Hara, the husband of Parbati, Nilakanth, Biswabasa, Mahadev, Shiva.

Stanza 43
O' Shiva, give me a place on your lotus-like feet and I will remain like a large black bee (*satpada*) under your lotus feet.

SECOND CANTO

Musical mode 'Asadha sukla' [usually sung during the light fortnight of Asadha Month]

Stanza 1
O' good souls' holders, hear me attentively; I will describe the details of Kadamba kings' dynasty of Bonai State. From the navel cord of Lord Vishnu one lotus flower has blossomed on which Brahma has taken His birth and

staying there. His son is sage Duttatriya. His eyes tears fell on the sea and from the sea the moon was born.

Stanza 2
The son of the moon is King Budha, who resides among the planets. The son of Budha is Puroraba, who is most famous. Saint Oudha is his son. His son is Naghosha, who was born from the semen of Saint Oudha.

Stanza 3
Naghosha became Indra, the king of Heaven, and remained there as king for seven lakh years and ruled the world. His son is Yayati. His son is Manadhata, who became an emperor in this world and ruled like a God King.

Stanza 4
Emperor Manadhata had six sons–Ganga, Gargya, Soma, Dibakara, Bhoja and Kadamba. They ruled this world in six different Kshatriya clans. They are famous in the four eras.

Stanza 5
Kadamba Kesari was the king of Singhal Island. He was the most powerful to rule this world. A few generations after him, King Viru was born along with seven brothers. They ruled Singhal Island with love.

Stanza 6
The eldest six brothers had no sons. Only the youngest brother had a son. Because of this Viru's mind became indifferent. He thought that a life without a son was meaningless. I must go to foreign lands leaving behind all duties of the world.

Stanza 7
The name of his Queen was Sushila. She was calm, beautiful and endowed with excellent qualities. King Viru went to her and said: 'O' queen, because I am sonless my life is meaningless. I do not want to rule anymore. It is not necessary for me.'

Stanza 8
By handing over the charge of my state in the hands of my younger brother's son, I will proceed to Nilachala Dham [Puri] (where Lord Jagannath is staying). You shall stay here. Never quarrel with my brothers.

Stanza 9
You will take care of the son of my brother just as your own life. You must be loving to all friends and relatives. You must keep my brothers happy. You must serve God and Brahmins. I am going away. Please remember me, O' my beloved wife.

Stanza 10

Hearing this Sushila was astonished. She said: O' my dear husband, what are you saying? You are my life's life. Without you my life is useless. I will leave the houses of our brothers and friends and I come along with you.

Stanza 11

At whose face shall I look as I spend my days? The house will become like a barren garden. Hearing this the king of Singhal Island became saddened and told his wife Sushila with loving words, if the wife is with the husband in a foreign land then many kinds of dangers can befall them.

Stanza 12

Wandering in foreign countries I will go to Nilagiri and see the holder of the blue wheel (Lord Jagannath). After visiting the Orissa kingdom (Odra rashtra) I will come back. So my beloved, do not be sorrowful and give me permission to go.

Stanza 13

After addressing Sushila thus, the king entered the room of his brothers' son. He clasped the child to him and showered him with kisses and then sitting down, king Viru told him, O' my dear son I am going to a foreign land.

Stanza 14

I surrender all to you as ... I have no other legal heir except you. You will take care of my queen, love her. Inform her and consult her at the time of suffering and happiness.

Stanza 15

You become the king and enjoy well. You need not to be afraid if you depend on Hari and eat His offerings (*prasad*). If you are at the side of Dharma (righteouness), you will be victorious, if you are not on the side of Dharma then your clan will be destroyed, the Earth will not tolerate it. Taking all the troubles upon yourself, rule your subjects.

Stanza 16

If the king is happy at the happiness of his subjects, the glorious flag of the king will fly in the world. At the time of need, rain comes from the Heaven and when agriculture improves, it stops raining. So, my son, if someone commits a crime then you judge the case properly and give the required punishment.

Stanza 17

Send your messenger to enquire about the right and wrong. Those who are extremely wicked and violent cut-off their heads. If you do so, you will not be judged guilty. Laxmi (Goddess of wealth) will be always be with you. After telling this the king called the secretary and explained to him everything.

Stanza 18

O' secretary hear my words. I have handed over the full charge to my son. You know everything about my past. You listen to the prayer of right men and in that way you must take care of the younger king (child).

Stanza 19

After saying this, the king performed the coronation ceremony of the Rajkumar and made him King. He informed all his subjects about it and met them in a field. He sent messengers to summon all his brothers too.

Stanza 20

The messenger went hurriedly and informed the six brothers. On hearing this, the brothers came rushing to meet the king. Saluting him they asked politely.

Stanza 21

'Where are you going O' Singhaleswar! Who has done any harm to you that you are leaving your wife and brother's son.

Stanza 22

When you have become indifferent and have decided to go, we all six brothers will also come along with you. Whatever you have decided is our fate, so give a proper judgement. Gopinath Brahmana is telling that whatever they have decided that is right.

THIRD CANTO

Musical mode 'Desakshya' [sung while driving a bullock cart]

Stanza 1

The younger brother of King Viru said: 'O' king, hear me. I will go to Nilasekhara and see Devaraj [Lord Jagannath] and salute Him.

Stanza 2

If I see Dinabandhu [the friend of poor people] Jagannath, I will be liberated. This is my main aim of going with you, O' my brother, please hear.'

Stanza 3

On hearing this, the younger brothers were also interested in accompanying. They readied their bags and baggages and hurriedly came forward to leave.

Stanza 4

They took with them a pure round pebble, each representing the idol of Gopal [Vishnu], one garland, a sword (*khanda*) and came out forming one group.

Stanza 5
Each of them rode on one white horse and uttering the name of Hari they started their journey along the road, which the people of the state saw.

Stanza 6
The people say earnestly, 'O' the king of Singhal please hear, where are you going and how shall we live without looking at our Chhatrapati (king)'.

Stanza 7
Singing your divine glory day and night we were living, now we have become helpless. To whom we shall go to now?

Stanza 8
By giving the charge of the state to your younger son you will go to foreign countries, but we the poor and hungry people of the state would belong to whom?

Stanza 9
We all will go with you and serve you and if you deny it then we will mix '19 and 1'[1] and eat it and die.

Stanza 10
Saying all this the men and women started to cry, tears from their eyes and sorrowfully they all sunk like a fish without water.

Stanza 11
Hearing the sorrowful words of his subjects King Viru said: O' my dear people, please bid us farewell smilingly so that we shall see Nilagiri and come back.

Stanza 12
By your holy kindness and our right appearance the pure, spotless Soma clan has been famous in the whole world.

Stanza 13
Tell me, I am perplexed, bid me farewell happily, so that I will come back within one year and again be with you.

Stanza 14
Here Brahmana Gopinath is telling, by giving consolation, the seven brothers went away and reached near the sea.

FOURTH CANTO

Musical mode 'Malaba' [usually sung while giving a garland to the God of the Sea, Varuna]

Stanza 1
Sitting on a boat they crossed the salty sea and reached 'Setu-Bandh' on an auspicious moment. They entered the Rameswar Temple where both Sri

Ram and Iswara Sambhu [Shiva] reside. They worshipped them and prayed for a happy journey.

Stanza 2

Shiva, the husband of Uma holds the moon on his head and river Ganga flows from his matted hair. Panchanana [Shiva] is holding the endless holy mountain. So O' God! be kind on us and give liberation. By praying like this they poured water hastily.

Stanza 3

They took *mahaprasad* [the great offering to God] and halted there for five days to serve Lord Shiva. From that place they proceeded towards the north on horseback and reached Cuttack after facing a lot of difficulties on the way.

Stanza 4

It took two days from Cuttack to Bhubaneswar. They started on a holy moment and the entire way they prayed and recited the name of Lingaraj. They worshipped the God having 15 eyes (Lingaraj).

Stanza 5

They halted for three days at Bhubaneswar before proceeding forward. On the way they saw the Sakhi Gopinath idol. After finishing their bath in the Kedar reservoir they started their journey towards Chandrabhaga happily.

Stanza 6

In Chandrabhaga they worshipped the Sun God. Then on horseback again the seven warriors went from there to Purushottam Kshetra [Puri].

Stanza 7

On the way at the eighteen canals (*athara nalas*) there were security guards who were collecting tax. 'Pay tax, or else we will not let you cross', they told the seven brothers.

Stanza 8

The brothers refused saying: O' guards, we are Rathors and good Kshatriyas and we belong to the Kadamba clan. We are not fools.

Stanza 9

We have no devotion for anyone, we do not salute anyone, we never stay under anybody's control, we are warriors only. We will only see the lotus holder [Jagannath] and return to our own native state.

Stanza 10

After doing hard labour we reached here, but by coming to this place we fell in great danger. We are not businessmen so why should we pay tax;

we have come only with a hope to see the husband of Kamala [Laxmi], Jagannath.

Stanza 11

So go and inform Gajapati that if he does not permit us then we will go back. Hearing this the guards went to Gajapati and informed him.

Stanza 12

Seven members of Kshatriyas have come and they do not agree to pay tax. They say, we are Rathors and we never pay tax, we never respect anyone, we are not servants of anyone.

Stanza 13

We only wish to see Lord Jagannath with our own eyes, otherwise we will go back to our own state. Hearing this the Gajapati of Orissa told, if they are really Rathor Kshatriyas then do this.

Stanza 14

Fix up a saw on the way and tell them to go by that way. If they go on that way by riding on horses then you will know that they are Rathor Kshatriyas of Kadamba clan.

Stanza 15

Hearing this, the guards returned and buried pillars by the side of the saw, 'Go this way if you are the Kshatriya Kumars of the Rathor clan'.

Stanza 16

Otherwise go back to your state. Gajapati has given this order. On hearing this the warriors thought sorrowfully in their mind that Jagannath has given this trouble.

Stanza 17

In the hope to see him we have covered such a long distance and now this obstacle has befallen us. If we do not go on that way then our clan will be blamed and if we go we cannot escape from death.

Stanza 18

The seven warriors thought for a while and ultimately decided to go because death seemed a better choice rather than giving blame to the clan. The Rajkumar who gives bad name to the clan, for him death is better than life.

Stanza 19

By telling so they concentrated their mind under the feet of Krishna and said: O' destroyer of sorrows, save us from this danger. If you do not save us then we will be helpless, and the name of 'Dinabandhu' will be disgraced.

Stanza 20
You saved the deer from danger, O' Murari, you saved Draupadi's chastity and O' Prabho it was a very simple work for you to destroy the large sea of Kauraba [family of Kurus] soldiers easily.

Stanza 21
O' Achuta, Kesaba, Rama, Gobinda, Hari, husband of Satyabhama, O' Madhaba Murari, O' Narayana, Hrusikesa, O' Dambodara, O' God, save us from this great danger.

Stanza 22
Otherwise you will be held responsible for this murder, we will not go back to our state. The troubles King Gajapati is giving to us, you punish him by giving the right judgement.

Stanza 23
We never go back for the fear of death. But we have come so near to Jagannath and the Gopinath is telling us that the hope is lost to see His lotus face?

FIFTH CANTO

Musical mode 'Kanada' [sung at the time husking grains]

Stanza 1
The name of Hari, King Viru sat on his horse and was blessed his brothers. Speedily ran past with his horse but fell on the saw and was immediately beheaded. His horse was torn to seeing this his brothers cried so sorrowfully that it cannot be explained, O' King.

Stanza 2
His next brother out of anger rode his horse speedily over the saw. He too fell down and was killed. Then another brother too also went on his horse on that way and fell on the saw and was killed; the next brother also rode his horse on that way and fell on the saw and died. Seeing this, the next brother ran along with his horse out of anger immediately and he too fell on the saw and was killed along with his horse.

Stanza 3
Witnessing all this, the security guards immediately ran to the remaining three brothers and said: 'Please do not ride on this way. We will go and inform the king about your borthers immediately. Your four brothers have gone to "Yamalok". You do not do this please and hurt our already sorrowful mind and heart.' Saying so the guards started immediately and met the king.

Stanza 4
O' Gajapati, king of Orissa (Orissadhiswar), please hear about the activities of the Kshatriya brothers. We killed four brothers. The remaining three

brothers were also attempting to ride their horses on that way, but we have stopped them, O' king. The four brothers who fell down there along with their horses never feared to die. They told that if they go back out of fear then their glory will be lost in the world O' king.

Stanza 5
Hearing this, Gajapati was satisfied and said, 'I will go and meet them at once and try and persuade them not to jump and also console them. Saying this the king reached them at once. Seeing the four brothers lying dead, the king too became very sorrowful. He said that the warriors had kept their glory in the world by dedicating their lives.

Stanza 6
The three brothers seeing the Gajapati king, a senior man, calmed down and saluted him and said: 'You gave us this sorrow. We all seven brothers jointly came here to see and worship Jagannath, but because of the fruits of our *karma* we failed, O' king. Four of our brothers died and the Almighty had written this in our fate to see such sorrow and sufferings O' king.'

Stanza 7
Hearing that Gajapati consoled them and said, 'Hear me O' Kshatriya heroes (*veer*), the Almighty had written it in their fate and so they went away, but why are you in distress, O' royal sons. See this world is full of illusions– our house, our friends, our brothers, etc. Who belongs to whom, for this false thing you are crying sorrowfully, O' royal sons!

Stanza 8
You cry day and night to see them. But as per their own fate (*karma*) they have left for their places. They are now calling you, which means they are pouring cold water on your sorrowful life, O' kings. King Gajapati then asked them about their genealogy and the Kshatriya qualities. Rudradev took offence at this and angrily said.

Stanza 9
O' king, we are born in the Soma clan. We are Rathor kings and very tough by nature. Our birth place and house is the Singhal Island. Staying in Kadamba clan we are ruling our state. We worship the idol of Raghunath who is our tutelary God, O' king. Raghunath is staying with us and we are serving him day and night. We never stay anywhere, nor eat anybody's rice nor do we serve to anyone, O' king.

Stanza 10
The Gajapati king of Orissa who was most powerful said: O' warrior group listen to me. You are pure Kshatriyas. O' royal sons stay with me in my

palace. I will look after you as my friends, I will give you villages and zamindaries, so that you will be serving Dinabandhu [Jagannath] daily. The royal sons refused and went with the king to Nilagiri.

Stanza 11
Entering the temple first they saw the son of Binita (Garuda), the chariot of Lord Vishnu, and they saluted him. In the western side they saw the black body (Jagannath). His strong hands were clearly visible. His lotus eyes were looking to the sorrows and sufferings, O' king. The sweet laughter in his colourful lips is driving the anger away.

Stanza 12
O' Hari, be kind to us. You are the destroyer of diseases of distressed people. O' ocean of kindness Gadadhara (one who holds the mace in his hand). In *kali juga* (era) your incarnation is that of the Bouda. You are offering boons to your devotees by opening your hands, O' Kesaba. O' Prabhu. Our sorrows are very scanty. In your strong hand the Sudarsan wheel is moving. By looking at your black face, our sorrows and sufferings are driven away and life seems saved, O' Kesaba.

Stanza 13
O' Nilamber [Balaram] you are holding the plough and the club and you are the husband of Rebati. We salute you. O' Hari, you are also known as Kampala and Haladhara. You have killed the demons called Amba, Kadamba, Pralamba, etc., and you enjoy smoking. O' Kesaba. O' the holder of mountain, be kind to us. Our sorrows and sufferings are not unknown to you. Your flag is visible in the whole world because you are uplifting the poor distressed persons, so your flag is known as *patita tarana bana*, O' Kesaba.

Stanza 14
They saluted and came out, then they ate the offerings of God Jagannath, because their invincible desire has been fulfilled on seeing Jagannath. But, only due to the sad demise of their four brothers their mind was full of sorrow. Outside the boundaries they saluted once again and they went and saw the Gajapati's house. Here the writer Gopinath is telling, being distressed O' Madhuhari [Jagannath] save me. O' [Kesaba].

SIXTH CANTO

Musical mode 'Ramkeri' [sung while riding a horse]

Stanza 1
While halting for three days at Srikshetra, the Kshatriya Kumars thought in their minds, 'What work is their any more in our life'.

Stanza 2

We came by saying 'All seven brothers would now come back, losing four brothers how can we go back'?

Stanza 3

What will we say when people of the state ask us about them? How will we see with our own eyes queen Sushila's sorrowful state?

Stanza 4

Thinking like this the Rajkumars gave up the idea of going back home and instead they wandered about Orissa happily.

Stanza 5

At first they visited Jajpur town and the three Rajkumars saw and worshipped Goddess Biraja.

Stanza 6

Then they reached Singhbhum and one of them was made a king there, because he had killed a lion. He named his clan as Kesari and happily settled there.

Stanza 7

With a very sorrowful heart, the Kesari king made his next brother the zamindar of Saranda.

Stanza 8

Only Rajkumar Pratap Rudra remained. He was spending his time in much distress at Singhbhum town.

Stanza 9

Once he quarrelled with his two brothers and in a distressed state of mind left that place.

Stanza 10

He had heard that in Bonai town, Baneswar Linga has been established, and when someone is in distress the priests give offerings (*prasad*).

Stanza 11

So he decided to go and worship Baneswar. At first he came across the beautiful sight of river Brahmani.

Stanza 12

The holy fountain is flowing towards the northern side. The clean white scented sand is looking beautiful.

Stanza 13

In the midst of stones inside the water, water is flowing, producing a sweet sound as if a music player is playing his musical instrument.

Stanza 14

The side of the river bank is filled with flowers and fruits and some flowering plants having creepers have touched the river water.

Stanza 15

The birds sitting are producing *hulhili* sounds which is very sweet to hear and is like the sound of the great trumpet.

Stanza 16

In that beautiful flower garden the grass is beautifully decorated as if done by the Almighty for the pleasure of visitors.

Stanza 17

Seeing it, the Rajkumar felt very happy and after crossing the river he started going to the western side of the bank of the river Brahmani.

Stanza 18

Seeing the temple he understood that it is the abode of God Biswanath [Baneswar/Shiva], and hurried to reach the spot.

Stanza 19

Pratap Rudra worshipped Baneswar of Bonai with the river water and flowers and took shelter beneath the feet of Baneswar.

Stanza 20

He halted there for a few days, eating sweet edible roots and serving Baneswar day and night.

Stanza 21

At that time Banasur was the king of Bonai State and everyday he was worshipping Lord Baneswar.

Stanza 22

The second ruler was a Bhuiyan zamindar. He was in-charge of all the forest areas of Bonai and took care of it.

Stanza 23

One day Banasur saw the royal son inside the temple and many things crossed his mind.

Stanza 24

He was sure that by serving Hara [Baneswar] in such a dedicated manner one day this royal son would become the king. Considering me his enemy he may drive me out from this place.

Stanza 25

Definitely my enemy has come to this place and is staying here. By saying this he charged towards him with a sword in order to kill him.

Stanza 26
Seeing a Kadamba tree nearby the Rajkumar quickly hid inside the hollow of the tree and while Banasur was pursuing him.

Stanza 27
A peacock who was grazing nearby finding the Rajkumar hiding in the tree fled from there.

Stanza 28
During his flight the peacock disfigured the footprints of the Rajkumar, and made the field plain and himself hid inside a dense creeper.

Stanza 29
Just at that time Banasur reached that place. He searched for the Rajkumar everywhere but not finding him he was fed up.

Stanza 30
Where could my enemy have hidden, he thought? I did not get anywhere, so I know the husband of Parbati (Shiva) has himself kept him.

Stanza 31
By saying this Banasur returned came back to his palace disappointed.

Stanza 32
At this time the peacock came out from behind the dense creeper and danced and sang happily.

Stanza 33
By raising his head Pratap Dev saw that the peacock has hidden (mixed) his footprint and was dancing happily.

Stanza 34
If the peacock had not erased the footprints, the wicked Banasur would have surely caught him.

Stanza 35
Surely he would have killed him, so out of gratitude he kept the sign of the peacock on his head.

Stanza 36
Because the peacock had saved the first man of Kadamba clan, the peacock sign still continues in the Kadamba royal emblem.

Stanza 37
Since the Rajkumar was able to save his life by hiding in the hollow space of a Kadamba tree, people of the Kadamba clan never cut the Kadamba tree.

Stanza 38
From that day onwards they have stopped cutting the Kadamba tree and also discontinued wearing the Kadamba flower garland on their necks.

Stanza 39
Out of fear, the royal son remained hidden, in the hollow of the Kadamba tree and the peacock kept vigil the whole night under that Kadamba tree.

Stanza 40
Staying there in fasting he concentrated his mind on Hara [Baneswar]. Seeing his sorrowful state the husband of Girija was pleased with him.

Stanza 41
In the midnight in a dream Baneswar told him, O' Rajkumar hear me, tomorrow you shall be the king of Bonai State.

Stanza 42
The wicked Banasur has became prideful and he has now started killing his own subjects. So tomorrow I shall make you the king by driving him out from this place.

Stanza 43
Only you will be in my service, day and night. So without any hesitation, come to my temple.

Stanza 44
By telling this Panchanana [Baneswar] vanished and in the same night he met the Bhuiyan king in a dream.

Stanza 45
In the dream he told him there is a Rajkumar in my temple. Tomorrow you shall make him the king of Bonai State.

Stanza 46
If you do not make him king tomorrow and complete his coronation ceremony then I shall have to destroy your race.

Stanza 47
Then Baneswar entered into the palace of Banasur and told the king, tomorrow early morning you must leave the Bonai State.

Stanza 48
You will go to Baranasi [Varanasi] and stay there as a 'Bhairab' or else you will be killed.

Stanza 49
After telling this Baneswar entered back into his temple, the Brahmin Gopinath is telling, there will be a new king.

SEVENTH CANTO

Musical mode 'Basanta mangala' [sung during the beautiful spring season]

Stanza 1
Pratap Dev arose from the hollow space of the Kadamba tree. After getting the orders of Baneswar his sleep was broken.

Stanza 2
For a moment he has silent and quite bewildered. But he could know that definitely Panchanana [Baneswar] has been kind enough on me.

Stanza 3
Early morning dreams unually turn out to be true. And the dream seems as if the events are happening in reality.

Stanza 4
I must go, even if the demon will kill me, this he thought and came out from the hollow of the Kadamba tree.

Stanza 5
Thinking like this the Rajkumar came out of the hollow of the Kadamba tree and immediately entered the temple.

Stanza 6
Banasur rose at once as he could know that this was the furious order of Lord Baneswar.

Stanza 7
When Banasur was going towards the temple, the husband of Uma [Baneswar] held him back with his left hand.

Stanza 8
Roughly Baneswar told him: O' Banasur go from this place and at once remain in Kasi Kshetra in the garb of a Bhairab.

Stanza 9
The world cannot tolerate your oppression anymore. Taking your family immediately go away from this place.

Stanza 10
Hearing this Banasur took his family and fled to Baranasi [Varanasi] and remained there.

Stanza 11
He is still there under the clutches of Bhairab and the husband of Uma [Baneswar] accepting his devotion has kept him there.

Stanza 12
Baneswar had given him a boon to be immortal, so he took him to his place so that he will be worshipped in the world.

Stanza 13
So the Bhuiyan zamindar without making any delay came out because he knew that Chakradhar [Baneswar] had ordered him in the dream.

Stanza 14
One who will be in the temple I will make him king, and thinking like this he went towards the Shivalaya (temple).

Stanza 15
He saw that Pratap Dev was inside the temple and was worshipping Baneswar with full devotion.

Stanza 16
He told him that Panchanana [Baneswar] had ordered him in the dream to make him the king in Bonai state.

Stanza 17
We will go now and first we will select a place and after that we will construct a fort there.

Stanza 18
While discussing this both came out of the temple and their eyes fell on the bank of Brahmani River which was looking most beautiful.

Stanza 19
On all four sides there was water and in the middle of it there was an elevated land filled with many trees and creepers.

Stanza 20
Finding that place as suitable they constructed a fort there and also brought along some subjects.

Stanza 21
At first the great royal court (*durbar*) was constructed, where this royal clan is still functioning.

Stanza 22
Pratap Rudra Dev became king and sat there on the throne. Seven idols made of clay of the state have been kept there.

Stanza 23
In this way the maternal uncle Mithuna reached the zodiac sign (*rashi*) Sagittarius–9th sign (Dhanu) and then came the day of Pousa Purnima.

Stanza 24
That zamindar in order to make him the king arranged all the formalities of the coronation ceremony of the new king.

Stanza 25
They took Pratap Dev and made him sit on the throne of the Bonai king and after decorating him, handed over to him the charge of the Bonai State.

Stanza 26
They put a mark of vermilion on his forehead and at first they raised the umbrella in the name of Baneswar and worshipped Him.

Stanza 27
They then took that umbrella and raised it on the head of the king, and all saluted him by addressing him as the king of Bonai.

Stanza 28
The general public unitedly uttered his victorious sound chanting 'Sri Pratap Rudra Dev the king of kings'.

Stanza 29
As the zamindar has made him king all are worshipping him by addressing him 'Matiswar', the king of Bonai State.

Stanza 30
The King Rudradev sat on the throne and surrounded by many kings he ruled the state.

Stanza 31
By cutting the forests he established villages and constructed new corn fields for cultivation.

Stanza 32
He married the daughter of the king of Bhanjanagar. She possessed all the good qualities of a queen and loved him greatly.

Stanza 33
He developed friendship with the kings of Gangpur, Bhanjabhumi, Samalaipur, Surguja, Khadial and Swarnapur.

Stanza 34
And also developed friendship with the kings of Patna, Bamanda and the states of Singhbhum and ruled peacefully and happily.

Stanza 35
His brothers' sons are staying in Keonjhar, Bhanjabhumi, Bamanda, Patna and Sambalpur which they decided as best places.

Stanza 36

Besides these states, his brothers' sons of this clan are not staying in any other state.

Stanza 37

Gopinath, the Rajpurohit of that clan, has blessed him with a long life and is working under him.

EIGHTH CANTO

Musical mode 'Chakrakeli' [sung while playing by rotation]

Stanza 1

The name of the zamindar was Indra, who made Rudra Dev a king.

Stanza 2

Only this much he begged from the king, 'In my name, you become king'.

Stanza 3

By accepting his words, Pratap Rudra Dev became king by adding the title of 'Indradev' to his name.

Stanza 4

He ruled Bonai State for 34 years and managed himself by tolerating too many sorrows, etc., as per his *karma* (fate).

Stanza 5

His son Dinamani Dev became the king after him and he also served Sadashiva [Baneswar].

Stanza 6

At that time, one Kolha was living in Jharagada, whose name was Mahabir.

Stanza 7

He had six brothers who were rogues and criminals and were not obeying the king.

Stanza 8

The king decided to kill all six of them. So he kept himself well equipped with weapons always.

Stanza 9

As soon as king Dinamani got the information, he killed Mahabir.

Stanza 10

He killed two more persons staying there and knowing this the other four fled.

Stanza 11

The king followed them and intercepted them at Gharbuda.

Stanza 12
He beheaded two of them and threw their bodies in the forest.

Stanza 13
He followed the other two immediately with high speed and killed another of them in village Jangada.

Stanza 14
Chandra managed to flee and entered the Pallahada forest.

Stanza 15
The king then ran into the forest, caught him and raised his sword to kill him.

Stanza 16
Seeing that Chandra fell down at his feet, and said, O' king please do not kill me, I have something to tell you.

Stanza 17
The three persons whom you killed in the fort (*garh*), please worship them in your palace.

Stanza 18
When you are in grave danger, they will come out as warriors and save your clan as well as your state.

Stanza 19
In my name keep your royal insignia on your head, and happily rule the state without any obstacle.

Stanza 20
After granting my request you can behead me, then there will be no danger to your clan.

Stanza 21
As he told like this, his head was cut by king Dinamani Dev, who then returned back.

Stanza 22
The king believed in the words of Chandra and worshipped the three brothers in his palace.

Stanza 23
So he kept 'Chandra Dev Pata' as a royal sign on his head and ruled Bonai State for 63 years.

Stanza 24
After him his son Madhusudana became the king of Bonai State.

Stanza 25
Once a fisherman named Gobinda attempted to kill the king.

Stanza 26
He entered the king's palace by force, and caught hold of the king's hand.

Stanza 27
He said, 'I must kill you, see I am holding a sword in my hand'.

Stanza 28
While he was telling all this the king overpowered him and snatched away his sword and attempted to kill him with the same sword.

Stanza 29
Gobinda started trembling with fear and said, please spare me this time.

Stanza 30
Or else bearing my name you will be king and rule your state.

Stanza 31
By telling this he started running away, but the king held him by following swiftly.

Stanza 32
In the north-west corner in the forest when a storm was raging the king killed him with the sword which he was holding.

Stanza 33
As yet that place is having a sign of 'fisherman killing' (*keuta maruni*) and nowadays people refer to that place as 'keuta maruni'.

Stanza 34
He accepted the words of Gobinda and kept 'Gobinda Dev Pata' in his name.

Stanza 35
In this way the Gobinda Dev Pata continued for three generations and Kshatriya kings ruled the state quite ruthlessly.

Stanza 36
He ruled ... years two months and nine days and left this world and reached his place in the other world.

Stanza 37
In this way three generations passed and the Brahmin Gopinath composed these cantos.

NINTH CANTO

Musical mode 'Malaba' [usually sung while giving a garland to the God of the sea 'Varuna' and nowadays in this musical mode sung in the Island 'Malwa']

Stanza 1

The son of king Dinamani was Ramchandra Indra Dev. He became king and ruled eight years three months in Bonai State.

Stanza 2

Then his son Kirtibas Indra Dev became the king and he ruled ... years two months in Bonai State.

Stanza 3

Paramesti Chandra Dev was the son of Kirtibas Indradev, he became the king after his father and ruled for fifteen years having very cordial relations with his subjects.

Stanza 4

Mukunda Govind Dev was his son. He became king for seven years two months.

Stanza 5

Giridhari Suradev was his son. He ruled well by taking the responsibilities of the Bonai State for twenty-two years and nine months.

Stanza 6

Then Dotmakurtidhar Sasadhar Dev ruled forty years before departing from this world.

Stanza 7

The Dambarudhar Gobinda Dev became the king and ruled Bonai State for six years one month.

Stanza 8

Then his son Biswaswar Indra Dev became king and he ruled for fifty-one years then he went to the other world leaving his body behind.

Stanza 9

Then his son Nilakantha Chandra Dev became king and ruled for twenty-three years in Bonai State.

Stanza 10

Then his son Narayan Govinda Dev became king and ruled for ten years and one month.

Stanza 11
Then his son Hrusikesh Indra Dev became king and ruled for twenty-three years and two months.

Stanza 12
Then his son Jadumani Chandra Dev became king and he ruled for twenty-five years.

Stanza 13
Then his son Giridhari Govinda Dev became king and he ruled for seven years before he went to the other world leaving his body behind.

Stanza 14
Then his son Mukunda Alyaya Raj Dev became king and he ruled for fifty-two years.

Stanza 15
Then his son Tribikram Chandra Dev became king and he ruled for more than twenty years.

Stanza 16
Then his son Kumar Gobinda Dev Kampal became king he ruled only for four years one month.

Stanza 17
After him Indra Dev Biranchi became king and he ruled for fifty-seven years carefully.

Stanza 18
Then his son Dhaba Sudhansu Dev became king and ruled for more than twenty years.

Stanza 19
Then his son Basudev holding the 'Pata' of Gobinda Dev and he ruled the earth.

Stanza 20
He ruled for fifty-five years and nine months and leaving behind everything went to the other world.

Stanza 21
Then his son Mahindra Dev became king and ruled the state by holding the title of Bajradhar.

Stanza 22
Being a king he ruled for forty years, eight months and three days before he went to the other world.

Stanza 23
Then his son Gadadhar Chandra Dev ruled for eighteen years.

Stanza 24
Then his son Makaradwaja Gobinda Dev became king and ruled for seven years before expiring.

Stanza 25
During his reign there were big cracks on the walls, deep pools, ditches and tanks. The fort was covered in four sides.

Stanza 26
Only there were three gates on three sides, and by closing them, all were safe.

Stanza 27
The name of the first door was Khetrapal, and one *veer* (hero) named Dwarasuni was the watchman of the the gate.

Stanza 28
He is still worshipped there. This is the glory of the king Makaradwaja Dev.

Stanza 29
By the second big door there was a great warrior, he was watching there along with his brother.

Stanza 30
By the third door they established Goddess Andhari, and the name of that door was Andhari.

Stanza 31
In the fort there was no fear of enemy of any kind, and all the people were living happily inside.

Stanza 32
His son Indradev Paramananda became king after him and he ruled the state for fifty-six years and three months.

Stanza 33
His second queen's son Chandra Dev became king after him and he ruled the state twenty-three years two months.

Stanza 34
His son Purusottam Dev by holding the Pata of Gobinda Dev took over the charge of the state and became king.

Stanza 35
Then his son Purandar Dev became king as per the old customs and manners and ruled his subjects.

Stanza 36
It was first decided that Purandar Dev would hold the 'Gobinda Dev Pata' and by sitting on the throne he will rule his subjects.

Stanza 37
But whosoever the king who was holding the 'Gobinda Dev Pata' did not rule too long in ruling and many of them went under the control of 'Kala', the king of Death.

Stanza 38
Out of that fear they have stopped holding the 'Gobinda Dev Pata' anymore, and sitting on the Pata of Indradev they started completing their coronation ceremony.

Stanza 39
From that day onwards the 'Gobinda Dev Pata' was stopped, and both the Indra and Chandra Pata were taken into consideration.

Stanza 40
He (Purandar Dev), the king ruled the state for fifty-seven years two months and one day and then he went away to his place by leaving this world.

Stanza 41
After thirty-one patas (generations) this system was stopped and Brahmin Gopinath composed this in cantos.

TENTH CANTO

Musical mode 'Bangalashree' [Bengali tune sung in praise of the Goddess Laxmi]

Stanza 1
Padmanava Dev Chandradev is the son of Purandar Dev who became the king of Bonai State after him. He ruled for fifteen years, eleven days.

Stanza 2
His son Kumar Indradev Veer Padmalochan became king after him. He followed the qualities of his father and ruled for twenty years and three months.

Stanza 3
After him Debandra Pratap Chandradev became king, and ruled for nine years two months and three days.

Stanza 4
Then his son Kumar Indradev Veer Kadamba Kesari became king, he ruled for fourteen years and nine months.

Stanza 5
Then Ramchandradev Nrupa Indra became king, he ruled his subjects for seventeen years and fifteen days.

Stanza 6
Since the time of his forefather Kumari Devi was their tutelary goddess in the northern side of the fort, and her temple was constructed on the banks of the Brahmani River.

Stanza 7
Her idol was established in that temple. She was a most powerful goddess and he was worshipping her with full devotion by keeping his sword there.

Stanza 8
The king of Keonjhar sent his spies and the sword was stolen by them. Being antagonistic towards one another, war took place between the two kings.

Stanza 9
King Sekhar of Keonjhar was defeated in the battle and out of fear of his life he brought back that sword to Ramachandra, the king of Bonai.

Stanza 10
From that day he did not keep the sword in Kumari Temple and out of fear of the spies the sword was kept in his palace.

Stanza 11
Then Veer Jadumani Indradev, the son of Ramchandra, became king. He constructed one temple near Bonai and established Jagannath idol there.

Stanza 12
He had brought the Salagram pebble of his tutelary god from Raghunathpur and kept it carefully in Jagannathpur for worshipping.

Stanza 13
In order to perform the Gundicha Jatra [car festival of Lord Jagannath] he had given property of two villages to the temple. He ruled ..... years two months ten days and left for the other world.

Stanza 14
Then Udayanarayan Dev, the son of Jadunath, became king by holding the title of Chandradev and continued twenty-four years on the throne of Bonai.

Stanza 15

During the reign of his son Kalia Chandadev Indradev, there took place a war in between Bamanda and Bonai when there was boundary dispute between them.

Stanza 16

By entering the fort of Bonai, the king of Bamanda was attacking the people and was taking away their properties, but the king of Bonai attacked them and they fled.

Stanza 17

Out of fear the soldiers of Bamanda king left their royal umbrella and till now it is worshipped by all the people of Bonai.

Stanza 18

The soldiers who remained were slain by the Bonai soldiers and their heads were seen rolling on the ground after which they fell under the edge of a tank and as such the name of that tank has been kept as 'munda gada bandh'.

Stanza 19

Only the king of Bamanda fled out of fear for his life and the same dispute for boundary area is yet remaining between Bamanda and Bonai.

Stanza 20

Kalachandra Dev ruled as a king for forty-four years and eighteen days before he left this earth forever.

Stanza 21

Sri Kalia Chandra Kumar by holding the title of Sri Birakeswari Deba Indradev and by taking over the charge of the state ruled smoothly.

Stanza 22

He ruled for a period of fourteen years eleven months and seven days and fell on the trap of 'Kala' (the Death) and went away.

Stanza 23

His son Kumar Balunkeswar Dev Indradev became king and ruled the state for twenty-two years, seven months and nine days.

Stanza 24

His son Kumar Veer Baneswar Sasadhar Dev became king after him and he ruled for twenty-nine years and eleven months.

Stanza 25

Then his son Govinda Indradev became king and ruled for thirty-three years before gone away to the other world.

Stanza 26

His son Kumar Narahari Dev Chandradev became king after him. He ruled Bonai State for fourteen years seven months and nine days.

Stanza 27

During the reign of his son Gopinath Indra Dev, there arose a boundary dispute between Nagara and Bonai.

Stanza 28

But that dispute was resolved when the king of Gangpur became a mediator and he suggested pillars be constrncted to determine the line of control.

Stanza 29

The king Gopinath Dev ruled for twenty-three years two months and six days before leaving this world he and going away to the other world.

Stanza 30

His son Ram Kari Chandra Dev became the king of Bonai for a period of four years and then fell in the hands of 'Kala' (the death) and went away.

Stanza 31

His son Raghunath Indradev became the king of Bonai and ruled for fourteen years three months and six days.

Stanza 32

Then his son Bhikari Chandra Dev became the king. During his period he measured the area of the State.

Stanza 33

He established the *linga* in Kupeswar temple, but he had not constructed the temple. His Dewan's friend had constructed the temple.

Stanza 34

He had arranged landed property for the temple. He ruled for seven years and then left this world and went to the other world.

Stanza 35

Then his son Veer Pitamber Indradev became the king. He established a Brahmin locality and gave them villages in lieu of worship in the temple.

Stanza 36

But in exchange [for the temple worship—authors] he gave the village Pitamberpur, he ruled for twenty-three years and died.

Stanza 37

Then his son Bhagirathi Dev Chandradev became the king and he ruled for seventeen years and died.

Stanza 38
Then his son Sibanarayan Indradev became the king. He gave Sibanarayan sasan [village] to Gangagarva (the son of Ganga).

Stanza 39
He established Brahmin villages and ruled there with full devotion. He ruled twenty-nine years two months and six days and then expired.

Stanza 40
Then Chandra Sekhar Chandradev became king. He ruled for thirteen years and then expired.

Stanza 41
Then the son of Chandra Sekhar, Kumar Sridhar Indradev became king. He ruled for thirty-three years and then expired.

Stanza 42
Then his son Kumar Dileswardev Chandradev became king. He ruled for three years and three months and died.

Stanza 43
Sri Dharanindhar Indradev became the king of Bonai in the year 1901. He was a very kind king.

Stanza 44
Here the writer expressed his inability to describe the clan of King Dharanidhar Indradev and with whatever information he had got, he went on writing.

Stanza 45
Here the writer prays that he may kindly be excused if he has made any mistake, like a swan drinking only milk and leaving the water behind (the reader should pick the best parts and ignore the mistakes).

Stanza 46
The writer is again telling that if he will visit foreign countries then the learned people should help him, he is asking for this repeatedly to the king.

Stanza 47
He is praying to Baneswar who is holding a trident to bless the king Dharanidhar Indradev and how he will acquire unfailing glory.

Stanza 48
He is again praying to the Goddess of Learning [Saraswati] to sit on the tongue of the king and let the glorious flag of Indradev fly from country to country.

Stanza 49

He is again praying to Hari to bless king Dharanidhar Indradev and he wishes him a long life.

Stanza 50

At last the writer has a desire to submit under the feet of the king and Brahmin Gopinath composed the cantos giving blessing to king.

THE END

Assisted by: Kabi Pradhan (Kisan Caste)
Sri Gangadhar Rout,
Village: Similia,
PO: Manjuri,
Dist.: Baleswar   Dated 24.02.39

NOTE

1. 19+1 = 20 – 20 in Oriya is *bisa*, and *bisa* also means poison.

CHAPTER V

କାଦମ୍ବ ଗାଥା

ଉତ୍ସର୍ଗ ପତ୍ର

ମହିମା ସାଗର ଗୁଣିଗଣ ଅଗ୍ରପୁଜ୍ୟ ।
ବଣାଇଁ ଦୁର୍ଗ ନରେଶ ଶ୍ରୀ ଧରଣୀଧର ।
ଇନ୍ଦ୍ରଦେବ ପଦଧ୍ୱଜା ଉଡୁଛି ଜଗତେ ।
ଶାନ୍ତ ଗୁଣେ ସାଗର ର ସମତା ଯାହାର ।
ନିତାନ୍ତ ଅର୍ଥ ବିହୀନ ଗରିବ ସନ୍ତାନ ।
କିଧନେ କରିବି ପୂଜା ଛାମୁଙ୍କ ପୟରେ ।
କେବଳ ଭକ୍ତି କୁସୁମ ସ୍ନେହ ଚନ୍ଦନକୁ ।
ଅର୍ପଣ କରିବା ଆସେ ସେହି ପୂଜ୍ୟନାମେ ।
ବହୁ ଆଗ୍ରହ ଥିବାରୁ ତବ ବଂଶାବଳୀ ।
ଛାନ୍ଦ ରୁପେ ବିରଚନ କରୁଅଛି ମୁହିଁ ।
ନାହିଁ ବିଦ୍ୟା ବୁଧିମୋର ତୋଷ କରିବାକୁ ।
ଏକେ ଶ୍ୱୟଂ ରାଜକବି ବିଦ୍ୟାର ଆଗାର ।
କେବଳ ପବିତ୍ର ନାମେ କରି ଉତ୍ସର୍ଗଣ ।
ଏ ଭକ୍ତି ପୁଷ୍ପ ଚନ୍ଦନ ଦେଲି ଶ୍ରୀ ପଦରେ ।
ଦୋଷା ଦୋଷ ଥିଲେ ତାହା କ୍ଷମା କରିବାକୁ ।
ଏକାନ୍ତ ବିନିତ ଚିତ୍ତେ କଲି ନିବେଦନ ।

ଅନୁଗତ

ରାଜ ପୁରୋହୀତ ଗୋପିନାଥ ମିଶ୍ର

ପ୍ରଥମ ଛାନ୍ଦ

ରାଗ – ବସନ୍ତ ବରାଡ଼ି

ଜୟ ଜୟ ବିଘ୍ନ ବିନାଶନ ଗଜାନନ ।
ଯୋଗେଶ ପରମାନନ୍ଦ ପାର୍ବତୀ ନନ୍ଦନ ॥ ୧ ॥
ମହା ବ୍ରହ୍ମ ଯୋଗେଶ ସିନ୍ଦୁରେ ମୁଖମଣ୍ଡି ।
ଜୟ ଜୟ ଶ୍ରୀ ଚନ୍ଦ୍ର ଶେଖର ଦେବ ଖଣ୍ଡି ॥୨॥
ଦେବ ଯୁଦ୍ଧେ ବନ୍ଧ ଯହୁଁ ନୋହିଲା ତ୍ରୀପୁର ।
ତବ ବୁଦ୍ଧି ବଳେ ନାଶ କଲେ ଦେବ ହର ॥୩॥
ତୋଶେବର ଦେଲେ ତହୁଁ ଶିବଦେବ ରାଜା ।
ସକଳ ଭୁବନେ ତେଣୁ ପାଉଅଛୁ ପୂଜା ॥୪॥
ଗିରିଜା ନନ୍ଦନ ସତରଜ ତମସ୍ଥାନ ।
ଯୋଗେ ମହାଯୋଗି ସଦା ନନ୍ଦର ନନ୍ଦନ ॥୫॥
ଚୈତନ୍ୟ ପୂରୂଷ ତୁ ଅଜଣା ଯୋଗେଲୟ ।
ଶରଣ ରକ୍ଷଣ ସର୍ବ ଜନେ ତୁ ସହାୟ ॥୬॥
କରୁଣାମୟ ପତାକା ଶରଣ ବିରଧୁ ।
ସଂସାର ଜନଙ୍କ ତୁ କରୁଣାମୟ ସିନ୍ଧୁ ॥୭॥
ବିସ୍ତାର ଉଦର ତୋର ଜ୍ଞାନ ଯେ ଅସଂଖ୍ୟ ।
ପୃଥୁଳ ଉଦର ଯେ ଅଭୟ ପିଙ୍ଗକାକ୍ଷ ॥୮॥
ଶିଖାଖଣ୍ଡ ମଉଳି ବତିଶ ଗୁଣେ କଳା ।
ତାଣ୍ଡବ ରସନାୟକ ନୃତ୍ୟ ରଙ୍ଗ ଭୋଳା ॥୯॥
କର ଅନୁଗ୍ରହ ମୋତେ ବାମଦେବ ସୁତ ।
କହିବି କଦମ୍ବବଂଶ ବଂଶାନୁ ଚରିତ ॥୧୦॥

ନମାମି ଅମ୍ବିକା ସୁତ ତାତ ପଂଚାନନ ।
କ୍ଷୀଣ ଶଶୀ କଳାଧର ବୃଷଭ ବାହନ ॥୧୧॥
ଅନ୍ଧକ ନାଶନ ଜୟ ମଦନ ଅଇରି ।
.....ଗେ ବ୍ୟାଘ୍ରାମ୍ବର ପାଂଶୁ ସୁର ନଦୀଧାରି ॥୧୨॥
ଧାତାବରେ ସାଗର ତନୟ ଜଳନ୍ଧର ।
ତ୍ରୀପୁର ବିଜୟୀ ହୋଇ କରିଲା ସମର ॥୧୩॥
....ଜ ଗଣ ଘେନିରଣେ କରିଲ ବିନାଶ ।
ମହିଭାର ନାଶି ରକ୍ଷା କରିଛ ତ୍ରୀବଶ ॥ ୧୪ ॥
... ହ ଭାନୁ ଭାନୁ ଭାନୁ ନେତ୍ର ଜଟାଧର ।
ତ୍ରୀଶୁଳ ଡମ୍ବରୁ ଧାରୀ ଉମାପତି ହର ॥ ୧୫ ॥
.... ମ୍ଭି ଦକ୍ଷ ଜଜ୍ଞେ ଯହୁଁ ନକଲା ବରଣ ।
ରାଗେ ଉମା ପିତ୍ରାଳୟେ କରିଲେ ଗମନ ॥୧୬ ॥
ବହୁ ଅପମାନ ଯହୁଁ ଦେଲେ ପ୍ରଜାପତି ।
ଜଜ୍ଞ ହୁତାଶନେ ପ୍ରାଣ ବିଶର୍ଜୀଲେ ସତୀ ॥ ୧୭ ॥
ସେହିରାଗେ ଦକ୍ଷପ୍ରଜାପତି ମୁଣ୍ଡହାଣି ।
ଛାଗ ମସ୍ତକ ଲଗାଇ ହେଲେ ଶୂଳପାଣି ॥ ୧୮ ॥
କ୍ରୋଧ ହୋଇ ଶାଶୁ ଆଗେ ଦେଖାଇଲ ଅଣ୍ଡ ।
ସେ ଅଣ୍ଡେ ପୁଜିଲେ ତେଣୁ ଅଶେଷ ବ୍ରହ୍ମାଣ୍ଡ ॥୧୯॥
କିରାତ ରୁପେ ଅର୍ଜୁନ ଗଣ୍ଡାବଧ କଲା ।
ଧନୁ ହୁଳ ବେକେ ଦେଇ ଶୂନ୍ୟେ ବୁଲାଇଲା ॥୨୦॥
ସନ୍ତୋଷ ହୋଇଣ ପାଶୁପତ ଅକ୍ଷତୃଣ ।
.........ବର ସହ କରିଲ ପ୍ରଦାନ ॥୨୧॥

ଉଷା ହରଣେ ଯାଦବେ ବିବାଦି ହୋଇଲ ।
ସମର କରିଣ ବାଣାସୁରେ ରକ୍ଷାକଲ ॥୨୨॥
କାମ ବିନାଶନେ ତେଜ୍ୟା କରି କପିଳାଶ ।
କାଶି କ୍ଷେତ୍ରେ ବିଜୟ କରିଛ ବିଶ୍ୱବାସ ॥୨୩॥
ବାରାଣସି ପୁରେ ବାଣା ତାଣ୍ଡବ ନୃତ୍ୟରେ ।
ସନ୍ତୋଷ କରିଣ ଥିଲା ପତ୍ନି ସହିତରେ ॥୨୪॥
ସେ ତୋଷେ କହିଲ ବର ମାଗ ବାଣାସୁର ।
ପୂର୍ବରୁ ତୋ ତ୍ରୀଜିବୀ ହୋଇଛି ଦେହତୋର ॥୨୫॥
କହଇ ଶୃଣିତାଧୀପ ଶୁଣ ତ୍ରିଲୋଚନ ।
ତେବେ ମୋପୂରକୁ ଦେବ କରନ୍ତୁ ଗମନ ॥୨୬॥
ଇଷ୍ଟଦେବ ପୁରେରଖି ସେବାମୁଁ କରିବି ।
ଚରଣେ ଶରଣ ପସି କୃତାର୍ଥ ହୋଇବି ॥୨୭॥
ତଥାସ୍ତୁ ବୋଲି ଧୂର୍ଜଟି କହିଲେ ବାଣାକୁ ।
ଅଗ୍ରେ ଅଗ୍ରେ ଜାତକରି ଚଳତୋ ପୁରକୁ ॥୨୮॥
ତୋ ନୁପୁର ନାମ ଶୁଣି ଜିବି ପଛେ ମୁହିଁ ।
ବିଳମ୍ବ ନକରି ବାଣା ଚଳ ବେଗହୋଇ ॥୨୯॥
ଶୁଣି ବାଣାସୁର ବୀର କରିଲା ଗମନ ।
ପଛେ ବିଯେକଲେ ବଳଘେନି ପଂଚାନନ ॥୩୦॥
ନୁପୁର ଶବଦେ ବୃଷ ଗତିକରି ଗଲା ।
ଶୃଣିତ ନଦରେ ଯାଇ ପ୍ରବେଶ ହୋଇଲା ॥୩୧॥
ଉତ୍ତର ବାହିନୀ ବ୍ରାହ୍ମୀ ନଦୀ ପୂର୍ବ ତୀରେ ।
ଗଙ୍ଗାସମ ନଦୀନୀର ଭାବିଲେ ଶଙ୍କରେ ॥୩୨॥

ବୋଇଲେ ଏ ଭଲସ୍ଥାନ ନିର୍ଜନ ଶ୍ମଶାନ ।
ତୀର୍ଥ ସମ ସ୍ଥାନଦେଖି ରହିଲେ ଈଶାନ ।।୩୩।।
ବୃଷର ଘଂଟି ଶବଦ ଯହୁଁ ନଶୁଣିଲା ।
ଲେଉଟୀଣ ବାଣାବୀର ପଛକୁ ଚାହିଁଲା ।।୩୪।।
ବୋଇଲେ ଶଙ୍କର ବାଣା ଲେଉଟି ଚାହିଁଲୁ ।
ଏହିଠାରେ ଜାଣ ଆମ୍ଭେ ନିଶ୍ଚୟ ରହିଲୁଁ ।।୩୫।।
ଉତ୍‌ତମ ସ୍ଥାନଏଠାରେ ରହିବା ଉଚିତ ।
ବ୍ରାହ୍ମୀତୀର ଶ୍ମଶାନ ଏସ୍ଥାନ ଆନନ୍ଦିତ ।।୩୬।।
ତୋହର ନାମାନୁସାରେ ଏହିଠାରେ ରହି ।
. . . . ଣ ଇଶ୍ୱର ନାମକୁ ବୁଲାଇବି ମୁହିଁ ।।୩୭।।
ତୋ ନାମ ଧରିଯେ ମୋତେ ପୂଜନ କରିବ ।
ଅଇଶ୍ୱର୍ଯ୍ୟ ଫଳପାଇ ମୋପୁରେ ରହିବ ।।୩୮।।
ଯାଅ ବାଣାସୁର ଏବେ ମୋହର ବାସକୁ ।
ବୋଲି ତୋଷି ପଠାଇଣ ଦେଲ ଅସୁରକୁ ।।୩୯।।
ତାହାର ଭକ୍ତିରେ ରହି ଶୁଣିତ ନବରେ ।
ବିଖ୍ୟାତ ହୋଇଛି ନାମ ଜଗତ ମଧ୍ୟରେ ।।୪୦।।
ଏହିରୁପେ ଜଣାଇଁ ଦୁର୍ଗରେ ବାଣେସର ।
. . . ପ ଭୁପଗଣେ ରକ୍ଷାକର ନିରନ୍ତର ।।୪୧।।
ଆହେ ଗଙ୍ଗାଧର ହର ପାର୍ବତୀ ବଲ୍ଲଭ ।
ନୀଲକଣ୍ଠ ବିଶ୍ୱବାସ ମହାଦେବ ଶିବ ।।୪୨।।
ତୁମ୍ଭପଦ ଅରବିନ୍ଦ ଷଟ୍‌ପଦ ହେବାକୁ ।
ସ୍ଥାନ ଦିଅ ଦ୍ୱିଜ ଗୋପୀନାଥର ମନକୁ ।।୪୩।

ଦ୍ୱିତୀୟ ଛାନ୍ଦ

ରାଗ – ଆଷାଢ ଶୁକ୍ଳ

ଶୁଣ ସୁଜନେ ଦେଇ ମନକର୍ଣ୍ଣ ।ନୃପ ଭୂପତୀ ଙ୍କ ବଂଶ ବର୍ଣ୍ଣନ

ବିଷ୍ଣୁ ନାଭି ପଦ୍ମୁଧାତା ଜନମ । ଦାତ୍ରେୟ ମୁନି ତାଙ୍କ ନନ୍ଦନ ।

ତାଙ୍କ ନେତ୍ରନୀରୁ । ଜନମ ହୋଇଲେ ଶଶୀ ସାଗରୁ ।।୧।।

ସୋମତନୟ ବୁଧ ଅଧିପତି । ଗ୍ରହଗଣେ ମିଶିରହି ଅଛନ୍ତି ।

ବୁଧ ତନୟ ପୁରୋରବା ଖ୍ୟାତ । ଅଭଧ ମୁନି ତାଙ୍କଠାରୁ ଯାତ ।

ନଘୋଷ କୁମର । ଜନମ ହୋଇଲେ ତାଙ୍କ ବୀର୍ଜର ।।୨।।

ସର୍ଗେ ସେପୁଣି ଇନ୍ଦ୍ର ହେଲେଯାଇ ।ସାତଲକ୍ଷ ବର୍ଗ ପାଳିଲେ ମହୀ

ନଘୋଷ ସୁତ ଅଟନ୍ତି ଯଜାତୀ । ତାଙ୍କଜ ମାନଧାତା ଚକ୍ରବତର୍ତୀ

ଏ ମହୀ ମଣ୍ଡଳେ । ସୁରରାଜ ସମ ଜଣ କାଶିଲେ ।।୩।।

ମାନଧାତାଙ୍କ ଛଅଟି କୁମର ।ଗର୍ଗ, ଗାର୍ଗ୍ୟ ଯେସୋମ ଦିବାକର

ଭୋଜ କଦମ୍ବ ଏରୂପ ଛପୁତ୍ର । କ୍ଷେତ୍ରୀୟ ଆଦି ଷଡ୍‌ବଂଶ ସମ୍ଭୁତ

ପୃଥିବୀ ମଧ୍ୟରେ । ବିଖାତ ହୋଇଛି ଚାରିଯୋଗରେ ।।୪।।

ସଂହଳ ଦ୍ୱିପେ କଦମ୍ବ କେଶରି । ମହିପାଳିଲେ ହୋଇ ଦଣ୍ଡଧାରି

ତାଙ୍କର କେତେ ପୁରୁଷ ଉତ୍‌ତାରୁ ।ଜନମି ଥିଲେ ନରପତି ଭୀରୁ ।

ସପ୍ତ ଭାତୃସହ । ପାଳନ୍ତି ସିଂହଳ ବହୀ ସେନେହା।।୫।।

ଜ୍ୟେଷ୍ଟ ଛଅଙ୍କ ନୋହିଲା ତନୟ । ସାନଭାଇର ହେଲାଏକ ପୁଅ

ଦେଖି ଭୀରୁ ମନହେଲା ଉଦାଶ । ପୁତ୍ର ବିହୁନେ ପ୍ରୟୋଜନ କିଶ

ପୃଥିବୀର ଭାର । ତେଜି ନିଶ୍ଚୟ ଜିବି ଦେଶାନ୍ତର ।।୬।।

ଶୁଶୀଳା ନାମେ ତାହାଙ୍କର ରାଣୀ । ଶାନ୍ତ ଗୁଣବନ୍ତ ଚାରୁ ରୂପିଣୀ

ତାଙ୍କପାଶେ ଯାଇ ଭୀରୁନରେଶ ।ବୋଇଲେ ରାଣୀ ଶୁଣମୋର ଭାଷ ।

ସୁତହୀନେ ପ୍ରାଣ । ରାଜତ୍ୱ ଗଣେ ନାହିଁ ପ୍ରୟୋଜନ ।୭।।

ସାନୁଜ ପୁତ୍ରେ ରାଜ୍ୟ ଭାର ଦେଇ ।ନିଳାଚଳ ଯାତ୍ରା କରିବି ମୁହିଁ

ମୋପ୍ରାଣ ପ୍ରୀୟା ସହଧର୍ମିଣି । ତେଣୁ ଏକଥାକୁ ଦେଲି ଜଣାଇଁ ।
ନିଜପୁରେ ଥିବୁ । ଭାଇଙ୍କ ସଙ୍ଗେ ବିବାଦୀ ନୋହିବୁ ।।୮।।

ପୁତ୍ରକୁ ପାଳିବୁ ଜିବନପରି । ବନ୍ଧୁ କୁଟୁମ୍ବେ ସ୍ନେହଥିବୁ ଧରି ।

ଭାଇଙ୍କୁ ମୋରି ସୁଖି କରିବୁ । ଦେବ ବ୍ରାହ୍ମଣେ ସୁଶୃଷା ବିହିବୁ ।
ଯାଉଅଛି ମୁହିଁ । ମନେରଖିଥିବୁଟି ପ୍ରାଣସହି ।।୯।।

ଶୁଣି ଶୁଶୀଳା ହୋଇ ଆଚମ୍ଭିତ । ବୋଇଲେ କିକଥା କହୁଛନାଥ

ତୁମ୍ଭେ ମୋହର ଜୀବନ ଜୀବନ ।ତୁମ୍ଭ ବିନେ ମୋ କିଶପ୍ରୟୋଜ
ଭାଇ, ବନ୍ଧୁ ଘର । ଉପେକ୍ଷା କରି ଜିବି ସଙ୍ଗତର ।।୧୦।।

କାହା ମୁଖ ଚାହିଁ କାଟିବି ଦିନ । ସଦନ ହେବ କାନନ ସମାନ ।

ଶୁଣି ସିଂହଳାଧୀପ ଦୁଃଖମନେ । କହନ୍ତି ଶୁଶିଳ ପ୍ରୀୟ ବଚନେ

ପତ୍ନି ସଙ୍ଗେ ଥିଲେ । ନାନା ବିପଦ ପଡେ ବିଦେଶରେ ।।୧୧।।

ବୁଲି ବିଦେଶ ଜିବି ନିଳଗିରି । ଦର୍ଶନ କରିବି ଗଦାବ୍ଜଧାରି ।

ଓଡ୍ର ରାଷ୍ଟ୍ର ଭୁମି ଭ୍ରମଣ କରି । ବାହୁଡି ଆସିବି ନିଜ ନଗରି ନ
ହୋଇ ବିରସ । ଅନୁମତି ଦିଅ ରମଣି ଇଶ ।।୧୨।।

ଯତନେ ସଂବୋଧି ଶୁଶୀଳାମନ ।ପ୍ରବେଶ ହେଲେ ପୁତ୍ର ସନିଧାନ

ଚୁମି ବଦନ ପୁତ୍ରେ କୋଳକରି । ଆସନେ ବସି ଭୀରୁ ଦଣ୍ଡଧାରି ।

ଭାଷିଲେ ଏବାଣି । ଯାଉଛି ବିଦେଶ କୁମରମଣି ।।୧୩।।

ସମର୍ପୀ ଦେଉଛି.......................................

ତୋ ବିନା ମୋର କେହିନାହିଁ ଆନ ।ରାଣିଙ୍କୁ ମୋର କରିବୁ
ପାଳନ ଆଦର କରିବୁ , ବିପଦ ସ୍ୱଚ୍ଛନ୍ଦେ ଜଣାଉ ଥିବୁ ।।୧୪।।

ଉତ୍ତମ ଭୋଗକର ରାଜାହୋଇ ।ହରି ପ୍ରସାଦେ କିଛିଭୟ ନାହିଁ
ଧର୍ମରେ ଥିଲେ ହେଉଥିବ ଜୟ ।ଅଧର୍ମ କଲେ ବଂଶ ହେବକ୍ଷୟ
ନସହିବ ମହି । ପ୍ରଜାପାଳିବୁ ନିଯେ ଦୁଃଖ ସହି ।।୧୫।।

ପ୍ରଜା ସୁଖରେ ସୁଖି ହେଲେ ରାଜା ।ଜଗତେ ଉଡଇ କୀରତି ଧ୍ୱଜା
ଉଚିତେ ବୃଷ୍ଟି କରେ ଶୁନାଶୀର । କୃଷି ଉପୁଜିଲେ ହୁଅଇସ୍ଥିର
ଦୋଷକଲେ ବାବୁ । ଉଚିତ ବିଚାରେ ଦଣ୍ଡବିହିବୁ ।।୧୬।।

ଦୂତପେଶି ବୁଝି ବିଧି ଅବଧି । ଦୁର୍ଦ୍ଦାନ୍ତ ଲୋକ ପକାଇବୁ ଛେଦି ।
ତେବେ ସେ ତୋତେ ନଲାଗିବ ଦୋଷ । ନିଶ୍ଚଳେ ଲକ୍ଷ୍ମୀଥିବେ
ତୋର ପାଶ ରାଜାଏହା କହି । ସଚିବେ ଡକାଇ ଦେଲେ
ବୁଝାଇ ।।୧୭।।

ଶୁଣହେ ଶଚିବ ମୋର ଗିର । ପୁତ୍ରଙ୍କୁ ପ୍ରଦାନ କଲି ଭୂଭାର ।
ତୁମୋର ପୁରାତନ କଥା ଯାଣୁ । ଉଚିତ ଲୋକର ଗୁହାରିଶୁଣୁ
ସେହିପରକାରେ । ପାଳନ କରିବୁ ଶିଶୁ ରାଜାରେ ।।୧୮।।

ଏତେକହି ରାଜ ଆଶନନପରେ । ଅଭିଷିକ୍ତ କଲେ ରାଜକୁମାରେ
ପୁରବାସୀଙ୍କୁ ଖବର ଜଣାଇ ।ତୋଟା ଜଗତିରେ ମିଳିଲେ
ଜାଇଁ
ଦୂତପଠାଇଲେ । ଭାଇଙ୍କୁ ମୋର ଡ଼ାକରେ ବୋଇଲେ ।।୧୯।।

ଚଳିଲା ଚାର ହୋଇ ଖର ଖର ।ଛଅ ଭାଇଙ୍କୁ ଦେଲା ସେଖବର
ଶୁଣି ଭାଇଗଣ ଅଧିର ହୋଇ ।ରାଜନ ସମୀପେ ମିଳିଲେ
ଜାଇ
ନମସ୍କାର କଲେ । ବିନୟ ହୋଇ ବଚନ କହିଲେ ।।୨୦।।

କାହିଁ ଯାଉଅଛ ସିଂହଳେଶ୍ୱର । କିଏ କିଦୋଷ କରିଛି ତୁମ୍ଭର ।

....

ପତ୍ନୀ ଭାଇ ପୁଅ । ଯେହେବ ହେଉ ଏଗଣ ନିଶ୍ଚୟ ॥୨୧॥

ଯେବେ ଉଦାଶେ କରିଛ ଗମନ ସଙ୍ଗତେ ଜିବୁଁ ଆମ୍ଭେଛଅଜଣ

ତୁମ୍ଭ ଇଣତିଟି ଗତି ଆମ୍ଭର । ଏଥିକି ଉଚିତ ବିଚାରକର ।

ଦ୍ୱିଜ ଗୋପୀନାଥ । ବୋଲେ ଉଚିତ ତାଙ୍କ ମନୋରଥ ॥୨୨॥

ତୃତୀୟ ଛାନ୍ଦ

ରାଗ ଦେଶାକ୍ଷ

ଶୁଣଧୀରେ ଭୀରୁରାଜ ଭାଷନ୍ତି ଶୁଣ ସାନୁଜ ।

ନିଜ ଶେଖରକୁ ଯାଇଣ ଦର୍ଶନ କରିବି ମୁଁ ଦେବରାଜ ॥୧॥

ଦିନବନ୍ଧୁ ଜଗନ୍ନାଥ ଦେଖିଲେ ହେବି ମୁକତ ।

ଏହିମୋ ନିଶ୍ଚୟ ଗମନକାର ଶୁଣହେ କନିଷ୍ଟ ଭ୍ରାଥ ॥୨॥

ଶୁଣି ସାନଭାଇଗଣ ସଙ୍ଗରେ ଜିବାକୁ ମନ ।

ସାଜି ବୁଜୁଳିକା ଉଦବେଗ ହୋଇକଲେ ଶୀଘ୍ର ଆଗମନ ॥୩॥

ଶୁଦ୍ଧ ଶାଳଗ୍ରାମ ଶିଳା ଗୋପାଳ ମୁରତୀ ମାଳା

ଖଣ୍ଡା ତରବାରି ଏକ ଏକ ଧରି ବାହାରିଲେ ହୋଇ ମେଳା ॥୪॥

ଶ୍ୱେତ ଅଶ୍ୱ ଆରୋହଣେ ବାହାରିଲେ ଜଣେ ଜଣେ ।

ହରିପଦ ଧ୍ୟାଇ ପଥ ବହିଗଲେ ଦେଖିଲେ ନଗର ଜନେ ॥୫॥

ବୋଲନ୍ତି ହୋଇ ବିନତୀ ଶୁଣହେ ସିଂହଳ ପତୀ ।

ଜାଉଅଛ କାହିଁ କେମନ୍ତେ ବଂଚିବୁ ନଦେଖି ଛତ୍ରପତି ॥୬॥

ତୁମ୍ଭର ବିମଳ ଯଶ ଗାଇଣ ନିଶି ଦିବସ ।

ବଂଚୁଥିଲୁଁ ଏବେ ଅନାଥ ହୋଇଲୁଁ କାଆଗେ କହିବୁକିଶ ।।୭।।
ଶିଶୁ ପୁତ୍ରେ ରାଜ୍ୟଭାର ଦେଇ ଜିବ ଦେଶାନ୍ତର ।
ଦୁଃଖି ଭୋକି ସର୍ବ ପୁରବାସିଜନ ଆମ୍ଭେ ହୋଇବୁ କାହାର ।।୮।।
ତୁମ୍ଭ ସଙ୍ଗେ ସର୍ବେ ଜିବୁଁ ଉଚିତ ସେବା କରିବୁଁ ।
ଅନ୍ୟଥାକଳେ ଉଣୋଇଶେ ଏକ ମିଶାଇ ଖାଇ ମରିବୁଁ ।।୯।।
ଏତେ ଭାଷି ନରନାରି ନୟନୁ ବୁହାଇ ବାରି ।
ଦୁଃଖ ସରିତରେ ବୁଡିଲେ ସକଳେ ଜଳହୀନପରି ।।୧୦।।
ପ୍ରଜାଙ୍କ ବିକଳ ବାଣି ଶୁଣି ଭୀରୁ ନରମଣି ।
ଦେଖି ନୀଳଗିରି ଆଶିବୁଁହେ ଫେରି ହସେ ଦିଅ ମେଲାଣି ।।୧୧।।
ତୁମ୍ଭ ପବିତ୍ର ଦୟାରେ ଆମ୍ଭର ଶୁଭଯୋଗରେ ।
ଶୁଦ୍ଧ ନିଷ୍କଳଙ୍କ ଶୋମବଂଶ କ୍ଷାତ ହୋଇଅଛି ଜଗତରେ ।।୧୨।।
କୁହ ଅଧିର କାତରେ ବିଦାଦିଅ ଆନନ୍ଦରେ ।
ବରଷ ଭିତରେ ଲେଉଟି ଆସିମୁଁ ରହିବି ତୁମ୍ଭସଙ୍ଗରେ ।।୧୩।।
ପ୍ରଜାଙ୍କୁ ସାନ୍ତ୍ୱନା ଦେଇ ଚଳିଗଲେ ସାତଭାଇ ।
ସମୁଦ୍ର ନିକଟେ ପ୍ରବେଶ ହୋଇଲେ ଦ୍ୱିଜ ଗୋପୀନାଥ
କହି।।୧୪।।

ଚତୁର୍ଥ ଛାନ୍ଦ

ରାଗ – ମାଳବ

ପୋତେ ବସି ପାରିହେଲେ ଲୁଣି ସାଗର ।
ପ୍ରବେଶିଲେ ସେତୁ ବନ୍ଧେ ଶୁଭ ଯୋଗର ।
ଶ୍ରୀରାମ ଇଶ୍ୱର ସମ୍ଭୁ ଦେଉଳେ ପସି ।

ଦର୍ଶନ କରିଲେ ନିଜ ଶୁଭ ମନାସୀ ॥୧॥
ଯୟ ଉମାଧବ ଶିତ ଅଶୁଁ ଧାରଣ ।
ଅନନ୍ତ ପବିତ୍ର ଧର ଫଂଚାନନ ।
. . . . .ଅନୁଗ୍ରହ ନାଥ ଦିଅ ମୁକତି ।
. . . . .ହା ବୋଲି ପ୍ରକ୍ଷିଣ କଲେ ଝଟତି ॥୨॥
ମହା ପ୍ରସାଦ ଭକ୍ଷଣ କରି ସେଠାରେ ।
ରହିଲେ ଫଂଚ ଦିବସ ଶିବ ଶେବାରେ ।
ସେଠାରୁ ଉଠେ ମୁଖେ ଘୋଟକ ଯୋଗେ ।
ପ୍ରବେଶ ହେଲେ କଟକେ ବିଷମ ଭୋଗେ ॥୩॥
କଟକୁ ଭୂବନେଶ୍ୱର ଦୁଇଦିନରେ ।
ପଥ ବହିଗଲେ ସର୍ବେ ଶୁଭଯୋଗରେ ।
ଲିଙ୍ଗରାଜ ପଦେ ମନଦେଇ ଶତତ ।
ଦର୍ଶନ କଲେ ସେଠାରେ ପନ୍ଦର ନେତ୍ର ॥୪॥
ଦିନା ତିନି ରହି ଜମନିକରୁ ଗଲେ ।
ସାକ୍ଷୀ ଗୋପିନାଥ ମୂର୍ତୀ ପଥେ ଦେଖିଲେ ।
ତହୁଁ କେଦାର କୁଣ୍ଡରେ ସ୍ନାହାନ ସାରି ।
ଚନ୍ଦ୍ରଭାଗା ଯାତ୍ରାକଲେ ପ୍ରମୋଦ ଭରି ॥୫॥
ଚନ୍ଦ୍ରଭାଗା ସୂର୍ଯ୍ୟଦେବ ସେବାକରିଲେ ।
ହୟେବସୀ ସପ୍ତବୀରେ ସେଠାରୁଗଲେ ।
ପୁରୁଷ ଉତ୍ତମ କ୍ଷେତ୍ର ନାମ ଯାହାର ।
ସେଠାରେ ପ୍ରବେଶ ହେଲେ ସପତବୀର ॥୬॥
ଅଠର ନଳାରେ ଥିଲେ ଯଗୁଆଳିଏ ।

ମାଶୁଲ ଅଶୁଲ କରୁ ଥିଲେ ସଭିଏଁ ।
ଦେଖି ପଥ ରୁଦ୍ଧ କରି କହିଲେ ଯାଇ ।
ମାଶୁଲ ନଦେଲେ ଆମ୍ଭେ ଛାଡିବୁ ନାହିଁ ।।୭।।
ଗଲେଯାଅ ଥିଲେଥାଅ ଏହାନିଶ୍ଚୟ ।
କହିଲେ ସପତ ବୀରେ ଶୁଣ ଯାଗୁଅ ।
ରାଠୋର କଠୋର ପ୍ରଜ୍ଞା କ୍ଷତ୍ରୀ ଉତ୍‌ତମ ।
କଦମ୍ବ ବଂଶୀକ ଆମ୍ଭେ ନୁହୁ ଅଧମ ।।୮।
ନକରୁ ଭକତି କାରେ ପ୍ରଣାମ ନୋହୁଁ ।
ଅଧୀନତାରେ ନରହୁଁ ବୀର ବୋଲାଉଁ ।
କେବଳ ଦର୍ଶନ କରି କମଳ ଧାରି ।
ବାହୁଡିଣ ଜିବୁଁ ଆମ୍ଭେ ନିଜ ନଗରି ।।୯।।
କେତେ ପରିଶ୍ରମେ ଆସି ଏଥି ମିଳିଲୁଁ ।
ଏଥିଆସି ମହାବିପଦରେ ପଡିଲୁଁ ।
ନକରୁ ବାଣିଜ୍ୟ କିପାଁ ଦେବୁ ଟେକସ ।
କେବଳ ଦେଖିବା ଆଶା କମଳାଈଶ ।।୧୦।।
ଗଜପତିଙ୍କ ଛାମୁରେ ଜଣାଇ ଦିଅ ।
ନବୋଇଲେ ଆମ୍ଭେ ଫେରି ଜିବୁଁ ନିଶ୍ଚୟ ।
ଶୁଣି ବାଣି ପ୍ରହରିଏ ଚଳିଲେ ଖରେ ।
ପ୍ରବେଶି ବୋଇଲେ ଅବଗତ ଛାମୁରେ ।।୧୧।।
ସାତଜଣ କ୍ଷତ୍ରୀଦେବ ଆସିଅଛନ୍ତି ।
ଟେକସ ଦେବାକୁ ଅସୀକାର କରନ୍ତି ।
କହନ୍ତି ଆମ୍ଭେ ରାଠୋର ନଦେଉ କର ।

ମାନ୍ୟ ନକରୁ କାହାରେ ନୋହୁଁ ଚାକର ॥୧୨॥
କେବଳ ଦେଖିବୁ ନେତ୍ରେ ଜଗତନାଥ ।
ଅନ୍ୟଥା ସପୁରେ ଫେରି ଜିବୁଁ ନିୟତ ।
ଶୁଣି ଓଡଷାଧିପତି ବୋଲନ୍ତି ବାଣୀ ।
ସେ ଯେବେ ରାଠୋର କ୍ଷତ୍ରୀ ବୁଝ ଏକ୍ଷଣି ॥୧୩ ॥
କରତ ପଥରେ ତୁମ୍ଭେ ବସାଇ ଦିଅ ।
ଏହିପଥେ ଯାଅବୋଲି ତାହାଙ୍କୁ କହ ।
ଯେବେ ସେହି ପଥେ ଜିବେ ଚଳାଇ ଅଶ୍ୱ ।
ଯାଣିବ ରାଠୋର ଛତ୍ରୀ କଦମ୍ବ ବଂଶ ॥୧୪॥
ଶୁଣି ପ୍ରହରିଏ ଫେରି ସତ୍ୱରେ ଗଲେ ।
ଖମ୍ବ ପୋତି ପଥରେ କରତ ଆଡଲେ ।
ବୋଇଲେ ଏପଥେ ତୁମ୍ଭେ ଗମନ କର ।
ଯଦ୍ୟପି ରାଠୋର ବଂଶି କ୍ଷତ୍ରୀ କୁମର ॥୧୫॥
ନହେଲେ ବାହୁଡି ଯାଓ ନିଜ ପୁରକୁ ।
ଗଜପତି ଏ ଆଦେଶ ଦେଲେ ତୁମ୍ଭକୁ ।
ଶୁଣି ବୀରେ ଦୁଃଖ ଭରେ ମନେ ପାଂଚିଲେ ।
ଜଗନ୍ନାଥ ଆମ୍ଭକୁ ଏ କଷଣ ଦେଲେ ॥୧୬॥
ତାଙ୍କ ଆଶେ କେତେ ପଥ ଚାଲି ଆସଲୁଁ ।
ଶେଷେ ଏ ମହା ବିପଦେ ଆଶି ପଡିଲୁଁ ।
ପଥେ ନଗଲେ ବଂଶକୁ ନିନ୍ଦା ହୋଇବ ।
ଗଲେ ନିଶ୍ଚୟ ମରଣୁ ବଂର୍ଚିନ ଜିବ ॥୧୭॥
ସପ୍ତବୀରେ ବିଚାରି ବୋଇଲେ ଗମିବା ।

ମରଣେ ଉତ୍ତମ ବଂଶେ ନିନ୍ଦା ନଦେବା ।
ବଂଶକୁ କଳଙ୍କ ଦିଏ ଯେଉଁ କୁମର ।
ଜିବନୁ ମରଣ ଅଟେ ଉତ୍ତମ ତାର ।।୧୮।।
ଏତେ ବୋଲି କୃଷ୍ଣପାଦେ କରିଲେ ଧ୍ୟାନ ।
ଏ ବିପଦୁଁ ରକ୍ଷାକର ଦୁଃଖ ନାଶନ ।
ତୁମ୍ଭେ ନରଖିଲେ ଆମ୍ଭେ ହେବୁ ଅନାଥ ।
ଦିନବନ୍ଧୁ ନାମେ ହେବ କଳଙ୍କ ଯାତ ।।୧୯।।
କରି ହରିଣି ବିପଦ ତାରଣ କାରୀ ।
ଦ୍ରୌପଦୀ ଲଜ୍ଜା ରକ୍ଷକ ଆହେ ମୁରାରୀ ।
ଆମ୍ଭଏ ବିପଦ ପ୍ରଭୋ କେତେ ମାତର ।
ବଂଚିତେ ନାଶିଲ କୁରୁ ଶନ୍ୟ ସାଗର ।।୨୦।।
ଅଚ୍ୟୁତ କେଶବ ରାମ ଗୋବିନ୍ଦ ହରି ।
ସତ୍ୟ ଭାମା ଧବ ହେ ମାଧବ ମୁରାରି ।
ନାରାୟଣ ହୃଷିକେଶ ହେ ଦାମୋଦର ।
ଏ ମହା ବିପଦୁଁ ଦେବ ଉଦ୍ଧାର କର ।।୨୧।।
ନ ହେଲେ ଏ ହତ୍ୟାଦେବ ହେବତୁମ୍ଭକୁ ।
ଲେଉଟି ନଜିବୁଁ ଆମ୍ଭେ ନିଯ ପୁରକୁ ।
ଗଜପତି ରାଜା ଦୁଃଖ ଦେଉଛି ଯେତେ ।
ତାହାକୁ ବିହିତ ଶାସ୍ତି ଦେବ ଉଚିତେ ।।୨୨।।
ଜିବନେ ମରଣେ ଆମ୍ଭେ ନୁହୁ ବିମୁଖ ।
କେବଳ ଦେଖି ନପାରି କମଳ ମୁଖ ।
ନିକଟେ ଆଣି ଜିବନ ହରାଇ ଦେଲୁଁ ।

ବୋଲେ ଗୋପୀନାଥ ଆଶା ବିଫଳ କଲୁଁ ।।୨୩।।

ପଂଚମ ଛାନ୍ଦ

ରାଗ – କନଡା

ହରି ଚିନ୍ତା କରି, ଭୀରୁଦଣ୍ଡଧାରି, ଘୋଟକ ଉପରେ ବସିଲେ ।
ଭାଇ ଗଣଙ୍କୁ କଲ୍ୟାଣ ବିହିଲେ ।
ଧ୍ୱଆଁଇ ଘୋଟକ କରତ ଉପରେ ପଡି ଦ୍ୱିଖଣ୍ଡିତ ହେଲେସେ । ।।ରାଜନ।।
ଘୋଡା ସହିତେ ଛିଡିଣ ପଡିଲା । ପିଣ୍ଡୁ ପରାଣ ଛାଡି ଉଡିଗଲା ।
ଦେଖି ଭାଇଙ୍କର, ହୃଦୟ ବିକଳ, କହୁଁ କହୁଁ ନସରିଲା ହେ ।
।।ରାଜନ।। ।।୧।।

ତାଙ୍କର ଅନୁଜ, ଧରି ଗରୁତେଜ, ରାଗେ ଅଶ୍ୱକୁ ଧୁଆଁଇଲେ ।
ସେହି ପୁଣି ପଡି ପ୍ରାଣ ଛାଡିଲେ । ତହୁଁ ତଳ ଭାଇ ଅଶ୍ୱକୁ ଚଳାଇ
ତହୁଁ ତଳ ଭାଇ ଅଶ୍ୱକୁ ଚଳାଇ କରତ ଦାଢେପଡିଲେ ସେ ।
।।କୁମାର।।
ଦେଖି ତବାନୁଜ ହୋଇ କୁପିତ । ଚଳାଇଲେ ସେ ଅଶ୍ୱକୁ ତୁରିତ ।
କରତ କବଳେ ପଡି ପ୍ରାଣଛାଡିଗଲେ ଘୋଟକ ସହିତ ସେ ।
।।କୁମାର।। ।।୨।।

ଦେଖିଣ ପ୍ରହରି, ଗଣ ଖର କରି, ଦଉଡି ପହଂଚିଲେ ଖରେ ।
ଅବଶେଷ ତିନିଭାଇ ପାଖରେ ।
ନଚଳାଅ ଅଶ୍ୱ, ଯାଇରାଜା ପାଶ, ଯଣାଇଁ ଦେବୁ ସତ୍ୱରେ ହେ ।
।।କୁମାର।।
ଚାରିଭାଇଗଲେ ଯମପୁରକୁ । ତୁମ୍ଭେ ନକରାଅ ଶୋକ ମନକୁ ।

କହି ପ୍ରହରିଏ, ଜାଇ ତରତରେ,ମିଳିଲେ ରାଜା ପାସକୁ ସେ ।।୩।।

ଶୁଣଦଣ୍ଡଧର, ଓଡିଶାଧିଶ୍ୱର, କ୍ଷତ୍ରୀୟ ଗଣଙ୍କ ଚରିତ । ଚାରି ଭାଇଙ୍କୁ ନାଶିଲା କରତ ଚଅବଶେଷ ତିନି ଉଦ୍ୟତ ହୁଅନ୍ତେ ଅଟକାଇଲୁ ତ୍ୱରିତ ହେ

।। ନରେଶ ।। ।

ଅଶ୍ୱ ସହିତ ସେଠାରେ ପଡିଲେ । ମରିବାକୁ କିଛି ଭୟ ନକଲେ ।

ଡରି ଫେରିଗଲେ ଅପଯଶଧ୍ୱଜା ଉଡେ ଜଗତେ ବୋଇଲେ ହେ ।

।। ନରେଶ ।।୪।।

ଶୁଣି ଗଜପତି, ହୋଇ ତୋଷମତି, ବୋଇଲେ ଜିବାତାଙ୍କ ପାସ ।

ବୋଧି କରିବା ତାହାଙ୍କୁ ସନ୍ତୋଷ ।

ବୋଲି ଚଳିଯାଇ ପ୍ରବେଶ ହୋଇଲେ ଅଡାକର ତର ପାସ ହେ ।

।। ରାଜନ ।।

ଚାରି ଭାଇ ପଡିଛନ୍ତି ଦେଖିଲେ । ମନେ ବହୁତ ସନ୍ତାପ ଲଭିଲେ ।

ବିରେ ମରି ଯଶ ଭୂମିପରେ ରଖି ହତ୍ୟାରେ କାରିଣି କଲେ ସେ ।

।। ରାଜନ ।।୫।।

ବୟବୃଦ୍ଧ ଚାହିଁ, ସିତ ପ୍ରଣାମ କଲେ ନରେଶଙ୍କୁ କହିଲେ ଏଦୁଃଖ ଦେଲ ଆମ୍ଭଙ୍କୁ

ସାତଭାଇ ରମା ସାଇଁ ଦର୍ଶନରେ ଆସି ମିଳିଲୁଁ ଏଠାକୁ ହେ ।

।। ରାଜନ ।।

କର୍ମଫଳେ ସେ ବିଫଳ ହୋଇଲା । ଚାରି ଭାଇ ଜୀବନ କାଳ ନେଲା ।

ଆମ୍ଭ କର୍ମରେ ଏ ଦୁଃଖ ଦେଖିବାକୁ ବିଧାତା ଲେଖିଥିଲା ହେ ।

।। ରାଜନ ।।୬।।

ଶୁଣିଗଜପତି, ପ୍ରବୋଧି କହନ୍ତି, ଶୁଣ କ୍ଷତ୍ରିୟ ବୀର ମାନେ ।

ଧାତା ଲିଖନ ଯେ ଥାଇ କରମେ ।

ସେ ଫଳ ନେଇ ସେମାନେ ଚଳିଗଲେ ଦୁଃଖ କିପାଁ ତୁମ୍ଭମନେ ହେ

॥ କୁମାରେ ॥

ଦେଖ ମାୟାମୟ ଏହି ସଂସାର । ଘର ବନ୍ଧୁ ଭାଇ କିଏ କାହାର ।

ମିଛ କଥା ପାଇଁ ରୋଦନ କରୁଛ ମନରେ ହୋଇ ଅଧିର ହେ ।

॥ କୁମାରେ ॥୭॥

ଭାଇ ବୋଲି ନିଶି ଦିବସ କାନ୍ଦିଲେ ଦେଖିବାକୁ ସେହି ମାନଙ୍କୁ ।

କର୍ମେ ଚଳିଲେଣି ନିଜପୁରକୁ ।

ପ୍ରୀତି ସମ୍ବୋଧନେ ତାପିତ ଜୀବନେ ଦେଲେ ଶୀତଳ ନୀରକୁସେ ।

॥ରାଜନ॥

ବଂଶାବଳୀ କ୍ଷତ୍ରିୟ ଗୁଣ ମାନ । ପଚାରିଲେ ଗଜପତି ରାଜନ ।

ଶୁଣି ରୁଦ୍ରଦେବ, ବହି କ୍ରୋଧଭାବ, ଭାଷିଲେ ଏହି ବଚନ ହେ ।

॥ରାଜନ॥୮॥

ଶୁଣ ନୃପନାଥ, ସୋମବଂଶଜାତ, ରାଠୋର କଠୋର ନୃପତି ।

ଯନ୍ମୁ ସିଂହଳ ଦ୍ୱୀପ ଆମ୍ଭ କ୍ଷିତୀ ।

ନିପବଂଶ ବହୀ, ପାଳୁଅଛୁ ମହୀ, ଇଷ୍ଟ ରଘୁନାଥ ମୂର୍ତୀ ହେ ।

॥ରାଜନ॥

ଦେଖ ରହିଛନ୍ତି ଆମ୍ଭ ପାଶରେ । ସେବା କରିଥାଉଁ ନିଶୀ ବାସରେ ।

ପର ଅନ୍ନ ଖାଇ ନରହିବୁ କାହିଁ ଶେବାନକରୁ କାହାରେ ହେ ।

॥ରାଜନ॥୯॥

ଓଡୀଷ ଭୂଦେବ, ବୀର ବାସୁଦେବ, କହିଲେ ଶୁଣ ବୀରଗଣେ ।

ଶୁଦ୍ଧ କ୍ଷତ୍ରୀୟ ଅଟ ତୁମ୍ଭେମାନେ । ବନ୍ଧୁପଣେ ନିତି ଶେବାମୁ କରିବି ରହ
ମୋହର ଭବନେ ହେ ।।କୁମାରୋ।।

ଗ୍ରାମ ଜମୀଦାରୀ ଦେବୀ ତୁମ୍ଭଙ୍କୁ । ଶେବା କରୁଥିବ ଦୀନ ବନ୍ଧୁଙ୍କୁ ।
ନାସ୍ତୀକରି ବୀରେ ରାଜା ସହିତରେ ଚଳିଲେ ନୀଳଗିରିକୁ ।
।।କୁମାରୋ।।୧୦।।

ଦେଉଳ ଭିତରେ ପଶି ପ୍ରଥମରେ ଦେଖିଲେ ବିନିତା ନନ୍ଦନ ।
ବିଷ୍ଣୁବାହ ବୋଲି କଲେ ପ୍ରଣାମ ।
ପର୍ଶ୍ଚିମ ମୁଖରେ ଅନାଇ ଦେଖିଲେ ଦିଶୁଛି କଳା ବଦନ ହେ ।
।।କେଶବା।।

ଫିଟି ଦିଶୁଛି ବଳିୟାର ଭୂଜ । ଦୁଃଖ ଦେଖୁଅଛି ନେତ୍ର ପଙ୍କଜ ।
ରଙ୍ଗୀମା ଅଧର ମଧୁରହାସରେ ପଳାଉଛି ତମ ରାଜ ହେ ।
।।କେଶବା।।

କୃପାକର ହରି ଆରତ ନାଶନ । କରୁଣା ସିନ୍ଧୁ ଗଦାଧର ।
କଳିଯୁଗେ ବଉଦ ଅବତାର ।
ଭୂଜ ପ୍ରସାରିଣ ଭକତ ମାନଙ୍କୁ ଯାଚି ଦେଉଅଛ ବର ।
।।କେଶବା।।

ଆତ୍ମଦୁଃଖ ପ୍ରଭୁ କେତେ ମାତର । ଶୁଦର୍ଶନ ଭ୍ରମୁଛି ଦକ୍ଷକର ।
ଦେଖିକଳା ମୁଖ, ଖଣ୍ଡି ଭବଦୁଃଖ ଜୀବନ ହେଲା ଉଦ୍ଧାର ହେ ।
।।କେଶବା।।୧୨

ନମୋ ନୀଳାମ୍ବର, ମଉ ନନ୍ଦଧର, ରେବତୀ ବଲ୍ଲଭ ମୁଷଳୀ ।
କାମପାଳ ହଳଧର ହେ ହଳୀ । ଅମ୍ବା କଦମ୍ବା ପ୍ରଳମ୍ବା ନିବାରକ
ଧୁମ୍ରପାନେ କୁତୁହଳି ହେ ।।କେଶବା।।

ମହୀଧର ଧାରୀ କର କରୁଣା ଆମ୍ଭ ଦୁଃଖକି ତୁମ୍ଭଙ୍କୁ ଅଜଣା ।
ଜଗତ ଜାକରେ ଫିଟି ଦିଶୁଅଛି ପତିତ ତାରଣ ବାନା ହେ ।
॥କଶବ॥୧୩

କରିନମସ୍କାର ଅଇଲେ ବାହାର କଲେ କଇବଲ୍ୟ ପାରଣ ।
ମନକାମନା ହୋଇଲା ପୁରଣ । କେବଳ ଭାତୃ ନିଧନ ଶୋକେ ମନ
ହଉଛି ଛନ୍ନ ଛନ୍ନ ସେ । ବେଢ଼ା ବାହାରେ ଦରଶନକରି ଯାଇ
ଦେଖିଲେ ଗଜପତି ପୁରି । ବୋଲେ ଗୋପିନାଥ ହୋଇଣ ଦୁଃଖିତ
ରକ୍ଷାକର ମଧୁହାରି ହୋ ॥ କେଶବ॥୧୪

ଷଷ୍ଠ ଛାନ୍ଦ ।

ରାଗ – ରାମକେରୀ

ଦିନା ତିନି ରହି କ୍ଷେତ୍ରରେ କ୍ଷେତ୍ରି କୁମାର ମାନେ ।
ମନେବିଚାରିଲେ କିକାର୍ଯ୍ୟ ଆଉ ଅଛି ଜୀବନେ ॥୧॥
ସାତ ଭାଇ ଫେରି ଆସିବା ପାଇଁ ଆସିଲୁଁ କହି ।
ହଜାଇଣ ଚାରି ଜଣଙ୍କୁ ଆମ୍ଭେ ଜିବା କିପାଁଇ ॥୨॥
ପୁର ବାସିଏ ପଚାରିଲେ କିସ ବୋଲି କହିବା ।
ଶୁଶୀଳା ରାଣୀଙ୍କ ବିକଳ କିପାଁ ନେତ୍ରେ ଦେଖିବା ॥୩॥
ଏମନ୍ତ ବିଚାରି କୁମାରେ ଗୃହ ଜିବା ମାନସ ।
ବିନାଶି ଓଡୀଷୀ ଭ୍ରମଣ କଲେ ହୋଇ ହରଷ ॥୪॥
ପ୍ରଦକ୍ଷିଣ କରି ପ୍ରଥମେ ଜାଜପୁର ନଗର ।
ବିରଜା ଦର୍ଶନ ଲଭିଲେ ତିନିରାଜ କୁମାର ॥୫॥
ତହୁଁ ସିଂହଭୂମେ ପହୁଂଚୀ ଜଣେହେଲେ ନରେଶ ।

ସିଂହ ବନ୍ଧ କରି କେଶରୀ ବଂଶ, ହେଲେ ସରସ ॥୬॥
ତହୁଁ ତଳଭାଇ ସାରଣ୍ଡା ଜମିଦାର ରୂପରେ ।
ରଖାଇଲେ କେଶରୀ ଭୂପ ଅତି ଦୁଃଖମନରେ ॥୭॥
କେବଳ ରହିଲେ ପ୍ରତାପ ରୁଦ୍ର ରାଜ କୁମାରେ ।
ଦୁଃଖେ ବଂଚୁଥାନ୍ତି ଦିବସ ସିଂହଭୂମ ନଗରେ ॥୮॥
ଏକଦା ଭାଇଙ୍କ ସଂଗତେ ବହୁ ବିବାଦୀ ହୋଇ ।
ସ୍ଥାନ ତ୍ୟାଗକେଲେ ମନରେ ବହୁ ସନ୍ତାପ ବହି ॥୯॥
ଶୁଣିଲେ ବଣାଇ ନଗରେ ବାଣଇଶ୍ୱର ଲିଙ୍ଗ ।
ଅକର୍ମିଗଣ ଦୁଃଖ ଦେଖି ଦିଅନ୍ତି ଅପବର୍ଗ ॥୧୦॥
ଦର୍ଶନ କରିବା ମାନଶ ତହୁଁ ହେଲା ତାଙ୍କର ।
ଆଶିଣ ପ୍ରଥମେ ଦେଖିଲେ ରମ୍ୟବ୍ରାହ୍ମଣିତୀର ॥୧୧॥
ଉତ୍ତର ମୁଖେ ଶ୍ରୋତସତୀ କରିଅଛି ଗମନ ।
ଶୁଭ୍ର ଶ୍ୱେତ ବାସ ବାଲୁଙ୍କା ଦିଶୁଅଛି ଶୋଭନ ॥୧୨॥
ଜଳମଧ୍ୟସ୍ଥିତ ପ୍ରସ୍ଥରେ ଜଳ ଯାଉଛି ବହି ।
କଳ କଳ ସ୍ୱନ ବାଦ୍ୟକି ବାଦ୍ୟକାର ବଜାଇ ॥୧୩॥
ତଟ ବିଟପିଏ କିସୁମ ଫଳେ ହୋଇ ଭୂଷିତ ।
ପୁଷ୍ପାଞ୍ଜଳି ନଦୀ ଗର୍ଭକୁ କରିଛନ୍ତି ଆଗତ ॥୧୪॥
ଡୁଳ ଡୁଳି ଦେଉଅଛନ୍ତି ବସି ବିହଙ୍ଗ ଗଣ ।
ଅଥବା ବୀର ତୁରୀପରି ଶୁଭୁ ଅଛି କୂଜନ ॥୧୫॥
ସୁରମ୍ୟ କାନନେ ପଲ୍ଲବ ତୃଣ କରି ସଜ୍ଜିତ ।
ରଖି ଦେଇଛନ୍ତିକି ବିଧାତା ବାଟୋଇଙ୍କ ନିମି ॥୧୬॥
ତାହା ଦେଖି ବହୁ ହରଷ ହୋଇ ରାଜ କୁମାର ।

ନଦୀ ପାର ହୋଇ ପଶ୍ଚିମ ତୀରେ ହେଲେ ବାହାର ॥୧୭॥
ଦେଉଳ ଦେଖିଣ ବୁଝିଲେ ବିଶ୍ୱନାଥ ନିବାସ ।
ଆସିଣ ତ୍ୱରିତ ମିଳିଲେ ବାଣ ମନ୍ଦିର ପାସ ॥୧୮॥
ନଦୀ ଯଳ ବନ ଫୁଲରେ କରି ବହୁ ପୂଜନ ।
ବଣାଇଁ ଈଶ୍ୱର ଚରଣେ ପସିଲେ ସେ ଶରଣ ॥୧୯॥
ଶାଳ କନ୍ଦ ମୂଳ ଭକ୍ଷଣେ ରହି କେତେ ଦିବସ ।
ଶେବା କରୁଥିଲେ ଦିବସ ନିଶି ଗିରିଜା ଈଶ ॥୨୦॥
ସେ ସମୟେ ବାଣା ଅସୁର ଥିଲା ବଣାଇ ରାଜା ।
ପ୍ରତିଦିନ ବାଣେଶ୍ୱରଙ୍କୁ କରୁଥିଲା ସେ ପୂଜା ॥୨୧॥
ଦ୍ୱିତୀୟ ଜଣେ ଭୂଇଁଆଁ ତାହାର ଜମୀଦାର ।
ହୋଇପାଳୁଥିଲେ ଜଙ୍ଗଲ ମୟ ବଣାଇ ଭାର ॥୨୨॥
ଏକଦିନେ ବାଣା ଅସୁର ସେହି ରାଜ ପୁତ୍ରଙ୍କୁ ।
ଦେଉଳ ଭିତରେ ପଶିଣ ଭାବେ ନିଜ ମନକୁ ॥୨୩॥
ଶେବାକରି ଏହି ହରଙ୍କୁ ଏବେ ନରେଶ ହେବ ।
ଶତ୍ରୁପଣେ ପରେ ମୋତେକି ଏହୁ ଘଉଡି ଦେବ ॥୨୪॥
ନିଶ୍ଚୟ ମୋହର ଅଇରି ଏଥି ଆସି ରହିଲା ।
ଏତେ ବୋଲି ଖଡ୍ଗଧାରଣେ ମାରିବାକୁ ଧାଇଁଲା ॥୨୫॥
ତ୍ରାସ୍ଥେ ଧାଇଁ ନୃପ କୁମାର ଦେଖି କଦମ୍ବ ଗଛ ।
କୋଟ ଭିତରେ ପସିଗଲେ ବାଣା ଧାଉଁଛି ପଛ ॥୨୬॥
ବନୁଆଁ ମୟୂର ଗୋଟିଏ ଚରୁଥିଲା ସେଠାରେ ।
କୁମାର ଲୁଚିବା ଦେଖିଣ ଦଉଡିଲେ ସତ୍ୱରେ ॥୨୭॥
ତାହାଙ୍କ ଚରଣ ଚିହ୍ନକୁ କେକୀ ଦେଲା ମେ ାଇ ।

ଲତା ଅଭ୍ୟାନ୍ତରେ ରହିଲା ସେହି ଗୁପତ ହୋଇ ।।୨୮।।
ଏ ସମୟେ ବାଣା ସେଠାରେ ଆସି ପ୍ରବେଶ ହେଲା ।
ଖୁଜି ଖୁଜି କାହିଁ ନପାଇ ବଡ ଦୁଃଖ ଭାବିଲା ।।୨୯।।
ଶତ୍ରୁ କେଉଁ ପାଶେ ଲୁଚିଲା କାହିଁ ପାଇଲି ନାହିଁ ।
ଜାଣିଲି ତାହାକୁ ରଖିଲେ ନିଯେ ପାର୍ବତୀସାଇଁ ।।୩୦।।
ଏତେ ବୋଲି ବାଣା ଅସୁର ଫେରି ସେଠାରୁ ଗଲା ।
ଆପଣା ନବରେ ନିରାଶ ମନେ ପ୍ରବେଶ ହେଲା ।।୩୧।।
ଏ ସମୟେ ଲତା ବନରେ ବାହାରିଲା ମୟୂର ।
କେକାରବ କରି ନାଚିଲା ହୋଇ ହରଷ ଭର ।।୩୨।।
ମସ୍ତକ ଟେକିଣ ପ୍ରତାପ ଦେବ ଦେଲେ ଅନାଇଁ ।
ପଦଚିହ୍ନ ଗୁପ୍ତ କରିଣ ବନ ପ୍ରୀୟ ନାଚଇ ।।୩୩।।
ସେକାଳେ ମୟୁର ପାଦର ଚିହ୍ନ ମେଣ୍ଠି ନଥିଲେ ।
ଦୁରାଚାର ବାଣା ଅସୁର ତାଙ୍କୁ ଧରନ୍ତା ଭଲେ ।।୩୪।।
ନିଶ୍ଚୟ ବିନାଶ କରନ୍ତା ସେହି ରାଜ କୁମାର ।
ସନ୍ତକ ମସ୍ତକେ ବହିଲେ ତେଣୁ ସେହି ମୟୁର ।।୩୫।।
ଅବଧି ମୟୁର ସନ୍ତକ ରାଜବଂଶେ ରହିଛି ।
ନୀପ ବଂଶ ଆଦି ପୁରୁଷେ ଯେଣୁରକ୍ଷା କରିଛି ।।୩୬।।
କ୍ରୋଟେ ବଂଚାଇଣ ରଖିଲା ଯେଣୁ ରାଜ ପୁରୁଷ ।
ତେଣୁ ନିପ ବୃକ୍ଷ ସ୍ପରସ ନକରିନ୍ତି ଏ ବଂଶ ।।୩୭।।
ନୀପ ପୁଷ୍ପ ଗଳେ ଧାରଣ ସେହି ବୃକ୍ଷ ଛେଦନ ।
କରଣେ ସେହି ଦିବସରୁ କରିଛନ୍ତି ବାରଣ ।।୩୮।।
ଭୟେ ରାଜପୁତ୍ର ରହିଲେ ସେହିକ୍ରୋଟ ଭିତରେ ।

ଜଗି ରହିଥିଲା ମୟୁର ମୂଳେ ନିଶି ବାସରେ ।।୩୯।।
ତହିଁ ଉପବାସେ ରହିଣ କଲେ ହରଙ୍କ ଧ୍ୟାନ ।
ଦୁଃଖ ଦେଖି ତାଙ୍କ ଗିରିଜା ପତି ହେଲେ ପ୍ରସନ୍ନ ।।୪୦।।
ନିଶାରେ ସପନେ କହିଲେ ଶୁଣ ରାଜକୁମାର ।
କାଲିଏ ବଣାଇଁ ରାଜ୍ୟରେ ହେବ ନର ଈଶ୍ୱର ।।୪୧।।
ଦୁଷ୍ଟ ବାଣାସୁର ଦର୍ପରେ ନରହନ୍ତି ପରଜା ।
କାଲି ଏଥୁଁ ତାକୁ ଘଉଡି ତୋତେ କରିବି ରାଜା ।।୪୨।।
କେବଳ ମୋହର ସେବାରେ ଥିବୁ ନିତି ଦିବସ ।
ନିଶ୍ଚିନ୍ତ ହୋଇଣ ପ୍ରଭାତେ ମନ୍ଦିରେ ଆସ ।।୪୩।।
ଏହାକହିଣ ଅନ୍ତର୍ହୀତ ହେଲେ ପଂଚ ବଦନ ।
ଭୂଇଁୟା ରଜାକୁ ରାତ୍ରୀରେ ପୁଣି ହେଲେ ସପନ ।।୪୪।।
ବୋଇଲେ ମୋହର ମନ୍ଦିରେ ଅଛି ରାଜ ପୁରୁଷ ।
କାଲିତୁ ବଣାଇ ରାଜ୍ୟରେ ତାକୁକରି ନରେଶ ।।୪୫।।
କାଲି ତାକୁ ନୃପ ପଣରେ ଅଭିଷିକ୍ତ ନକଲେ ।
ନିଶ୍ଚୟ ତୋହର ବଂଶକୁ ନାଶିବି ମୁଁ ଭଲେ ।।୪୬।।
ତହୁଁ ବାଣାପୁରେ ପ୍ରବେଶି ତାକୁ କହିଲେ ହର ।
କାଲି ତୁହି ଏହି ନବରେ ପ୍ରତୁଃ ହୁଅ ବାହାର ।।୪୭।।
ଭୈରବ ସରୁପେ ରହିବୁ ଯାଇ ବାରଣସିରେ ।
ନହେଲେ ତୋହର ନିପାତ ହେବ ଏହି ନବରେ ।।୪୮।।
ଏତେ କହି ନିଜ ମନ୍ଦିରେ ଯାଇ ହେଲେ ପ୍ରବେଶ
ଦ୍ୱିଜ ଗୋପିନାଥ ଭାଷଇ ହେବେ ନବ ନରେଶ ।।୪୯।।

ସପ୍ତମ ଛାନ୍ଦ ।

ରାଗ – ବସନ୍ତ ମଙ୍ଗଳ

ଯାଣିଲେ ପ୍ରତାପ ଦେବ କ୍ରୋଟ ମଧ୍ୟେ ଥାଇ ।
ଭାଙ୍ଗିଗଲା ନିଦ୍ରା ବାଣେସର ଆଜ୍ଞାପାଇ ॥୧॥
ଆଚମ୍ବିତ ହୋଇକ୍ଷଣେ ରହିଲେ ମଉନେ ।
ଯାଣିଲେ ନିଶ୍ଚୟ ଦୟାକଲେ ପଂଚାନନେ ॥୨॥
ପ୍ରଭାତ ସପନ କେବେ ଅନ୍ୟଥା ନହୁଏ ।
ପ୍ରତ୍ୟକ୍ଷ ଘଟିଲା ପ୍ରାୟ ମନପ୍ରତେ ହୁଏ ॥୩॥
ଦେଉଳେ ଜିବାକୁ ଆଜ୍ଞା ଦେଇଗଲେ ହର ।
ଜିବି ନିଶ୍ଚୟ ମାଇଲେ ମାରିବ ଅସୁର ॥୪॥
ଏତେ ଭାବି କ୍ରୋଟରୁ ଉତୁରି ବୀରବର ।
ଦେଉଳେ ପସିଲେ ଯାଇ ହୋଇ ଖର ଖର ॥୫॥
ତେଣେ ବାଣାସୁର ଶୀଘ୍ର ତେଜିଣ ଉଠିଲା ।
ଇଶ୍ୱର କୋପ ଆଦେଶ ବୋଲିଣ ଯାଣିଲା ॥୬॥
ଦେଉଳକୁ ଚଳନ୍ତେ ଧାଇଁଲେ ଉମାପତି ।
ଅସୁର ଦକ୍ଷିଣ କରେ ଧଇଲେ ଝଟତି ॥୭॥
ସରୋସେ ବୋଇଲେ ବାଣାସୁର ଏଥୁ ଯାଓ ।
ଭୈରବ ସରୁପ ଧରି କାଶୀ କ୍ଷେତ୍ରେ ଥାଓ ॥୮॥
ତୋହର ପ୍ରତାପ ସହି ନପାରିବ ମହି ।
କୁଟୁମ୍ବ ଧରିଣ ଏଥୁ ଯାଅ ବେଗ ହୋଇ ॥୯॥
ଶୁଣି ବାଣାସୁର ନିଜ କୁଟୁମ୍ବକୁ ଧରି ।
ପଳାଇ ରହିଲା ଯାଇ ବାଣାରାଶି ପୁରି ॥୧୦॥

ଭୈରବ ସରୁପେ ଅବିଯାଏ ଅଛି ରହି ।
ଭକ୍ତି ଘେନି ପାଖେ ରଖିଛନ୍ତି ଉମାସାଇଁ ।।୧୧।।
ଅମରବର ଇଶ୍ୱର ଦେଇଥିଲେ ତାଙ୍କୁ ।
ଜଗତେ ପୂଜ୍ୟ ହେବାକୁ ନେଲେ ସେ ପାଖକୁ ।।୧୨।।
ତେଣୁ ଭୁୟାଁ ଜମିଦାର ହୋଇ ଖର ଖର ।
ଯାଣିଲା ସପନେ ଆଜ୍ଞା ଦେଲେ ଚକ୍ରଧର ।।୧୩।।
ଯେ ଥିବ ମନ୍ଦିରେ ତାଙ୍କୁ କରିବି ରାଜନ ।
ମନେ ଭାବୀ ଶିବାଳୟେ କରିଲା ଗମନ ।।୧୪।।
ଦେଖିଲା ପ୍ରତାପଦେବ ଦେଉଳ ଭିତରେ ।
ପୂଜା କରୁଛନ୍ତି ଭକ୍ତିଭରେ ବାଣେଶ୍ୱରେ ।।୧୫।।
ବୋଇଲେ ସପନେ ଆଜ୍ଞା ଦେଲେ ପଂଚାନନ ।
ବଣାଇଁ ରାଜ୍ୟରେ ତୁମ୍ଭେ ହୋଇବ ରାଜନ ।।୧୬।।
ଯାଇ ପ୍ରଥମରେ ସ୍ଥାନ ନିଶ୍ଚୟ କରିବା ।
ଭଲ ସ୍ଥାନ ଦେଖି ତହିଁ ଗଡ ବନାଇବା ।।୧୭।।
ଏତେ କହି ବେନିଜନେ ହୋଇଲେ ବାହାର ।
ଆଶି ଦେଖିଲେ ପ୍ରାଚୀରେ ରମ୍ୟ ବ୍ରାହ୍ମୀତୀର ।।୧୮।।
ଚତୁର୍ଦୀଗେ ଜଳମୟ ମଧ୍ୟେ ଉଚ୍ଚ ସ୍ଥାନ ।
ନାନା ବୃକ୍ଷଲତାରେ ହୋଇଛି ପରିପୂର୍ଣ୍ଣ ।।୧୯।।
ଭଲ ସ୍ଥାନ ଦେଖି ତହିଁ ଗଡ ବନାଇଲେ ।
କିଛି ପ୍ରଜା ଆଣି ସେଥି ବସତି କରିଲେ ।।୨୦।।
ପ୍ରଥମେ ଗଠିତ ହେଲା ବଡ ଦରବାର ।
ସେଥିପାଇଁ ଆଜିଯାଏ ଏରାଜବଂଶର ।।୨୧।।

ନରେଶ ହୁଅନ୍ତି ସେହି ସୁଶାସନେ ବସୀ ।
ସପ୍ତ ମୂର୍ତୀକା ସେଠାରେ ରଖାଯାଇ ଅଛି ॥୨୨॥
ଏପରି ମିଥୁନ ମାମୁଁ ଧନୁଯାଏଗଲା ।
ପୌଷ ପୂର୍ଣ୍ଣମୀ ଦିବସ ପ୍ରବେଶ ହୋଇଲା ॥୨୩॥
ନୃପତୀ କରିବା ପାଇଁ ସେହି ଜମୀଦାର ।
ଆୟୋଜନ କଲେ ଅଭିଷେକର ସମ୍ଭାର ॥୨୪॥
ବଣାଇ ନୃପ ଆସନେ ପ୍ରତାପ ଦେବଙ୍କୁ ।
ନୃପତି ଗଣରେ ସାଢି ସମର୍ପିଲେ ତାଙ୍କୁ ॥୨୫॥
ମସ୍ତକେ ଲଗାଇ ଦେଲେ ସିନ୍ଦୁରର ଚିତା ।
ପ୍ରଥମେ ବାଣେସରଙ୍କୁ ଟେକାଇଲେ ଛତା ॥୨୬॥
ସେହିଛତ୍ର ନେଇ ରାଜା ମସ୍ତକେ ଟେକିଲେ ।
ବଣାଇଁ ନରେଶ ବୋଲି ନମସ୍କାର କଲେ ॥୨୭॥
ପ୍ରଜା ପୁଞ୍ଜ ମିଳି ମୁଖେ କଲେ ଯୟ ଧ୍ୱନୀ ।
ଶ୍ରୀ ପ୍ରତାପରୁଦ୍ର ଦେବ ନୃପଶିରୋମଣି ॥୨୮॥
ଅବଧି ସେ ଜମିଦାର କରିଛନ୍ତି ରାଜା ।
ମାଟିଶ୍ୱର ବୋଲି ସର୍ବେ କରୁଥାନ୍ତି ପୂଜା ॥୨୯॥
ନୃପ ପଣେ ବସି ରୁଦ୍ରଦେବ ନରପତି ।
ପରିକ୍ଷ ନୃପତି ସମ ପାଳିଲେକ କ୍ଷିତୀ ॥୩୦॥
କାଟି ଜଙ୍ଗଲ ପରଜା ବସତି କରିଲେ ।
ନୂତନ ନୂତନ ଧାନ୍ୟ କ୍ଷେତ୍ର ବନାଇଲେ ॥୩୧॥
ବିବାହ ହୋଇଲେ ଭଞ୍ଜ-ଭୂମି ନୃପ ସୁତା ।
ପତିପ୍ରାଣା ସୁଲକ୍ଷଣି ସର୍ବଗୁଣ ଯୁତା ॥୩୨॥

ଗାଙ୍ଗପୁର ଭଞ୍ଜଭୂମି ସମଲାଇ ପୁର ।
ମୁରଗୁଜା ଖଡିଆଳ ଆଉ ସର୍ଣ୍ଣପୁର ॥୩୩॥
ପାଟଣା ବାମଣ୍ଡା ଆଉ ସିଂହଭୂମି ଦେଶେ ।
ବନ୍ଧୁତ୍ୱ ପ୍ରକାଶ କରି ରହିଲେ ହରଷେ ॥୩୪॥
କେନ୍ଦୁଝର ଭଞ୍ଜଭୂମି ବାମଣ୍ଡା ପାଟଣା ।
ସମ୍ବଲପୁର ଉତ୍‌ତମ କରିଣ ଗଣନା ॥୩୫॥
ରହିଛନ୍ତି ଏହିବଂଶ ଭାଇପୁଅ ମାନେ ।
ଏହାଛଡା ଅନ୍ୟଦେଶେ ନାହାନ୍ତି ସପନେ ॥୩୬॥
ସେହିରାଜ ବଂଶ ପୁରୋହିତ ଗୋପିନାଥ ।
ଦିର୍ଘାୟୁ କାମନା କରି ରହିଛି ଶତତ ॥୩୭॥

ଅଷ୍ଟମ ଛାନ୍ଦ

ରାଗ – ଚକ୍ରକେଳୀ

ଯମୀଦାରର ଥିଲା ଇନ୍ଦ୍ରନାମ ।
ରୁଦ୍ର ଦେବଙ୍କୁ ଯେ କଲାରାଜନ ।୧।
କେବଳ ସେହିଏତିକି ମାଗିଲା
ମୋର ନାମେ ରାଜା ହୁଅବୋଇଲା ।୨।
କଥାମାନି ପ୍ରତାପ ରୁଦ୍ର ଦେବ ।
ଇନ୍ଦ୍ରଦେବ ପଦେହେଲେ ରାଜିବ ।୩।
ଚଉତ୍ରୀଂଶ ବର୍ଷ ପାଳିଲେ ମହି ।
କର୍ମେ ଚଳିଲେ ନାନା ଦୁଃଖସହି ।୪।
ତାଙ୍କ କୁମର ଦିନମଣୀ ଦେବ ।

ରାଜା ହୋଇ ସେବନ୍ତି ସଦାଶିବ ।୫।
ମହାବୀର ନାମେ କୋହ୍ଲ ଗୋଟିଏ ।
ଝରାଗଡରେ ବାସ କରିଥାଏ ।୬।
ତାରସଙ୍ଗେ ଛଅଟି ଭାଇଥିଲେ ।
ଦୁଷ୍ଟ ପଣେ ରାଜାଙ୍କୁ ନମାନିଲେ ।୭।
ନରେଶ ବିନାଶ ମନରେ ଧରି ।
ହୋଇଥିଲେ ସେ ସଦା ଶସ୍ତ୍ରଧାରୀ ।୮।
ଖବର ପାଇ ନୃପ ଦୀନମଣୀ ।
ମହାବୀରଙ୍କୁ ପକାଇଲେ ହାଣି ।୯।
ଦୁଇଜଣଙ୍କୁ ସେଠାରେ ମାଇଲେ ।
ବାକୀ ଚାରିହେଁ ଯାଣି ପଲାଇଲେ ।୧୦।
ରାଜା ଗୋଡାଇଲେ ବ୍ୟଗ୍ର ଗତିରେ ।
ଯାଇ ଭେଟିଲେ ଘରବୁଡାଠାରେ ।୧୧।
ଦୁଇଜଣଙ୍କୁ କରିଶିରଛେଦ ।
ପକାଇ ଦେଲେ ସେହି ବନ ମଧ୍ୟ ।୧୨।
ପୁଣି ଗୋଡାଇଲେ ଅତିଖରେ ।
ଜଣେ ମାଇଲେ ଯାଙ୍ଗଡାଗ୍ରାମରେ ।୧୩।
କେବଳ ଚନ୍ଦ୍ର ପଲାଇଣଗଲା ।
ପାଲ ଲହଡା ଜଙ୍ଗଲେ ପସିଲା ।୧୪।
ଧାଇଁ ନୃପତାଙ୍କୁ ତହିଁ ଧଇଲେ ।
ମାରିବାଙ୍କୁ ଖଡଗ ଉଠାଇଲେ ।୧୫।
ଦେଖି ଚନ୍ଦ୍ର ପାଦ ତଳେ ପଡିଲା ।

ମୋତେ ନ ମାର କହୁଛି ବୋଇଲା ।୧୬।

ଯେଉଁ ତିନିଙ୍କୁ ମାଇଲ ଗଡରେ ।

ତାଙ୍କୁ ପୂଜାକର ନିଜ ନବରେ ।।୧୭।

ଘୋର ବିପଦେ ବୀର ରୁପ ବହି ।

ରକ୍ଷାକରିବେ ତବ ବଂଶ ମହି ।୧୮।

ମୋର ନାମେ ପାଟ ରଖି ମସ୍ତକେ ।

ସୁଖେ ରାଜ୍ୟତୁ କର ନିଷ୍କ କେ ।୧୯।

ଏହି ମାଗୁଣି ଦେଇ ଶିର ଛେଦ ।

କେବେ ନୋହିବ ତୋବଂଶେ ବିପଦ ।୨୦।

କହୁଁ କହୁଁ ତାହାରି ମୁଣ୍ଡହାଣି ।

ଫେରି ଆସିଲେ ନୃପ ଦୀନମଣି ।୨୧।

ଚନ୍ଦ୍ର କଥାକୁ ବିଶ୍ୱାସ ରଖିଲେ ।

ତିନିଭାଇଙ୍କୁ ନବରେ ପୂଜିଲେ ।୨୨।

ଚନ୍ଦ୍ର ଦେବ ପାଟ ମସ୍ତକେ ବହି ।

ତେଏ ଷଠ ବର୍ଷ ପାଲିଲେ ମହି ।୨୩।

ତାଙ୍କର କୁମର ମ୍‌ଧୁସୁଦନ ।

ତହିଁ ଉତ୍‌ତାରୁ ହୋଇଲେ ରାଜନ ।୨୪।

. . ମଳା ଗତେ ଗୋବିନ୍ଦ କୈବର୍ତ୍ତ ।

ମାରିବାକୁ ସେ ହୋଇଲା ଉଦ୍ଧତ ।୨୫।

. . ନେବଳେ ପସି ପୁର ଭିତରେ ।

ଝପଟିଧାଇଲା ନରେଶ କରେ ।୨୬।

ବୋଇଲା ନିଶ୍ଚୟ ମାରିବି ତୋତେ ।

ଦେଖ ଖଡଗ ଧରିଅଛି ହାତେ ।୨୭।

କହୁଁ କହୁଁ ଖଣ୍ଡା ଉଛୁଡି ନେଲେ ।

ସେହି ଅସ୍ତ୍ରେ ମାରିବାକୁ ବସିଲେ ।୨୮।

ଦେଖି ଗୋବିନ୍ଦ ହୋଇଲା କେତର ।

କାନ୍ଦି କହିଲା ବାରେ ରକ୍ଷାକର ।୨୯।

ଅଥବା ମୋର ନାମକୁ ବହିବୁ ।

ନରେଶହୋଇ ପୃଥିବି ପାଳିବୁ ।୩୦।

. . ହା କହି ପଳାଇଲା ଦଉଡୀ ।

ନୃପତୀ ଧଇଲେ ତାକୁ ଘଉଡି ।୩୧।

. . ର୍ଗ ବାୟବ୍ୟେ ଜଙ୍ଗଲ ଭିତରେ ।

ତାକୁ ମାଇଲେ ହସ୍ତ ଖଡଗରେ ।୩୨।

. . . ଅବଧି ସେସ୍ଥାନ ଚିହ୍ନ ଘେନୀ,

ହୋଇ ରହିଛି କେଉଟ ମାରୁଣି ।୩୩।

କିନ୍ତୁ ଗୋବିନ୍ଦ କଥାକୁ ମାନିଲେ ।

ଗୋବିନ୍ଦ ଦେବ ପାଟକୁ ବହିଲେ ।୩୪।

ଏହି ରୁପରେ ବହି ତିନି ପାଟ ।

ପାଳିଲେ ମହୀ କ୍ଷେତ୍ରିୟ ମୁରାଟ ।୩୫।

. . ପେ ନାବ୍ଦ ବେନି ମାସ ନ ଦିନ ।

ମହିପାଳି ଚଲିଲେ ନିଜସ୍ଥାନ ।୩୬।

ଏହିରୁପେ ତିନି ପାଟ ହୋଇଲା ।

ଦ୍ୱିଜ ଗୋପୀନାଥ ଛନ୍ଦେ ରଚିଲା ।୩୭।

ନବମ ଛାନ୍ଦ

ରାଗ – ମାଳବ

ଦିନମଣି ସୁତ ରାମ   ଚନ୍ଦ୍ରଇନ୍ଦ୍ରଦେବ ।
ଆଠବର୍ଷ ତିନିମାସ ହୋଇଲେ ଭୋଦେବ ।୧।
ତାଙ୍କ ସୁତ କୀର୍ତୀବାସ ଇନ୍ଦ୍ରଦେବ ରାଜା ।
. . . ନୀ ଶାବ୍ଦ ଦୁଇ ମାସ ପାଲିଲେ ପରଜା ।୨।
କିର୍ତୀବାସ ସୁତ ପରମେଷ୍ଠି ଚନ୍ଦ୍ରଦେବ ।
ପନ୍ଦର ବର୍ଷ ପାଲିଲେ   ବହି ସଦଭାବ ।୩।
ମୁକୁନ୍ଦଗୋବିନ୍ଦ ଦେବ ତାଙ୍କର ନନ୍ଦନ ।
ସାତ ବର୍ଷ ଏକମାସ ହୋଇଲେ ରାଜନ ।୪।
ଗିରିଧାରି ସୁରଦେବ ତାଙ୍କର କୁମର ।
ବାଇସ ବର୍ଷ ନମାସ ପାଳିଲେ ଭୁଭାର ।୫।
ଦୋମୃକୁର୍ତୀଧର ଶଶଧର ଦେବ ।
ଚାଳିସ ବର୍ଷ ରାଜତ୍ୱ ଗଲେନିଜ ଠାବ ।୬।
ଡମ୍ବରୁଧର ଗୋବିନ୍ଦ ଦେବ ମହିପତି ।
ଛଅ ବର୍ଷ ଏକମାସ ପାଳିଲେ ଏ କ୍ଷିତୀ ।୭।
ବିଶ୍ୱେଶ୍ୱର ଇନ୍ଦ୍ରଦେବ ତାଙ୍କର ତନୟ ।
ଏକାବନ ବର୍ଷ ପାଳି ତ୍ୟାଗକଲେ ଦେହ ।୮।
ନିଳକଣ୍ଠ ଚନ୍ଦ୍ରଦେବ ତାଙ୍କର କୁମର ।
ତେଇଶ ବର୍ଷ ପାଳିଲେ ବହୀ ମହୀ ଭାର ।୯।
ନାରାୟଣ ଗୋବିନ୍ଦ ଦେବ ସୁତ ତାଙ୍କର ।
ଦଶ ବର୍ଷ ଏକମାସ ହେଲେ ନୃପବର ।୧୦।

ହୃଶିକେଶ ଇନ୍ଦ୍ରଦେବ ତାଙ୍କର ନନ୍ଦନ ।
ଦ୍ୱାତ୍ରିଂଶାବ୍ଦ ଦୁଇମାସ ହୋଇଲେ ରାଜନ ।୧୧।
ତାଙ୍କ ସୁତ ଯଦୁମଣି ଚନ୍ଦ୍ରଦେବ ରାଜା ।
ପଚିଶ ବରସ ସେହି ପାଳିଲେ ପରଜା ।୧୨ ।
ଗିରିଧାରି ଗୋବିନ୍ଦ ଦେବ ତାଙ୍କର ପୁଅ ।
ସାତ ବର୍ଷ ରାଜା ହୋଇ ତ୍ୟାଗ କଲେ ଦେହ ।୧୩ ।
ମୁକୁନ୍ଦ ଅବ୍ୟୟ ରାଜ ଦେବ ତାଙ୍କ ସୁତ ।
ବାଉନ ବରସ ସେହୁ କରିଲେ ରାଜତ୍ୱ ।୧୪ ।
ତାଙ୍କ ସୁତ ତ୍ରିବିକ୍ରମ ଚନ୍ଦ୍ରଦେବ ରାଜା ।
... ଇସ ବରସ ରାଜ୍ୟେ ଉଡ଼ାଇଲେ ଧ୍ୱଜା ।୧୫ ।
ତାଙ୍କ କୁମର ଗୋବିନ୍ଦ ଦେବ କାମପାଳ ।
ଚାରିବର୍ଷ ଏକମାସ ହେଲେ ମହିପାଳ ।୧୬ ।
ତଦୁ ।ରେ ଇନ୍ଦ୍ରଦେବ ବୀରଂଚୀ ରାଜନ ।
. . .ବାବନ ବର୍ଷ ମହି ପାଳିଲେ ଜତନ ।।୧୭।।
. . .ଧବ ସୁଧାଂଶୁ ଦେବ ତନୟ ତାଙ୍କର ।
. . . ଇଶ ବର୍ଷ ପାଳିଲେ ବହିମହୀ ଭାର ।।୧୮।।
ତାଙ୍କର ତନୟ ବାସୁଦେବ ନୃପମଣୀ ।
ଗୋବିନ୍ଦ ଦେବ ପାଟରେ ଶାଶିଲେ ଧରଣୀ ।୧୯।।
ପାଂଚ ବର୍ଷ ନଅମାସ ଏକ ଦିବସରେ ।
ଭବଲୀଳା ତ୍ୟାଗକରି ଗଲେ ନିଯ ପୁରେ ।।୨୦।।
ତାଙ୍କ କୁମର ମହିନ୍ଦ୍ର ଦେବ ନରପତି ।
ବଜ୍ରଧର ଦେବପଦେ ପାଳିଲେ ଧରିତ୍ରୀ ।।୨୧।।

ଚାଳିଶ ବରଶ ଆଠମାସ ତିନିଦିନେ ।
ଭବଭୂମି ତ୍ୟାଗ କରି ଗଲେ ନିଜ ଧାମେ ॥୨୨॥
ଗଦାଧର ଚନ୍ଦ୍ର ଦେବ ତାଙ୍କର କୁମର ।
ଅଠର ବର୍ଷ ପାଳିଲେ ବହୀ ମହୀ ଭାର ॥୨୩॥
ମକର ଧ୍ୱଜ ଗୋବିନ୍ଦ ଦେବ ତାଙ୍କ ପୁଅ ।
ସାତ ବର୍ଷ ରାଜପଣେ ତ୍ୟାଗକଲେ ଦେହ ॥୨୪॥
ଏହାଙ୍କ ରାଜତ୍ୱେ ଖଣା, କଟା, ଖାଇ, ବନ୍ଧ ।
ଗଡ ଚାରିପାଶ କାନେ କରିଥିଲେ ବନ୍ଦ ॥୨୫॥
କେବଳ ତିନିଟି ଦ୍ୱାର ଥିଲା ତିନିପାଶେ ।
କପାଟ ଦେଇ ଭିତରେ ରହୁଥିଲେ ସୁଖେ ॥୨୬॥
କ୍ଷେତ୍ରପାଳ ନାମେ ଥିଲା ପ୍ରଥମ ଦୁଆର ।
ଦ୍ୱାର ଶୁଣି ନାମେ ଜଗୁଥିଲେ ଏକ ବୀର ॥୨୭॥
ଅବଧୀ ସେଥିରେ ଦେବଙ୍କ ପୂଜା ପାଉଛନ୍ତି ସେହି ।
ମକର ଧ୍ୱଜ ଦେବଙ୍କ କୀରତୀ ଅଛଇ ॥୧୮॥
ଦ୍ୱୀତୀୟରେ ବଡ ଦ୍ୱାରେ ଥିଲେ ମହାବୀର ।
ଭାଇସହ ଜଗୁଆଳି ଥିଲେ ସେହିଠାର ॥୨୯॥
ତୃତୀୟ ଦୁଆର ପାଶେ ଅନ୍ଧାରି ଥାପିଲେ ।
ଅନ୍ଧାରି ଦୁଆର ବୋଲି ନାମରଖି ଦେଲେ ॥୩୦॥
ଶତ୍ରୁ ଭୟ ଭିତି କିଛି ନଥିଲା ନବରେ ।
ସୁଖେ ବାସ କରୁଥିଲେ ପୁରବାସୀ ନରେ ॥୩୧॥
ତାଙ୍କ ସୁତ ଇନ୍ଦ୍ରଦେବ ପରମ ଆନନ୍ଦ ।
ଛପନାବ୍ଦ ତିନିମାସ ହୋଇଲେ ନରେନ୍ଦ୍ର ॥୩୨॥

ଦୋମୃଜଶୀର ପାଣୀ ଚନ୍ଦ୍ରଦେବ ରାଜା ।
ତେଇଶ ବର୍ଷ ଦ୍ୱିମାସ ପାଳିଲେ ପରଜା ।।୩୩।।
ପୁରୁଷ ଉତ୍ତମ ଦେବ ତାଙ୍କର କୁମର ।
ଗୋବିନ୍ଦ ଦେବ ପାଟରେ ବହି ରାଜ୍ୟ ଭାର ।।୩୪।।
ତାଙ୍କ ସୁତ ପୁରନ୍ଦର ଦେବହେଲେ ରାଜା ।
ପୂର୍ବ ରିତୀ ଅନୁସାରେ ପାଳିଲେ ପରଜା ।।୩୫।।
ଗୋବିନ୍ଦ ଦେବ ପାଟରେ ନୃପତି ହେବାକୁ ।
କଥାଥିଲା ବସି ପ୍ରଜା ଦେଶ ପାଳିବାକୁ ।।୩୬।।
କିନ୍ତୁ ଏପାଟ ନରେଶ ଅଳ୍ପ ରାଜତ୍ୱରେ ।
ଚଳୀଲେ ଅନେକ ରାଜା କାଳ କବଳରେ ।।୩୭।।
ସେହିଭୟେ ଗୋବିନ୍ଦ ପାଟକୁ ଉଠାଇଲେ ।
ଇନ୍ଦ୍ରଦେବ ପାଟେ ବସି ଅଭିଷେକ ହେଲେ ।।୩୮।।
ରହିଲା ଗୋବିନ୍ଦପାଟ ସେହିଦିନଠାରୁ ।
ଇନ୍ଦ୍ର ଚନ୍ଦ୍ର ବେନିପାଟ ହେଲେଏ ଏ ଉତ୍ତାରୁ ।।୩୯।।
ସତାବନ ବର୍ଷ ବେନିମାସ ଏକଦିନ ।
ପାଳି ମହୀ ଭାଳି ଚଳିଗଲେ ନିଜ ସ୍ଥାନ ।।୪୦।।
ଏକତ୍ରିଂଶ ପାଟେ ଏହି ପାଟ ଉଠିଗଲା ।
ଦ୍ୱିଜ ଗୋପିନାଥ ଛଳ ବଳେ ବିରଚିଲା ।।୪୧।।

ଦଶମ ଛାନ୍ଦ

ରାଗ- ବଙ୍ଗଳାଶ୍ରୀ

ପୁରନ୍ଦର ସୁତ ପଦ୍ମନାଭ ଦେବ ଚନ୍ଦ୍ରଦେବ ନୃପମଣୀ ।

ପନ୍ଦର ବରସ ଏଗାର ଦିବସ ପାଳନ କଲେ ଧରଣୀ ।୧।
ତାଙ୍କର କୁମର ଇନ୍ଦ୍ରଦେବ ବୀର ପଦ୍ମ ଲୋଚନ ନରେଶ ।
ପୀତା ଗୁଣ ଘେନି ପାଳିଲେ ଅବନୀ ବିଂଶ ବର୍ଷ ତିନିମାସ ।୨।
ଦେବେନ୍ଦ୍ର ପ୍ରତାପ ଚନ୍ଦ୍ରଦେବ ନୃପ ହୋଇଲେ ତାଙ୍କ ଉତ୍ତାରେ ।
ନବବର୍ଷ ବେନି, ମାସ ଦିନାତିନି, ପାଳିଲେ ପ୍ରଜା ନିକରେ ।୩।
ତାଙ୍କର କୁମର ଇନ୍ଦ୍ରଦେବ ନୃପ ବୀର କଦମ୍ବ କେଶରୀ ।
ଚଉଦ ବରଷ ନଅଗୋଟି ମାସ ହୋଇଲେ ଦଣ୍ଡଧାରି ।୪।
ରାମଚନ୍ଦ୍ର ଦେବ ନୃପଇନ୍ଦ୍ର ତହିଁପରେ ହେଲେରାଜା ।
ସତର ବରଷ ପନ୍ଦର ଦିବସ ପାଳିଲେ ଦେଶ ପରଜା ।୫।
କୁମାରି ତାଙ୍କର ଆଦି ପୁରୁଷରୁ ହୋଇଥିଲେ ଇଷ୍ଟ ଦେବୀ ।
ଦୁର୍ଗ ଉ ରରେ ବ୍ରାହ୍ମଣୀ ତୀରରେ କରିପୁର ଅନୁଭବୀ ।୬।
ବଶାଇଲେ ନେଇ ନବ ପୁତୁଳିକା ଶୀଳାଧାନ ଯତୁ ମୟୀ ।
ପୂଜା କରୁଥିଲେ ତୁଷ୍ଟ ମାନସରେ ତରବାରି ରଖିତହିଁ ।୭।
କେଉଁଝର ନୃପ ପେଶି ଚୋରଦୂତ ଚୋରାଇନେଲେ ଅସ୍ତ୍ରକୁ ।
ହୋଇଲା ସମର ବେନିରାଜାଙ୍କର ବିରୁଦ୍ଧ ରଖି ମନକୁ ।୮।
ହାରି କେନ୍ଦୁଝର ନୃପତୀ ଶେଖର ଜୀବନ ହତ୍ୟାଭୟରେ ।
ସେହି ତରବାରୀ ଦେଲେଆଣିକରି ରାମଚନ୍ଦ୍ରଙ୍କ ଛାମୁରେ ।୯।
ସେହି ଦିବସରୁ କୁମାରି ମନ୍ଦିରେ ନରଖିଲେ ତରବାରି ।
ରାଜଭରନରେ ରଖାଯାଉଥିଲା ଗୁପ୍ତଚରଭୟକରି ।୧୦।
ରାମଚନ୍ଦ୍ର ସୁତ ବୀର ଯଦୁନାଥ ଇନ୍ଦ୍ରଦେବ ନୃପବର ।
ପୁର ନିକଟରେ ଜଗନ୍ନାଥ ମୂର୍ତ୍ତି ସ୍ଥାପିଲେ କରି ମନ୍ଦିର ।୧୧।
ଇଷ୍ଟ ଦେବ ଶାଳ ଗ୍ରାମଶୀଳା ରଘୁନାଥ ଦେଶୁଆଣିଥିଲେ ।

ଯଗନ୍ନାଥ ପୁରେ ରଖିଲେ ଜତ୍‌ନରେ ପୂଜାବିଧି ନିମିରେ ।୧୨।

ଗୁଣ୍ଡିଚା ଯାତ୍ରାଦି ଥିଲେସେ ସମ୍ପାଦି ଦେଇଥିଲେ ଦୁଇଗ୍ରାମ ।

. . . ପନାବ୍ଦ ବେନିମାସ ଦଶଦିନେ ଚଳିଗଲେ ନିଜ ଧାମ ।୧୩।

ଉଦେ ନାରାୟଣ ଦେବ ନୃପରାଣ ଯଦୁନାଥଙ୍କର ସୁତ ।

ଚନ୍ଦ୍ରଦେବ ପଦେ ଚବିଶ ବରଷ କୋଇଥିଲେ ନରନାଥ ।୧୪।

ତାଙ୍କ କୁମର କାଳିୟା ଚନ୍ଦ୍ରଦେବ ଇନ୍ଦ୍ରଦେବ ସମୟରେ ।

ବାମଣ୍ଡା ବଣାଇଁ ହୋଇଲା ଲଢାଇ ସିମାନାର ବିଷୟରେ ।୧୫।

ଗଡମଧ୍ୟେ ପସି ବାମଣ୍ଡା ନରେଶ ଲୋଟୁଥିଲେ ପୁରଜନ ।

କରି ଆକ୍ରମଣ ବଣାଇରାଜନ କରିଦେଲେ ଛିନ୍ନ ଭିନ୍ନ ।୧୬।

ଭୟେ ରାଜଛତ୍ର ଛାଡି ପଳାଇଲେ ବାମଣ୍ଡା ସୈନିକ ବଳ ।

ଅବଧି ସେ ଛତ୍ରେ ଥାପୀତ ଦେବଙ୍କୁ ପୁଜନ୍ତି ଜନ ସକଳ ।୧୭।

ଯେତେ ସନ୍ୟଥିଲେ ସମସ୍ତ ମାଇଲେ ଗଡାଇଲେ ମୁଣ୍ଡଯହିଁ ।

ମୁଣ୍ଡଗଡା ବନ୍ଧ ବୋଲି ଆଜିଯାଏ ନାମଅଛିତାର ରହି ।୧୮।

କେବଳ ନୃପତି ପଳାଇଲେ ଏକା ନିଜ ପରାଣ ଭୟରେ ।

ଆଜିଯାଏ ଗୁଳମାଳ ଚଲୁଅଛି ଶିମାନାର ବିଷୟରେ ।୧୯।

ଚୌରାଳିସ ବର୍ଷ ଅଠର ଦିବସ ରାଯାପଣେ ପାଳି ମହି ।

କଳାଚନ୍ଦ୍ର ଦେବ ଭବଲୀଳା ତେଜି ଶୂନ୍ୟପଥେଗଲେ ବହି ।୨୦।

ଶ୍ରୀବୀରକୀଶ୍ୱରି ଦେବଦଣ୍ଡଧାରି କାଳିୟାଚନ୍ଦ୍ର କୁମାର ।

ଇନ୍ଦ୍ରଦେବପଦେ ବସି ନିର୍ବୀବାଦେ ଚଳାଇଲେ ରାଜ୍ୟଭାର ।୨୧।

ଚଉଦ ବରଷ ଏକାଦଶମାସ ସାତଦିନ ପାଳି ଭୁବୀ ।

ଚଳିଲେ ସପୁରେ କାଳ କବଳରେ ନିଯପଥ ଅନୁଭବୀ ।୨୨।

ତାଙ୍କ କୁମର ବାଲୁକେଶ୍ୱର ଦେବ ଇନ୍ଦ୍ରଦେବ ନୃପମଣି ।

ବାଇସବର୍ଷ ସାତବର୍ଷ ନଅଦିନ ପାଳିଲେ ଜାଣ ଧରଣୀ ।୨୩।
ତାଙ୍କ କୁମର ବୀର ବାଶେଣସର ନୃପ ଶଶଧର ଦେବ ।
ଉନବିଂଶ ବର୍ଷ ଏଗାରଟି ମାସ ହୋଇଣଥିଲେ ରାଜନ ।୨୪।
ତାଙ୍କ ନନ୍ଦନ ଗୋବିନ୍ଦଇନ୍ଦ୍ରଦେବ ନୃପତି ହେଲେ ଏଠାରେ ।
ତେତ୍ରିଂଶବର୍ଷ ରାଜତ୍ୱ ଭୋଗକରି ଚଳିଗଲେ ନିଜ ପୁରେ ।୨୫।
ତାଙ୍କର କୁମର ହରିଦେବ ଚନ୍ଦ୍ରଦେବ ନୃପମଣି ।
ଚଉଦବର୍ଷ ସାତମାସ ନଦିନ ଶାଶିଲେ ଏହି ଧରଣି ।୨୬।
ତାହାଙ୍କର ସୁତ ବୀର ଗୋପୀନାଥ ଇନ୍ଦ୍ରଦେବ ସମୟରେ ।
ହେଲା ଗୋଳମାଳ ନାଗରା ବଣାଇଁ ସିମାନାର ବିରୁଦ୍ଧରେ ।୨୭।
କିନ୍ତୁ ସେ ବିରୁଦ୍ଧ ହେଲାନିର୍ବୀବାଦ ବଙ୍ଗପୁର ନୃପବଳେ ।
ଥାପିଲେ ସିମାନା ଖମ୍ବ ସ୍ଥାନେସ୍ଥାନେ ନିଜମଧ୍ୟସ୍ଥ ପଣରେ ।୨୮।
ତେଇଶବର୍ଷ ଦୁଇମାସଛଦିନ ପାଳିମହିରାଜ ପଣେ ।
ଛାଡି ଭବଲୀଳା ଗୋପୀନାଥଦେବ ଚଳିଲେ ନିଜଧାମେ ।୨୯।
ତାଙ୍କସୁତ ରାମ କରି ଚନ୍ଦ୍ରଦେବ ଚାରିବର୍ଷ ହୋଇରାଜା ।
ଚଳିଲେ ସପୁରେ କାଳକବଳରେ ତେଜିସଜନ ପରଜା ।୩୦।
ତାଙ୍କ ସୁତ ରଘୁନାଥ ଇନ୍ଦ୍ରଦେବ ହେଲେ ବଣାଇଁ ରାଜନ ।
ପାଳିଥିଲେ ଦେଶ ଚଉଦବରସ ତିନିମାସ ଛଅଦିନ ।୩୧।
ତାଙ୍କ ତନୟ ଭୀଖାରି ଚନ୍ଦ୍ରଦେବ ପ୍ରକାଶକଲେ ରାଜତ୍ୱ ।
ମାପକଲେ ଦେଶ ହଳବାଳିକରି ମାଣଗୁଣ୍ଠ ଚଉବିଂଶ ।୩୨।
କୁପେଶ୍ୱର ଦେବ ମନ୍ଦିର ପ୍ରତିଷ୍ଠା କରିଣ ଥାପିଲେ ଲିଂଗ ।
କିନ୍ତୁ ସେ ଦେଉଳ ନିଜକୃତ ନୁହେ ତାଙ୍କର ଦେଓ୍ୱାନର ସଙ୍ଗା୩୩।
କରିଖଞ୍ଜାବାଡୀ ନିଯୋଗ ଯୋଗାଡି ସାଧାରଣ ବିଚାରରେ ।

ସପତ ବରସ ପାଳି ନିଜଦେଶ ଚଳିଗଲେ ନିଜପୁରେ ।୩୪।
ତାଙ୍କର କୁମର ବୀର ପିତାମ୍ବର ଇନ୍ଦ୍ରଦେବ ନରପତି ।
କଲେ ଦେବଗ୍ରାମ ଶାଶନ ପ୍ରଦାନ କରି ବ୍ରାହ୍ମଣ ବସତି ।୩୫।
କିନ୍ତୁ ସେହିଗ୍ରାମ ବଦଳରେ ପୁଣି ପୀତାମ୍ବର ପୁର ଦେଲେ ।
ତେଇଶ ବରସ ହୋଇନରଇଶ ବିଶ୍ୱଲୀଳାତ୍ୟାଗକଲେ ।୩୬।
ତାଙ୍କର ତନୟ ଭାଗିରଥିଦେବ ଚନ୍ଦ୍ରଦେବ ନୃପରାଣ ।
ସତରବରଷ ପାଳିଏହିଦେଶ ଚଳିଗଲେ ନିଜଧାମ ।୩୭।
ତାଙ୍କର ନନ୍ଦନ ଶିବନାରାୟଣ ଇନ୍ଦ୍ରଦେବ ନୃପବର ।
ଶିବନାରାୟଣ ଶାଶନ ପ୍ରଦାନ କରିଲେ ଗଙ୍ଗାଗଉରା ।
ବ୍ରାହ୍ମଣ ବସତି କରି ସେହିସ୍ଥାନେ ପାଳିଲେ ଭକତିଭରେ ।
ଉନବିଂଶାବ୍ଦ ଦୁଇମାସଛଦିନେ ଚଳିଲେ ନିଜପୁରରେ ।୩୯।
ଚନ୍ଦ୍ରଶେଖର ଚନ୍ଦ୍ରଦେବ ନୃପତି ତହିଁପରେ ହେଲେରାଜା ।
ତେଏର ବରଷ ପାଳିନିଜଦେଶ ଭବ ଭୂମିକଲେତେଜ୍ୟା ।୪୦।
ଚନ୍ଦ୍ରଶେଖରଙ୍କ କୁମର ଶ୍ରୀଧର ଇନ୍ଦ୍ରଦେବ ନୃପବର ।
ତେତ୍ରିଶ ବରଷ ପାଳିଲେଦେଶ ଚଳିଲେ ଶୂନ୍ୟପୁର ।୪୧।
ତାହାଙ୍କ କୁମର ଡିଲେଶ୍ୱରଦେବ ଚନ୍ଦ୍ରଦେବ ନୃପମଣି ।
ତିନିବର୍ଷ ତିନିମାସ ରାଜାପଣେ ଶାଶିଲେଏହି ଧରଣୀ ।୪୨।
ଖ୍ରୀଷ୍ଟ ଅବ୍ଦ ଉନବିଂଶ ଶତଏକ ସାଲରୁ ହେଲେ ନରେଶ ।
ଦୟାର ଆଗାର ଶ୍ରୀଧରଣୀଧର ଇନ୍ଦ୍ରଦେବ ନରଇଶ ।୪୩।
ବିଶେଷ ତ ଭାବେ ଏ ବଂଶ ବର୍ଣ୍ଣନା କରିବାକୁ ମୁ ଅକ୍ଷମ ।
କିନ୍ତୁ ଯାହାଥିଲା ଲେଖନୀଧରିମୁ କଲିଲେଖନ ଚାଳନ ।୪୪।
ଥିଲେ ଦୁଶା ଦୁଶ ତ୍ୟାଗ କରିବାକୁ ଏତିକି ପ୍ରାର୍ଥନା ମୋର ।

ଯଥା ରାଜହଂସ କ୍ଷୀର ପାନକରି ତ୍ୟାଗ କରିଦିଏ ନୀର ।୪୫।

ତଥା ବିଜ୍ଞନରେ ଦୋଶପର୍ଯ୍ୟନରେ ହୋଇବେ ବୋଲି ସହାୟ ।

ନରଇନ୍ଦ୍ରପଦେ ଏତିକି ମାଗୁଣୀ କରୁଅଛିଁ ଅହରହ ।୪୬।

ତ୍ରିଶୂଳଧାରଣ ହେରମା ରମଣ କରିତାଙ୍କୁ ଅନୁଗ୍ରହ ।

ସୁବିପଳ କୀର୍ତୀ ପ୍ରକାଶ କରଣେ ଉଦ୍ଦିପନ କରପୁଅ ।୪୭।

ସଧନେ ଇନ୍ଦିରା ହୁଅନ୍ତୁ ଅଧୀରା ବାଣୀ ବସି କଣ୍ଠ ଦେଶେ ।

କୀରତି ପତାକେ ଇନ୍ଦ୍ରଦେବ ପଦେ ଉଡୁଥାଉ

ଦେଶେଦେଶେ।୪୮।

ଖଗବରଧାରୀ ବିଶ୍ୱଜେତା ହରି ହୋଇଥାନ୍ତୁ ସୁପ୍ରଶନ୍ନ ।

ଧରଣୀଧର ଇନ୍ଦ୍ର ଦେବ ନୃପତି ଲଭନ୍ତୁ ଦୀର୍ଘ ଜୀବନ ।୪୯।

କରି ଶୁଭ ବାର୍ତା ଯାହାଥିଲାଇଛା ଦେଇନରେଶ ପୟରେ ।

ଦ୍ୱିଜ ଗୋପିନାଥ ଛଳେ ବୀରଚିତ କରି ଆଶୀର୍ବାଦକରେ ।୫୦।

ସଂପୁର୍ଣ୍ଣ

ସହାୟକ – କଲେଇ ପ୍ରଧାନ (କିଷାନ ଜାତି)

CHAPTER VI

Kadamba Gatha by Madan Mohan Mishra

Secript prepared by* Pandit Madan Mohan Mishra Jail Road, Keonjhar 1, Orissa, India

The great sage Dattatreya was born from the 'Nabhi Padma' of Lord Bishnu. His son was Budha and Budha's son was Puroraba. His son was Nahusha. From him Yayati was born. His son was Mandhata. Mandhata had six sons. They were Ganga, Gargya, Soma, Dibakar, Bhoj and Kadamba. This Kadamba reigned on the island namely Simhala, that is Ceylon. After ruling for several generations, one king namely Bhiru reigned at Simhala with his six brothers. King Bhiru and his five brothers were issueless. Only the youngest brother Kadamba had a son. At this the eldest son Bhiru and other brothers had in mind:

Sutahine prana
Rajatwapune nahin prayojana

It means that what is the use of remaining alive without a son. Again, it is useless to have the kingship and thereby ruling a princely state without having a son. It is absolutely of no use.

Considering from this point of view, the eldest Bhiru and the other five brothers entrusted the youngest brother Kadamba and his son in ascending the royal throne of Simhala. And bidding farewell to queen Sushila, the eldest Bhiru along with other five brothers set out for the present-day Nilanchal Dham, i.e. Puri, leaving behind their estate Simhala. After crossing the sea in a ship, they reached Rameshwar. After having the *darshan*, of god Shri Rameshwar, they stayed there for five days then proceeded onwards on horses. Thus, they reached Cuttack. After that they reached Bhubaneswar. From there, they proceeded to Sakshigopal (present-day Satyabadi or Sakshigopal locality in Puri district en route to Puri). From there, they advanced to Chandrabhaga (present-day Konarak) where they worshipped the Sun God. After that, they proceeded towards present day Puri and by and by reached 'Atharnala', i.e. a very old bridge having eighteen culverts.

At the checkpost the security personnel demanded tax for entering Puri. At this, the eldest Bhiru and other brothers said:

*The English explanations have been edited for this volume.

rather Kathor Prajna kshatri uttama
Kadamba Banshika Ambhe nohu adhama
Nakara Bhakti Kare Pranam Nohun
Adhinatare navahun Bira Bolaun
Kebal Darshan Kari Kamaladhari
Bahuding jiban Ambhe nija nagari

It means that we are Kshatriyas, i.e. warriors by caste. Our heroic recognization is as Rathore who are very strong in warfare. We are born in the great race namely Kadamba. We are not fools. We never pay salutation to anybody with our hands. We are never subservient before anybody. We do maintain our warrior status. After having a look at Lord Sri Jagannath, who holds a lotus in His hand, we shall return to our own township.

Hearing this, the guard informed the Gajapati king of Orissa about this. The Gajapati, on hearing this matter, passed orders in this sense:

Kavata pathare humbnle basai dig
ehi pathe lao bati tahanku kuha
Jibe sehi pathe jibe chalai Ashwa
Jamiba rather chhhatri Kadamba Vamsha

It means: arrange a path of the edge of blades. After that tell them to proceed riding their respective horses. If they become successful in this attempt of proceeding in that style, then you should be sure that these people are of Kshatriya origin of the Rathore clan. Thereby it will be decided that these people are of Kadamba family as they claim. On hearing of this cruel test, the eldest Bhiru and other brothers became sorrowful and remembered Lord Shri Krishna. After that they started proceeding on the very sharpened edge of the blades, riding on horseback. Two brothers died while moving forward. On seeing such a tragic end of the two, the security persons did stop the other three brothers in moving in a likewise manner. Immediately, they informed the Gajapati king about the tragic end of the innocent princes. The Gajapati at once paid a visit to the spot and became extremely sorry on seeing such an incident. He was now sure about their real family position and turned sympathetic towards them. He:

shudha Kshatriya tumbhemane
Bandhupane niti seba mun karibi
Raha mohar Bhabane
He Kumare

It means: O young princes ! Now I have come to realize that all of you are indeed of pure Kshatriya clan. Henceforth I shall serve you as my personal friend. Please come and stay in my palace.

But the princes did not agree to stay and instead went with him to have a *darshan* of the Lord. There, they took the *prasad*, i.e. the sacred food of the Lord. After that they went around the palace of Gajapati.

After the tragic death of their brothers they had no desire to return to their native country. Neither they wished to stay on Puri as per the request of the Gajapati. So proceeded to Jajpur to have a *darshan* of the famous Goddess Biraja there. After that they proceeded towards Singhbhum. One of the brothers was made the king of Singhbhum. Another brother became king of the Serenda region. Another brother Pratap Rudra was passing his time with a heavy heart at Singhbhum. Once he had altercation with his brothers as a result of which, he left. He proceeded towards Bonai city. At that time he heard:

shunile Banai Nagare
Bana Ishwar Linga
Akarmi gana Dukha dekhi
Dianti apavarga

It means that while moving towards Bonai city, the prince heard that there has been established a Shiva Linga in Banai, by the name of Baneshwar. This Lord is so kind to his devotees that He bestows all kinds of happiness to them in the time of their distress or misfortune.

Thereafter the prince went there and did stay in the forest taking only wild fruits as his food and offering forest flowers for the worship of Lord Baneshwar. In this way his days were passing.

One day, when the king of Banaigada, Banasura, happened to be there to worship Lord Baneshwar as per his daily routine he saw the prince there was about to kill the prince thinking that the prince would snatch away the kingship of Banaigada from him by satisfying the Lord with his intense devotion. Realizing that he would be killed the prince fled and running as far as he could, he did hid himself in the hollow of a Kadamba tree. Fortunately, just at that time a peacock appeared there and instantly the footprints of the prince was wiped away, with his long tail. He too hid from the king behind a cluster of creepers. Banasura followed the prince, but in vain. He could not find any trace of the prince. Disappointed, he returned to his palace. After that the prince came out of the hole of the Kadamba tree. The peacock too came out from his hiding and started dancing before him.

As grateful gesture of it, the Kshatriya kings of the Kadamba Vamsha do not touch the Kadamba tree and still have a peacock as their royal insignia.

Still remaining in his hideout, the prince continued to meditate upon

Lord Baneshwar. The Lord was very pleased and realizing the state of the mind of the prince told him in a dream.

Kali e Banai Rajyare
Heba Nara Ishwar
Kebala Mohari Sebare
Thiba niti Dibasa

It means: 'O' Prince! Tomorrow you will become the king of the Banai Rajya (state). After becoming king you will continue to worship me without negligence.'

Side by side, Lord Baneshwar also passed an order in a dream to the Bhuiyan king (most probably the King Banasura [comment by M.M. Mishra, but the authors disagree here])

Baile Mohara Mandire
Achhi Maha Purusha Kali tu Banai Rajyare
Taku kari Naresha
Tahun Banapure Prabeshi
Taku Kahile Hara
Kali Tuhi Ehi Nabare
Pratun Hua Bahara
Bhairaba Swarupe Rahibu
Jai Baranasire
Nahel Tohar Nipata
Heb ehi Nabare

It means: 'In my temple, a great man is staying. Tomorrow you should make him the king of this Banai kingdom.'

Again, entering into King Banasura's dream he told him 'tomorrow you must leave Banai city in the morning, and go to Banaras where you should stay as a Bhairaba, an attendant of Lord Shiva. Otherwise, you would face your death in this city.

It has been said in the scriptures that a dream one has while sleeping never becomes true. So taking it as the kindness of the Lord Baneshwar, the prince became assured and did enter into the temple of the Lord.

Similarly, taking the dream as truth, king Banasura started moving towards the prince inside the temple. But Lord Baneshwar stopped him at once and strictly ordered him to quit Banai city and proceed towards Banaras with his family. After that

Shuni Banasura nija kutumba ku dhari
Palai asila jai Banasura puri [comment M.M. Mishra: perhaps Baranasi]
Bhairaba Swarupe aji aajae achhi rahi

Bhatki gheni pakhe
Rakhichhnti Um sin

It means: On hearing this order of Lord Baneshwar, the king Banasura, along with his family members did flee to the Banaras city. Hence forward he did remain there as a Bhairaba, a noted attendant of the Lord Shiva and he continues himself in the same rank till today. Lord Shiva, in return, keeps him in that position due to his devotion to him he did offer. Uma is the wife of Lord Shiva. Her husband is called Uma-Sain, i.e. Lord Shiva.

Moreover, as directed in the dream, the Bhuiyan king rushed to the temple and met the prince there. The Bhuiyan king also invited the prince, who was styled as the future king of Bonai, to ensure that proper land for construction of the newly-created kingdom. It so happened, the Gada [also fort–the authors], i.e. the township of the kingdom, was completed in construction in between the Hindu month Ashadha to Paush, within one year.

Prince Pratap Dev changed his name to Indradev and ascended the throne of the Bonai state. Afterwards he engaged himself in the wholehearted worship of Lord Baneshwar with devotion and started maintaining the affairs of the kingly estate Bonai along with bringing happiness and prosperity to his subjects.

After that, he married the princess of Bhanja Bhumi and led a happy married life. In this way he reigned for thirty-four years, fully enjoying the kingship of Bonai Rajya. During his reign:

Gangapur bhanja Bhumi Sambalpur
Suragaja Khadiala Au Swarnpur
Patna Bamanda au Singha Bhumi Deshe
Bandhutwa Prakash Kari Rahile Hareshe

It means: He did keep and maintain very good relationship and goodwill connection with the neighbouring states and others such as Gangapur, Bhanja Bhumi, Sambalpur, Surguja, Khadiala and Swarnpur, Patna, Bamanda, and the Singhbhum region. Thus having very good personal relationship with these states, he did pass his time happily.

Another noteworthy matter took place during his reign and after him. That is:

Keonjhar Bhanja bhumi
Bamanda Patna
Sambalpur Uttama Desh Karina Gamana
Rahi chhanti ehi Deshe Bhai pua mane
Ehachhada Anya deshe Nahanti swapane

It means: In course of time this Kadamba Raj family became extended. The other Kadamba Raj family members did wish to settle in other larger areas and line move freely and independently. Accordingly, they preferred the areas in and around Kendujhar Bhanja Bhumi, Patna, Bamanda and Sambalpur and started settling in these areas of the states. From this point of view, it may be ascertained that there are no other places, except these states in Orissa, where the Kadamba royal brothers can be found.

After Indra Deb, his son Dinamani and grandson Madhusudan reigned in the Bonai state. After them, Ramachandra Deba, Kirtibasa, Mukunda Gobinda Deba, Giridhari Sura Deba, etc., came keeping the great prestige of the Kadamba Raj family in tact all through in the course of time.

Thus rendering the best administration during their reigning in the Bonai Rajya, the Rajas also keep the Kadamba memory bright and intact in the kingly areas of entire Orissa. And finally:

Khrist Abda Unabinsha Ekashata Salame hele Neresha
Dayara Agara Shri Dharanidhar Indra deba Nara Isha

It means: This is the providence of continuity of the Kadamba Royal administration in Banai Rajya, there did appear a king, namely Shree Dharanidhar Indra Deba, who is just like a storehouse of kindness.

From this quotation, it is revealed that in the year of 1901 sal, Shree Dharanidhar Indra Deba became king in the Kadamba Royal family. Most probably, the British government, did raise the question of his family's old tradition or with a view to write down the Kadamba Raj family, Raja Dharanidhar did get the *Kadamba Gatha Pothi* composed by one pandit Gopinath Mishra after 1901.

Hence, the prepared historical Kabya (book in poetry form) may be surely ascertained that it has been composed in the twentieth century.

Such are the facts regarding the establishment of the Kadamba Raj in Bonai State.

But, it seems to be very much fantastic except for some events.

The real creation of the Kadamba Raj in Bonai Rajya has been illustrated in the previous lines which is assured to be true from the historical point of view.

CHAPTER VII

Kadamba Gatha: Synopsis by Surendranath Mishra (Original English Text)[1]

NOTE

The book *Kadamba Gatha* in verse consisting of eighteen chapters was compiled by Sri Gopinath Purohit in 1914, when he was a teacher in the Rajbati Primary School. In 1947, the then Raja Dharanidhar Indra Deo Deb donated the State grant of Rs.150/- and the manuscript was sent to the Manager, Saraswat Press along with the grant money by the then Headmaster, Raja D.D. High School, who went on transfer to Dhenkanal on 21st August 1948.

Thereafter the next Headmasters or the Administrators remained silent about the publication. The book was published but never delivered to the author or the Orissa Government. Steps were being taken to realize[2] the grant money from the author, who had to produce the printed copy in proof stage to Sri G.N. Das as a proof for publication.

The manuscript is lost for the author and the book might have been still kept in the press or destroyed. The second chapter written on the past history speaks of Nanda empire extending upto Tumkela on the Bramhani [*sic*] River. The agitation for Kharswan and Saraikela may be the main cause for stopping the publishing of the book or non-delivery of it.

This note is prepared from synopsis made by the author on which he had based his poems.

Sri S.N. Mishra, the translator has prepared this note while he was Headmaster at B.S. High School, Sundargarh in 1967. A typed copy of the translation is intended to be sent to the Sambalpur University museum.

Sundargarh (6.9.67.) S.N. Mishra

N.B. The *Kadamba Gatha* contains the reignal years of the various Rajas and the same years have been rendered into dates of the Christian era by the translator as per the direction of the original writer.

KADAMBA GATHA BY G.N. PUROHIT

The Kadambas were the scions of the Nandas. They claim to have their origin from the revered sage Koundinya and were Bramhins [*sic*] by birth and Kshtriyas [*sic*] by profession.

In the early Gupta Age, they had built a stronghold at Annegundi in South Kanara and King Mayur Sarman was a contemporary of Samudra Gupta. They had cordial relation [*sic*] with the Guptas. When the Guptas dwindled and the Vakatakes tried again to establish their hegemony, the Kadambas migrated to the south and flourished under the patronage of the Sailandra kings of the Srivijaya Rajya of Srilanka.

After the rise of the Cholas, seven Kadamba chieftains with their mercenaries joined the Cholas army and advanced to the north about the year 1067 A.D. After the invasion, the chieftains moved further north and reached Nilachala by 1077 A.D. after ten years of escapades in the surrounding regions.

The Ganga king of Puri arranged a contest for them to test their valour. Seven big saws were placed in an area of 18 ft. by 10 ft. and they were asked to jump over them. Out of the seven brothers four perished during the jump and only three surviving brothers were allowed to visit the old Jagannath temple.

After this the three brothers migrated further north and defeated the Bhuyas,[3] established supremacy over Podahat and Saranda in Singhbhum. When the king of Saranda died issueless, Saranda was divided into two portions and added to Podahat and Bonai in 1403 A.D [*sic*].

The third brother Sri Pratap by name migrated to Bonai via Keonjhar in the year 1081 A.D. He was a worshipper of a Salagramsila, known as Raghunath. He carried the lord in a pouch tied to his neck. On his head, he was carrying a sword which was afterwards known as the Kauri Prasad.

Bonai was previously known as Kodalak Mandal, which extended up to the Mahanadi in the South. The Nand kings had their sway over it, though they were not known in the areas south of the Mahanadi. As it appear [*sic*] from the Bonai Copper Plate No. 1 and No. 2 now kept in Patna museum, the kings of the Barah dynasty known as Vijay Barah, Uday Barah ruled over it. They donated a village to Harsanal. Talai near Barkot was their capital. They used the deer as their official symbol and they had spreaded [*sic*] the Buddhist culture in the area.

After the Barahas the Tungas became supreme over the region. By the beginning of the 11th century, they faced the rebellions of the Kondhs and the Bhuyas and being defeated fled to the south to receive the patronage of the Gajapati king of Orissa. Their descendants are still found in the Dhenkanal and Cuttack Districts of Orissa.

By 1081 A.D., Bonai was divided into two parts. The north-east of Bramhani was ruled by Indra Samanta, a Bhuya and the south-west Bramhani was ruled by Bana, an aboriginal Kandh, who worshiped Lord Baneshwar at Deogaon. A number of small stone built temples were built in the south-west. There was ill feeling between the two rulers and Sri Pratap came to know of it while passing through Koira. He developed friendship with Indra Samanta, who promised to help him.

With a band of mercenaries, he crossed the Bramhani at Kenapalii and reached Sondhikona in the evening. Bana coming to know of it sent his men to find out and kill him.

Sri Pratap coming to know of it ran away and took shelter in the hollow of a Kadamba tree. Meanwhile a peacock coming out of the nearby jungle wiped out his footprints. The packs [*sic*][4] of Bana killed all the men of Sri Pratap and returned back to Deogaon.

At night Sri Pratap had to worship Raghunath in the hollow. He was asked by the Lord to use peacock in a Kadamba tree as his royal insignia and worship Lord Baneshwar, the Sthanadhipati[5] before he undertakes the second invasion.

Sri Pratap with a few thousand [*sic*] of Bhuya and Kohl packs [*sic*] attacked Bana once again in the month of August or Sravana the same year in 1081 A.D. He managed to cross the river upon dug out canoes. Deogaon being surrounded by the river on three sides Bana could not gather enough men. Sri Pratap and Indra Samanta defeated Bana, who fled to the Kapilas region, now known as Biramitrapur in Sundargarh District. He established two Siva images at Deogaon and Vedavyas, which stand till now in a reformed and new way.

After the victory, Indra Samanta, the Matiswar[6] placed Pratap on a stone platform at the Bada Darbar and placing the turban and the vermilion over his head acknowledged him as the over lord [*sic*]. Indra Samanta was given a fief of about 50 square miles with thirteen villages in it.

After ruling for more than five years Sri Pratap died in 1086 and his son Dinamonichandra Deo who was aged about fifty ascended the Gadi. He granted some concessions to the Bhuyas of Paudi region round about Khandadhar. Feeling difficult to maintain himself, he brought a number of Bhuyas from Phuljhar area and made them Rajaudi Bhuyas.

These Bhuyas were gradually absorbed in the Aryan faction of the society though their brothers in Pabudi remained untouchables as before.

Dinamani ruled for more than twenty years and died at the ripe old age of 73 in the year 1106 A.D.

Madhusudan was the third kind [*sic*][7] of the line. He ruled for 26 years from 1106 to 1132 A.D. He made arrangements for the worship of Lord Baneshwar.

He brought a number of Bhuyas from Kalaiposh and gave them lands in Deogaon. They were given the right to perform pujas at the Baneshwar temples, though they were not given the Aryan status.

Seeing the special privileges of the Rajaudi Bhuyas, the Keuts of Kenapali headed by Govinda Keut claimed to be treated as aryans. The ruler was not willing to give them any concession.

Govinda headed a group of agitations and wanted to set fire to the mud fort. Madhusudan drove him out of the fort and killed him at Keut marani[8] in Gharbuda patala about 2 kilometres from the town. Then he assumed the name of Madhusudan Govinda Deb.

The three sons of Madhusudan ruled for 41 years, Sri Chandan Indra Deo for 12 years, Kurtibas Chandra Deo for 22 years and Paramesh Govinda Deo for 7 years. These three constructed a thick mud wall around the fort and planted bamboo trees around the fort to a depth of one-fourth of a mile to make the fort impenetrable for an attacking army.

The next kind [*sic*] Mukunda Indra Deo ordained that the Kadamba rulers of Bonai will have the three titles; Indra Deo, Chandra Deo and Govinda Deo in consecutive orders. He built the three gate ways [*sic*]. The Samanta of Kalaiposh remained in charge of Badadwar with Kumari as the presiding deity of that gate. The Mahapatra Jagirdar of Khuntgaon remained in charge of Pattadwar with Andhari as the presiding deity. The third gate way [*sic*] with Dwarsuni as the presiding deity was placed under the Jagirdar of Bijakuli, which had the title of Dandapat. The three with their packs [*sic*] guarded the gates of the fort which had a Bhitar Dwar, the interior where the kind[9] lived with his men and a Bahargarh the outer ring where the artisans and workers lived.

Mukunda Indra Deo ruled for twenty-three years from 1172 to 1194 A.D. He had no natural born issue. So his brothers Sridhar Chandra Deo, Srinibas Govinda Deo, Dambarudhar Indra Deo and Kurtibas Chandra Deo ruled for four years, three years, six years and two years consecutively up to 1210 A.D. The illegitimate sons of Mukunda plotted against those brothers and have them murdered to get power for themselves.

Nilakantha Govinda Deo was the twelfth king of the line. He was son of Kurtibas. He went to Allahabad with a number of retinues to perform worship there for his departed father and uncles. He remained in the Bhardwaj

Ashram for a time. He brought the two brothers Digambar and Pitambar to perform puja for him in Bonai. Those bramhins [*sic*], who were Nath Sharma's [*sic*] were Bhardwaj Gotris. They brought Goddess Basuli with them.

The next kind [*sic*] Narayan Indra Deo ruled for 21 years upto 1242 A.D. He went to Bhimanagari to meet Anangabhima Deo the Gajpati who had gone there to atone for his sins. He excavated deep ditches on the border of his kingdom and placed big brass pots filled with salt and saw dust in them. The Bhuyas of Koira rebelled against him and he quelled the rebellion.

His son Hrushikesh Chandra Deo ruled for four years upto 1246 A.D. He married a daughter of the Bhanja king of Mayurbhanja. He had two sons, Jadumani Govinda Deo after ruling for eight years went to Mayurbhanja on adoption and his brother Sirapani Indra Deo became king of Bonai for 13 years from 1254 to 1266 A.D.

Mukunda Chandra Deo, son of Sirpani ruled for seven years upto 1272 A.D. He constructed the ramparts around the mud fort, Mohana, a Kondh rebelled against him. With great difficulty, he could kill him. The Kondh had a large sword which the king could get after victory. He ordained the sword in his armoury and worshiped it as Mohana Durga.

The 18th king Bikram Govinda Deo ruled for four years and the 19th king Kampal Indra Deo ruled upto 1289 A.D.

The 20th king Biranchi Narayan Chandra Deo ruled from 1289 to 1303 A.D. A number of Rajputs came to take shelter under him when they were much oppressed by the Khilji kings of Delhi. Fearing for troubles, he would not keep them in his kingdom but helped them to establish themselves in the neighbouring regions comprising up [*sic*] Ranchi and Purulia districts. The houses of Rautu, Bansarigarh and Jagnathpur were founded by them. He maintained matrimonial relations with them.

The 21st king Madhab Govinda Deo ruled for only three years from 1300 to 1303 A.D. when Pathan Sultanate of Delhi and Bengal were at the peak of their powers [*sic*]. He had maintained cordial relation [*sic*] with the Gajpati kings of Orissa and sent a contingent to help the Gajpati against the Bahamani invasion of South Orissa.

The next king Banudeb Indra Deo ruled for 34 years from 1303 to 1336 A.D. He maintained a number of Sawars to help his packs [*sic*] to fight against the marauders [*sic*] from Chaibasa who entered through Champus and ravaged the adjoining territory. He married Bhabani Debi, a Chowhan princess from Sambalpur. He removed Goddess Chandi from the mud fort and placed him on a jungle on the east of the Bramhani river during an epidemic when 50 per cent of the inhabitants of the fort died.

The 23rd king Mahendra Chandra Deo ruled from 1336 to 1346 A.D. He supported the cause of Kala against his brother Kapil to be the Samanta of Kalaiposh. There was a fight between the two parties at Ladam, where Goddess Kalapat is worshiped till now. He assessed the land and realized regular taxes from people in the shape of Cowries and grains. He enunciated the weekly worship of Kumari on all thursdays and 52 villages were asked to supply the articles of worship turn by turn. He helped his brother Ramanchandra Singh of Saranda when Abhiram Saha of Rautu invaded Saranda.

His three sons Sridhar Govind Deo, Makar Indra Deo and Paramananda Chandra Deo ruled for nine years, 11 years and 12 years upto 1377 A.D. Makar and Paramananda were instigated by the then king of Bamra to plot against the elder brother Sridhar Govinda Deo. This was a period of unrest. The Kols of Jharakandal guided by the Mohapatra of Balanda spread havoc in the Bhimgad region and the rulers of Bonai were unable to cope with it.

Sirapani Govind Deo was the 27th king of the line. He ruled for five years from 1377 to 1382 A.D. His brother Hadu Deo went to Bamra and became king there being the grandson of Raghunath Sudhal Deb who had to shift his fort from Purunagarh to Balam because of the rebellion of Ghatual Kondh. The two brothers became enemies because of a virgin known as Sita Debi. There was a fight between them. Hadu Deb came from Balam and crossing Chapbahal and Bijakul fought a battle at Patjadi.[10]

The Bonai forces were not a [*sic*] match for the Bamra forces and suffered terrible losses. The king with Chandra Amant worshiped [*sic*] Goddess Kumari and Andhari, and could finally defeat them at Mundgala. Hadu Deo left his royal umbrella at Patjadi and fled away. The replica of the umbrella is worshipped till now in the month of Sravan every year.

The next king was Purusottam Indra Deo, who ruled from 1382 to 1408 A.D. for about 27 years. His younger son Kurtibas Kuar went to Rairakhola and became king there, when the Raja of Saranda died issueless in 1403 A.D., he added half of Saranda to his realm.

Ugrapratap Chandra Deo was the 29th king of the line. He ruled from 1408 to 1432 A.D. He submitted to the suzerainty of the Chawhan rulers of Sambalpur and promised to pay a tribute of 2,000 tankas a year. His son Chitrabhanu Govind Deo did not keep that promise. So Raja Baliar Singh had to attack Bonai in 1442 A.D. Chitrabhanu ruled for nine years from 1432 to 1442 A.D. He died immediately after [*sic*] war with Baliar Singh as he was wounded in the battle.

Chitrabhanu Govind Deo died issue-less. He ordained that rulers of Bonai shall use two titles of Indra Deo and Chandra Deo and no one should use the title of Govind Deo hereinafter [*sic*].

After the death of Chitrabhanu there was chaos in the state for 11 years from 1446 to 1457 A.D. Padmanabh Indra Deo, Trilochan Chandra Deo and Indra Pramath Indra Deo, all of whom were the nephews of the king in quick succession. In 1448 A.D Mahmmad [*sic*] Shah of Janupur after conquering Tirhut and Rauta invaded Gangpur, Bonai and Bamra and after defeating the forces of the three rulers captured 30 elephants from them and returned with a large body [*sic* probably 'booty'].

Kadamba Keshari Chandra Deo was the 34th king of the line. He went on a pilgrimage to Puri. He brought Pandit Srikar [*sic*] Mishsra from Sriramchandrapur Sasan in Puri and made him his Rajpurohit, Srikara Mishra was given 30 acres of land in Bisri Palli now known as Bisipali. His descendants enjoyed the said land till 1710 A.D. when Sasan Nilambarpur[11] was granted to them.

Bonai had no Agharias till then. He brought a number of Agharias from Sambalpur and allotted them lands in Bisipalli, Gurundu Palli and Baramusa. The tanks known as Patbandh, Pastabandh, Jharibandh were excavated by them. They remained near the village around the...[12] [*sic*]

Those Agharias remained there till the beginning of the eighteenth century. Some families perished because of an epidemic. So they fled to Jarda and the neighbouring regions around Jharsuguda where a scion of the Barpalli family related to Madhukar Sai of Sambalpur had his Zamindary [*sic*].

The thirty-fifth king was Purandar Indra Deo. He ruled from 1466 to 1488 A.D. He sent a contingent of packs [*sic*] under Damodar Jena to fight with the army of Baliar Singh of Sambalpur in the aid of Gajpati of Orissa. In 1486 he adopted Pratap Rudra Bijay Singh of Talcher to be his successor. He accepted the Jaganath cult of worship and constructed a mud temple in the palace to worship the three deities.

Bijay known as Sriramchandra Chandra Deo, the thirty-sixth king, donated Jaganathpur now known as Thakurpalli [and] Subhadra Palli, now known as San-Bhaludungri[13] for the worship in Jaganath temple in the fort. He ruled from 1483 to 1509 A.D. A Pathan General of the Nawab of Bengal passed through Champua and Keonjhar to attack the coastal districts. He went to fight against him and joined the army of the Raja of Keonjhar. They could not check the forces of Ismail who could go right upto Puri.

While returning from the battlefield after loosing [*sic*] half of his army, he fell sick and died on the way.

Raghunath Indra Deo, the next king, ruled from 1509 to 1526 A.D. He built the Baseli[14] image and placed it out side [*sic*] the fort, which still stands near the present Bonaigarh post office. Goddess Baseli was placed under a thatched shed. Some weavers from Keonjhar and some copper smith [*sic*] from Dhenkanal came to Bonai. They were untouchables. They remained in the new area around Kopeswar temple, then known as Raghunathpur. Some of them were entrusted with the Puja of Baseli. He also built the Digikata out side [*sic*] the fort and during the car festival, the deities from the fort were taken out through a path in between Digi and Andhari Kata.

Krushna Das Mahanta, a Sadhu from Puri, came to Bonai during this reigh [*sic*].[15] He was given a place in Raghunathpur. The sage constructed an altar and worshiped Sri Gopalji there. His decendants are still worshipping them. He was given some lands in Bisi Palli for the maintenance of the temple. Under the influence of Krushna Das, Raghunath Indra Deo began Doljatra in Bonai.

Uditnarayan Chandra Deo, the next king, ruled from 1526 to 1554 A.D. His younger son Hiramoni Bajradhar went to be the Raja of Talcher on adoption. Ever since the Raja of Talcher is showing respect to the Raja of Bonai as his elder brother.[16] He fixed that Dasara Anukul should be made in the following manner.[17]

Friday and Sunday	East	Tumkala.
Tuesday	South	Uparpada.
Saturday and Monday	West	Jibika Narendra.
Wednesday, Thursday	North	Arikela.

Anukulia and Baktria will start to [*sic*] the villages mentioned above and shall get five Khandis of paddy (about 100 seers) and ten annas from the Gountia's concerned. The Anukulia and Baktria were each given ten acres of land from the royal Khamar for this duty.

The four brothers Mira, Khamra, Mahabira and Hamra, helped him to crush the Bhuyan rebellion at Ladam. Getting direction from Goddess Kumari, he worshiped their [*sic*][18] in the Kumar Purnima[19] to commemorate their death in the Ladam battle. Kalapat, another hero killed in the battle, was also worshiped at Ladam. Two he-buffaloes were killed at Kumari Gudi and Kalapat on the Kumar Purnima day.

The next king, Kalia Indra Deo, ruled from 1554 to 1579 A.D. and his son Bir Keshari Chandra Deo ruled from 1579 to 1592. Bir Keshari Chandra Deo attended the Durbar of Mansingh at Barbati Fort, and acknowledged the Moghul supremacy. He gave his daughter Rajsri Debi to the Raja of Surguja. Khamar Satkuta was founded by him. The marriage party on their journey remained at Satkuta for a week.

Their camp in Bonai was fixed at Bandhatota in Bisipalli, where they had planted about 300 Mango [*sic*] trees. The new groove was pledged to the local Brahmin for a sum of rupees ten only. The descendants of that Bramhin [*sic*] still enjoy the ownership of the mango groove, [*sic*] where there is not a single tree at present.

He founded the Hatipilthana Kothi.[20] A number of ryots were given lands in the Baramusa and Upurda to supply paddy and straw for the royal elephants. Banrei, a Sadhu from Simlipal in Mayurbhanj, came and lived near the Andhari Gudi in Pattadwar. In the sixth year of his reigh [*sic*], there was an epidemic and six out of nine elephants died. Banrai,[21] the Sadhu could save the the [*sic*] other three elephant by treatment. He was honoured and he was worshiped in the elephant stuble [*sic*] as a deity after his death.

Balunkeswar Indra Deo was the forty-first king of the line, who ruled from 1592 to 1611 A.D. for twenty years. He founded the villages of Laxminarayanpur and Indrapur and ceded [*sic*] them two learned Brahmins from Puri. The village Naxmimnarayanpur [*sic*][22] was later given to Rajguru Narasinha Rath from Sasan Biswanathpur in the year 1733 A.D. The village Indrapur became the Khurposh grant of his colaterals. He spent the last two years of his reigh [*sic*] at Kamarposh Balang putting [*sic*] the rebellions of the Kols there. Banapati, the leader of the Kols, evaded his packs [*sic*] and spread havoc in the adjoining region. Finally he selected six Bhuyans to be Chchanaik or the six Sardars, giving them military fiefs to guard the frontiers. The Chachnaik pragana [*sic*] still exists.[23]

Baneshwar Chandra Deo, the next king, ruled from 1611 to 1622 A.D. He is said to have built the Baneshwar temple at Deogaon in the sixth year of his son. Ghana Maharana, a builder from Khandapara, was the chief builders [*sic*]. He also constructed the stone temple of Khireswar at Gogua, which was afterwards washed away by the flood of the Mahanadi. He was married in the Chouhan family of Sambalpur and brought a number of Kultas from Sambalpur to Bonai. They were given lands in the villages of Kenabheta, Govindpur, Kantasara and Ghosra.

Gobinda Indra Deo was the 43rd ruler who ruled from 1622 to 1646 A.D. He [helped][24] the Raja of Gangpur in his border conflict with the Raja of Bamra. The Raja of Gangpur being defeated ceded Bandhabaria pragana [*sic*] to Bamra. The Bonai Raja got a number of villages near Jodabandha[25] for his help. He married the daughter of the Raja of Gangpur. His Rani Champabati excavated the Raja Bundh at Pandrisila. A number of Naga [*sic*] came from Arda and they were assigned lands at Nagadihi and Adadihi near modern Tunia Palli. Within a few years they became troublesome to the people and Narsingha Dandapat, the Jagirdar, tried to drove them away. It is said that he invited a number of Sanyasis to his fort for a religious worship and branded their bodies with red hot sickles. After that the Nagas fled away leaving their lands and homes to the Gond packs [*sic*] of the Jagirdar.

He did not pay *peskis* to the Deputy Nawab of Orissa Taki Khan for the year 1636. The Deputy Nawab sent a number of Sawars in 1937 [*sic*] A.D. under a Foujdar named Ghazi Khan. He came to the fort of Bonai and realised the *peskis* for two years. Being requested by Gajpati Sriram Chandra of the Bhoi dynasty, he sent some woods [*sic*] and stones through the water route of the Brahmani [*sic*] river. Those materials were utilized in the Jagannath temple. Raja Gobind in turn got the privilege to enter the Jaganath temple with Chchatra and Kahali.[26]

The forty-fourth king was Narahari Chandra Deo, who ruled from 1646 to 1651 A.D. His brother Gopinath Indra Deo plotted against him and his men killed Narahari Chandra Deo in his sleeping chamber in his palace. His Rani Sumitra fled to Rairakhol with her only daughter.

Dullav Deo of Barma after reducing the Jit Jamindar crossed the Bramhani at Singhsal and attacked Kantasara. Talcher forces aided by Damodar came to help the Raja of Bonai.

Intervention of the following Brahmins, Ramachandra Mohapatra, Somanath Nanda and Loknath Misra led to peace among the warring forces.

Gopinath Indra Deo ruled from 1651 to 1673 A.D. The early years of his reign were marked with great unrest. Like the other rulers of North and West Orissa. [*sic*] He withheld tribute to the Moghuls. Mirzumla was sent to Orissa in 1667 A.D. He along with the Raja of Keonjhar went to Karanjia to fight against the Moghul army. When Raja Keshen Bhanj of Mayurbhanj was killed, the rulers of Keonjhar and Bonai left the field and thereafter they sent their *peskises* to the Khani Dourani at Cuttack.

The Raja of Kanika was his brother-in-law. He was imprisoned by the Subedar for withholding tribute.

The Raja of Bonai stood surety [*sic* peace] for him and had him released from prison. Kanika Raja was brought to Bonai. He was a very keen hunter and he remained in a place known as Raja Basa for more than two years. Two elephants and four sawars were allotted to him with a few attendant servants. His son-in-law, the Raja of Khalikot, acknowledged the supremacy of the Moghuls and lived in place [*sic* peace] with them.

Ramhari Chandra Deo was the 46th ruler of Bonai who ruled for less than ten years from 1673 to 1686 A.D. He maintained friendly relation [*sic*] with Raja Mukunda Dev 2nd of Orissa. He had been to Puri on a pilgrimage. He returned with Raja Mukunda Deva upto Jajpur. At Jajpur, Makunda Dev died of small pox [*sic*]. He returned from Jajpur via Anandapur, Champua and Barbil. He also contacted [*sic*] small pox [*sic*] and died at Birat Palli Basti, now known as Barsuan. He was brought to the fort on an elephant and was cremanted [*sic*] in the fort.

His son Raghuraj Indra Deo ruled from 1686 to 1709 A.D. for a period of fifteen [*sic*] years. He married the daughter of Jayant Singh, the Maharaja of Rautu. He had a son Bhikari Chandra Deo and a daughter Gouri Debi by name. Gouri Debi was married in Surguja. She is famed to have built the Gouri Tank near the Sadar Police Station, Bonaigarh.

His brother Harinarayan Chandra Deo ruled for a few months and died in an accident during hunting in 1709 A.D.

The next ruler was Bhikari Indra Deo. He donated the Baramusa Sasan to his Raj Purohit in 1710 A.D. The receiver of the Grant was one Nilamar Das [*sic*] from Sriramchandrapur, who was adopted into the Raj Purohit family of Bonai State. The present author is related to him in the following way as his eighth descendant.

1. Nilambar.
2. Maheswar.
3. Bhagirathi.
4. Raghunath.
5. Narayan.
6. Purusottam.
7. Madan Mohan.
8. Gopinath.

Bhikari Indra Deo ruled from 1709 to 1732 for more than 22 years. He established 22 villages in Labangbar Pragana[27] [*sic*]. Labang Naik, a local chieftain was entrusted to do the work. Putuli Banias, a kind of local merchants from Khurdha and Cuttack were coming to Bonai to sell salt and Ayurvedic medicines. They were allowed to carry on tax free business. They were allowed to remain in State rest-sheds during their journey. He also granted a few privileges to the Bhuyans of Pabudi for Panguli[28] worship and for grazing their cows and buffaloes in the state forests.

From his time scribes were appointed to write the royal orders on palm leaf. Previous to this, there was a Bakul tree in the Bhitar Gambhir. The peons and Sawars went to villages with leaves from that tree on which a peacock was inscribed by Lekhan. That sign on the leaf was a sufficient royal order for the tenants of the State.

Pitambar Chandra Deo, the next ruler, ruled from 1732 to 1749 A.D. He was a contemporary of Raja Ramachandra Deb II of Khurdha, who married Fatima Bibi, the daughter of Nawab Suja Khan. The Sasani Brahmans of Raichakradharpur, Harekrusnapur and Dand Makundapur vehemently opposed the entry of the Puri Raja to the temple of Jaganath [*sic*]. The men of the [*sic*] Gajpati oppressed them. As a result of the oppression, sixteen Brahmin families of those sasans left their home and fled to the neighbouring states of Nayagarh, Dhenkanal, Talcher, Bonai, etc. Raja Pitambar Chandra donated the Pitambarpur Sasan now known as Tankjoda to them on the eclepse [*sic*] day of Baisakh Purnima in 1734 A.D. Their descendants were enjoying those mafi lands till the Mafi abolition in 1965 A.D. He ordered that the Brahmins should do Chandi Patha for the ruler and offer Suna Patha[29] to the ruler in lieu of the Mafi grants given to them.

A number of Karanas headed by Gangadhar Patnaik came to Bonai during his reigh [*sic*]. He called them Oriya Karan and allotted them lands inside the Palace. They acted as scribers [*sic*] of the ruler. Some of them founded Chahalies in Bhitar Garh and Bahar Garh to teach Oriya and arithmetic. Gopi Bbhara, Kesheb Koeli and Bhagabat were tought [*sic*] beside arithmetic and mensuration. Some of those Chahalies continued till 1926. When the Bharat Chandra Naik was the Dewan of the state, some families of Karanas with the title of Dhgara [*sic*] and Dwari to remain in charge of the watch and ward of the fort.

He also imported from Ranchi and Singhbhum, a number of goldsmith families and some of them were appointed as Dandias and Gahandals to act as modern Peons and Sepoys.

Bhagirathi Indra Deo was the fifty-first ruler, who ruled from 1749 to 1781 A.D. and died after the third battle of Panipath [*sic*] when the Marhattas were supreme over Orissa. He had to submit to the ravages of Raghuji Bhonsola [*sic*] and paid tribute and Chouth[30] to him. He did not help the Raja of Bamra when he was attacked by the Marhattas. Finally Gajpati Birkishore Deb II ceeded [*sic*] the 14 Garjats to the Marhattas and Bonai being one of them remained under the Marhattas till 16th August 1826 A.D. for about one hundred years.

He checked the advance of Raja Dhanunjay Narayan Bhanja Deo at Ambagaon when after his victory over Barma at Thiamal he wanted to enter Bonai by the Southern rout [*sic*]. The fact is corroborated in *Ambika Bilas*.[31]

In 1776 A.D. Bhagirathi Birbar Harichandan of Talcher took Baikuntha Das, father of Petu Das from Bonai, to do the puja at Bhanaghar in Talcher. Previously his relatives were doing the worship but as they became traitors he had the colaterals killed. The village Kuarmunda was given to Petu Das.

The next ruler Raghunath Chandra Deo, who [*sic*] ruled from 1781 to 1802 A.D. He built the temple of Kopeswar Mahadeb and founded the Basti now known as Patna. He founded the Gundicha Mandap near the Kopeswar temple where the present post office stands. A number of Telis (oil men) from Maldihi were accommodated in Patna Basti by him.

During his reigh [*sic*] Ghosra was subjected to frequent epidemic. [*sic*] Hari Sadhu, a tantric yogi from Rambha told him to worship Hanuman. He set up the Hanuman image made by Fakir Maharana at Ghosra and arranged for its worship.

He appointed Brahmins to do puja in the houses of Hansis and Kansaries who were who were [*sic*] considered to be non aryans till that time. A second batch of Karanas came from Sambalpur under the direction of Rani Mohan Kumari being oppressed by Bhup Singh. They were accommodated at Patna Basti founded by him.

Sibnarayan Indra Deo the 53rd king ruled from 1802 to 1831 A.D. He married Rani Padmabati from Keonjhar and got Koira as his dowry. He founded the sasan of Sibnarayanpur now known as Pandrisila.[32] His son Dinabandhu married in the Chowhan family a daughter of Madhukar Sai and got Samasingha as dowry. Sibnarayan had two queens and Padmanabha was the son of the elder queen. Moughlal Chandra was younger in age.

Raja Sib Narayan led an army upto Bhanja Mardan Bhadi in Balanda to punish Padmanabha but the Raja of Bamra intervened and he had to return back.

He offered shelter to Narayan Singh, who was given a place in the fort to start a shop for trading in Maghi tobacco leaf. As he knew to treat elephants for diseases [*sic*], he was asked to look after them. Chchatak Singh later became the Moharir for elephants.

Chandra Shekhar Chandra Deo was the 54th king of the line and he ruled from 1832 to 1850 A.D. for about 18 years. One of his daughters was married to Chitrabhanu Sai, son of Surendra Sai of Khinda. He was a ruler with a loose [*sic*] brain and he was known as the Baya Raja.

He gave Amatpalli to the Sud Pujaree. They were untouchables, but they enjoyed a number of privileges.

When Narayan Singh was selected to be king of Sambalpur he sent him on 7.10.1833 with an elephant and four attendants via Jarda and Jharsaguda to be the king of Sambalpur on 10.10.1833.

He attended the marriage of Jema Ashakumari with Raja Udit Pratap of Kalahandi in 1844 as per the special invitation of Maharaja Narayan Singh.

He ratified the Deogaon treaty made by Damnikoh, his father's representative, on August, 1926 [*sic*] A.D. and began to pay regular tribute to the British Government. Some Marwaries from Raigharh were sent to Bonai by Ghansam Sing [*sic*] in the year 1831 but he did not allow them to carry on any trade in Bonai.

Dinabandhu Deb, son of Sibnarayan, was the son of the eldest queen but he was younger in age to Chandra Sekhar Chandra Deo who became ruler in 1832.

Dinabandhu and his mother fled to Ambagaon with the golden image of Laxmi Narayan and other valuable properties of the palace.

Raja Balunka Brushabab Deb of Bamra welcomed them and gave them lands and shelter near Barkot.

Dinabandhu married in the family of Madhukar Sai of Sambalpur and got Samasigha as his dowry, which village his descendants enjoyed till 1953.

Dayanidhi Indra Deo was the 55th king of the line, who ruled from 1850 to 1898 A.D. He went to Ranchi along with Jalandhar Sekhar Deo, the Raja of Gangpur, to give witness in favour of Bir Surendra Sai of Khinda. He brought his brother-in-law Chitrabhanu Sai, son of Vir Surendra from Hazaribag jail and remained surety [*sic*] for him. From 1904 to 1922 Chitrabhnu Sai remained in Koira and in 1926 he was taken to Khinda after the death of his wife. Chitrabhanu married a second time but as he was made impotent, no son or daughter was born. Finally he died in 1946 after adopting Fakir Sai as his heir.

Hari Sadhu mentioned above was a tantric Sadhu. He made a Devijantra for his worship. The hut of the Sadhu was washed away and he was killed in a flood which took place in 1852. The jantra of the Sadhu was discovered by a Harijan, who used that as the Sama of his Dhenki. He could get equal amount of rice when paddy is [*sic*] crushed. The Raja heard of it, brought the Jantra and worshiped it in Kumari Gudi. The deity in a dream asked the Raja to send Him back to the forest. The deity was taken to a cave in Khandadhar Parbat. On the 2nd day of the Sukla Paksha, the Bhuyan Dehuri brought the deity to Bonaigarh via Jala, Khuntgaon, Jakeikela. When they reached Bonai, the Raja went to Kantajori to receive the deity. The Bhuyan Dehury of Pabudi fled on seeing the king and his men. The Raja asked the Amat to do the Puja in Bonaigarh. After the Raja [*sic* puja] was finished the deity was handed over to the Pabudi Bhuyan at Nimachakuli. The Bhuyan Dehuty took the deity in a circulous [*sic*] route passing through Tankajoda, Bramhangaon and Kaleiposh, etc. That happened in the year 1862.

A Satpathy Brahmin from Sohela came to Bonai and he became Rajvaidya. Sautipalli near Indrapur was given to him. Jaideb Satpathy of that family became his Diwan for about 18 years.

In 1894, he started a tol in the fort with Pandit Padmanabha Sarangi as teacher. Bhagaban Sarangi and six others were taught Karm Kanda, astronomy and Sanskrit. With his death in 1898, the tol[33] was abolished and the Pandit went away.

The Zamindar of Kaleiposh had full powers over the jungles in his area. He appointed a Tahsildar, Manager and a Forester and tried to realize half of the revenue and the forest cess. Krushna Samanta and his brother Krupa Samanta rebelled and the Raja had to bring reserve forces from Chaibasa to check their raids. Babu[34] Manikar Deo a scion of Shib Narayan helped the

Raja against the Bhuyans and received a sword and a robe from the British Government. Patayat Bisweswar Deo accused Tikayat Nilambar Deo to have connection with the Bhuyans. The Tikayat was rebuked but finally excesed [*sic*] on the intervention of the Raja Sahib of Saraikela and the Thakur Saheb of Dungi who had weilded [*sic* excused] great influence with the Collector, Chaibasa.

The Raja had Banla[35] Bedi in God Vitar[36] where some learned men as Danai Jena, Markanda Mishra and Hari Bisi attended to discuss the Puranas and the Chchandas. The Raja had strong faith on Lord Siva and he went to the temple on all Mondays to worship there. He excavated the second tank near the Baneshwar temple. He gave Khurposh grants to the newly imported Kshatriyas[37] at Rautani and Nuagaon, which their descendants are still enjoying.

In 1861, Bonai was taken away from Orissa and placed under Ranchi.

In 1877, just before the Delhi Durbar, Raja Dayanidhi got the title of Raja Bahadur for his help during the Bhuyan rebellion of Keonjhar.

In 1896, he undertook a journey to Puri. While returing, he remained at Talcher. He gave Ram Bux, the tusker and two white stallion to Raja Bhagirathi Harichandan of Talcher.

In 1867, Krushna Samanta and Krupa Samanta of Kalaiposh rebelled. Raja Dayanidhi had to supress them with British forces from Ranchi and Chaibasa.

Sri Manikar Deo, his nephew was awarded a sword and a robe for his work in the rebellion.

Towards the close of the nineteenth century, the Christian missionaries came to Bonai and he restricted their preaching areas on [*sic*] the north of the Bramhani [*sic*] river.

In a social case he decided that Sutar,[38] Ojha and Maharana[39] should be regarded as offspring of one caste and they can intermarry among themselves. A Brahmin was appointed for them.

Nilambar Chandra Deo was the 56th king of the line, who ruled from 12.11.1898 to 12.2.1901 A.D. He was the author of *Kautak Kalanidhi*[40] and the book was published in 1893. His son was married to Rani Amarabati, a daughter of Raja Sir Basudeb Sudhal Deo. Lal Nrupalal Singh Deo of Barpalli was his friend. Nrupalal and Nilambar married two sisters of Raja Sriram Chandra of Mayurbhanja.

The Raja gave his daughter to Raja Dinabandhu Mahendra Bahadur of Dhenkanal. A few Kondhs headed by Santha Joutikia were allowed some privileges allowed for Aryans and they were sent to Dhenkanal with his daughter, the Maharani Annapurna of Dhenkanal.

One of his sons Kumar Jadumani was sent to Rairakhol in 1902 to be Raja there and he ruled over Rairakhol for 41 years till merger from 1907 [*sic*]. Raja Jadumani died in 1973.

In 1902, there was a fire at the Jadunath temple and the thatched house was gutted. Out of the three Gods, only Jadunath known as Bhudha Gossain was saved. He started the building of the new Jagarnath [*sic*] temple which was completed in year 1904.

He founded the Chadak[41] Jatra and that was [*sic*] regularly held from 6th April to 14th April every year. Kapila Patra, the head of the Hanshi caste was given lands for service in Chadak Jatra. The Choudhury [*sic*] takes the pictured image of Baseli to the Puja Pandal for nine days and various festivals are observed for nine days.

In February 1901, the Raja was going with his son to Deogarh for his marriage. At Kantajodi, a black cat crossed the road in front of his elephant. One kilometre away, the branch of a mango tree suddenly fell on the way. At the 7th mile from the fort the Raja fell sick of diarrhoea and was taken back to the Baneshwar temple. On 19.2.1901, the Raja died and the marriage was stopped. Three months later, the marriage was again celebrated and Bhiku Purohit, the father of the writer, was highly praised by Raja Sri Basudeb for his work as Purohit. He was given a pair of robes, some gold ornaments and a pair of bullock [*sic*].

He gave one of his daughters Bindumati Debi to Lal Sonmukuta Saha Deo and his grandson Lal B.N. Saha Deo died while working as Subjudge [*sic*] in Sundargarh District in 1964. Another daughter was married to the Raja of Aul who died in a boat disaster. He kept Harinath and Narinath of Aul in his fort for more than four years.

Raja Dharanidhar Indra Deo Deb, the 57th Raja ruled from 1902. He died on the 4th July 1949 at Swarga dwar at Puti [*sic*].[42] The modern town of Bonai was his own planning. On the second year of his reign, he was sent to Ranchi for training for his suspicious linking [*sic*] with a murder case in the palace. Sri Sarat Chandra Roy, M.A., B.L. was his guardian tutor.

After returning from Ranchi in 1913, he started the 1st M.E. School in the State. The late Joykrushna Mahapatra, who retired from Capital High School, Bhubaneshwar unit III was the first headmaster of the school. The first High School was started in 1938, but the scheme was dropped. The second High School was started in 1944. Colonel J.H. Todd laid the foundation stone of the Raja D.D. High School in 1946. Major Iskander Mirza opened the hostel building in 1945.

The court building and the jail were constructed in 1918 and the present Girls' High School building was completed in 1926.

The Raja established the rest houses at Jangra, Banki, Darjing, K. Balang and S. Balang.

He was a poet himself. Poetic contests were organised. He published the three *Badgitikas* containing about 1,000 poems.

After his return from Ranchi, he built the temporary roads upto [*sic*] Banki/Koira, Sarsara and Jarda.

Gangpur and Bonai were placed under the A.G.G. Ranchi and afterwards they were placed under the Political Agent of Sambalpur and the Resident of Eastern States at Calcutta.

He inaugurated the Chandan Jatras at Jangra in 1941 and offered prizes to the competitors in Palla and Kirtan.

In 1926, he had established 26 Primary Schools in the State. In each school, he had a teacher from Puri or Cuttack District to teach language to the students. In 1936 he started a *tol* [*sic*] where Dinamani Mishra and others were reading. The *tol* was abolished in 1938.

Raja Dharanidhar was a Nationalist and he had full sympathy for the freedom movement. He did not oppress his people to raise funds for the war in the years 1914 to 1918 and 1939-1945. So he was not in the good book [*sic*] of the British Government. When the Prajamandal movement was started in 1946 under the leadership of late Bharat Charan Mohanty, Aanadi Dandpat[43] and Bhajan Chandra Mahanta, he did not give orders for firing or arrest though the Diwan pressed for it.

The Sundhies and the Kalwars approached him to treat them as Aryans. He appointed special Brhmins [*sic*] to perform Puja in their houses but they remained untouchable as before. He founded the Jatiya Mahasabha[44] consisting of members from all castes to decide religious and social matters. In 1942, he fell sick of diabetes and lost the thumb of the left hand.

After signing the merger agreement on 14.11.1947, he went from Cuttack to Puri and remained there till his death. He never returned to the state and the Diwan Rai Sahib H.P. Deb handed over the charge of the state to Sri G.N. Das on 1.1.1948.[45]

Raja Dharanidhar founded the Dharanidhar Club in 1926 A.D. He founded a theatre party in 1928 and appointed Sri Dibyasingh Sarangi of the Balanga party as the music master. He also started the water supply and the electric supply schemes for the palace and the civil lines in 1932 [*sic*]. When Mr. A.J. Ollenbatch retired Deputy Commissioner, Angul and Kondmal was his Diwan.

In 1938,[46] he adopted Kadamba Keshari Deo as his heir apparent and sent him to the Rajkumar College at Raipur. He died at the ripe old age of sixty-five. He was benevolent and popular with his subjects.

Raja Kadamba Keshari Chandra Deo ascended the Gadi on 7th July 1949. He married Maharajakumari Gita Devi in 1947. He was enjoying privy purses and privileges till January, 1973.

ADDENDA

1. Khandadhar–It is a water fall 800 ft. in hight [*sic*] about 16 kilometres east of the Bonaigarh town. According to tradition, Nakul brother of Yudhisthir tested the edge of his sword on a Sal tree on the eastern side of Khandadhar while going on a hunting [*sic*]. The edge of the sword struck the mountain and a spring came out. The place of origin is known as Nakulchua and the stream is known as Khandadhar.
2. Makadnacha is a mountain about 4000 ft. high. It is rich in iron ores [*sic*]. The aboriginal Bhuyans living in it had the hobby to rear monkeys to dance on ceremonial occasions. Sita was pleased to see the dance of the monkeys during their marriage. The Bhuyans living there were the Pundabas. All the brothers in a family had one wife to run the housekeeping. That custom in restricted forms [*sic*] still remains.
3. Baneshwar at Deogaon was the Sthanadhipati and the Samanta of Kalaiposh was the Thaneswar or Matiswar. There is a Usha Medh on the south of the temple associated with the legend of Banasur the demon king. Tirtha ghat [*sic*] on the Brahmani on the north of the Temple had a number of small temples, which were submerged in the Brahmani river. In the Brahmani at Tirtha Ghat, some times natural stones with images of deities are found. The Kisans [*sic*] living in Bonai regarded Brahmani as their Gangas and throw the bones of their ancestors there.
4. Kumari along with her six sisters was the presiding deity of the fort. Kumari prasad a sword ordained in the name of Goddess Kumari, is worshiped till now in the temple on the north-east of the palace. She is worshiped on all Thursdays. Special worship is done on Kumar Purnima and sometimes buffaloes were sacrificed.
5. Andhari is a Goddess which guarded the south of the fort. The image of the Goddess is a fine specimen of medival art of Orissa. The image is the finest image of Bonai. There was a small Jogini temple at the place Deodhuda in Deogaon. When that temple was destroyed, the Jogini images were brought to a place known as Nilji Gudi towards the end of the 17th century.

   At the beginning of the 18th century, some of the images were worshiped as Andhari, Dwarsuni and Baseli in different parts of Bonaigarh town.
6. Kantasara: It is a village 14 kilometres south of the town. Goddess Kant Kumari was discovered there.

J.N. Sahu

NOTES

1. Footnotes and commas have been added by the authors for a better understanding of the text otherwise the text has not been changed. If not indicated otherwise, the comments are based on interviews with the late Rajasahib, Sri Kadamba Kesari Chandra Deb.
2. In the text it is 'nealize', but probably a typing mistake.
3. The author prefers the spelling Bhuya, while Bhuiyan is used more commonly in the region.
4. Probably 'Paiks'.
5. Dandia: *adhipati* = Raja—as Jagannath for Orissa.
6. Probably 'Lord of the Soil' derived from *mati* = soil, indicating that the Samanto was the original owner of the place or that he is giving a *tika* of soil/*mati* during the coronation ceremony.
7. Probably 'king' here.
8. As G.N. Dandia argued, it's a place on the road to Bamra via Barkot (close to Kendrikala, left side). The Raja mentions that Keut Deo is worshipped by the *amat* during all auspicious occasions such as weddings or sacred thread ceremonies, who also worships Mayur Deo (peacock god) on such occasions.
9. Probably king.
10. A place on the road from the market to Bisipali—before the village there is a bamboo tree and that place is named Patjodi.
11. Place not known to the present Raja. The Dandia believes that it is Tankjoda—the name was changed from Nilambarpur to Tankjoda during Kelly settlement.
12. This sentence remained incomplete in the original.
13. Situated between Baramusa and Jakeikala.
14. The Goddess is usually referred to as 'Basuli'.
15. Probably 'reign'.
16. This is rather doubtful according to the present Raja.
17. Probably when the Dossomi Day fall on a Friday the Ankulia started towards the east, while on a Tuesday towards south, etc.
18. Probably 'there' or 'them'.
19. On Kumar Puni the Rajpurohit performs the puja at the Kumari Mandir—in particular the *jagya/homa*. Not the *amat*.
20. Staple for the elephants (formerly on the side of the old Jagmohan Temple).
21. There are different spellings of the name in the original text.
22. The village is usually referred to as Laxminarayanpur.
23. According to G.N. Dandia it is the K-Balang area. Other Pargana: Koira Pargana, Banki Pargana, Sola Pradhan, Chou Naik, Labangbar Pargana.
24. Added by the authors.
25. Near Banki on the way to Rourkela.

26. A kind of flute.
27. Area near Gomlei, Brahmingaon.
28. G.N. Dandia: a jungle devta, i.e. a *khunt.*
29. Should be *paita* according to present Raja.
30. A gift of money or tribute, thereby recognizing the supremacy.
31. G.N. Dandia: a book—possibly: the *Satchidanand Ganthaboli* or *Badkumar Ganthaboli.*
32. Near Baramusa—on the way towards Barkot.
33. Old term for a school.
34. Here: Babu—relative of the Raja.
35. *Baṇla*—meaning permanent.
36. Probably a spelling mistake and it should be: *Ghar Bhitor*—inside the fort.
37. Babus from Bamra and other states, who were given land.
38. Probably a spelling mistake: It should be sutas, who vaccinated people against smallpox, etc.
39. Caste of brass smiths, but also carpenters.
40. Collection of songs. Most likely lost. Dandia: Part 1 of the Bada Gitika.
41. Probably a spelling mistake: It should be *Cheitra. Chadak* means 'lightning', but the present Raja has never heard that term used for Cheitra Jatra.
42. Puri.
43. Related to the Dandpat family in Bijakuli. Had to stay outside Bonai for some years. Not because the Raja had anything against him, but rather the Political Department, which referred the matter to the Raja, who had to react to that kind of 'order'.
44. There were one or two meetings, the present Raja remembers, which were called upon in order to develop the state. It was a kind of assembly. The Raja saw it as a way to come to know about the opinion of the people. Where was a school needed, where roads, etc., so that the concerned departments could take action.
45. Who came as an administrator.
46. According to the late Raja, Sri Kadamba Kesari Chandra Deb it was on 13.5.1935.

APPENDIX

Chapter XIV of *Kadamba Gatha*

SURENDRANATH MISHRA

After the *Panji* (*Madla*) of Bonai was published, many archaeologists of different places of Orissa, being curious, have asked some questions. My limited knowledge has got no such strength to answer these questions. Still whatever I know I am describing that in the fourteenth chapter.

As per the prevailing custom of Bonai State, on the day of Kumar Purnima (full moon day of Dasara month), lines are drawn on the granite-stone Kumari temple and astrological calculations are done. On that day in the Kumari temple the details of the previous astrological calculations of the king are written in a book and that book is kept in the Kumari temple. The 22nd (twenty-second) forefather of the compiler, Srikara Mishra, had started this *Madla Panji* writing. The *Madla Panji* which he had written was kept in the Jagannath temple. The Bhuiyas stole the Kumari Prasad Khanda (Tarabari) from the Kumari temple, so the Tarabari (sword), after procuring it again, and that ancient scripts (*pothi*) were kept in Jagannath temple. In the year 1904 when there was a fire in Jagannath temple the said book (*pothi*) was burnt.

Later on, in the year 1909, the genealogist (*panjia*) Damodar Satpathi wrote the *Madla* of Bonai. In the beginning of the 18th century Bhagban and Damodar, the two brothers had came from Sohella, Sambalpur to Bonai. They had married the two daughters Susila and Malati of Maheswar Mishra, the eighth forefathers of the compiler. Bhagban Satpathy being Raj Kabiraj got Sountipali village and Damodar became the genealogist.

The first ten chapters of the *Madla* were written by Damodar Dwija. The queen, late Rani Saheba Amarabati Devi (the daughter of Bamunda King Sir Basudev Sudhaladev K.C.I.E.), had kept the book (*pothi*) on her Bhagbat throne. In the year 1914 as per the directions of the British government, the Bihar government had asked some questions to the then king of Bonai Sri Dharanidhar Indradeo Dev about his genealogy. The Raja Saheb told Gopinath Purohit, the father of the author, to give one explanatory note along with the copy of the *Madla*. The *Bonai Madla* and the history of Kadamba clan were submitted to the government along with the explanatory notes. The history of Kadamba clan (*Kadamba Gatha*) was printed at the Saraswat

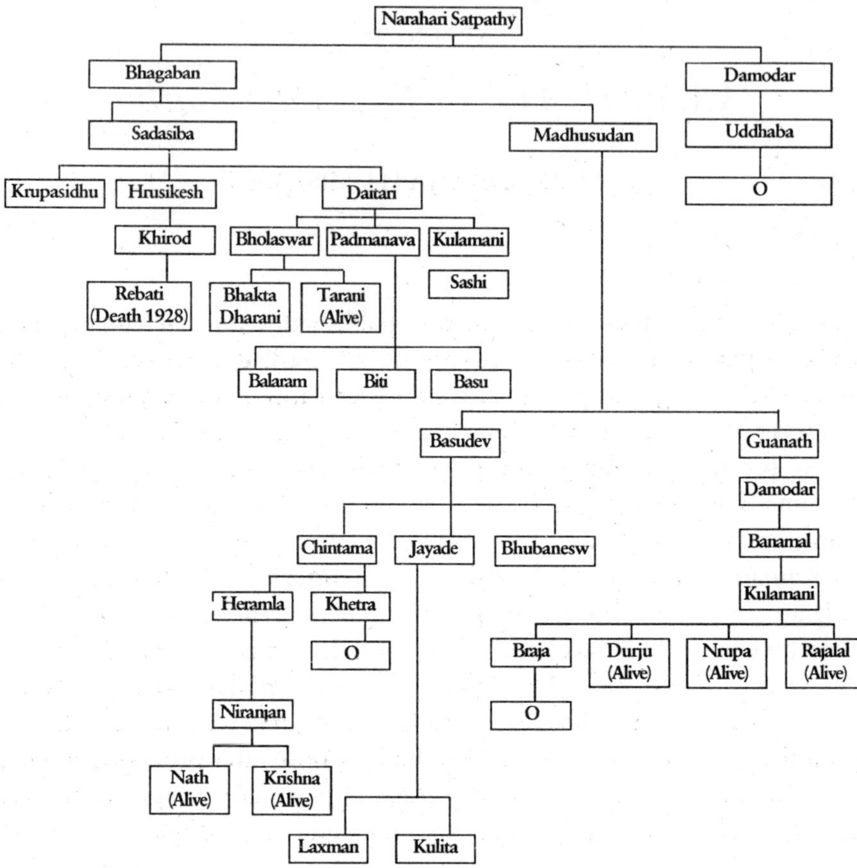

Press in the year 1947. The compiler in his capacity as headmaster, Dharanidhar High School had sent the said book to the press along with an advance of Rs.150 only. On 22.8.1948 the compiler was transferred to Dhenkanal. For certain reasons that book could not come out from the press. In the year 1949 Gopinath Purohit wrote *Kadamba Gatha* (History) B which is with me. In the 2nd chapter of the original *Kadamba Gatha* it was described that all the areas till Barkot of Deogarh Subdivision were under the Maurya and Nanda Dynasty. Like the ancestors of the Nandas of Jeypore of Orissa the Kadambas were the legal heirs of the Nandas. All these matter related to the possession and inheritance were known from the Kadamba rulers of the southern region which was later on declared by the author in a public meeting after the merger of the state. As a result of which it was taken for granted that it was against Orissa, and as such the book could not come to light. Out of the twelve forts that were constructed by the Nanda kings Barkot is one of them.

The first chapter of the *Madla* is traditional. Banasur was the king of Harkenia city situated on the bank of Kashyapa Sea. He belonged to the clan of Hiranyakasyapa. He was the pioneer of Baneswar of Bonai. On the south-west side of the temple there is the decorated seat of the idol of Usha. His (Banasur's) fort was situated in front of the temple. While digging a tank in front of the temple at least twenty hands length depth under the ground, the foundation made by the big sizes of stems of *sishu* and *sala* (timber trees) of a city was discovered. Due to the fear that the precipitous bank of the river would slip down suddenly, the fort was constructed on the bank with the support of wooden pillars. On the rock situated by the eastern side of the temple and on the south-west side doorways up to now the vincible bead (*jet-kanthi*) of different colours were available and now also it is found. These were like artificial diamonds in appearance. For the above reasons the tradition is believed. How Banasur came from the bank of the Kaspiyan Sea to Bonai is unknown till now.

In second chapter of *Madla,* Baraha Rule and in the third chapter Tunga Rule are described. There were two copper plate inscriptions in the Jagannath temple of Bonai. The first one was Bonai copper plate No. 1 and the second was copper plate No. 2. The first copper plate was the deed of the Baraha king's gift and the second copper plate was the deed of the Tunga king's gift. Rai Bahadur Sarat Chandra Roy, M.A., B.L. took the said two copper plates from Jagannath temple in the year 1916 and printed one essay in the Research Journal of Bihar and Orissa. He had submitted the two copper plates in Patna Museum. The writer when he was in Patna College everything has been given to him. In the June 1916 magazine the lesson of the copper plates were printed there, but that was not read.

In the fourth chapter Dr. J. Jourlaw Dubsiel and Prof. E.I. Rapson have described that as per the *Mughal Purana,* the first Kadamba King of Bhima Karnata in the year 350 in Gupta yuga had established Mayurdarsan Kadamba states in Kanara. In the year 1631 Dudhadev, the King of Mysore and the King of Bonai had seen Jagannath along with Mukunda Dev, the king of that time. Both had admitted that they as Kadambas are rightful heirs of the Nandas.

A few days after the said events Mukunda Dev permitted the Britishers to carry on their business at Marichpur, Patia, Pipili and other places.

PANEGYRIC OF BONAI KING

The name and fame of the Bonai king with his title is noted here. He was highly prosperous. He has tolerated all the troubles and enlarged his kingdom. He worshipped all deities such as Sri Baneswar Debagana, Sri Kumari Devi and he had taken shelter under the feet of the mother Kumari Devi. He received a boon after offering prasad of Sri Kopeswar. So his name was as such Sri Bonai Chalisi Sahasuasur Stanadhipati Rajadhiraj Rajeswar Trilokya Mandalaswar (king of the places where forty thousand demons reside, king of kings who is the trinity) Sri Sri Sri Dayanidhi Indra Dev Maharaja. This is the address to the Maharaja of Bonai.

From this it is known that the famous gods of Bana Durga (fort) were Baneswar, Kumari, Kopeswar. Long ago Baneswar was established by Banasur and was worshipped. Kumari is the goddess of Bhuyan pitha (permanent seat/religious centre). She was the beloved goddess [tutelary deity] of Samanta. The Kadamba clan established Kumari as the 'Goda Chandi' (Chandi of the fort). Kopeswar is worshipped in the heart of the town. The Kadamba king had established him. In the year 1728 at Raghunathpur Patna the king of that time and Nata Sadangi had constructed his temple.

Sri Pratap, the first king who came to Bonai, had wrapped one Salegram named Raghunath in a piece of black silk cloth and had tied that around his neck. It was a Salegram Sila (stone) having 3½ inch diameters. Here there was a small hole. There is a sign of a trident (*trishul*) on its back. This *sila* (stone) is worshipped with the *mantra* of Ramchandra. Besides this, the first king had brought one big sword named *Patkhanda*. The said sword is worshipped at the time of Dasahara or at the time of the coronation ceremony of a new king. In the olden days many animal sacrifices and human sacrifices (*nara bali*) were given. The said sword is worshipped with the *mantras* of 'Bana Durga'. Also he had received Mohana Khanda by killing Mohana Kondh. Further he had received Kalapat Khanda from Kaleiposh and the Kumari Prasad Tarabari (*khanda*), which are also worshipped.

The signs of the Kadamba kings were the Kadamba tree and the peacock. If anybody was found cutting a Kadamba tree or killing a peacock he was punished with jail and fine. This was in force till 1.1.1948.

In terms of social development, Bonai was progressive. The 56th king Sri Dayanidhi Indra Deo had united twelve houses of Bhuyans and two houses of Kondhs with the Aryas by performing *jagya* in the Baneswar temple. For Hansi and Kansaries he had arranged Brahmins.

One hundred years ago this state was administered by one learned man (*manisa*) and twelve riders (*swars*). At that time there was no pen, ink and paper. The *swars* were drawing peacock sign on a Boula leaf or palm-leaf with a pen-like stick (*lekhani*) and showing the same to the people on the High Court Pendal (Bada Darabara Mandap) and intimating the king's orders. On 18.1.1882 King Dharanidhar, the third son of King Nilambar was born. The same year ink and paper came to Bonai. The ink pen was used. In the year 1882 the Forest Department was formed by hiring fourteen employees. The salary of all the employees was Rs.1,200 per year but the annual profit were Rs.4,800, excluding the staff's salary. In the year 1882 the revenue was enhanced unto Rs.8,000 and this was approved by James Walt. In the year 1913 J.D. Kelley enhanced the revenue up to Rs.22,000 and approved that. By 1936 the annual income of this state was Rs.1,39,000.

COMPILER'S GENEALOGY

11. Nilamber – In 1709 Barahmusa Rule supporter.
10. Chintamani
9. Bhagban
8. Maheswar
7. Bhagirathi

Genealogy:

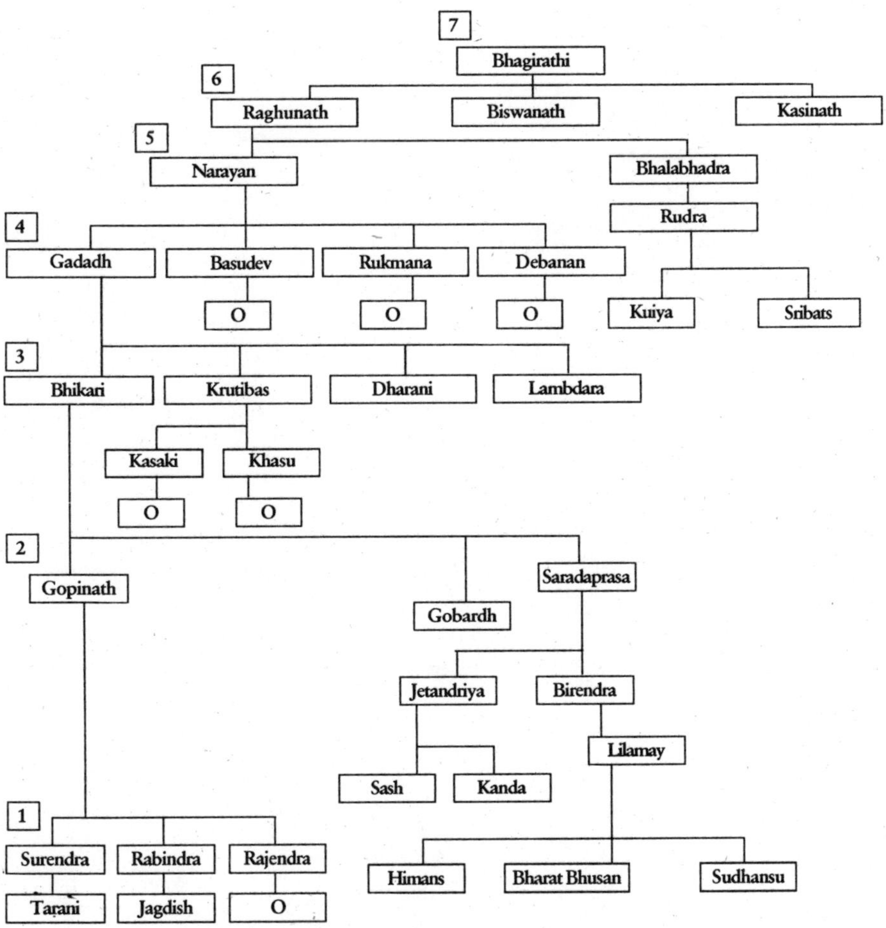

Whatever I had to say I said. The readers by thinking will excuse me if I committed any mistakes.

Sd/-
Surendranath Mishra
M.A., O.E.S.

Length - 34 cm
Width - 3.5 cm
In each page 6 lines written
Writing place 27 cm
In both sides 3 cm
Total pages 102
Numbers of palm leafs 102
In the middle parts in between writings there are pictures of Ganesh and Durga Printed.